Using Turbo

RECENT COMPUTER SCIENCE TITLES FROM PWS PUBLISHING COMPANY

Using Turbo Pascal

6.0–7.0

THIRD EDITION

Julien Hennefeld

Brooklyn College—City
University of New York

PWS PUBLISHING COMPANY

I(T)P AN INTERNATIONAL THOMSON PUBLISHING COMPANY

Boston • Albany • Bonn • Cincinnati • Detroit • London • Madrid • Melbourne • Mexico City
New York • Pacific Grove • Paris • San Francisco • Singapore • Tokyo • Toronto • Washington

PWS PUBLISHING COMPANY
20 Park Plaza
Boston, Massachusetts 02116-4324

Dedication
To Maggie, Dan, Marianne, and Zoe.
And, to my parents
Lillian and Edmund.

Copyright © 1995, 1992, and 1989 by PWS Publishing Company, a division of International Thomson Publishing Inc.

 International Thomson Publishing
The trademark ITP is used under license.

 This book is printed on recycled, acid-free paper.

For more information, contact:

PWS Publishing Co.
20 Park Plaza
Boston, MA 02116

Nelson Canada
1120 Birchmount Road
Scarborough, Ontario
Canada M1K 5G4

International Thomson Publishing GmbH
Königswinterer Strasse 418
53227 Bonn, Germany

Thomas Nelson Australia
102 Dodds Street
South Melbourne
Victoria, Australia

International Thomson Editores
Campos Eliseos 385, Piso 7
Col. Polanco
11560 Mexico D.F., Mexico

International Thomson Publishing Europe
Berkshire House I68-I73
3205 High Holborn
London WC1V 7AA
England

International Thomson Publishing Japan
Hirakawacho Kyowa Building
2-2-1 Hirakawacho
Chiyoda-ku, Tokyo
Japan

International Thomson Publishing Asia
31221 Henderson Road
#05-10 Henderson Building
102 Singapore 0315

Library of Congress Cataloging-in-Publication Data
Hennefeld, Julien O.
    Using Turbo Pascal 6.0-7.0 / Julien Hennefeld.—3rd ed.
        p.   cm.
    Rev. ed. of: Using Turbo Pascal 4.0-6.0. 2nd ed. c1992.
    Includes index.
    ISBN 0-534-94398-5
    1. Pascal (Computer program language)   2. Turbo Pascal (Computer file)   I. Hennefeld, Julien O.   Using Turbo Pascal 6.0-7.0.
    II. Title.
    QA76.73.P2H463   1995   94-21767
    005.13'3—dc20   CIP

IBM PC® is a registered trademark of International Business Machines Corporation.
Turbo Pascal® is a registered trademark of Borland International, Inc.

Sponsoring Editor: *Michael J. Sugarman*
Developmental Editor: *Susan McCulley Gay*
Production Editor: *Monique A. Calello*
Editorial Assistant: *Benjamin Steinberg*
Marketing Manager: *Nathan Wilbur*
Manufacturing Coordinator: *Ellen Glisker*

Interior Designer: *Monique A. Calello*
Cover Designer: *Julia Gecha*
Compositor: *Modern Graphics Inc.*
Cover Photo: *Jose Fuste Raga, © The Stock Market, Inc.*
Cover Printer: *Henry N. Sawyer Co., Inc.*
Text Printer: *R.R. Donnelley & Sons–Crawfordsville*

Printed and bound in the United States of America
97 98 99—10 9 8 7 6 5 4

Contents

Preface

• • • There are many books that provide thorough coverage of programming principles and Pascal syntax. A big need, however, always exists for a book that does so in a readable format, since comprehensive coverage does not necessarily mean *comprehensible coverage*. A serious difficulty facing any technical writer is that the reader might read with little assimilation of the material, just turning the pages, even though the discussions are coherent and packed with information.

In writing *Using Turbo Pascal: 6.0-7.0, Third Edition,* I have given serious thought to how readers actually assimilate technical material. My goal has been to make this book clear, concise, and focused by stripping down the discussion to what is essential, since too much explanation can be just as bad as too little. Most importantly, I have employed a variety of pedagogical devices that make the reader an active participant and not just a passive page-turner.

To foster *active* reading, *Using Turbo Pascal* introduces new topics by means of short programs whose outputs the reader is asked to determine before reading on. For many of the longer programs, the reader, informed of what the programming is to accomplish, is asked to fill in one or two blank program lines. This self-testing approach gives readers a basis for determining whether they need to review some of the earlier material before moving on. It also provides positive reinforcement for correct responses. Perhaps most importantly, it creates a framework that can facilitate the readers' entry into the material.

Many books reproduce in great detail the chain of thought the author uses in arriving at solutions to complex programming problems. The disadvantage of this approach is that an author's chain of thought is too idiosyncratic to be immortalized in this way. Furthermore, although this sort of extended treatment can be effective in a classroom setting, on the printed page the result is frequently tedious, unfocused, and visually overwhelming. Accordingly, I have tried to keep discussions of program development focused and streamlined.

The extremely clear and concise writing style makes this book suitable for courses ranging from a computer literacy course to an introductory college course for computer science majors. In a computer literacy course, a gentle pace is suggested, with only a portion of the book being covered and lectures following the book closely. By contrast, in a course for computer science majors, most or all of the book could be covered. Because the chapters are bite-sized, they can be taken up in an order different from the one given.

CHANGES FOR THE THIRD EDITION

The most significant improvements in the third edition involve the treatment of *procedures,* the inclusion of *debugging exercises on disk,* the increased emphasis on *how to write a program,* and the revised discussion of *sorting algorithms.*

The discussion of procedures begins much earlier than in the second edition, starting in Chapter 4 with the use of procedures as a way of implementing top down design, and providing a bridge for material from Chapter 10 on parameters to be covered earlier in the course, if so desired. Moreover, structure charts are now included in the discussion of procedures and data flow.

Many chapters now have a debugging exercise section, containing various erroneous programs on disk. For some of these programs, the student is guided through the reasoning and debugging techniques that an experienced debugger might use. For other programs, the student can practice these techniques, and is given no guidance beyond a description of what the program was supposed to do. Increased attention has also been given to hand tracing with the addition of some new, more challenging tracing exercises in the regular Exercise Sections.

The issue of how to write a program is addressed more directly than in the second edition. General guidelines, stressing top down design, are given in Chapter 4 and illustrated throughout the book. The two chapters on while loops and repeat-until loops have been reorganized. Chapter 7 discusses the three basic types of applications, considering repeat and while versions together. Along the way, the guidelines suggested for writing programs are applied to constructing General Task Controlled Loops. Chapter 8 considers more specialized topics and introduces the concept of loop invariants.

The chapters on searching and sorting have major revisions. Searching now comes before sorting. The binary search exposition has been improved. The first sort presented is the selection sort (new), and the two versions of the bubble sort are now the "nested for loop version" (new) and the "early exit version." A new section in Chapter 28 discusses the Big O analysis of sorting algorithms and explains why the quick sort tends to be so much faster than an elementary sort on large arrays. Finally, the order of Chapters 18 and 19 has been reversed so that the chapters on one- and two-dimensional arrays are consecutive.

Turbo 7.0 is taken as the primary version. Chapter 2 has been reorganized so that students can find out what they need to know more readily, and also so that Sections 2.2 and 2.3 walk the students through the basics, step-by-step. Appendix H and material on disk provide hands-on tutorials on the following topics: the basics of DOS and subdirectories, the basics of the Turbo Editor, block operations, and search and replace. Solutions are provided in the Solutions Appendix for selected exercises, whose numbers are printed in black rather than blue.

Diskette   The diskette that is bound into the book contains:

- The debugging programs listed in the end of chapter exercises.
- Lab tutorials (to be used in conjunction with Appendix H) on DOS and the Turbo 7.0 system.
- Most of the sample programs from the text.

Supplements

- An Instructor's Manual containing solutions to all exercises, transparency masters, and test banks.
- Accompanying solutions/test bank diskette free to adopters only.

ACKNOWLEDGMENTS

• •

I am enormously indebted to Naftaly Kleinman for the extraordinary amount of help that he gave me in revising and rewriting material for the third edition. I am also very grateful to Eva Cogan and Ira Goldfine for functioning in a similar capacity for the second edition (Ira also helped during the early phase of reorganizing the third edition). I would also like to thank Indira Malik who has been extremely helpful in making a range of improvements in the third edition; and Jeff Grunstein, who has been very helpful during the final stages of work on the book.

I would like to extend my appreciation to the following reviewers, whose comments and criticisms helped shape the book:

Earl L. Adams
Illinois Central College

Charles Burchard
Penn State Erie, Behrend College

Donald Burlingame
Potsdam College

Sue DeLay
Donnelly College

Jeanne Douglas
University of Vermont

Gerdika Elberfeld
Front Range Community College

George Hamer
South Dakota State University

Martin Osborne
Western Washington University

William Peters
San Diego Mesa College

Wayne Wallace
University of Wisconsin

Thomas E. Wolf
University of Pittsburgh—Greensburg Campus

Janet Urlaub
Sinclair Community College

In addition, I would like to thank Mike Sugarman, my editor, and Susan McCulley Gay, my developmental editor, at PWS Publishing Company for a superb job of guiding this project; and to Monique Calello, also at PWS, for her excellent work as production editor, and for creating the stunning new interior design of the book.

Finally, I would like to thank my wife, Marianne, my children, Dan and Maggie, and my canine associate, Zoe, for bearing with me and sustaining me during the difficult stretches of work on the book.

Julien Hennefeld

INTRODUCTION: OVERVIEW OF COMPUTERS AND PROBLEM SOLVING

BRIEF HISTORY

Computers have become so pervasive in today's world that it is easy to forget what a recent development they are. The first general-purpose, purely electronic digital computer, called ENIAC, was not built until 1946. ENIAC was a large, cumbersome device that contained 18,000 vacuum tubes, occupied a space of 50 feet by 30 feet, and weighed 30 tons. ENIAC was built for the U.S. Army to make calculations for weather predictions and ballistics tables. UNIVAC I, the first real commercial computer, was introduced in 1951.

Since those early days, there have been enormous advances in electronics technology. Perhaps the most remarkable breakthrough was the miniaturization of electronic circuits, allowing a circuit containing hundreds of thousands of switches to be etched onto a silicon chip the size of a fingernail. Today a computer that sits on a desktop, known as a microcomputer, can cost under $1,000 and yet have more computing power than did earlier computers that filled entire rooms and could be afforded only by a large organization.

COMPUTER LANGUAGES

In order to have a computer accomplish something useful, such as solve a problem or process information, you must provide it with a precise list of instructions. This list of instructions is called a ***program.*** The program must be written in a form that is appropriate for the computer—that is, in one of the computer languages.

Each computer comes equipped with its own ***machine language,*** which is the only language that the computer can "understand" directly. Instructions in machine language consist of sequences of 0s and 1s. For example, a typical instruction in a machine language might be

0100 1010 0101 0011

In the early days, all computer programs were written in machine languages. Now, however, much programming is done in **high-level languages** such as Pascal, BASIC, PL1, FORTRAN, C, or COBOL. High-level languages are much easier to program in since their instructions are similar to ordinary English. For example, a typical instruction in Pascal might be

```
wage := hours * rate;
```

Compiler All the programs in this book will be written in *Turbo Pascal*, which is a specific version of Pascal. You might wonder how a computer can understand a program written in the high-level language Turbo Pascal, if it can only understand its own machine language. The answer is that the computer must be supplied with a translating program—called a **compiler**—that translates the Turbo Pascal program (referred to as source code) into a list of instructions in machine language (referred to as object code). In other words, a compiler converts source code into object code. At the start of a programming session, you will load the Turbo compiler into RAM by using a diskette containing a copy of the Turbo compiler and an appropriate command.

HARDWARE VERSUS SOFTWARE

The term **hardware** means the physical components of a computer system. (By contrast, **software** means programs.) There are five basic types of hardware: (1) input devices, (2) output devices, (3) the central processing unit, (4) internal computer memory, and (5) external storage devices. Let us consider each of these in greater detail.

Input Devices When using a microcomputer, you usually input your program by typing it at the computer keyboard. Other input devices include a mouse, a scanner, and a joystick.

Output Devices Two important output devices are the video screen and the printer. Current printers come in three main varieties: dot matrix printers, ink spray printers, and laser printers.

CPU The central processing unit, or CPU, can be considered the brain of the computer. The CPU contains the arithmetic and logical circuitry and is responsible for all the actual processing of data.

Internal Computer Memory When your program and its data are input to the computer, they are stored in the computer's internal memory. In running a program, the CPU processes and manipulates what is in its internal memory.

All information in memory is represented in a series of bits, or binary digits (0s and 1s). A *byte* contains eight bits. For example, 01001011 is a typical byte. Since *one* byte can store a very limited amount of information (that is, a single letter or number no greater than 255), the storage capacity of a computer is discussed in terms of *K* (for *kilobytes*) or *meg* (for *megabytes*) where one K is approximately 1,000 bytes and one meg is approximately 1,000 K. Typically, a microcomputer will come with 640 K or 1 or more meg of internal memory.

Internal memory is divided into two types. *ROM* stands for read only memory. ROM is permanent memory; its contents are fixed by the manufacturer and cannot be altered by your programs. ROM contains information that helps guide the CPU in its internal functioning. It is not available for storing your programs.

The part of internal memory that is used as workspace to store your current program and its results is called *RAM,* which stands for random access memory. RAM is not permanent. In fact, whenever the computer is turned off, the contents of RAM are completely erased.

External Storage Devices   Suppose that you have just typed a program into the computer. How do you save this program for future use? (Recall that when the computer is turned off, your program will be completely erased from internal memory.) You save the program on an external storage device. Microcomputers generally use a *disk drive* and *diskette* for that purpose. A diskette is a plastic disk on which information can be stored in magnetically coded form. The disk drive functions something like a cassette recorder—programs can be stored and retrieved in much the same way as music can be recorded and played back using a cassette recorder.

There are three basic kinds of diskettes (and accompanying disk drives):

- *5¼-inch diskette* These diskettes are also known as floppy diskettes because they bend. A floppy diskette is fragile and should be handled with care since the information stored on it might be totally lost if the diskette is damaged.

- *3½-inch diskette* These are encased in hard plastic. Their main advantages over floppies are their greater durability and greater storage capacity.

Both the 5¼-inch and the 3½-inch diskettes are removable.

- **Hard disk** A hard disk is not removable. It is usually permanently installed by the time the computer is purchased. It looks like a large round platter, though you can't see it without unscrewing the casing that houses it. Its two big advantages over a diskette are its greater speed and its much larger amount of memory. A computer with a hard disk will generally also have at least one diskette drive.

PROBLEM SOLVING USING A COMPUTER
• •

Computers Cannot Think   Computers are incredibly fast (some can execute hundreds of millions of operations per second) and accurate, but they are also very dumb. Computers can do only what they are explicitly told to do. Moreover, they cannot recognize what you must have meant when you make a slight mistake in communicating with them. For example, if you were to mistype the `write` command as `wrrite`, the computer would have no idea what you meant and would not be able to execute your command.

Programmer's Role   To write a program in a language like Pascal to solve a particular problem, you (not the computer) must come up with the method for solving it. The computer will merely carry out the step-by-step list of instructions given in your program.

Stages in Problem Solving

1. ***Understanding the problem***   It is foolish to try to develop a solution before one understands the problem. It must be clear exactly what needs to be accomplished. The consequences of blindly charging ahead can be lost time and costly mistakes.

2. ***Developing an algorithm***   An ***algorithm*** is a detailed list of instructions that when carried out will lead to a solution for a particular type of problem. For example, a recipe to bake a cake is an algorithm. Or if our problem is to find the area of a circle, the formula $a = pi * r^2$ is the algorithm that gives the answer. Similarly, for any given problem, we need to develop the list of steps (or algorithm) that when followed provide the solution. In trying to solve a complicated problem, it is often a good idea to subdivide the problem into smaller more manageable subtasks—such an approach is called ***top down*** design.

3. ***Implementation and coding***   After an algorithm is developed, we need to apply the steps that are listed in the algorithm. In the case of writing a program, implementation means translating the algorithm into working commands or instructions in the specific computer language being used.

4. ***Testing and debugging***   The mere fact that you got a result or wrote a program that ran and produced an output does not necessarily mean that it is correct. The solution should be tested for other sets of input, designed to cover all types of cases.

In Chapter 4, we consider in greater detail problem solving in relation to writing programs.

What Good Is the Computer? Beginners often ask, "What good is the computer, if you are the one who really has to solve the problem?" The simple answer to this question is that the computer's incredible speed and accuracy can be enormous assets. Many tasks involve a large number of complex calculations that humans perform slowly and not very reliably but that a computer can be programmed to perform with great speed and 100 percent accuracy.

Even for tasks of a conceptual nature, the computer can be a great asset because much of conceptual analysis is nothing more than trial-and-error consideration of a large number of cases.

• • • • • • • • •
Question   Let us suppose that the Celtics and the Lakers are about to play in the championship basketball series—the first team to win four games wins the series. As you probably know, playing at home is a big advantage. Let us suppose that the Celtics and the Lakers are evenly matched in that, for any given game, the home team has a 75 percent chance of winning. Let us also suppose that games 1 and 2 are to be played in Boston; games 3, 4, and 5 (if necessary) are to be played in Los Angeles; and games 6 and 7 (if necessary) are to be played in Boston. The question is: Under these assumptions, which team if any has the advantage? Even more specifically, what is the probability for each team of winning the series?

Answer   One of the teams has a distinct advantage. One way of determining which team has the advantage is to make an exact calculation of the probability of each team's winning the series. If you are not familiar with the necessary mathematical techniques, there is a second way in which you might proceed— use the techniques of computer simulation from Chapter 14.   • • •

Artificial Intelligence   As we have mentioned, a computer can do only what it has been explicitly programmed to do by a human. In this sense, a computer cannot think. Nevertheless, there is a branch of computer research called ***artificial intelligence*** that is devoted to programming the computer to perform tasks that would seem to require real "intelligence." Developments in artificial intelligence (for example, chess-playing programs, language translation programs, and expert systems such as computer medical diagnoses) have been quite impressive. Although there is no general agreement among computer scientists concerning the significance of these results, clearly the distinction between human thought and what a computer can achieve is not as cut and dried as was once believed.

INTRODUCTION TO TURBO PASCAL

• • • A *computer program* consists of a list of instructions written in a *computer language.* All the programs in this book are written in Turbo Pascal, a version of the computer language Pascal. In this chapter, we will go over some of the basics of Turbo Pascal. In Chapter 2, you will learn how to sit at the computer and type in your programs. • • •

1.1 A FIRST PROGRAM

Example

```
program HeightInInches;
var feet, inches: integer;

begin
  feet := 6;
  inches := feet * 12;
  writeln ('Height in inches is ', inches)
end.
```

When this program is ***run*** (see Chapter 2 for the details of running a program using the Turbo system), the computer screen will display

```
Height in inches is 72
```

The first line of the program is the program header. This gives the program a name. The second line declares that the two variables, `feet` and `inches`, will have `integer` values. The ***body*** (the action part of the program) starts with the word `begin`. The first statement in the body assigns the value 6 to `feet`. The next statement takes the value of `feet`, multiplies it by 12 and assigns this result to the variable `inches`. The `writeln` statement produces the screen output.

Keywords   Certain words, such as the `writeln` command to produce output, have built-in meanings in Turbo Pascal and are known as ***keywords.*** Note that within the program `HeightInInches`, we italicized each keyword.

Variables   In processing data, a computer program usually must keep track of the values of various quantities—these quantities can be referred to by names known as ***variables.***

Legal Variable Names   A variable name must begin with a letter and may contain only letters, digits, and the underbar (_). One further restriction is that a special class of keywords, known as reserved words, cannot be used as variable names. (In Turbo Pascal 7.0, a color monitor will display a program's reserved words in white. See Appendix A for a list of all reserved words.) If a variable name has more than 63 characters, only the first 63 matter. Some legal variable names are

```
feet  sum  Tax1993  FINAL  average_score
```

Some illegal names for variables are

`1993Tax`	Doesn't begin with a letter
`average.score`	Periods are not permitted
`average score`	Blanks are not permitted

Declaration of Variables   Every variable that appears in the body of a program must have its data type declared. This is done by listing all these variables and giving their data types in the `var` section, which begins with the keyword `var`. In the previous program, the statement

```
var feet, inches: integer;
```

declared the variables `feet` and `inches` as type `integer` variables. Variables of type `integer` can take on as values only whole numbers such as 7, 45,

0, or −36. Moreover, values of type `integer` must be between −32,768 and 32,767. In this chapter, we will consider only variables of type `integer`. In later chapters, we will consider other data types.

Assignment Statements   An assignment statement assigns a value to a variable. For example,

```
feet := 6;
```

is an assignment statement that assigns the value 6 to `feet`. The first two statements of the main body of the program `HeightInInches` are assignment statements.

The general form of an assignment statement is

```
variable := expression;
```

where the expression might be a constant, a variable, or a more complicated arithmetic expression.

When the computer reaches an assignment statement, it evaluates the expression on the right side of the assignment symbol (:=) and assigns the result to the single variable on the left of the symbol.

In Pascal, the symbols for addition and subtraction are the usual symbols, but the symbol for multiplication is *. There are two division operations, **div** and /. (They will be discussed in Chapter 3.)

writeln Statements   A **writeln** statement is used to send information to the screen or printer. For now, we just discuss outputting to the screen. (Writing to the printer is discussed in Section 2.3.)

You may use `writeln` to output a message. To do so, enclose the message in single quotes. The single quote mark that is used for messages is on the same key as the double quote mark. This key is used for both open and closed quote marks.

Screen

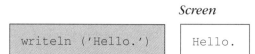

```
writeln ('Hello.')
```

```
Hello.
```

Or you may use a `writeln` statement to output the value of a variable or an expression.

Screen

```
x := 7;
writeln (x);
writeln (x + 9);
```

```
7
16
```

A writeln statement can also combine messages, variables, and expressions in any order. Just use a comma to separate the parts. For example, in the first program, the statement

```
writeln ('Height in inches is ', inches)
```

outputs the message that was in quotes followed by the value of the variable inches, thus writing

```
Height in inches is 72
```

Be aware that different parts in a writeln statement will be output one after another with no space between them. One way to have a space appear between the message and the value of the variable is to include a blank space in the writeln statement just before the closing quote mark. This blank is part of the message.

Example   Suppose the variable area has the value 20. The statements

```
writeln ('area of rectangle is ', area);
writeln ('area of rectangle is', area);
```

will produce the output

```
area of rectangle is 20
area of rectangle is20
```

Note that blank spaces outside the quote marks (like the blank after the comma) are ignored.

Question   What will be the output of the following program segment?

```
x := 8;
y := 6;
writeln (x, y);
writeln (x, ' ', y);
```

Answer

```
86
8 6
```

• • •

write versus writeln Writeln has the computer output what is in parentheses and then go to the start of the next output line.

By contrast, the **write** statement has the computer output what is in parentheses and then stop there without going to the next line. The difference between write and writeln is illustrated in the next question.

• • • • • • • • • •
Question What will be output by each of the following?

(a)
```
yards := 8;
feet := yards * 3;
write (yards, ' yards is');
write (feet, ' feet');
```

(b)
```
yards := 8;
feet := yards * 3;
writeln (yards, ' yards is');
writeln (feet, ' feet');
```

Answer

(a)
```
8 yards is24 feet
```

(b)
```
8 yards is
24 feet
```

• • •

Empty writeln Statements The writeln statement may be used alone, without an output list, if the programmer wishes to send only a carriage return to the screen—in other words, drop the cursor to the beginning of the next output line. If the cursor is already at the beginning of a screen line, an empty writeln statement will cause the computer to skip a line in the output.

• • • • • • • • • •
Question What will these segments output?

(a)
```
writeln ('Yes');
writeln ('No');
```

(b)
```
writeln ('Yes');
writeln;
writeln ('No');
```

(c)
```
write ('Yes');
write ('No');
```

Answer

(a)
```
Yes
No
```

(b)
```
Yes

No
```

(c)
```
YesNo
```

• • •

Question   What will be output on the screen by the following complete program? Give it with the *exact* messages and spacing.

```
program NickelDime;
var nickels, dimes, TotCents: integer;

begin
  nickels := 3;
  dimes := 7;
  TotCents := (nickels * 5) + (dimes * 10);
  writeln (nickels, ' nickels and ', dimes, ' dimes');
  writeln ('= ', TotCents, ' cents')
end.
```

Answer

```
3 nickels and 7 dimes
= 85 cents
```

. . .

1.2   PUNCTUATION AND STYLE
. . . .

Correct punctuation is essential for running a program. By contrast, the spacing or indentation within a program won't affect whether it runs though it does affect how easy it is for a person to understand the program.

Period   The period after the last end in a program is used to mark the end of the entire program.

Semicolons   A semicolon is used to separate two consecutive statements in a Pascal program. Note that in the two full programs you have seen so far most but not all lines end in a semicolon. For now, the rule for semicolons is to put them after every line *except*

1. begin
2. the last end (it gets a period)
3. comments (discussed at the end of this section)
4. the line before an end (semicolon is optional here)

. . . .
Question   Put the appropriate punctuation in the following program, and then give the output.

```
program YdsToFeet
var feet, yards: integer
begin
   yards := 8
   feet := yards * 3
   writeln (feet)
end
```

Answer

```
program YdsToFeet;
var feet, yards: integer;
begin
   yards := 8;
   feet := yards * 3;
   writeln (feet)
end.
```

The output will be 24 .   • • •

REMARK   It is optional whether to put a semicolon after the statement `writeln (feet)`. We will, however, follow the style of always omitting a semicolon after a statement that immediately precedes the keyword `end`.

• • •

Commas   Commas are used to separate items in a list, such as the variables of one type in a declaration statement or several print elements in a `writeln` statement.

Use Meaningful Variable Names and Identifiers

Any name that you make up for use within a program is known as an ***identifier.*** For example, each variable name is an identifier; so is the program name. The same rule for legality that was stated for variable names in Section 1.1 also applies to any identifier made up by the programmer.

In making up a name for a variable or some other identifier, you should use a name that is not only legal but also meaningful (the name should remind you of what it refers to). Thus, `inches` would be a better variable name than `x` would be to keep track of the number of inches.

Reserved Words versus Standard Identifiers   Keywords are words with a built-in meaning in Pascal. There are two kinds of **keywords.**

1. **Reserved words** are keywords that may *never* be used for an identifier that you make up. For example, `begin`, `end`, and `var` are reserved words. See Appendix A for a complete list. Recall also that a color monitor will display reserved words from your program in white.

2. **Standard identifiers** consist of all other keywords. For example, `writeln` and `integer` are standard identifiers. See Appendix A for a list of some of the most commonly used standard identifiers. Although it is legal to use a standard identifier for a name that you make up, it is better not to do so since that will interfere with the identifier's built-in meaning within that program.

Blank Spaces and Indenting   With regard to blank spaces, two rules that must be followed are (1) at least one space must separate any two distinct identifiers in the program, and (2) no spaces may be placed in the middle of an identifier or in the middle of compound symbols such as := (thus : = would be an error).

Additional spaces, especially in the form of indentation and line breaks, can and should be used to make the program easier to read. Note, however, that this is only for the human eye since the computer is guided solely by punctuation and Pascal keywords in determining where one statement ends and the next one begins. Thus, program `YdsToFeet` would run perfectly well even if it were typed as

```
program YdsToFeet; var feet, yards:
integer; begin yards := 8; feet :=
yards * 3; writeln (feet) end.
```

Comments   Another important method for making a program easier to understand is to include **comments.** Comments are simply messages to whoever is reading the program. They may explain the purpose of the program or even clarify individual steps. They are completely ignored by the compiler.

To place a comment in a program, enclose the message in braces { }. Because a comment is not considered a statement, no additional semicolons are needed. You should always place a comment after the program header of a program to explain the purpose of the program. Here is the first program from Section 1.1 with a comment.

```
program HeightInInches;
{converts 6 feet into inches}
var feet, inches: integer;
begin
   feet := 6;
   inches := feet * 12;
   writeln ('Height in inches is ', inches)
end.
```

Capitalization and Identifiers   The Turbo compiler does not distinguish between uppercase and lowercase letters in identifiers. Thus, it would not matter if you typed the reserved word end as end, End, or END. As a matter of style, however, in this book reserved words and predeclared identifiers will be typed entirely in lowercase.

In making up variable names, you may use capitalization to improve clarity if the name is a compound word. For example, you could declare a variable with the name ClassAverage. Note that ClassAverage is easier to read than classaverage. Although the compiler would not object if within the same program you sometimes typed ClassAverage and other times typed classaverage (the compiler would treat these as exactly the same variable), doing so would be considered poor style. The compiler would object, however, if you typed ClassAverage as class_average, since the underbar makes it a different variable.

Capitalization and Strings   A *string,* also called a *literal,* is a value consisting of a sequence of characters. For strings, the compiler is sensitive to whether letters are uppercase or lowercase. Hence, writeln ('ABC') will have a different effect than writeln ('abc').

1.3 MEMORY CELLS AND MORE ON ASSIGNMENTS

• •

When a program is run, each variable declared in the var section is given a memory location (which you can think of as a memory cell). For example, when program NickelDime of Section 1.1 is run, three memory cells are created. After the first three assignment statements, memory can be depicted as follows:

nickels	dimes	TotCents
3	7	85

Changing the Value of a Variable The memory cell of a variable will hold just the current value of the variable.

Question What will be output by the following program?

```
program drill;
var x: integer;

begin
  x := 6;
  x := 8;
  writeln ('x is ', x)
end.
```

Memory

```
   x
 ┌─────┐
 │  6̸  │
 │  8  │
 └─────┘
```

Answer *Output*

```
x is 8
```

Note that x is first assigned the value 6. Then the next assignment statement assigns x the new value 8 (erasing the previous value of x). The `writeln` statement prints just the current value of x. ● ● ●

Only Variable on Left Affected Recall that an assignment statement assigns a value to the variable to the left of the assignment symbol (: =). Thus, a statement like

```
num1 := num2;
```

assigns to num1 whatever value num2 has; it does not affect the value of num2.

Question What will be output by the following program fragment?

```
num1 := 5;
num2 := 14;
num1 := num2;
writeln (num1);
writeln (num2);
```

Answer In the line-by-line memory trace given to the right, a dash means the variable has not had its value changed by the current statement.

Output

```
14
14
```

```
num1 := 5;
num2 := 14;
num1 := num2;
writeln (num1);
writeln (num2);
```

num1	num2
5	—
—	14
14	—
—	—
—	—

• • •

Same Variable on Both Sides   The variable on the left side may also appear on the right. In this case, the variable's old value is used in the expression on the right side to calculate its new value.

• • • • • • • • • •
Examples

(a)   count := count + 1   {increases the value of count by 1}

(b)   sum := sum + x   {increases the value of sum by x; it does not change the value of x}

(c)   num := 3 * num   {triples the value of num}

CAUTION   The left side of an assignment statement must consist of a single variable. Thus,

     x + 4 := y   {is illegal}   • • •

• • • • • • • • • •
Question   What will be printed by the following fragment?

```
hours := 40;
rate := 5;
pay := hours * rate;
writeln (hours, ' ', rate, ' ', pay);
rate := rate + 1;
writeln (hours, ' ', rate, ' ', pay);
pay := hours * rate;
writeln (hours, ' ', rate, ' ', pay);
```

Answer

```
40 5 200
40 6 200
40 6 240
```

                                          • • •

REMARK   Notice that the original value of pay (200) was printed by the second writeln statement because at that point pay had not been assigned a new value yet. The statement, `rate := rate + 1`, changes the value of `rate`. The value of `pay` is not changed until the second time that the statement `pay := hours * rate` is executed.   • • •

1.4 INTERACTIVE PROGRAMS

Obviously, the `HeightInInches` program in Section 1.1 is not very useful. Every time it is run, it will perform the same computation and produce the same output. A more useful program would allow the *user* (the person who runs the program) to enter a value of his own choosing for `feet`. Such a program is called ***interactive.***

readln Statements   A **readln** statement allows values to be entered from a source external to the program. One type of `readln` statement allows the user to type in value(s) from the keyboard while the program is running.

When the computer comes to a `readln` statement during the run of a program, it will halt until the user types in a value (or values) and hits the ENTER key.

• • • • • • • • • •
Example

```
program FeetToInches;
{converts input number of feet to inches}
var feet, inches: integer;

begin
   write ('enter number of feet ');
   readln (feet);
   inches := feet * 12;
   writeln (inches, ' inches')
end.
```

When this program is run, the computer will display on the output screen the prompt

```
enter number of feet
```

and will halt with the cursor blinking. The computer is waiting for the user to enter a value for `feet`. After the user types a value and presses the ENTER key, the computer will assign that value to `feet` and then resume the running of the program. For example, typing 5 and pressing the ENTER key would have the same effect as `feet := 5;`.

After the run is complete, the output screen can be recalled (by pressing ALT-F5). The final display will be

```
enter number of feet 5
60 inches
```

Prompts   In writing an interactive program, you should precede each `readln` statement with a `write` or `writeln` statement that will display a message to let the user know what kind of value to enter. That was the purpose of

```
write ('enter number of feet ')
```

in the previous program.

Generally, you should use the `write-readln` combination instead of `writeln-readln`. The advantage of `write-readln` is that it uses less screen space since the value that is entered will appear on the same screen line as the prompt. (With `writeln-readln`, the entered value would appear on a line by itself.)

Input Lists   The general format of a `readln` statement is

```
readln (input list);
```

where `input list` is a list of one or more variables separated by commas. Thus, it would be permissible to use a statement like

```
readln (nickels, dimes);
```

Of course, the associated prompt should mention that values for several variables are to be entered—for example

```
write ('enter number of nickels and dimes ');
```

When the statement `readln (nickels, dimes)` is executed, the user should type two integer values, separated by at least one space, and then press ENTER after both values have been typed.

• • • • • • • • •

Question   Suppose we want a program to convert an input number of nickels and dimes into a total number of cents. For example, if the user inputs 3 and 7 for the number of nickels and dimes, respectively, the screen display at the end of the run would be

```
enter number of nickels and dimes 3 7
3 nickels and 7 dimes = 85 cents
```

Complete the blanks in the following program to produce the output shown:

```
program NickelDime;
{converts input number of nickels and dimes into cents}
var nickels, dimes, TotCents: integer;

begin
  write ( _____ );
  readln (nickels, dimes);
  TotCents := (nickels * 5) + (dimes * 10);
  writeln ( _____ )
end.
```

Answer   The prompt for `readln (nickels, dimes)` is obviously

```
write ('enter number of nickels and dimes ');
```

To determine what the `writeln` statement is, let us analyze the second line of output by underlining what is printed verbatim and encircling what resulted from the value of a variable.

③ nickels and ⑦ dimes = ⑧⑤ cents

Thus, the `writeln` statement should be

```
writeln (nickels,' nickels and ', dimes,
                  ' dimes = ',Totcents,' cents')   • • •
```

read Statements   Turbo Pascal also provides a **read** statement. It is advisable, however, to use `read` statements only when reading from external files (Chapters 9 and 22). Don't use `read` for entering data from the keyboard.

• • • • • • • • •   **EXERCISES**
• •

1. Which of the following identifiers are legal? Which are illegal? Why?

(a) `FinalScore`   **(b)** `final score`

(c) `final_score`   **(d)** `Sales1987`

(e) `1987Sales`   **(f)** `m * 2`

2. Put the appropriate punctuation in the following program.

```
program prog8
var feet, inches integer

begin
   feet := 5
   inches := feet * 12
   writeln (inches)
end
```

3. What output will the following fragment produce?

```
x := 5;
y := 8;
writeln ('x equals ', x);
writeln (x, y);
writeln (x, 'equals x');
```

4. What output will the following fragments produce?

(a)
```
numb := 10;
x := 5;
write (numb);
write (x);
writeln (numb);
```

(b)
```
numb := 10;
x := 5;
write (numb, ' ');
write (x, ' ');
writeln;
writeln (numb);
```

(c)
```
x := 4;
y := 6;
y := y + x;
x := x + 1;
writeln ('x = ', x);
writeln ('y = ', y);
```

(d)
```
numb1 := 5;
numb2 := 9;
numb1 := numb1 + 1;
numb2 := numb2 + numb1;
writeln ('numb1 = ', numb1);
writeln ('numb2 = ', numb2);
```

5. Complete the following program fragment so that it produces the output given to the right.

```
dimes := 4;
pennies := 6;
TotCents := _____
_____
_____
```

```
4 dimes and 6 pennies
equals 46 cents.
```

6. Write an interactive program to convert yards into inches. Here are two typical runs.

Run 1

```
enter number of yards 4
4 yards = 144 inches
```

Run 2

```
enter number of yards 6
6 yards = 216 inches
```

7. Write an interactive program that asks the user to input a number of dimes and a number of quarters. The program should then calculate and output the cents total.

8. Write a program that asks the user to input the length and the width of a rectangle. The program should output both the area and the perimeter of that rectangle.

Chapter

2

USING THE TURBO SYSTEM

2.1 SOME BASICS

Keyboard   Take a moment to look at your keyboard. Find the ENTER key (↵). Then find the CTRL key (control), the ESC key (escape), and the ALT (alternate) key. Also find the 12 function keys marked F1 through F12.

CAUTION

1. Observe the row of number keys. Be careful not to confuse the letter O with the number 0, or the letter l with the number 1.

2. The same keystroke is used for both the open and closed quote marks in a statement like

```
writeln ('Computers never lie');
```

You must use the key ⌜"⌝ for that purpose.   • • •

Booting Up   When the computer is switched on, it carries out a startup process known as ***booting up.*** During the final step in the boot process, the operating system is loaded into the computer's memory. The operating system provides the basics necessary for the operation of the system. We will assume that the operating system you will be using is the ***DOS*** operating system. Once the system is started, you will be in the DOS environment where you can execute any of the DOS commands that you will use primarily for disk and file operations, or you can proceed to load other programs (like Turbo Pascal). You can tell that you are in DOS if you see a DOS prompt ending with the > symbol, for example, C:\> or A:>.

Disk Drives   The operating system, DOS, usually designates the diskette drive(s) for removable diskettes as drive A and drive B, and the fixed hard drive(s) as drive C and higher. If a computer has only one diskette drive, it is usually drive A. If a computer has two diskette drives, usually the upper (or left-hand) drive is drive A and the other is drive B.

Files   Information can be stored together in a unit known as a file. One important use of files is to save programs on a disk so that they can be recalled for future use. To facilitate their retrieval, each file is given a name by which the computer's operating system can recognize it. A file name consists of a first part beginning with a letter and containing up to eight characters that are letters or digits, and an optional second part (extension) consisting of a period followed by as many as three characters. For example, prog1.pas is a valid file name.

Formatting   A new blank diskette must be formatted before it can be used to store information. To format a blank diskette that is in drive A, at the DOS prompt (C:\>) you should type **format a:** then press **ENTER** and follow the screen instructions.

CAUTION   The format command will destroy any information that is previously on a diskette. Do not format the diskette that comes with this book since it contains various files that you will be using later.   • • •

2.2   A FIRST LOOK AT TURBO PASCAL

The exact procedures to get into Turbo Pascal depend on the configuration of your particular system. On many systems, you would either type tp7 at the DOS prompt or select tp7 from a menu. Record the method for getting into Turbo Pascal on your system here: _____

Edit Screen   When you have just loaded Turbo Pascal 7, the computer monitor displays the Edit Screen (top of page 24) with the cursor blinking inside the Edit Window. The Edit Screen must be displayed when you want to type in a program.

User Screen versus Edit Screen   The User Screen is a second mode that the monitor can display. Whereas the Edit Screen displays a program, the User Screen displays the output produced by running the program. To move from the Edit Screen to the User Screen, press ALT-F5 (that is, while holding down the ALT key press the F5 key). To return from the User Screen to the Edit Screen, simply press any key.

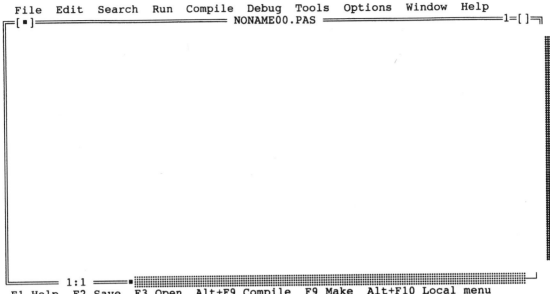

```
 File   Edit   Search   Run   Compile   Debug   Tools   Options   Window   Help
┌─[■]══════════════════════════ NONAME00.PAS ══════════════════════════1=[ ]─┐
│                                                                             ▓│
│                                                                             ▓│
│                                                                             ▓│
│                                                                             ▓│
│                                                                             ▓│
│                                                                             ▓│
│                                                                             ▓│
│                                                                             ▓│
│                                                                             ▓│
│                                                                             ▓│
│                                                                             ▓│
│                                                                             ▓│
│                                                                             ▓│
│                                                                             ▓│
│                                                                             ▓│
│                                                                             ▓│
│                                                                             ▓│
│                                                                             ▓│
│                                                                             ▓│
└══════ 1:1 ══════■░░░░░░░░░░░░░░░░░░░░░░░░░░░░░░░░░░░░░░░░░░░░░░░░░░░░░░░░░░░┘
 F1 Help   F2 Save   F3 Open   Alt+F9 Compile   F9 Make   Alt+F10 Local menu
```

Edit Screen

- Press **ALT-F5** to go to the User Screen. (Do so now.)
- Press **any key** to return to the Edit Screen. (Do so now.)

Pulling Down a Menu

The ten main submenus are listed across the top line of the Edit Screen. When the Edit Screen is displayed, you can pull down a desired submenu by holding down the ALT key and pressing the first letter of the desired submenu (or, using a mouse, by clicking the desired submenu).

Pulling Down the File Submenu

- Press **ALT-f** (or, using a mouse, click File).

Do so now. The File submenu (top of page 25) should appear in a box on your screen, containing 10 choices.

To close or get rid of a submenu without selecting from it,

- Press the **ESC** key.

Pulling Down the Window Submenu

- Press **ALT-w,** look at it, and then press **ESC** to close it.

Selecting a Choice from a Submenu

Pull-down method   You can select a choice from a submenu by first pulling down the submenu and then typing the highlighted letter of the desired

```
┌─────────────────────────────┐
│  New                        │
│  Open              F3       │
│  Save              F2       │
│  Save as...                 │
│  Save all                   │
│  -----------------          │
│  Change dir...              │
│  Print                      │
│  Printer setup...           │
│  DOS shell                  │
│  Exit             Alt+x     │
└─────────────────────────────┘
```

File Submenu

choice—note that it is not always the first letter. (Or if you are using a mouse, click the desired choice.) For example, you can exit from Pascal by selecting the Exit choice from the File submenu. Thus, to exit

- Press **ALT-f** and then **x**.

Hot-key method Some submenu choices can be selected by a shortcut known as the hot-key method. If the choice has a hot key and if the Edit Screen is displayed, you can select that choice by pressing its hot key(s) without having to pull down the submenu it is on. For example, you can exit from Turbo Pascal by pressing the hot-key combination ALT-x without pulling down the File submenu. Section 2.6 gives a list of the most commonly used hot keys. Note also that each of the pull-down submenus lists the hot-key method for a choice (if it exists) to the right of the choice. For example, in the File submenu, note that the hot key that corresponds to the **S**ave choice is F2.

2.3 TYPING AND RUNNING A FIRST PROGRAM IN TURBO PASCAL

· ·

Running the Program with Output on the Screen

We assume that you have a formatted diskette in the A drive and that you are already in Turbo Pascal with the Edit Screen displayed.

Step 1   Opening a File and Giving It a Name

- Press **F3**.

This is the hot key for the Open choice from the File submenu. In the Name box, you will type a file name for your program.

- Type **a:prog1** and press **ENTER.**

The part of the screen inside the double-lined box should be blank. (If it is not, you already have a program with file name prog1 on your disk; in that case, you should press F3 again and make up a different file name like examp1.) Note that the drive prefix a: is included as part of the file name since we want to save the file on the diskette in drive A. (You may omit the drive prefix a: in the file name if the current directory is a: See the discussion of the Change dir choice in Section 2.6.)

Step 2   Typing in Your Program

Type in the following program:

```
program drill
begin
   writeln ('Computers never lie');
   writeln ('2 + 2 = 5')
end.
```

Note we intentionally had you make a syntax error, omitting the semicolon after `drill`.

Step 3   Saving Your Program

- Press **F2.**

This is the hot key for the Save choice. A copy of your program is now saved on your diskette with the file name prog1.pas.

Step 4   Compiling Your Program

- Press **ALT-F9.**

(Recall that this means while holding down the ALT key press the F9 key.)

If the computer detects a syntax error such as a missing semicolon (see Section 3.6 for more on syntax errors), then it will display an error message at the top of the screen and return you to the Edit Screen with the cursor positioned where the compiler thinks the error occurred. Usually the error will be on the same line as the cursor or on the line above the cursor (that will be the case for the missing semicolon).

- Type ; (a semicolon) after the word *drill.*
- Press **F2** to save the corrected version.
- Press **ALT-F9** to compile.

If there are more errors, each one must be detected and corrected. Once your program has been successfully compiled, you will be prompted by a blinking cursor to press any key.

- Press **any key.**

Step 5   Running Your Program

- Press **CTRL-F9.**

The output will flash momentarily on the User Screen, and then Turbo will return you to the Edit Screen.

Step 6   Recalling the Output Screen

- Press **ALT-F5** to recall the output screen.

Now you will see

```
Turbo Pascal Version 7.0
Computers never lie
2 + 2 = 5
```

- Press **any key** to get back to the Edit Screen.

If you are using a color monitor, note that reserved words are in white, whereas the rest of your program is in yellow. As you will see later, this is a useful debugging feature.

REMARK   You can combine the compile step with the run step by pressing CTRL-F9 (without pressing ALT-F9 first). This automatically compiles the program, and if there are no syntax errors, the computer will proceed to run it.

• • •

Revising the Program So That Output Is Printed on Paper

Continuing from where we left off, we assume that your program is displayed on the Edit Screen. If you want some or all of a program's output printed on paper, you should do the following:

1. Include the declaration uses printer;.

2. Insert lst, into each writeln or write statement whose output you want to be printed on paper.

3. Rerun the program.

Thus, prog1.pas would be modified to

```
program drill;
uses printer;
begin
   writeln (1st, 'Computers never lie');
   writeln (1st, '2 + 2 = 5')
end.
```

After you have made these modifications, make sure the printer is turned on, and then press **CTRL-F9** to rerun your program. This time the output (for all the `writeln` statements with `1st`) will be printed on paper.

Printing the Program Itself on Paper

Make sure the Edit Screen is displayed and then

- Press **ALT-f** and then **p**.

2.4 RUNNING A SECOND PROGRAM

You should be aware of two minor complications. The first complication is that the window from the previous program will still be open unless you close it. At this stage, it is not worth keeping several file windows open, so before you type in your second program, you should close the window for the first one by pressing ALT-F3. Another complication is that the User Screen might contain outputs from previous runs. Suppose that you have just finished running a program and now you want to type in another program.

- Press **ALT-F3** to close the previous window.

- Give the program that you are about to type in a file name, type in the program, save it, and then run it. Do so for the following program, naming it a:prog2:

```
program drill2;
var n: integer;
begin
   n := 12;
   writeln (n, 'squared = ', n * n)
end.
```

After you press **ALT-F5,** the output screen will display.

```
Turbo 7.0
Computers never lie
2 + 2 = 5
12 squared = 144
```

REMARK   The output for your first program is still on the output screen immediately above the current output. If you find this inconvenient, you can declare the **crt** unit in the **uses** section and then include **clrscr** (for clear screen) as the first line in the body of the program. For example, make the following changes to program `drill2` and rerun the program:

```
program drill2;
uses crt;
var n: integer;
begin
  clrscr;
  n := 12;
  writeln ( n,' squared = ', n*n)
end.
```

Notice that the output has now been placed on a fresh screen.   • • •

An Alternative to ALT-F5   There is a way to keep the output screen displayed after a program run without pressing ALT-F5. If you include the statement

```
readln
```

as the last statement in the program (before `end.`), the output screen will remain displayed until you press the ENTER key.

2.5 LOADING AND VIEWING
EXISTING FILES FROM THE DISK
• •

Loading an Existing Program

• Press **F3** to bring up the Open dialog box.

The cursor will be blinking in the Name box, and the files with the .pas extension will be listed in the Files box. At this point, you can either

- Type in the file name like **a:prog1.pas** and then press **ENTER**.

or

- Press the **TAB** key to move into the Files box.
- Use the arrow key to highlight the desired file, and then press **ENTER**. (If the desired file is the first one listed in the Files box, you will need to press ENTER twice.)

.pas versus .bak When you save the current version of a program file such as prog1, Turbo saves it as prog1.pas and also saves the previous version, giving it the .bak extension. Thus, the previous version of prog1.pas would be saved as prog1.bak.

Viewing the Files on the Disk

If you would like to see a list of all files that are in the current subdirectory on your disk, press F3 and then type a:*.* in the Name box, and then press ENTER. Thus, if you typed and saved the two programs from the preceding sections on a newly formatted disk, the Files box would display

```
prog1.bak
prog1.pas
prog2.pas
```

2.6 MORE ON SUBMENU CHOICES

Hot-Key Method Hot keys are not available for all submenu choices. Here is a table of some of the most useful hot keys. (Hot keys should be pressed only when the Edit Screen is displayed; they won't work from the User Screen.)

Hot Key	Use
ESC	To cancel a current operation or close a dialog box
F2	To save the program in the active edit window
F3	To open a file
F5	To enlarge the active window to full size
F6	To make the next window active
SHIFT-F6	To make the previous window active
ALT-x	To exit from Turbo Pascal
ALT-F3	To close the active window
ALT-F5	To recall the output screen
ALT-F9	To compile a program
CTRL-F9	To run a program

CAUTION   Be aware that there are situations in which the computer will not respond to your next command until you first get rid of an open dialog box by pressing the ESC key.   ● ● ●

Save as   The Save as choice is useful if you want to save a copy of the program currently on the Edit Screen, giving it a new file name, without erasing the copy that was previously saved under a different file name. After selecting Save as, you will be prompted to enter a file name for a copy of the current program.

DOS Shell versus Exit   The DOS Shell temporarily transfers you to DOS. When you have completed what you needed to do in DOS, you can return to where you were in Turbo Pascal by typing exit at the DOS prompt. By contrast, using the Exit choice from the File submenu (or, equivalently, the ALT-x hot key) causes a permanent exit from Turbo Pascal and does not allow you to return to where you left off.

Change dir   The Change dir choice can be used either to merely look at what the current directory is or to actually change it. First, let us use Change dir to look at the current directory without changing it.

● Press **ALT-f** then **c**

The current directory will be displayed in the Directory name box. After looking at it, try to pull down the File submenu by pressing **ALT-f**. Nothing happens. What is wrong? You must first close the dialog box for the Change dir operation by pressing **ESC**.

Second, let us select the Change dir choice again, and this time use it to change to the main directory of drive A.

● Press **ALT-f** then **c** type **a:** and then press **ENTER**.

2.7 MORE ON EDITING

● ●

Cursor Movement   The four arrow keys (→), (←), (↓), and (↑) can be used to move the cursor in the direction indicated. Other keys that can be used to move the cursor are

HOME	Moves the cursor to the beginning of the current line
END	Moves the cursor to the right end of the current line
CTRL-END	Moves the cursor to the bottom of the screen (hold down the CTRL key while pressing the END key)
CTRL-HOME	Moves the cursor to the top of the screen

| PGUP | Moves the cursor up approximately one screen in the file |
| PGDN | Moves the cursor down approximately one screen in the file |

Deleting a Line   CTRL-y will delete the entire line on which the cursor is currently positioned. By contrast, CTRL-q-y will delete from the current cursor position to the end of the line.

Three Similar Keys   It pays to master the difference between the DEL (delete) key and the BACKSPACE (←) key. The DEL key erases the character at the cursor, whereas the BACKSPACE key erases the character to the left of the cursor. A further source of confusion is a third key, the left arrow key (←), which moves the cursor one space back to the left but *without erasing anything*. Although the left arrow key looks like the BACKSPACE key, you can recognize it by the fact that the four cursor arrow keys are next to one another on the keyboard.

Insert and Overwrite   Note that text can be entered in either of two editing modes—*insert* or *overwrite.* When you first enter the editor, you are in the insert mode by default.

When you are in the insert mode, any new characters you type will be entered at the current position of the cursor. Thus, existing text at the current cursor position and to the right of the cursor will be moved farther to the right as you type new text.

When you are in the overwrite mode, any new character(s) you type will replace the character at the current cursor position. You can tell that you are in the insert mode in Turbo 7.0 by the thin cursor (as opposed to the thicker cursor when you are in the overwrite mode).

The INS key acts as a toggle between the insert and overwrite modes.

Inserting a New Line Between Two Existing Lines   First make sure you are in the insert mode. Then move the cursor to the line just above where you wish the new line to be inserted.

• Move the cursor to the end of the line, and then press **ENTER**.

The cursor will then be at the left end of a blank line between the two existing lines. You can now enter the text for that new line.

2.8 TUTORIALS ON THE STUDENT DISKETTE

The diskette at the back of the book contains explanations and hands-on practice sessions for using the Turbo editor and commonly used DOS commands. (See Appendix H for a more detailed content listing and procedures for using the student diskette.)

• • • • • • • • • •   EXERCISES
• •

1. Type in and run the program given in Section 2.2, sending all the output to the screen. Then rerun it so that all the output is printed on paper, and print the program itself on paper.

2. Which screen does your program output appear on, the Edit Screen or the User Screen? Explain how to go back and forth between the Edit Screen and the User Screen.

3. What is another method to achieve the same effect as the F3 hot key? *Hint:* Pull down the File submenu and look at what F3 is equivalent to.

4. Suppose that the output screen is displayed giving the output for a program that you have just run but have not saved yet. Will pressing the F2 hot key at this point save your program?

5. Explain the difference between ALT-x and the DOS Shell choice from the File submenu.

6. How can you see what files are contained in your diskette?

7. How do you type in a new line of a program between two existing lines?

8. Pull down various submenus until you find one that contains the choice that F6 is a hot key for.

3

MORE ON THE ELEMENTS OF PASCAL

• • • So far the only data type we've used has been `integer`. In this chapter, we will expand our repertoire to include other built-in data types—`real`, as well as four additional data types for integers. The rules of precedence for operation symbols are also given. • • •

3.1 A FIRST LOOK AT SYNTAX ERRORS

Before a Turbo Pascal program can be run, a compiler must translate the program into machine language. As part of this process, the compiler checks to make sure there are no violations of the grammatical rules—such violations are called **syntax errors**. (They are also known as **compile time errors**.) Some common kinds of syntax errors are misspelled keywords, incorrect or missing punctuation, and undeclared variables.

Just the First Syntax Error   If you try to compile a program that contains one or more syntax errors, the compilation will terminate with an error message giving the compiler's "best guess" on the nature and location of *just* the first syntax error in the program.

• • • • • • • • • •
Example   The following program contains four syntax errors. Type it in, and try to compile it by pressing **ALT-F9**.

```
program drill;
var n: interger;              ←misspelled keyword integer

begin
  writeln ('Hello')           ←missing semicolon
  writeln ('How are you);     ←missing quote mark
  {Watch out)                 ←wrong symbol to close
  n := 2;                        comment
  writeln ('n eqalls ', n)    ←not a syntax error
end.
```

The compiler will detect just the first syntax error (the misspelling of `inte-ger`), and compilation will terminate with the error message

```
Error 3: Unknown identifier
```

with the cursor blinking at the `i` of "`interger`." You should correct this first error and then compile again (ALT-F9). Repeat this process of correcting the error that the compiler detects and then compiling again until compilation is successful. Note that misspelled words within quote marks in a `writeln` statement are not syntax errors.

REMARK   Usually when the compiler detects an error, the blinking cursor will be on the line of the error or the line immediately following the error. Occasionally, however, the blinking cursor will be positioned on a line far away from the actual error or the error message will be misleading. Note that the incorrect symbol for closing a comment can have this effect.   • • •

ALT-F9 versus CTRL-F9   It is not necessary for you to use ALT-F9 to try to compile a program. If you wish, you can use the hot keys for the run command (CTRL-F9) instead. CTRL-F9 will first attempt compilation, and then, *if compilation is successful,* it will also run your program.

3.2   **THE REAL DATA TYPE**
• •

Variables of type `integer` can have as their values only whole numbers that are between $-32,768$ and $32,767$. A variable of type **real** may be assigned integer values, but it also may be assigned fractional values or large values like

4.3   8/3 -52.1 4375200

Exponential Notation   When a `write` or `writeln` statement has the computer output a `real` value, that value will be written in exponential form unless formatting specifiers are included. (Producing output in ordinary decimal notation is discussed at the end of this section and in Section 5.3.)

• • • • • • • • • •
Example

Output

```
program drill;
var x, y: real;
begin
  x := 426.5;
  y := 0.5;
  writeln ('x is ', x);
  writeln ('y is ', y)
end.
```

```
x is 4.2650000000E+02
y is 5.0000000000E-01
```

The `E+02` means that 4.265 is to be multiplied by 10^2. This operation can be carried out by moving the decimal point two places to the right. Thus, `4.2650000000E+02` is indeed equal to 426.5.

    Similarly, the computer uses negative exponents for positive numbers less than 1. Thus, `5.0E-01` means multiply 5 by 10^{-1}, which is the same as moving the decimal point one place to the left.

CAUTION   It is illegal for a Turbo Pascal statement to contain a decimal value that begins with a decimal point because a leading decimal might be confused with the period to end a program. That is, you are not allowed to have

```
y := .5;     {illegal to begin with decimal point}
```

The correct way to type a positive value less than one is either with a leading 0 or in exponential notation.

```
y := 0.5        {legal}
y := 5.0E-01    {legal}
```
• • •

Output in Ordinary Decimal Form   Output in exponential form is hard for humans to read. The syntax form for producing output in ordinary decimal notation is

```
writeln (RealExpr: width : p);
```

where `RealExpr` is a real expression and `p` specifies the number of decimal places (rounded off). In this chapter, we will just use a zero for the width specifier—this will ensure that the output of `RealExpr` will not have any leading blanks. (See Section 5.3 for more on width specifiers.)

Example

```
x := 78.291;
writeln (x:0:1);
writeln (x:0:2);
writeln (x:0:0);
writeln ('x = ', x:0:3);
writeln (x:0:4);
```

Output

```
78.3
78.29
78
x = 78.291
78.2910
```

REMARK Rounding off for output does not alter the stored value of a variable. (See `round` and `trunc`, Section 5.5, for ways to round off the stored value.) ● ● ●

When Reals and Integers Can Be Mixed Mixing reals and integers in an assignment statement is legal only when the variable on the left side is `real`. That is,

1. It is illegal to assign to a variable of type `integer` an expression that contains any decimal values or any variables of type `real`.

2. On the other hand, it is permissible to assign to a variable of type `real` an expression containing `integer` values or variables.

The reason for this rule is that whereas the memory cell of a `real` variable can store `integer` values, *the memory cell for an* `integer` *variable has no capacity to store a number with a decimal part.*

Question With the following declarations, which statements are illegal?

```
var a, b: integer;
    r, s: real;

a := 4.0;
a := 12.8;
r := 10;
b := r + 1;
s := r + 1;
```

Answer The only legal statements are `r := 10;` and `s := r+1;`. All the other statements assigned to an `integer` variable are either an expression with a decimal value or a variable of type `real`.

Example   Mixing Reals and Integers

```
program InchtoCm;
{will convert inches to centimeters}
var inches: integer;
    centimeters: real;

begin
  write ('enter number of inches ');
  readln (inches);
  centimeters := 2.54 * inches;
  write (inches, ' inches equals ');
  writeln (centimeters:0:1, ' centimeters')
end.
```

A typical run might produce

```
enter number of inches 4
4 inches equals 10.2 centimeters
```

• • •

3.3   ADDITIONAL INTEGER DATA TYPES

The most useful additional `integer` type is **longint**, which can handle integers up to 2,147,483,647 as opposed to 32,767 for the data type `integer`. For example, to store the product of `2,000 * 2,000` (which is 4 million), you would use a variable of type `longint` rather than of type `integer`.

Output

```
var profit: longint;
   .
   .
   .
  profit := 2000 * 2000;
  writeln ('profit $', profit);
```

```
profit $4000000
```

You might wonder why we don't do away with the data type `integer` altogether since `longint` can handle a much larger range of values. The reason is that the type `longint` uses more memory and also slows down processing. Thus, when you are sure that type `integer` will suffice, it is better to use it than `longint`.

Turbo Pascal also provides the data types **byte**, **shortint**, and **word**. For programs in which the amount of memory or processing time are significant factors, you should be sure to use the data type with the smallest range that will be adequate for the potential data.

The Five Integer Data Types

Data Type	Range
byte	0 to 255
shortint	− 128 to 127
integer	− 32,768 to 32,767
word	0 to 65,535
longint	− 2,147,483,648 to 2,147,483,647

Mixing Different Types   Suppose m is of type integer and n of type longint. What type must p be declared for the statement

```
p := m + n;
```

to be legal? The variable p would have to be of type longint.

In general, when an operation involves different types, both types are converted internally into what is called the *common type*. The common type is the built-in type with the smallest range that contains the union of the values of both types.

3.4 NUMERICAL OPERATORS

The Operators +, −, and *   Pascal uses + for addition, − for subtraction, and * for multiplication with both integer and real variables.

It is also permissible to have a statement such as

```
wage := hours * 6.5;
```

where hours is of type integer. Note, however, that wage would have to be of type real. In general, when at least one of the operands is real, you should assume that the result will be of type real.

The Three Division Operators   Turbo Pascal contains three different division operators.

Division Operators

Operator	Use	Examples
/	Performs ordinary division; the result is type `real`. Operands can be either `real` or an `integer` type.	`9/2` equals 4.5.
div	Gives the largest whole number of times the second operand goes into the first. Both operands must be an `integer` type, and the result is an `integer` type.	`9 div 4` equals 2. `8.4 div 4` is illegal.
mod	Gives the remainder when the first operand is divided by the second. Both operands must be an `integer` type.	`9 mod 2` equals 1.

Note that for / the operands may be either `real` or an `integer` type, but for `div` and `mod` both operands must be an `integer` type. Also note that for expressions with /, the result is always `real`; however, for expressions with `div` and `mod`, the result is always an `integer` type.

Question   Evaluate each of the following.

(a) `26 mod 4`   **(b)** `26 div 4`   **(c)** `26/4`

Answer

(a) 2   (b) 6   (c) 6.5   • • •

Question   Give the output for

```
inches := 75;
feet := inches div 12;
writeln (feet, ' foot ', inches mod 12, ' inches');
```

Answer

```
6 foot 3 inches
```

• • •

Rules of Precedence

Question Consider 2 + 3 * 4. Is it equal to 20 because (2 + 3) * 4 = 20? Or is it equal to 14 because 2 + (3 * 4) = 2 + 12 = 14?

Answer It is equal to 14 because in Pascal multiplication has higher precedence than addition and so is performed first.

Precedence Table

Precedence	Numerical Operators
Higher	*, /, div, mod
Lower	+, −

• • •

(Operations with the Same Precedence) When an expression with no parentheses contains two operations of the same precedence, the computer performs the operations in order from left to right.

(Parentheses Take Precedence) Operations within parentheses are performed first. Parentheses are used when you need to alter the normal precedence order. Thus if you wanted the computer to multiply the sum *a* + *b* by *c*, you would use (a + b) * c.

Question Evaluate each of the following.

(a) 1 + 2 * 3 + 4
(b) 6 + 4 / 2 + 3
(c) 2 / 3 * 4   (Is it equal to 1/6 or 8/3?)

Answer

(a) 11
(b) 11
(c) Since operations with the same precedence are performed in order from left to right, it is equal to 8/3. The calculation is 2 divided by 3 and then multiply that result by 4.   • • •

Question How would you write $\dfrac{a + b}{c + d}$?

Answer (a + b) / (c + d) [*Note:* a + b/c + d is not correct because it would be interpreted as $a + (b/c) + d$.]

3.5 CONSTANTS

• •

User-Defined Constants   A *constant* is something that has a fixed value. The computer (that is, the Turbo compiler) does not have built-in knowledge of the constants used in mathematics and science (except for pi). Within a program, however, you may define constant identifiers by declaring their fixed values in a `const` declaration section such as the following:

```
const
   MetersPerYard = 0.9144;
   TaxRate = 0.06;
```

Note that you use an equal sign (rather than the `:=` you use with variables) because you are declaring, not assigning, values. Once declared, these values will remain fixed throughout the program. Statements within the body of a program should not attempt to alter the value of a constant.

• • • • • • • • •
Example   Consider the following program:

```
program YdsToMeters;
{converts input number of yards to meters}
const MetersPerYard = 0.9144;
var yards, meters: real;

begin
  write ('Enter distance in yards ');
  readln (yards);
  meters := yards * MetersPerYard;
  writeln ('Equals ', meters:0:2, ' meters')
end.
```

Here is a typical output.

```
Enter distance in yards 100
Equals 91.44 meters
```
                                                                • • •

When to Use Constants   There are two main reasons for using constant identifiers.

1. Referring to a certain fixed value by a descriptive name can help make a program more understandable. For example, for most readers

the descriptive name `MetersPerYard` would have more meaning than the number `0.9144` would.

2. Since constants are declared at the top, a constant can make it easier to update a program if, at a later date, the value of a certain relatively fixed quantity is changed. This is especially useful in connection with declaring data structures such as arrays (see Chapter 17).

The Built-In Constants MaxInt and MaxLongInt   The largest values of type `integer` and `longint` can be accessed by the ***built-in constant*** identifiers, `MaxInt` and `MaxLongInt`, respectively. Since these are built-in constants, they should not be declared. The following program will produce the output shown:

Output

```
program drill;
begin
  writeln (MaxInt);
  writeln (MaxLongInt)
end.
```

```
32767
2147483647
```

3.6 ERRORS

• •

The three general categories of errors are (1) syntax, (2) run-time, and (3) logical. As you will see, logical errors are the most dangerous because the computer does not know they are errors and thus gives no warning.

Syntax Errors   Syntax errors (violations of the grammatical rules of Turbo Pascal) were already discussed in Section 3.1.

The most common kinds of syntax errors are misspelling keywords, incorrect or missing punctuation, undeclared variables, and type mismatches in assignment statements.

Run-Time Errors   A ***run-time*** error (also called an *execution error*) is an error that is not caught during the compilation stage, but instead is caught during the running of the program. For example, the computer would not stop with an error message during the compilation stage if it encountered the statements

```
c := 0;
y := x/c;
```

When the program is run, however, execution would be terminated with a `division by zero` error message.

Logical Errors   A logical error is an error in the design of the program. Logical errors generally do not produce error messages. A simple example of a logical error is the use of an incorrect formula. For example, in computing the average for b and c, suppose your program used the formula

```
avg := b + c / 2;
```

Using this formula, the program would calculate that the average of 60 and 80 was 100. Although this calculation is incorrect, the computer would not provide any warning because none of the rules of Pascal were violated.

More complex kinds of logical errors often occur in looping or nesting situations (covered later in the book), where the actual logical flow might be quite different from what the programmer had intended.

In any event, logical errors are quite dangerous because they may produce output that you do not realize is incorrect.

CAUTION   (Wrap Around)   Recall that values of type `integer` must be in the range $-32,768$ to $32,767$. Consider the following two program fragments where `salary` and `bonus` are variables of type `integer`. Their purpose is to add a $5 bonus to salary.

```
salary := 32767 + 5;
writeln ('salary = $', salary);
```

```
bonus := 5;
salary := 32767 + bonus;
writeln ('salary = $', salary);
```

The left-hand fragment will produce a syntax error (`constant out of range`). Somewhat surprisingly, the right-hand fragment will not produce either a syntax or a run-time error. Instead, it will produce the output

```
salary = $-32764
```

The integer values *wrap around,* that is, after 32767 comes -32768, then -32767, then -32766, then -32765, then -32764.   • • •

EXERCISES

1. Write the following numbers in ordinary decimal notation.

(a) `1.437E+03`   (b) `5.462E-01`

(c) `5.462E-03`   (d) `1.437E+05`

2. Suppose x is of type `real` and has 824.176 as its value. Give the output for

```
writeln (x:0:1);
writeln (x:0:2);
writeln (x);
```

3. Find the error in the statement

```
x := y + .25;
```

4. Evaluate each of the following

(a) `8 * 6 / 3 * 4`   **(b)** `(8 * 6) / 3 * 4`

(c) `8 * 6 / (3 * 4)`   **(d)** `1 + 4 * 6 + 8 / 4 + 4`

5. Rewrite each of the following expressions in ordinary notation, simplifying as much as possible

(a) `y * 2 / 2 * y;`   **(b)** `(y * 2) / y * 2;`

(c) `y * 2 / (y * 2);`   **(d)** `(y * 2) / (y * 2);`

(e) `y * 2 / y * 2;`

6. Suppose a = 49, b = 5, and c = 3. Find

(a) `a mod b * c + 1`   **(b)** `a mod (b * c) + 1`

(c) `24 / c * 4`   **(d)** `a div b mod 2`

(e) `7 + 2 div c - 1`   **(f)** `48 / (c * 2) * 4`

7. Write a Pascal statement for each of the following algebraic expressions

(a) $\dfrac{x + y}{2w}$ **(b)** $\dfrac{1}{2}(5x - 3y)$

8. Describe the three kinds of errors in a program and when they are caught.

9. Find the error in each of the following programs and state what kind it is.

(a)
```
program drill;
  var x, y: integer;

begin
   x := 6
   y := x/2;
   writeln (x, ' ', y)
end.
```

(b)
```
program drill;
  var n, total: integer;
       avg: real;

begin
   n := 0;
   total := 50;
   avg := total/n;
   writeln (avg:0:1)
end.
```

10. If `bonus` and `salary` are both of type `integer`, what is wrong with the following fragment?

```
bonus := 4000;
salary := 30000 + bonus;
```

11. The program below has two syntax errors. What are they?

```
program drill;
var sum, score1, score2: integer;

begin
   writeln ('Speling musteaks');
   write ('Enter your 2 test scores ');
   readln (score1, skore2);
   total := score1 + score2;
   writeln ('Total of scores ', total)
end.
```

12. Fill in the blank so that the output will be 4 3 6.

```
num := 436;
ones := num mod 10;
tens := (num div 10) mod 10;
hundreds := _____;
writeln (hundreds, ' ', tens, ' ', ones);
```

Longer Assignments

13. Write an interactive program that converts kilograms to pounds (1 kilogram = 2.2 pounds). For an input of 6 kilograms, the output on paper should be

```
6 kilograms = 13.2 pounds
```

14. Write an interactive program that converts an input number of quarters and dimes into a dollar total. For an input of 5 quarters and 2 dimes, the output on paper should be

```
5 quarters and 2 dimes
equals $1.45
```

15. Write an interactive program that converts ounces into pounds and ounces (there are 16 ounces to a pound). For an input of 39 ounces, the output on paper should be

```
39 ounces = 2 pounds 7 ounces
```

16. Write a program that asks the user to input a three-digit number and then prints the number in reverse order. Thus, for an input of 592, the output would be 295. (Your program should use a variable for the reverse number and print the value of this variable—it should not print each of the digits separately.)

Lab Exercises   **DEBUGGING AND SYNTAX ERRORS**

Lab3-1.pas   Removing Syntax Errors
Lab3-2.pas   Formatting Numeric Output
Lab3-3.pas   Mixing Numeric Types and Wraparound
Lab3-4.pas   Subtle Syntax Error

Chapter

4

IF–THEN–ELSE AND
TOP DOWN DESIGN

• • • The programs discussed up to now have been quite limited in what they accomplished since only a few, simple Pascal commands have been presented so far.

In Sections 4.1-4.3, we introduce some new syntax, `if-then`, `if-then-else`, and boolean operators such as **and**, **or**, and **not**. This syntax gives a program the capacity to make decisions—that is, to perform a test and then take the appropriate course of action depending on the outcome of the test. This capacity is known as selection.

In writing more complicated programs, it is important to use a more systematic and disciplined approach. In Section 4.4, we apply problem-solving techniques to the writing of programs, emphasizing the use of ***top down design***—the strategy of subdividing the original problem into smaller, more manageable subtasks. In Section 4.5, we briefly introduce the Pascal syntax for ***procedures***. This syntax allows you to write your program in a way that displays the top down design that you used. • • •

4.1 ONE-WAY SELECTION (if–then)

An `if-then` statement is used when you want the computer to perform some action conditionally—that is, only when a certain condition is true. Here are two examples of `if-then` statements:

```
if age >= 18 then writeln ('may vote');
if a + b = c then count := count + 1;
```

The general syntax is

if {*condition*} then {*action statement*}

where the condition must be a boolean expression (an expression that evaluates to true or false). For example, age >= 18 is either true or false when the current value of age is "plugged in."

If the condition is true, the computer executes the action statement and then proceeds to the next statement in the program. If the condition is false, the computer proceeds directly to the next statement in the program.

Relational Operators   There are six relational operators.

Relational Operator*	Definition
>	Is greater than (comes after)
<	Is less than (comes before)
=	Is equal to
>=	Is greater than or equal to (at least)
<=	Is less than or equal to
<>	Is not equal to

*Note that >= consists of two keystrokes with no space in between. The same is true of <= and <>.

Question   When the fragment

```
if age >= 18 then writeln ('of age');
writeln ('good luck');
```

is executed, what will be printed for each given value of age?

(a) age = 25   **(b)** age = 14   **(c)** age = 18

Answer

(a)
```
of age
good luck
```

(b)
```
good luck
```

(c)
```
of age
good luck
```

• • •

Question   If x = 5 and count = 31 when the computer reaches the following fragment, what will be printed?

```
if x > 8 then count := count + 1;
write (count);
```

Answer

$\boxed{31}$

because the action statement is not executed. Thus, count remains at 31.

• • •

4.2 SELECTING FROM TWO ALTERNATIVES (if–then–else)

In one-way selection, the computer does either something or nothing at all depending on the outcome of the test. In two-way selection, the computer performs a test and then does something in either case. If the condition is true, the computer executes the **then** alternative. If it is false, the computer executes the **else** alternative.

Question When the fragment

```
if score >= 60
   then writeln ('You pass')
   else writeln ('You fail');
writeln ('Have a nice day');
```

is executed, what will be output for each value of score?

(a) score = 54   **(b)** score = 73

Answer

(a)
```
You fail
Have a nice day
```

(b)
```
You pass
Have a nice day
```

• • •

REMARK Note that there is no semicolon at the end of the then alternative because the entire **if-then-else** test is considered a single statement. Placing a semicolon at the end of the then alternative would produce a syntax error.

• • •

Question Suppose baseballs are priced at $6.50 each if at least 10 are purchased, and $7.00 each otherwise.

(a) Complete the if-then-else test in the program baseballs.

(b)   Suppose the user inputs <u>5</u> for the number of balls. Show what would appear on the screen versus what would appear on paper.

```
program baseballs;
uses printer;
var   number: integer;
      cost: real;

begin
  write ('enter number purchased ');
  readln (number);
  if number >= 10
    then cost := _____
    else _____
  writeln (lst, number, ' baseballs cost $', cost:0:2)
end.
```

Answer   **(a)**
```
if number >= 10
  then cost := number * 6.5
  else cost := number * 7;
```

Note that a semicolon is needed to separate the if-then-else statement from the writeln statement following it.

(b)   *Screen*   *Paper*

```
enter number purchased 5
```
```
5 baseballs cost $35.00
```

• • •

CAUTION   Your output on paper should give the value that was used as input (5 in this run). If the last line of the program body had been

```
writeln (lst, 'baseballs cost $', cost:0:2)
```

the input for the number of baseballs would not be printed.   • • •

Two Common Formats   So far we have used indentation Format 1 for an if-then-else statement. Another common format is Format 2.

Format 1

```
if {condition}
  then {statement 1}
  else {statement 2}
```

Format 2

```
if {condition} then
  {statement 1}
else
  {statement 2}
```

Compound then or else Alternatives   Whenever a `then` or `else` alternative contains more than one statement, we will use Format 2. Note that `begin-end` markers must be used for any branch with more than one statement.

• • • • • • • • • •
Example   Let us return to the baseball cost program, in which a discount is given for purchases of at least 10 balls. Suppose we wish to output not only the cost but also either the message `Discount` or the message `No Discount`. Since we will have two statements within both the `then` and the `else` alternative, we need to use `begin-end` markers as follows:

```
if number >= 10 then
  begin
    writeln ('Discount');
    cost := number * 6.5
  end {then}
else
  begin
    writeln ('No Discount');
    cost := number * 7
  end; {else}
```

REMARK

1. Do not place a semicolon after the keyword `end` of the `then` branch of an `if-then-else` statement. Doing so would cause a syntax error because the `else` branch would be misinterpreted as an entirely separate statement.

2. Within the `begin-end` markers, however, semicolons must be used to separate individual parts of each compound statement, as shown.

• • •

4.3 BOOLEAN EXPRESSIONS AND OPERATORS
• •

Boolean Expressions   A boolean expression is something that is either true or false. The condition in an `if` statement is boolean since when it is evaluated it will be either true or false. An `if` statement can have a simple boolean condition such as in

```
if age >= 21 then . . .
```

It can also have a compound expression such as in

```
if ((sex = 'f') or (age > 25)) and (years > 5) then . . .
```

Boolean Operators Compound boolean expressions are formed by combining boolean expressions using one or more of the boolean operators

```
and      or      not      xor
```

and Operator An expression of the form p and q has the value true only when both p and q are true; otherwise, it has the value false.

• • • • • • • • • •
Example

The ABC Company gives two tests to each job applicant. An applicant is hired if he scores at least 65 on both tests; otherwise, he is rejected. The following fragment uses the correct if-then-else test to determine whether an applicant is hired or rejected:

```
write ('enter two scores ');
readln (score1, score2);
if (score1 >= 65) and (score2 >= 65)
  then writeln ('Hire')
  else writeln ('Reject');
```

REMARK Note that when you use a compound boolean condition, you *must* enclose each relational condition in parentheses. You will see why this is necessary when the rules of precedence are discussed at the end of this section.   • • •

• • • • • • • • • •
Example

In the town of Poduka, a woman is eligible to be a firefighter if her height is between 65 and 75 inches, inclusive. Mathematically, we can write

$$65 <= \text{height} <= 75$$

To translate this expression into Pascal, however, we must use the **and** operator because there are two conditions on height.

```
if (height >= 65) and (height <= 75) then . . .
```

or Operator An expression of the form p **or** q is true provided at least one of p or q is true; otherwise, it is false.

• • • • • • • • • •
Example

The XYZ Company gives two tests to job applicants. At this company, however, an applicant is hired if she scores at least 90 on either test; otherwise, she is rejected. Here is the statement we could use.

```
if (score1 >= 90) or (score2 >= 90)
  then write ('hired')
  else write ('rejected');
```

not Operator   An expression **not** p has the opposite boolean value that p has. Thus, if p is true, then not p is false; if p is false, then not p is true.

xor (exclusive or) Operator   An expression of the form p xor q is true if one and *only one* of p or q is true; otherwise, it is false.

Truth Table for and, or, and xor

p	q	p and q	p or q	p xor q
true	true	true	true	false
true	false	false	true	true
false	true	false	true	true
false	false	false	false	false

Rules of Precedence   Following is an updated precedence table. Note that of the boolean operators, not has the highest precedence, and the second highest, and or the lowest. Further, all the boolean operators have higher precedence than the relational operators.

Precedence table

Precedence	Numerical Operators	Boolean and Relational Operators
Highest		not
Second highest	*, /, div, mod	and
Third highest	+, −	or, xor
Lowest		<, >, =, <=, >=, <>

REMARK   Evaluate from left to right when two operators have the same precedence.   • • •

(Putting Parentheses Around Relational Conditions)   You must place parentheses around a relational condition in a compound expression because boolean operators all have higher precedence than the relational operators. For example,

```
if a > b and b > c then . . .
```

would result in a syntax error because it would be interpreted as

```
if a > (b and b) > c then . . .
```

The correct form for this expression is

```
if (a > b) and (b > c) then . . .
```

(Overriding the Rules of Precedence)   Additional parentheses can be used to override the rules of precedence. For example, when one of the parts of a compound expression is itself a compound expression, parentheses may be used to force the computer to evaluate the expression in the desired order.

· · · · · · · · · ·

Example   A person is hired if he is at least 18 years of age and scores over 85 on either of two tests. Note that

```
if (age >= 18) and (score1 > 85) or (score2 > 85)
    then write ('hired');
```

is incorrect because a 15-year-old with a score of 88 on the second test would be hired. The problem stems from the fact that and has higher precedence than or, and thus the computer evaluates the expression as if it had been typed

```
if ((age >= 18) and (score1 > 85)) or (score2 > 85)
    then write ('hired');
```

Question   Use additional parentheses to write the correct if statement for the preceding hiring example.

Answer
```
if (age >= 18) and ((score1 > 85) or (score2 > 85))
    then write ('hired');
```
· · ·

4.4 PROBLEM SOLVING APPLIED TO WRITING PROGRAMS

· ·

We now consider the four general problem-solving stages first discussed in the Introduction (page 4) in relation to the task of writing programs.

1. **Understanding the Problem**   Do you understand what the program is supposed to do? What form should the output take? What information must be read in to produce the output?
2. **Developing an Algorithm**
   (a) *Consider specific cases.* For many problems, a way to get started is to work out by hand the outputs for several different

inputs. Can you describe the formula or process that you used to convert input into output?

(b) *Top down design.*   Try to subdivide the problem into smaller, more manageable subtasks, and then figure out how to accomplish each of these subtasks.

(c) *Imitating.*   You need not try to reinvent the wheel at each turn. Can you imitate a program that you've already seen, just changing some of the variable names and some of the fixed values? Are there any additional complications? If so, focus on how to handle these complications.

(d) *Pseudocode.* **Pseudocode** is a mixture of ordinary English and actual Pascal code. Writing a pseudocode draft of your program can act as a tool to develop the algorithm in a way that keeps you focused on the ultimate goal of writing the code. This enables you to write down some of the syntax decisions that you have already made, while leaving in somewhat vaguer form the details that need more work. Sometimes you might find it useful to write further pseudocode drafts (known as ***refinements***) with more of the details filled in.

3. **Coding the Algorithm**   You must ultimately translate your method of solution into a complete program using the correct Pascal syntax.

4. **Testing and Debugging**   Even when your program runs successfully for one set of input, this does not necessarily mean that your program is correct. It should be tested (that is, run) for other sets of input designed to cover all the types of cases. For example, when there is an `if-then-else` statement, make sure that you test not only the boundary value (the fixed value in the `if` condition) but also inputs on each side of the boundary value.

. . . .

Question   (Overtime)

An employee earns $5 per hour for the first 40 hours and $8 per hour for each hour over 40. Write a program to compute an employee's weekly wage. Here is the output on paper for a typical run.

```
43 hours wage $224
```

Writing the Program

1. **Understanding the Problem**   Make sure you see why 43 hours should give a wage of $224. Namely,

$$(40 * 5 \text{ for the first } 40 \text{ hours}) + (3 \text{ hours overtime at } \$8 \text{ per hour})$$

2. **Developing an Algorithm** Since overtime occurs only if hours is more than 40, this suggests the need for two different formulas and the following top down design:

input hours worked

if-then-else test to determine which formula to use

print the result

In the pseudocode given here note that the complication of how to handle overtime is described somewhat vaguely in ordinary English.

```
write-readln—to input hrs
if hrs <= 40
   then wage := hrs * 5
   else
      begin
         find overtime hours
         wage := (first 40 hours pay) + (overtime hours pay)
      end
output hrs and wage
```

3. **Coding the Algorithm** Fill in the missing lines in the following program. Note that an else branch of else wage := hours * 8; would be incorrect since it would pay the employee (working 43 hours) $8 per hour for all 43 hours.

```
program overtime;
uses printer;
var hrs, wage, hoursOT: integer;
begin
   write ('enter hours worked ');
   readln (hrs);
   if hrs <= 40 then
      wage := hrs * 5
   else
      begin
         hoursOT := _____
         wage := _____ + _____
      end;
   writeln (1st, hrs, ' hours wage $', wage)
end.
```

Answer

```
else
   begin
      hoursOT := (hrs - 40);
      wage := (40 * 5) + (hoursOT * 8)
   end;
```

4. ***Testing and Debugging***   Make sure that you run the program at least two times so that you first test an input of over 40 hours and then test an input of under 40 hours. Perhaps you should also test an input of exactly 40 hours.   • • •

4.5   USING PROCEDURES TO IMPLEMENT TOP DOWN DESIGN

Procedures

A procedure is a named block of code for performing a subtask. Procedures are positioned in the declaration section of a program after the `var` section (if there is one) and before the main body of the program. A procedure can be accessed by a main body statement that consists of the name of the procedure. (The Pascal syntax for a ***procedure*** makes it easier to carry out top down design.)

The format of the simplest kind of procedure is

```
procedure ProcedureName;
  begin
    statement(s);          {body of procedure}
  end;
```

Flow of Control   When a program is run, execution always begins with the first line of the main body of the program. When a statement consisting of the name of a procedure (a calling statement) is encountered, control is temporarily transferred to the procedure to execute the subtask as specified by the statements in the body of the procedure.

• • • • • • • • • •
Example   (Montezuma Sauce)

We want to write a program for Montezuma Sauce using the following top down design:

> give title of recipe
>
> list the ingredients
>
> give the cooking instructions

Let us begin by making up some procedure names (`LIST_INGRED` and `COOKING_INSTR`) for the second and third steps and then writing the main body as

```
begin {main}
  writeln ('Montezuma Sauce');
  LIST_INGRED;
  COOKING_INSTR
end.
```

Question   What will the output be for the following program? (Recall that execution always begins with the first line of the main body.)

```
program MontezumaSauce;
{sauce recipe}

procedure LIST_INGRED;
  begin
    writeln ('Ingredients:');
    writeln ('  5 cups sliced prunes  2 cups beans');
    writeln ('  1 cup water   1/2 cup brown sugar')
  end;

procedure COOKING_INSTR;
  begin
    writeln ('Cooking Instructions:');
    writeln ('  Put into a pot and bring to a boil');
    writeln ('  Let simmer for 45 minutes')
  end;

begin {main body}
  writeln ('Montezuma Sauce');
  LIST_INGRED;
  COOKING_INSTR
end.
```

Answer

```
Montezuma Sauce
Ingredients:
  5 cups sliced prunes  2 cups beans
  1 cup water  1/2 cup brown sugar
Cooking Instructions:
  Put into a pot and bring to a boil
  Let simmer for 45 minutes
```

• • •

REMARK   As a way of highlighting procedures, we have adopted the style of using all capital letters in their names. You are free to decide whether or not you also want to use this convention.   • • •

• • • • • • • • • •
Example   (Smiling or Frowning Face)

Complex objects can be constructed from simpler building blocks. The next program draws a face by dividing the job into the following subtasks: drawing the eyes, drawing a nose, and drawing a mouth.

This program has the flexibility to let the user choose between a smiling face and a frowning face.

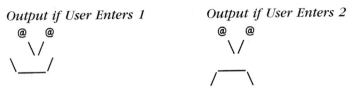

Output if User Enters 1   *Output if User Enters 2*

```
program faces;
var choice: integer;

procedure DRAW_EYES;
  begin
    writeln ('  @  @ ')
  end;

procedure DRAW_NOSE;
  begin
    writeln ('   \/   ')
  end;

procedure DRAW_SMILE;
  begin
    writeln (' \___/ ')        {\ 3 underbars /}
  end;

procedure DRAW_FROWN;
  begin
    writeln ('  ___  ');       {  3 underbars  }
    writeln (' /   \ ')        { /   \ }
  end;

begin {main}
  write ('enter 1 for happy face or 2 for sad face ');
  readln (choice);
  writeln;
  DRAW_EYES;
  DRAW_NOSE;
  if choice = 1
    then DRAW_SMILE
    else DRAW_FROWN
end.
```

REMARK   In Exercise 17, you are asked to modify this program so that the face will always be given hair (by DRAW_HAIR) and the user will have the option of giving it a beard. Thus, the modified program will have the flexibility of drawing four different faces: smiling with beard, smiling without beard, frowning with beard, frowning without beard. Here is a smiling face without a beard.

• • •

• • • • • • • • • EXERCISES

• •

1. Fill in the blank in the following statement so that it outputs whether or not age is under 21.

```
if _____
    then writeln (age, ' is under 21')
    else writeln (age, ' is not under 21');
```

2. The following program fragment is in poor style. Explain what is wrong with it and rewrite it.

```
if age >= 65 then
   writeln ('May retire');
if age < 65 then
   writeln ('May not retire');
```

3. Find the error in the following.

```
if age >= 18
    then writeln ('may vote');
    else writeln ('may not vote');
```

4. What will be the output when x = 1 and y = 5?

```
if not ((x < 2) and (y < 6))
   then writeln ('true')
   else writeln ('false');
```

5. What will be output by the following when x = 6, y = 6, and n = 7?

(a)
```
if (x > 5) and (y > 10) or (n > 10)
   then writeln ('okay')
   else writeln ('maybe');
```

(b)
```
if (x > 5) or (y > 10) and (n > 10)
   then writeln ('yes')
   else writeln ('no');
```

6. Find the outputs for parts (a) and (b) of Exercise 5 when x = 2, y = 3, and n = 12.

7. **(a)** Fill in the blank in the following program fragment so that someone who is less than 72 inches tall and heavier than 200 pounds is classified as overweight and all others are classified as maybeOK.

```
read (ht, wt);
if _____ then writeln ('overweight')
          else writeln ('maybe OK');
```

(b) Rewrite the fragment using an or operator in the condition.

Longer Assignments

8. Write a program in which the user inputs her age and the output states whether or not she is a teenager.

9. Shirts are on sale for $10 each if more than three are purchased and $12 each otherwise. Write a program that will read in an input number of shirts purchased and print out the total cost.

10. Write a program that will receive two distinct positive integers as input and will print the difference of the larger number and the smaller. Be sure that your program will print 6 both when 9 15 is input and when 15 9 is input.

11. Write a program that will receive two integers as input and then will print the message Opposite Signs only if one of the integers is positive and the other negative.

12. An employee is paid $7 per hour for the first 40 hours and $10 per hour for each hour over 40. Write a program to find an employee's pay. Run it twice; first with input of 42 hours, and then with input of 35 hours.

13. An employee is paid at her normal rate for the first 40 hours and three times her normal rate for each hour over 40. Write a program that receives two inputs: the `number of hours` worked and her `normal rate` of pay. Run it at least three times; the first time for input of 7 per hour for normal rate and 43 for hours. You make up the input for the other two runs.

14. Write a program that will receive the weight of a letter in ounces as input and will print the cost of postage calculated according to the following rule:

> First ounce costs $.29.
>
> Each additional ounce costs $.04.

15. At a state college, tuition charges are $50 per credit, with a maximum charge of $750 no matter how many credits are taken. Thus, a student taking 12 credits would pay $600, whereas a student taking 21 credits would pay the maximum charge of $750. Write a program in which the number of credits is input and the tuition charge is output.

16. At Poduka State University, veterans pay only $30 per credit, whereas everyone else pays $50 per credit. Write a program in which the user inputs the student's status (1 for veteran or 2 for regular) and the number of credits. The output should state whether the student is a veteran or a regular student and give the number of credits and tuition costs.

17. Write the face drawing program described in the Remark at the end of Section 4.5.

Lab Exercises **DEBUGGING AND SYNTAX ERRORS**

Lab4-1.pas	`if-then-else` Syntax Error
Lab4-2.pas	`if-then-else` Syntax Error
Lab4-3.pas	Voting Age
Lab4-4.pas	`and`/`or` Parentheses

Chapter

5

CHAR AND STRING DATA TYPES AND FORMATTING OUTPUT

• • • In the early days, computers were used almost exclusively for large-scale numerical calculations. Now, however, much of their use involves processing nonnumeric data for tasks ranging from making medical diagnoses to maintaining mailing lists.

This chapter introduces two new data types, `char` and `string`. It then discusses field specifiers for formatting output (especially in table form). Finally, it discusses built-in functions. • • •

5.1 VARIABLES OF TYPE CHAR

A variable of type **char** can store any single character value. Some familiar examples of a character value are a letter, a digit, or a punctuation mark. Character values in a program are enclosed in single quote marks—the same single quotes that are used for verbatim messages in `writeln` statements.

• • • • • • • • • •
Example In program `lettergrade`, `grade` is a variable of type `char`.

```
program lettergrade;
{prints your grade with a message}
var grade: char;

begin
  writeln ('Enter your grade');
  readln (grade);
  writeln ('You received the grade of ', grade)
end.
```

Typical output.

```
Enter your grade
B
You received the grade of B
```

• • •

REMARK   If you wanted to assign grade a value through an assignment statement, you would need to place single quote marks around the value, as in

```
grade := 'B';
```

• • •

5.2   A FIRST LOOK AT STRING VARIABLES

• •

Suppose you want a variable, let us call it LastName, to be able to hold someone's name as its value. A name is a sequence of characters. We call such a sequence a string. For example, the name 'Jones' is a string of five characters. Turbo provides the data type **string.** A variable declared to be of this type can store a string value of up to 255 characters. String values, like character values, are enclosed in apostrophes.

Example   With the declaration

```
var LastName: string;
```

the assignment statement

```
LastName := 'Jones';
```

would assign the value Jones to Lastname. You could visualize memory for LastName with the first 5 of the 255 memory cells filled

J	o	n	e	s		.	.	.	

Question   Suppose that the user entered M for `initial` and `Jones` for `LastName`. What screen display would be produced by program `name`?

```
program name;
{prints your last name and initial}
var initial: char;
    LastName: string;

begin
  write ('enter first initial: ');
  readln (initial);
  write ('enter your last name: ');
  readln (LastName);
  writeln (LastName, ', ', initial, '.')
end.
```

Answer

```
enter first initial: M
enter your last name: Jones
Jones, M.
```

When Quotes Are Needed

When entering a string or character value in response to a `readln` statement, you do not use quotes since the compiler is expecting a verbatim string or character value. By contrast, you must use quotes in an assignment statement like

```
LastName := 'Jones';
```

The quotes here inform the compiler that Jones is a string value and not an identifier. The following statement using two string variables is also legal:

```
name1 := name2;
```

CAUTION   For keyboard input, it is inadvisable to use a `readln` statement that contains *both* string and numeric variables. For example, if name is of type `string`, *don't use*

```
readln (name, score1, score2);
```

because an input of `Jones 80 90` would read in those 11 characters as the value of `LastName`.

| J | o | n | e | s | | 8 | 0 | | 9 | 0 | . | . | . |

Instead, you should use the two separate `readln` statements

```
readln (name);
readln (score1, score2);
```

• • •

Type string[n] In some situations, it is preferable to limit the number of characters that a string variable can hold to less than 255. The declaration

```
var name: string[10];
```

would allow the variable name to hold a value consisting of up to 10 characters. (One advantage of such a declaration is that it ties up far less memory than type `string` does.) Thus

```
name := 'John Doe'
```

would fill 8 of the 10 memory cells of `name`.

CAUTION Note that if the computer executed

```
name := 'Weatherspoon';
```

name would not be able to store the full 12 characters in Weatherspoon. Instead, name would hold only the first 10 characters. (Extra characters are truncated at the right.)

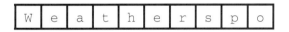

It also should be noted that the statement `name := ' Smith'` would assign to `name` a string consisting of six characters, with the first character being a blank.

• • •

Henceforth, for convenience, we will tend to use the data type `string` in preference to `string[ ]`. When conserving memory becomes a consideration (as in Chapter 17), however, we will sometimes declare variables of type `string [ ]`.

The length Function The Turbo `length` function returns the length of the current value stored in a string variable. That is, it gives the number of characters actually stored in the string variable (rather than the maximum number allowed in the declaration).

• • • • • • • •
Example

```
program how_long;
var message: string[100];
begin
  message := 'So Long';
  writeln (length (message))
end.
```

The output of `program how_long` is 7.   • • •

REMARK   Observe that the blank counts as a character.   • • •

5.3 FORMATTING OUTPUT USING ZONE WIDTH SPECIFIERS

Field *zone width* specifiers can be used to control the appearance of output. For example, they can be used to display output in table form. In this section, we discuss zone width specifiers for outputting string, integer, and real values.

Formatting Strings   In a statement of the form

```
writeln (StrExpr : width);
```

The value of the string expression `StrExpr` will be output in a zone of `width` spaces with its rightmost character at the right-hand edge of the zone. This is called *right-justified*.

• • • • • • • •
Question   Suppose the string variable `name` has the value `'Jones'`. What will be output by

```
writeln ('ABCDEFGH');
writeln ('NOW':6);
writeln (name:6);
```

Answer

```
ABCDEFGH
   NOW
 Jones
```

Note that NOW and Jones are both right-aligned under the F—that is, the sixth column—because the zone width was 6.

Formatting Integers   In a statement of the form

```
writeln (IntExpr : width);
```

the value of the integer expression, IntExpr, will be output in a zone of width spaces, with the rightmost digit of IntExpr at the right-hand edge of the zone. (As before, this is called right-justified.)   • • •

• • • • • • • • • •
Example   Let us contrast two different program fragments. Suppose the variables a, b, c, and d are of type integer and a = 14, b = 3254, c = 8, and d = 95. Note that program fragment (b) uses field specifiers.

(a)
```
writeln ('table');
writeln (a);
writeln (b);
writeln (c);
writeln (d);
```

(b)
```
writeln ('table');
writeln (a:5);
writeln (b:5);
writeln (c:5);
writeln (d:5);
```

Here are the results.

(a)
```
table
14
3254
8
95
```

(b)
```
table
   14
 3254
    8
   95
```
• • •

REMARK

1. Note that in program fragment (b), the zone width for each of the numbers is 5. Thus the rightmost digit of each number is written in column 5.

2. The format of (b) is preferable to that in (a) because the units' digits are aligned.   • • •

Formatting Reals   In a statement of the form

```
writeln (RealExpr : width : p)
```

the value of RealExpr will be output in a zone of width spaces rounded off to p decimal places and with the rightmost digit at the right-hand edge of the zone. Be aware that the decimal point uses one space.

Question   Suppose x and y are of type `real` and x = 29.431 and y = 57.128. What will be output by

```
writeln ('ABCDEFGH');
writeln (x:6:2);
writeln (y:6:2);
```

Answer

```
ABCDEFGH
 29.43
 57.13
```

Note that using the same values for `width` and `p` in both `writeln` statements produces alignment of the decimal points.   • • •

Values Too Long for Field Width   If a value to be output is too long for the specified zone width, the zone will be expanded to just enough spaces to fit the specified value. For example,

```
writeln (547:2);
writeln (89.463:1:2);
```

```
547
89.46
```

Note that this feature explains the behavior of the special syntax form

```
writeln (RealExpr:0:p);
```

from Chapter 3.

5.4   FORMATTING WITH SEVERAL ITEMS

Field zone width specifiers can be attached to any of the items in a `writeln` statement. The beginning of the zone for any item is the current output position.

In this section, we show how to produce tables in two kinds of situations.

1. When there is no mixing of numeric and string values within a `writeln` statement.

2. When there is mixing.

No Mixing

Question

Suppose a = 8, b = 12, c = 5. What will be output by

```
writeln ('NUMBER', 'SQUARED':10);
writeln (a:6, a*a:10);
writeln (b:6, b*b:10);
writeln (c:6, c*c:10);
```

Answer

```
NUMBER     SQUARED
     8          64
    12         144
     5          25
```

Note that there will be three blank spaces between the R of NUMBER and the S of SQUARED because SQUARED is seven characters long and right-justified in a zone of width 10 (3 = 10 − 7). Note also the unsquared numbers are aligned under the R of NUMBER. • • •

Mixing String and Numeric Values The `length` function can be used to produce a nicely formatted table for string and numeric values. Before we consider such an example, consider the following question.

Question

What will be output by the following fragment? *Hint:* K is the eleventh letter of the alphabet.

```
writeln ('ABCDEFGHIJK');
writeln ('Name', 'Age':6);
```

Answer

'Name' is output in the first four columns, then 'Age' is output right-justified in the next six columns. Thus, the 'e' of 'Age' will be in column 10 (4 + 6 = 10) and thus under the J.

```
ABCDEFGHIJK
Name    Age
```

• • •

Question   Suppose `name1 = 'Harriet'`, `name2 = 'John'`, `name3 = 'Henry'`, and `age1 = 25`, `age2 = 7`, `age3 = 18`. For the program fragment that follows

(a)   In which column will the `'e'` of `'Age'` be output?

(b)   Complete the blanks so that the fragment will produce the table to the right.

```
writeln ('Name', 'Age':10);
writeln (name1, age1: 14 - length(name1));
writeln (name2, age2: _____);
writeln (name3, age3: _____);
```

Name	Age
Harriet	25
John	7
Henry	18

Answer

(a)   The `'e'` of `'Age'` will be output in column 14 (10 + 4).

(b)   Note `length(name1) + 14 - length(name1)` equals 14. Thus, `age1` will be right-justified in column 14. The blanks are `14 - length(name2)` and `14 - length(name3)`, respectively.   • • •

5.5   BUILT-IN ARITHMETIC FUNCTIONS

The `length` function, which returns the length of the current value of a string variable, is called a ***built-in function.*** (See Chapter 13 for programmer-defined functions.)

Turbo Pascal also provides a number of purely arithmetic built-in functions. Recall from mathematics that when you supply a function with an argument, it returns a resulting value. For example, when you supply the square root function with the argument 9, it returns the resulting value 3.

sqrt and sqr Functions   The **sqrt** function returns the positive square root for a positive number. It always returns a value of type **real**. Its argument may be `real` or `integer`.

The **sqr** function returns the square of the argument. The argument may be `real` or `integer`. The result returned is of the same type as the argument.

Question   Give the output (exactly as it will be formatted) for the following fragment. *Hint:* $\sqrt{2}$ to three decimal places is 1.414.

```
writeln (sqrt(2):5:3);
writeln (sqrt(9));
writeln (sqr(9));
```

Answer   Note that the computer will treat $\sqrt{9}$ as a real value and output it in scientific notation.

```
1.414
 3.0000000000E+00
81
```

If you wanted $\sqrt{9}$ output as an integer, you could use

```
writeln (sqrt (9):1:0);
```

• • •

• • • • • • • • •

Question   Recall the Pythagorean formula for a right triangle with legs *a* and *b*.

$$\text{hypot}^2 = a^2 + b^2$$

Fill in the blank line in the program.

```
program Pythagorean;
var a, b, hypot: real;
begin
  write ('Enter the lengths of the two legs ');
  readln (a, b);
  hypot := _____;
  writeln ('Hypotenuse is ', hypot:6:3)
end.
```

Answer   hypot := sqrt (a * a + b * b);
          or   hypot := sqrt (sqr(a) + sqr(b));

• • •

Arithmetic Functions

Function	What It Calculates	Argument Type	Result Type
abs(x)	Absolute value of x	Integer or real	Same as argument
*arctan(x)	Arc tangent of x	Integer or real	Real
*cos(x)	Cosine of x	Integer or real	Real
exp(x)	e^x where $e = 2.718\ldots$	Integer or real	Real
ln(x)	Natural log of x	Integer or real	Real
†pi	π		Real
random	Discussed in Chapter 14		
round(x)	x rounded to nearest integer	Real	Integer
*sin(x)	Sine of x	Integer or real	Real
sqr(x)	x^2	Integer or real	Same as argument
sqrt(x)	$\sqrt{x}$	Integer or real	Real
trunc(x)	Truncates decimal part	Real	Integer

*For the trigonometry functions, angles are in radians not degrees.
†pi does not take an argument. The number of decimal places to which it approximates π depends on the compiler.

Raising to a Power Unfortunately, there is no built-in operator for raising a number to a general power—for example, if your program needed to calculate 5^n, with n a variable. Chapter 13 (Section 2 and Exercise 5) discusses two methods for achieving general exponentiation.

• • • • • • • • •
Example

Expression	*Its Value*
round(3.8)	4
trunc(3.8)	3
round(6.2)	6
round(8/3)	3
sqrt(abs(-16))	4.000
trunc(sqrt(15.9))	3
sin(pi/6)	0.5

• • •

• • • • • • • • •
Question (Precalculus) Complete the following fragment that will output the sine of an angle where the angle is input in degrees. (Note that angle must be converted into radian before the sin function can be applied to it.) *Hint:* Since an angle of one degree equals (π/180) radian, an angle of deg degrees will equal deg * (π/180) radian.

```
write ('enter angle in degrees ');
readln (deg);
radians := _____ * pi/180;
write ('sine of ', deg, ' degrees = ', _____ :6:3);
```

Answer   The first blank should contain `deg`. The second blank should contain `sin(radians)` since the `sin` function should be applied to the radian measure of the angle.   • • •

5.6   BUILT-IN CHAR FUNCTIONS

This section discusses the following built-in functions involving the data type `char`:

       `ord, chr, upcase`

ASCII Code Numbers   Each character in Turbo Pascal can be referred to by its *ASCII* (American Standard Code for Information Interchange) code number. Look at the ASCII chart in Appendix B and observe, for example, that R has ASCII number 82, r has ASCII number 114, and * has ASCII number 42.

ord and chr Functions   The `ord` function is applied to a `char` value and returns that character's ASCII number. For example, `ord('R')` equals 82. Inversely, the `chr` function goes in the opposite direction—it is applied to an ASCII number and returns the corresponding character. For example, `chr(82)` equals R.

Question   Look at the ASCII chart to determine what will be output by the following.

```
writeln (ord('B'));
writeln (ord('>'));
writeln (chr(78));
writeln (chr(63));
writeln (ord(chr(89)));
```

Answer

```
66
62
N
?
89
```

• • •

The Bell Some characters are invisible when output, but still may have some effect. One of the most useful in elementary programming is the character **BEL** whose ASCII value is 7. When executing the statement

```
writeln (chr(7));
```

the computer will emit a bell tone.

Comparing Characters We can compare characters using relational operators (like > or >=) that compare their ASCII values.

• • • • • • • • • •
Question What will be output by

```
if (symbol >= 'A') and (symbol <= 'M')
    then writeln ('Yes')
    else writeln ('No');
```

when

(a) symbol = 'g'
(b) symbol = 'G'
(c) symbol = 'R'
(d) symbol = 'r'

Answer Only in case (b) will `Yes` be printed since that is the only case in which `symbol` is between `'A'` and `'M'` (by ASCII value, between 65 and 77).

• • •

upcase Function The **upcase** function when applied to a letter will return the uppercase of the letter. For most other characters, upcase simply returns the character unchanged.

```
upcase ('g') returns 'G'

upcase ('G') returns 'G'

upcase ('4') returns '4'
```

Comparing Strings   The six relational operators (<, <=, >, >=, =, <>) can be used to compare two strings. Two strings are equal only if they are identical. For nonidentical strings, the comparison rule is similar to the dictionary ordering.

Two strings are compared character by character from left to right until the first occurrence of different characters—whichever string has the character with the lower ASCII number is "less than" the other string (thus, 'season' < 'send'). If two strings of unequal length agree on all the characters of the shorter string, then the shorter string is "less than" the longer one (thus, 'sea' < 'season').

CAUTION

1. Suppose word1 has the value 'baker' and word2 the value 'Charlie'. Then the test if word1 < word2 would yield the value false because b has a larger ASCII number than C.

2. This ordering does not work well for integer strings with different numbers of digits.

```
'99' > '200' because '9' > '2'
```

To overcome this potential problem, we can write both as three-digit numbers and we have

```
'099' < '200'
```

• • •

5.7 **THE + OPERATOR**

• •

The + operator will join string or character values. Thus, if first, last, and name are each of type string

```
first := 'John';
last := 'Bull';
name := first + ' ' + last;
writeln (name);
```

will output

```
John Bull
```

Question   If `card` is of type `string`, what will be output by

```
writeln ('7' + chr (3));
card := 'Q' + chr (4);
writeln (card);
```

Answer   7♡
           Q◇   • • •

EXERCISES

1. Give the outputs for

(a)
```
m := 431;
n := 57;
writeln ('ABCDEFG');
writeln (m: 6);
writeln (n: 6);
writeln (m: 4);
writeln (m: 2);
```

(b)
```
x := 3.8412;
y := 47.162;
writeln ('ABCDEFG');
writeln (x: 6: 1);
writeln (y: 6: 1);
writeln (x: 6: 3);
writeln (y: 3: 2);
```

2. Suppose k = 675, 1 = 42, m = 18, and n = 5. Give the output for

```
writeln ('ABCDEFGH');
write (k: 4);
write (1: 4);
writeln;
write (m: 4);
write (n: 4);
```

3. Give the output for

(a)
```
x := 32.75;
y := trunc (x);
z := round (x);
writeln (y, ' ', z);
```

(b)
```
A := -4;
B := abs (A);
D := sqrt (B);
writeln (B, ' ', D: 4: 1);
```

4. Give the value of each of the following.

    (a) `trunc (23/4);`   **(b)** `round (23/4);`

    (c) `sqrt (1 + 3);`   **(d)** `sqr (4 + 5);`

    (e) `upcase ('r');`   **(f)** `upcase (chr (100));`

5. Fill in the blanks so that if `LowLet` is a lowercase letter, `CapLet` will be assigned the value `upcase (LowLet)`.

         `CapLet := chr (_____ (Lowlet) - _____)`

6. Write an interactive program to have the following screen conversation with the user—the underlined values are typed by the user. To produce the last line of the output, the program should add five years to whatever age is input.

```
What is your name? Marge
How old are you Marge? 28
You look much older Marge.
I thought you were at least 33.
```

7. (a) Write a program that asks the user to input his last name and two initials and then produces output on paper as indicated by the typical run.

Screen   *Paper*

```
Enter last name      Jones       Jones, M. R.
Enter first initial  M           M. R. Jones
Enter middle initial R
```

(b) Modify the program so that if the user had entered a blank for the middle initial, the output on paper would have been

```
Jones, M.
M. Jones
```

8. Suppose num1 = 8, num2 = 10, and num3 = 3. Write a fragment to produce the table

```
Number    Its Square    Its Cube
     8            64         512
    10           100        1000
     3             9          27
```

9. Suppose name1 = Mark, name2 = Herman, name3 = Claudia; wt1 = 153, wt2 = 87, wt3 = 136; age1 = 21, age2 = 9, age3 = 20. Write a fragment to produce the table

```
Name     Weight    Age
Mark        153     21
Herman       87      9
Claudia     136     20
```

· ·

Lab Exercises   **DEBUGGING AND SYNTAX ERRORS**

Lab5-1.pas   readln, Strings and Integers

Lab5-2.pas   Trailing and Leading Blanks

Lab5-3.pas   String and Numeric Output in Table Form

Lab5-4.pas   Quadratic Formula $x = \dfrac{-b \pm \sqrt{b^2 - 4ac}}{2a}$

· ·

Chapter

6

FOR LOOPS

• • • In the programs considered so far, the computer has not executed any statement more than once. A powerful feature of the computer is its ability to execute the same group of statements a number of times. This process is called ***looping,*** and the group of statements executed repeatedly is called the ***loop body.***

It is advantageous to use a loop when essentially the same task is to be repeated a specified number of times. In such situations, the task *need be coded only once*—as the loop body. For example, in a program to calculate and print paychecks for 1,000 employees, it is not necessary to include 1,000 different groups of statements to perform the task of calculating and printing paychecks. Instead, a single group of statements can be used as a loop body to be repeated 1,000 times.

The three looping constructs available in Turbo Pascal are **for** loops, **while** loops, and **repeat-until** loops. This chapter will consider for loops, the simplest of the three loop structures. Usually, for loops are used when the number of iterations of the loop body is known in advance.

• • •

6.1 FOR LOOP SYNTAX

A for loop is used to execute a block of statements a specified number of times.

Example

```
for i := 1 to 3 do
   writeln ('John Doe');
```

The output will be

```
John Doe
John Doe
John Doe
```

Loop Body   The loop body in a `for` loop is the statement or group of statements that will be executed a specified number of times. In the preceding example, the loop body was the single statement

```
writeln ('John Doe');
```

Loop Header   The loop header determines how many times the loop body is executed. The variable immediately following the word `for` is called the *control variable.* In a `for` loop with a numeric control variable, the control variable must be an integer type. (A control variable of type `real` is not permitted.) Although an integer control variable must increase or decrease by steps of 1, it need not start at 1. The general form of an increasing `for` loop header is

for {*control variable*} := {*initial*} to {*final*} do

The loop body will be executed a number of times—once for each value (of the control variable) from initial to final, where *initial* and *final* are integers or integer expressions.

• • • • • • • • •
Example   In this example, the computer will print something different on each execution of the loop body. (Note that in this example the control variable appears in the body of the loop.)

```
for i := 1 to 4 do
   writeln (i, ' squared is ', i * i);
```

The output will be

```
1 squared is 1       ← printed when i = 1
2 squared is 4       ← printed when i = 2
3 squared is 9       ← printed when i = 3
4 squared is 16      ← printed when i = 4
```

In this example, first the loop body was executed with i = 1, then with i = 2, then with i = 3, and finally with i = 4. Be aware that i was *automatically* increased by 1 after each execution of the loop body. In fact, the body of a for loop should never contain any statement that assigns the control variable a new value.

downto   The control variable may also be made to decrease by steps of 1 through the use of the keyword downto. For example, the loop header

```
    for i := 5 downto 1
```

would cause i to take on the values 5, 4, 3, 2, and then 1.

Multiple-Statement Loop Body   The computer always takes the loop body to be the statement following the for header. To construct a loop body consisting of more than one statement, enclose the multiple statements in begin-end brackets. The compound statement will then be taken to be the loop body.

• • • • • • • • • •

Question   What output will be produced by the following program? (Note the different levels of indentation.)

```
program drill;
{loop with multiple statements in body}
var i,square : integer;

begin
  for i := 6 to 8 do
    begin
      square := i * i;
      writeln ('this time i equals ', i);
      writeln ('  its square is ', square)
    end; {for}
  writeln ('so long')
end.
```

Answer

```
this time i equals 6
   its square is 36
this time i equals 7
   its square is 49
this time i equals 8
   its square is 64
so long
```

• • •

REMARK

1. Note the semicolon after the `for` loop's end. This semicolon is needed to separate the `for` loop (which the computer treats as a single statement) from the statement `writeln ('so long')`.

2. We indent the loop body to make it stand out to the human eye. The computer ignores indentation in deciding what the loop body is—the computer is guided by the `begin-end` markers. Note that the statement `writeln ('so long')` is not indented but is aligned with the `for` header, since it come *after* the loop.

• • •

• • • • • • • • • •
Question   The Shirts-to-Go retail store has just received a new supply of shirts. Preliminary market research indicates that the profit obtainable at a given sales price *x* is given by the formula profit = $x(100 - 3x)$. Write a program that will produce the following tabular output for integer sales prices ranging from $10 to $30:

```
PRICE   PROFIT
   10      700
   11      737
   12      768
    .        .
    .        .
    .        .
   30      300
```

Before trying to write the program, decide what values the control variable should take on.

Answer   Here is the program.

```
program shirts;
{prints price-profit table for prices from $10 to $30}
var x, profit: integer;

begin
  writeln ('PRICE':5, 'PROFIT':10);
  for x := 10 to 30 do
    begin
      profit := x * (100 - 3 * x);
      writeln (x:5, profit:10)
    end {for}
end.
```

● ● ●

REMARK   Note that the use of the same field specifiers in the two `writeln` statements produces right alignment of the table headings and the columns of numbers.

● ● ●

Nonnumeric Control Variables   The control variable of a `for` loop can be of type `char`. For example,

```
for letter := 'A' to 'Z' do
  write (letter);
```

will produce the output

```
ABCDEFGHIJKLMNOPQRSTUVWXYZ
```

CAUTION

1. **Do Not Put a Semicolon after the** *do*   A semicolon after the `do` would cause the loop body to be the null statement, and any statements after that semicolon would be outside the loop body. Consequently, the "intended" loop body would be executed only *once.* For example,

```
for i := 1 to 4 do;
  writeln ('John Doe');
```

would first execute the null statement four times and then execute the `writeln` statement once, producing as output

```
John Doe
```

2. **Do Not Alter the Control Variable**   A statement in the `for` loop body should never assign a value to the control variable.

```
for i := 1 to 10 do
   begin
      writeln (i);
      i := i + 2        {don't do this}
   end;
```

3. **Don't Forget the `begin-end` Markers**   When you want the loop body to be a block of statements, the block must be contained within `begin-end` markers.

4. **A `for` Loop Will Be Skipped If Initial And Final Are Out of Sync**   That is, it will be skipped

   (a)   If it is an increasing loop (with `to`) and yet initial > final.

   (b)   If it is a `downto` loop with initial < final.

For example, the following loop would produce no output:

```
for i := 5 to 1 do
   writeln (i);
```

• • •

Internal Implementation   Here is the way the computer will implement an *increasing* `for` loop. `downto` loops are analogous.

   `if {initial} <= {final} then`

1.   The control variable is set to initial value.

2.   The loop body is executed a first time.

3.   While the control variable <> final value

   (a)   The control variable is increased by 1, and

   (b)   The loop body is executed again.

6.2 PROCESSING INPUT GROUPS OF DATA
• •

In the examples in the preceding section, the data item to be processed by the loop body was merely the current value of the control variable. In the examples in this section, during each execution of the loop body, new data will be input by the user and then processed. The control variable will go from 1 up to the number of groups of data.

Counting and Summing Variables   The following questions and examples show how counting and summing variables are implemented.

Question What is the output for each of the following fragments?

(a)
```
count := 0;
count := count + 1;
count := count + 1;
count := count + 1;
writeln (count);
```

(b)
```
sum := 0;
sum := sum + 8;
sum := sum + 3;
sum := sum + 11;
writeln (sum);
```

Answer (a) count is initially set to zero. It is then increased by 1 each time

```
count := count + 1;
```

is executed. This statement is executed three times; thus, the output is 3.

(b) The output is 22 because the values 8, 3, and 11 are added onto the initial value 0.

● ● ●

Example The following program uses a for loop to process the names and test scores of four students, which are input by the user.

```
program exam;
{mystery program}
uses printer;
var name: string;
    count, student, score: integer;

begin
  count := 0;
  for student := 1 to 4 do
    begin
      write ('enter name ');
      readln (name);
      write ('enter score ');
      readln (score);
      if score >= 90 then
        begin
          writeln (lst, name, ' ', score);
          count := count + 1
        end {then}
    end; {for}
  writeln (lst, count, ' with score at least 90')
end.
```

Question   If the user were to input scores for Smith, Chan, Kahn, and Jones so that the output screen displayed

```
enter name Smith
enter score 92
enter name Chan
enter score 85
enter name Kahn
enter score 95
enter name Jones
enter score 84
```

what would be printed on paper?

Answer   The program would print on paper the name and score for those students who scored at least 90. It would also print the count.

```
Smith 92
Kahn 95
2 with score at least 90
```

• • •

Initializing   A variable that is given a starting value *before* a loop is said to be *initialized.* For example, in the previous program, the statement

```
count := 0;
```

initialized `count` to 0. Counting and summing variables should *always* be initialized.

CAUTION   If you did not initialize `count` to 0, its starting value would be unreliable. It might be a value left over from a previously run program (see Exercise 5).   • • •

In general, a variable should be initialized if its update is calculated in terms of its previous value. Note that there is no need to initialize `score` to 0 since it is assigned a new value without regard to its previous value.

• • • • • • • • •
Example   The next program will use the variable `sum` to compute the sum of four numbers input by the user. For example, if the user were to input 17, 13, 20, and 8, here is what would appear on the screen.

```
enter number 17
enter number 13
enter number 20
enter number 8
The sum is 58
```

(Note that the program does not print anything on paper.)
Here is the program.

```
program summing;
{finds the sum of 4 input integers}
var i, number, sum: integer;

begin
  sum := 0;
  for i := 1 to 4 do
    begin
      write ('enter number ');
      readln (number);
      sum := sum + number
    end; {for}
  writeln ('The sum is ', sum)
end.
```

General Form   for loop programs to process input information for a certain number of people or items have the following top down design:

Before   initialize any variables that need initializing
            print any headings

During   for i := 1 to __ do
                begin
                    write-readln combination(s) to get the information
                        on one person or item
                    process that person's or item's information
                end; {for}

After   print any final tallies or results

Variable Limits   You can increase the flexibility of a program by using variable(s) as the upper or lower limit in the for header. A common application allows the *user* to specify how many groups of data will be entered.

Example   In the following program, the user is asked to input the number of employees (n) to be processed. Note the use of the variable n as the upper limit in the for header.

```
for employee := 1 to n do
```

Using n gives the program added flexibility—the user does not have to change any lines in the program to run it for different numbers of employees.

```
program payroll;
{finds each employee's wage and total payroll}
uses printer;
var n, employee, hours: integer;
    rate, wage, sum: real;
    name: string;

begin
  write ('enter number of employees ');
  readln (n);                              }← initialize
  sum := 0;
  for employee := 1 to n do
    begin
      write ('enter name of employee ');
      readln (name);                       }← get one employee's data
      write ('enter hours and rate ');
      readln (hours, rate);
      wage := hours * rate;

      _____      }← process that data
      _____

    end; {for}
  writeln (1st, 'total payroll $', sum:8:2)  ← print final result
end.
```

• • • • • • • • • •

Question   Fill in the blank lines in program payroll so that the output on paper will be each employee's name and wage and also the total payroll.

Answer
```
writeln (1st, name, ' $', wage:7:2);
sum := sum + wage
```
• • •

• • • • • • • • • •

Example   **(Finding Averages)**   To find the average of a group of values, you divide the sum of the values by how many values there were. The following program uses both a summing variable and a counter to keep track of the number of values.

Program AboveFreezing receives as input the noon temperature for each of the days in a week. It will find the average noon temperature for just those days on which the noon temperature was above freezing. A typical output would be

```
35 10 5 -4 20 36 31
Above freezing average = 35.5
```

```
program AboveFreezing;
{average noon temp for days when noon temp was above freezing}
var day, temp, count, sum: integer;
    avg: real;

begin
  sum := 0;
  count := 0;
  for day := 1 to 7 do
    begin
      write ('enter noon temp: ');
      readln (temp);
      if temp > 32 then
        begin
          sum := sum + temp;
          count := count + 1
        end {then}
    end; {for}
  if count > 0 then
    begin
      avg := sum/count;
      writeln ('Above freezing average = ', avg:4:1)
    end {then}
  else
    writeln ('No days above freezing at noon')
end.
```

REMARK   The test `if count > 0` was needed to avoid dividing by 0 in the event that there were no above-freezing temperatures.

   If you had been asked to find the average noon temperature for all seven days, you could have eliminated `count` and the `if-then` tests, and simply used `avg := sum/7`.   • • •

6.3 **MORE ON WRITING LOOPS**

In some `for` loop programs, the data value(s) to be processed by an execution of the loop body are input by the user. (For example, see the programs from Section 6.2.) In other programs, the control variable can be used to generate the value or term to be processed by the current execution of the loop body.

• • • • • • • •

Question   Write a program to find the sum of the squares of the first 100 integers—that is, the sum

$$1^2 + 2^2 + 3^2 + \cdots + 100^2$$

A very laborious method would be to have the user input each of these integers. A much better method would be to use the current value of the control variable to express the current term to be added on. Fill in the blank line in the following program:

```
program SumOfSquares;
{finds the sum of first 100 squares}
var i: integer;
    sum: longint;

begin
  sum := 0;
  for i := 1 to 100 do
  _____;
  writeln ('sum of 1st 100 squares is ', sum)
end.
```

Answer   Recall that for each execution of the loop body, we want to use the control variable i to express the term to be added to sum. Hence, the loop body should be

```
sum := sum + i * i;
```

Note that sum was declared to be of type longint because it will exceed 32,767.   • • •

• • • • • • • • •

Example   (Finding the Largest)   Suppose we wish to find the largest, or maximum, number from a list of five *positive* integers that are entered by the user. An algorithm can be developed using the following ideas.

Use a variable called maxsofar. Initialize maxsofar with the first number, then give each of the remaining numbers a chance to displace the current value of maxsofar. The final value of maxsofar will be the maximum.

Here is a pseudocode version of this algorithm.

Before   initialize maxsofar with first number

During   for i := 2 to 5 do
            read a number
            test whether it is larger than maxsofar,
                if so change the value of maxsofar

After   print the value of maxsofar

Here is the actual program.

```
program maxof5;
{finds the maximum of 5 input positive integers}
var maxsofar, i, numb: integer;

begin
  write ('enter first number ');
  readln (maxsofar);
  for i := 2 to 5 do
    begin
      write ('enter number ');
      readln (numb);
      if numb > maxsofar then maxsofar := numb
    end;
  writeln ('the maximum is ', maxsofar)
end.
```

REMARK

1. A shortcut we could use in the previous program would replace the first *three* lines of the program body with the following *two* lines:

```
maxsofar := -1;        {or maxsofar := -MaxInt}
for i := 1 to 5 do
```

In this method, instead of initializing `maxsofar` with the first input number, we initialize it with an artificially small value that we know will get bumped by the first input number. Note that the control variable goes from 1 to 5 instead of 2 to 5. A *danger* of this type of shortcut is that if the artificial initial value is never bumped, it will be printed as the maximum.

2. Whichever method is used, `maxsofar` should be given an initial value because the process of updating `maxsofar` depends on its previous value. ● ● ●

Problem   Suppose a gardener has 100 feet of fencing and wishes to enclose a rectangular garden alongside her house. Drawing a diagram, we find that the area of the garden equals $x(100 - 2x)$.

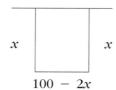

x x

$100 - 2x$

Write a program that will produce the following table of values and the maximum area. (Note that the user will have to scan the table to find the *x* that gives the maximum area.)

```
Value of x       Area
         10        800
         11        858
          .          .
          .          .
          .          .
         44        528
         45        450
Maximum area is 1250
```

(*Hint:* Determine what part of the proposed printout should be printed before, during, and after the loop.)

Answer   First write the pseudocode.

Before   print the table heading
           maxsofar := -1; {initialization}

During   for x := 10 to 45 do
               compute area produced by that x
               print x and associated area
               test area against maxsofar

After   print the maximum area

Here is the actual program. (See Exercise 13 for a program that finds the x which gives the maximum area.)

```
program maxarea;
{finds the maximum area for the garden}
var x, area, maxsofar: integer;

begin
  writeln ('Value of x':10, 'Area':10);
  maxsofar := -1;
  for x := 10 to 45 do
    begin
      area := x * (100 - 2 * x);
      writeln (x:10, area:10);
      if area > maxsofar then maxsofar := area
    end;
  writeln ('Maximum area is ', maxsofar)
end.
```

• • • • • • • • • •

Problem   Write the pseudocode for a program in which the user is asked to input the name, gender, hours, and pay rate for each of six employees. The first part of the printout on paper should give each employee's name and wage. The second part should give separate totals and separate average wages for male and female employees. The program should not assume that there are some employees of each gender.

On Screen

```
enter name          Old, John
    enter gender    m
    enter hrs rate  40 6.50
enter name          Smith, Jane
    enter gender    f
    enter hrs rate  50 6.00
        .
        .
        .
```

On Paper

```
Old, John $260.00
Smith, Jane $300.00
    .
    .
    .
Male total $____
Female total $____
Male average $____
Female average $____
```

Answer   We will use separate summing variables, `MaleSum` and `FemSum`. We will also use separate counters, `males` and `females`.

```
initialize summing variables and counters
for employee := 1 to 6 do
    read in an employee's data
    calculate that employee's wage
    print the name and wage on paper
    if sex = 'm' then
        add wage to MaleSum
        increase males by 1
    else
        add wage to FemSum
        increase females by 1
compute averages (use if-then-else tests to protect
                against dividing by 0)
print all the final tallies on paper
```

Writing the program based on this pseudocode is Exercise 14.   • • •

CAUTION   In an actual program, `begin-end` markers *must* be used to enclose multiple statements in `then` or `else` branches or loop bodies. In pseudocode, it is permissible to omit these begin-end markers and rely solely on indentation.   • • •

6.4 DEBUGGING STRATEGIES

• •

Let us suppose that your program either did not run at all or ran but gave an output that seemed incorrect. Here are some debugging steps you could take.

1. Reread the program to find any obvious errors such as incorrect syntax or kinds of errors that are common to the type of constructs that you are using. For example, when using a for loop, make sure that all variables that need to be initialized are done so correctly.

2. Do some sort of trace to determine the change in the values of important variables. There are three kinds of traces that you could use—the first two kinds are computer assisted, and the third is done entirely by hand.

   (a) *Inserting Extra writeln Statements*   Place them at various places in your program to determine the values of key variables at various times. Then rerun your program and analyze the trace. (Use writeln(lst, . .) if you want hard copy.) Once you've corrected your program, you should remove the extra writeln statements. **(See Lab Exercise Lab6-1.pas to be guided through the reasoning involved in using this method to debug an incorrect program to find the sum of the first 12 cubes.** Also see Lab6-2.pas for further practice at applying this debugging technique.)

   (b) *Using the Built-in Debugger*   This allows you to step through the program one statement at a time watching the effect each statement's execution has on any variables that you've flagged as watch variables. (See Appendix F for the details.)

   (c) *Hand Tracing*   This is an important tool, for there will be times when you do not have access to a computer and you will need to debug a piece of code. Furthermore, since skill at hand tracing increases your awareness of what pieces of program code will do, it will improve your ability to write programs that are freer of errors.

• • • • • • • • • •
Example   (Hand Tracing)

Suppose that when the following program fragment is executed, the user inputs the following six numbers: 5, 30, 10, 40, 15, and 29. What will the output on paper be?

```
for i := 1 to 3 do
   begin
      write ('enter a number ');
      readln (num1);
      num2 := num1 + 2;
      num1 := num1 - 1;
      writeln (lst, num1, ' ', num2);
      write ('enter a number ');
      readln (num2)
   end;
writeln (lst, num1, ' ', num2);
```

(Suggested Memory Table Method)   (1) Draw a column for each variable. A variable's current value will be the value *farthest* down in that variable's column. (2) Draw a horizontal line each time you are about to begin a new execution of the loop body or when you exit from the loop.

During a hand trace, each time you execute an assignment or `readln` statement, you should update the memory table. Each time you execute a `writeln` statement, you should write down the output it produces.

Here is what the memory table would look like at the time the first writeln statement is executed.

i	num1	num2
1	5	7
	4	

The first `writeln` prints 4 7. The total output on paper will be

```
4 7
9 12
14 17
14 29
```

By the time you have finished the hand trace, the memory table will be

i	num1	num2
1	5	7
	4	30
2	10	12
	9	40
3	15	17
	14	29

Note that you cannot determine what the output will be by just looking at the final version of the memory table because this table does not indicate where the `writeln` statements occurred.

EXERCISES

1. What will be output by each of the following program fragments?

(a)
```
for i := 1 to 3 do
   writeln ('hello');
   writeln ('good day');
writeln ('so long');
```

(b)
```
sum := 0;
for i := 1 to 4 do
   sum := sum + i * i;
writeln (sum);
```

(c)
```
for i := 1 to 4 do
   begin
      sum := 0;
      sum := sum + i
   end;
writeln (sum);
```

(d)
```
sum := 0;
c := 0;
for i := 1 to 4 do
   begin
      sum := sum + i;
      if i > 2 then c := c + 1;
   end;
writeln (sum / c :4:2);
```

2. How many times will each of the following loops print `Joe`? Note the semicolon after the word `do` in part (b).

(a)
```
for i := 5 to 15 do
   writeln ('Joe');
```

(b)
```
for i := 1 to 4 do;
   writeln ('Joe');
```

3. Is it always, sometimes, or never necessary to place a semicolon after the keyword `end` of a `for` loop body?

4. There is an error in style in the fragment shown here. What is it?

```
sum := 0;
wage := 0;
for i := 1 to 5 do
   begin
      write ('enter hours and rate ');
      readln (hours, rate);
      wage := hours * rate;
      sum := sum + wage
   end;
writeln ('Total payroll ', sum)
```

5. **(a)** Write a program to find the sum of the first 50 integers. Run it *twice*. Each run should produce exactly the same output.

(b) Now remove the initialization

```
sum := 0;
```

and run your program two more times. Explain why the outputs were incorrect.

6. In the hand tracing example of Section 6.4, what would the output on paper be if the fourth statement in the loop body were changed from num1 := num1 - 1 to num1 := num2 - 1?

7. Give the output for

(a)
```
x := 30;
for i := 1 to 5 do
  begin
    x := x-2;
    write ('x = ', x);
    if x mod 4 = 0
        then writeln ('OK')
        else writeln;
  end;
```

(b)
```
program drill;
var i, m, p: integer;
begin
  m := 5;
  for i := 1 to 3 do
    begin
      p := m - 2;
      m := m + p;
      p := p + 6;
      if m > p
          then writeln (p)
          else writeln (m)
    end;
  writeln (m, ' ', p);
end.
```

Longer Assignments

8. Write a program to produce the following table.

```
Yards   Inches
    1       36
    2       72
    3      108
    .        .
    .        .
    .        .
   10      360
```

9. Write a program to find the sum

$$1 + 1/2 + 1/3 + 1/4 + \cdots + 1/50$$

10. Write a program that will print a squares and cubes table (from 1 to 15) and then print

    The sum of the squares

    The sum of the cubes

    How many cubes were greater than 500

    A message stating whether or not the sum of the squares exceeded 2,000

    Format the table part of the output as follows.

NUMBER	SQUARE	CUBE
1	1	1
2	4	8
3	9	27
.	.	.
.	.	.
.	.	.
15	225	3375

11. *Trigonometry.* When a ball is thrown up at an angle of θ *degrees* and with initial velocity V_0 the height of the ball after t seconds is

    $$h(t) = V_0 t \sin\theta - 16t^2$$

    Using an initial velocity of 144 feet per second and $\theta = 60$ degrees, write a program to output a *table* giving the height of the ball for each value of t from 1 to 8.

12. 5! (read "5 factorial") is equal to the product $5 \cdot 4 \cdot 3 \cdot 2 \cdot 1$. Similarly, 8! is equal to the product $8 \cdot 7 \cdot 6 \cdot 5 \cdot 4 \cdot 3 \cdot 2 \cdot 1$. Write a program that will compute the factorial of an input positive integer. When this program is run with the user inputting 5, the output should be

    ```
    5 factorial is 120
    ```

    Rerun the program, inputting 8. (*Note:* 8! exceeds 32,767.) The output this time should be

```
8 factorial is 40320
```

13. Modify program `maxarea` from Section 6.3 so that it prints not only the maximum area but also the value of x that produces that area.

14. Write a payroll program based on the pseudocode given at the end of Section 6.3.

15. Write an interactive program for the Sales-R-Us Company to process and print out payroll information on its 10 employees. For each employee, the program should read in the employee's name, hours worked, base rate of pay, and age. For example, a typical data group might be

    Doe, Joe   50.0   5.00   57

    An employee's gross wage is computed at the regular pay rate for the first 40 hours and 1.5 times the regular rate for each hour over 40. Thus, an employee who worked 50 hours at $5 per hour would have a gross pay of $275. An employee's tax is withheld as follows: 10 percent on the first $200 and 20 percent on anything above $200.

    The first part of the printout on paper should give the relevant facts for each employee. (Skip a line between employees in the printout.) Format the output something like

```
Doe, Joe  Hrs worked 50.0   Base rate 5.00   Age 57
Gross $275.00   Tax $35.00   Net $240.00
```

    The second part should state

    The average gross for employees at least 55 years old

    The average gross for employees under 55 years old

    The name and the gross pay for the employee with the largest gross (you may assume that there is not a tie)

16. Write an interactive program to do the grading for a class of 10 students. For each student, the program should read in the student's name and three exam grades. The program should find each student's average and then determine if the student passed or failed, with an average of at least 60 needed to pass. The first part of the output on paper should give each student's name, three grades, average, and a message (`passed` or `failed`). The second part of the output on paper should give how many students passed and how many had an average of at least 80.

17. Write a program that asks the user to input the name and age for each of three employees. The output should be a table with a heading, formatted as follows. (*Hint:* See Section 5.4.)

```
Name              Age
Doe, John          25
Morgan, Jessica    31
Smith, James       19
```

Lab Exercises   **DEBUGGING AND EXPERIMENTING**

Lab6-1.pas	Summing cubes
Lab6-2.pas	Summing cubes
Lab6-3.pas	Finding lowest input score
Lab6-4.pas	Finding highest wage
Lab6-5.pas	Printable characters

Chapter

7

REPEAT-UNTIL AND
WHILE LOOPS

• • •   Although `for` loops are the easiest looping construct to use, there are looping situations in which they are not appropriate. (Recall that the number of times that the body of a `for` loop is to be executed must be known in advance—usually either by the programmer or the user.)

Turbo Pascal provides two more versatile looping constructs, **repeat-until** loops and **while** loops. Their greater versatility results from the fact that the number of executions of the loop body is controlled by a condition rather than merely a count, as in the case of a `for` loop.

In this chapter, we introduce `repeat-until` and `while` loops, subdividing them into the following three categories:

1. *Fixed Step-controlled loops with Integer Step.* These are very similar to `for` loops. (Steps of type `real` are covered in Section 8.4.)

2. *Data sentinel-controlled loops.* In interactive programs, these loops allow the user to decide when to stop entering data.

3. *More General Task-controlled Loops.* In loops of this kind, the exit condition tests for the completion of a task that is more general than either a count or a data sentinel.   • • •

103

7.1 INTRODUCTION TO WHILE AND REPEAT–UNTIL LOOPS

while Loops

Syntax for while Loops

```
while {test condition} do
   begin
      {body of loop}
   end;
```

Here is how a `while` loop works. The computer starts by testing the `while` condition. If the condition is true, the entire loop body is executed. Then control is returned to the top to retest the `while` condition. This process is repeated as long as the `while` condition is true. The first time the condition tests out as false, the computer exits from the loop.

Question   What will the output be for the following loop?

```
n := 7;
while n >= 0 do
   begin
      writeln (n);
      n := n - 5;
      writeln ('Hi ', n)
   end;
```

Answer

```
7
Hi  2
2
Hi  -3
```
{ 7, Hi 2 } ← printed during first execution of loop body
{ 2, Hi -3 } ← printed during second execution of loop body

REMARK   Note that the computer does not exit from the middle of the loop body. That is why the statement `writeln ('Hi ', n)` is executed even after n has become -3.

Fixed Step-Controlled while Loops Fixed step-controlled `while` loops closely resemble `for` loops in that there is a control variable that increases or decreases by a fixed step and the loop terminates after the loop body has been executed for the final value of the control variable. Unlike numeric `for` loops, however, the fixed step can be a value other than 1. The `while` condition usually tests whether the control variable has gone beyond its final value.

• • • • • • • • • •

Example (Increasing by Steps of 2)

Output

```
i := 1;
while i <= 9 do
   begin
      writeln (i);
      i := i + 2
   end; {while}
writeln ('so long');
```

```
1
3
5
7
9
so long
```

Note that in this kind of `while` loop, the control variable is initialized before the loop and incremented in the loop body by actual statements. Recall that in a `for` loop, both these things were handled automatically by the loop header.

• • • • • • • • • •

Question Fill in the blanks in the following program to find the sum

$$12^2 + 15^2 + 18^2 + 21^2 + 24^2 + 27^2 + 30^2$$

```
program SumofSquares;
var i, sum: integer;
begin
   sum := 0;
   _____
   while i _____ do
      begin
         sum := sum + (i * i);
         _____
      end;
   writeln ('Sum is ', sum)
end.
```

Answer   Note that i starts at 12 and goes up by steps of 3 to 30 as a final value. The lines with blanks should be

```
i := 12;
while i <= 30 do
    i := i + 3
```

A general form for fixed step-controlled while loops with i an increasing control variable is

```
i := first value;
while i <= final value do
    begin
        process current value of i
        i := i + increment
    end;
```

For loops with steps of type real, like 0.1, see Section 8.4.   • • •

repeat–until Loops

Syntax for repeat–until Loops

```
repeat
    {body of loop}
until {test condition}
```

Here is how a repeat-until loop works. The entire loop body is always executed a first time no matter what. Then the until condition is tested. If the condition is false, the entire loop body is executed again, after which the condition is tested again. The process is repeated until the condition is true. The first time the condition is true, the computer exits from the loop.

• • • • • • • • • •
Question   What will the output be for the following loop?

```
n := 7;
repeat
    writeln (n);
    n := n - 5;
    writeln ('Hi ', n)
until n < 0;
```

Answer

```
7
Hi  2      } ← printed during first execution of loop body
2
Hi  -3     } ← printed during second execution of loop body
```

• • •

Fixed Step repeat–until Loops

These are similar to fixed step `while` loops in that there is a control variable, which goes up by a fixed step, and the loop terminates when this control variable goes beyond (or in some cases merely reaches) a final value.

• • • • • • • • • •

Question   What will be the output for the following loop?

```
n := 1;
sum := 0;
repeat
   sum := sum + (n * n);
   n := n + 2
until n > 7;
writeln ('sum = ', sum);
```

Answer   *Output*

```
sum = 84
```

Trace

sum	(calculation for sum)	n
0		1
1	$(0 + 1^2)$	3
10	$(1 + 3^2)$	5
35	$(10 + 5^2)$	7
84	$(35 + 7^2)$	9

In summary, this loop found the sum $1^2 + 3^2 + 5^2 + 7^2$.   • • •

Comparison of while and repeat–until Loops

while	repeat–until
Test condition checked before body of loop is executed. Therefore, there might be no executions of the loop body.	Test condition checked after body of loop is executed. Therefore, body of loop is always executed at least once.
Body of loop is repeated when the test condition is true.	Body of loop is repeated when the test condition is false.

Question   Give the output produced by each of the following loops. *Hint:* It will not be the same for both loops.

(a)
```
x := 99;
repeat
   writeln (x);
   x := x + 1
until x > 1;
```

(b)
```
x := 99;
while x <= 1 do
   begin
      writeln (x);
      x := x + 1
end;
```

Answer   A `repeat-until` loop body is always executed at least once since it is bottom tested. Segment (a) will produce output 99, whereas segment (b) will produce no output.   • • •

7.2 DATA SENTINEL-CONTROLLED LOOPS

When a `for` loop is used to process groups of input data, the `for` loop header must specify in advance how many groups of data there will be. By contrast, in a data sentinel-controlled loop, the user can terminate data entry when he or she chooses by entering an appropriate signal known as a sentinel. In this section, we present three different types of sentinel-controlled loops, which we call types A, B, and C.

Type A: Using a y or n Question

Suppose that on this run the user wishes to find the sum

   15 + 47 + 43 + 64

In the following program, the user notifies the computer that there is no further data by entering an `n` in response to the prompt `type y to continue, n to stop`.

```pascal
program FindSum;
{finds the sum of any number of input numbers}
var sum, numb: integer;
    ans: char;

begin
  sum := 0;
  repeat
    write ('enter number ');
    readln (numb);
    sum := sum + numb;
    write (' type y to continue, n to stop ');
    readln (ans)
  until (ans = 'n') or (ans = 'N');
  writeln ('The sum is ', sum)
end.
```

Here is what would appear on the screen.

```
enter number 15
  type y to continue, n to stop y
enter number 47
  type y to continue, n to stop y
enter number 43
  type y to continue, n to stop y
enter number 64
  type y to continue, n to stop n
The sum is 169
```

REMARK   Note that the condition

```pascal
until (ans = 'n') or (ans = 'N');
```

is a form of error trapping. This allows the user to type the response in either uppercase or lowercase.

Alternatively, you could use the upcase function in

```pascal
until upcase (ans) = 'N';
```                                    • • •

Type B: repeat Loop with (Phony Value) Data Sentinel

One disadvantage of the previous program is that for each value entered, the user was required to make two inputs—the actual value and the answer (y or n) to the question whether he or she wished to continue. The following loop reduces the amount of data entry by the user, eliminating the y or n question. Instead, the user signals an end to data entry by typing the phony value -1 as a sentinel.

```
sum := 0;
repeat
  write ('enter number or -1 to stop ');
  readln (numb);
  if numb <> -1 then
    sum := sum + numb;
until numb = -1;
writeln ('The sum is ', sum);
```

When this loop is run to find the sum of 15, 47, 43, and 64, the output screen will display

```
enter number or -1 to stop 15
enter number or -1 to stop 47
enter number or -1 to stop 43
enter number or -1 to stop 64
enter number or -1 to stop -1
The sum is 169
```

REMARK   Note the purpose of the if-then test in the loop body—so that -1 is not processed (added to sum).   • • •

Type C: while Loop with Phony Data Sentinel

The following while loop is similar to the type B repeat-until loop that uses − 1 as a sentinel. The screen display and the demands on the user are identical to the type B version.

Priming the Pump   In the following while loop, note the write-readln combination that appears before the while loop. This is known as priming the pump since any variable in the while condition must already have a value when the loop is first encountered.

```
sum := 0;
write ('enter number or -1 to stop ');
readln (numb);
while numb <> -1 do
   begin
      sum := sum + numb;
      write ('enter number or -1 to stop ');
      readln (numb)
   end;
writeln ('The sum is ', sum);
```

REMARK

1. Note the two occurrences of the same `write-readln` combination, once before the loop and once at the bottom of the loop body. The `write-readln` at the bottom gets the next value of numb so that it is ready to be tested by the `while` condition.

2. Note that the `while` condition prevents processing the sentinel (adding −1 to sum.) Thus, the `if-then` test that was used in the type B loop is not needed.   • • •

Example (Sales Receipt)

As input for `program receipt`, a cashier enters in the data for each of the customer's purchases. Each data group consists of an item name, the price of the item, and the quantity of that item being purchased. The data sentinel `xyz` is used instead of an item name. Here is the screen display for a typical run that would also produce a printed sales receipt.

```
enter item name or xyz to stop   rake
   enter price per item and quantity   19.50   1
enter item name or xyz to stop   shovel
   enter price per item and quantity   14.50   2
enter item name or xyz to stop   light bulbs
   enter price per item and quantity   3.50   6
enter item name or xyz to stop   xyz
```

• • •

Question   Fill in the missing lines.

```
program receipt;
{prints a sales receipt-- type C version}
uses printer;
var item: string;
    quant: integer;
    price, cost, sum: real;

begin
  sum := 0;
  write ('enter item name or xyz to stop ');
  readln (item);
  while item <> 'xyz' do
    begin
      write (' enter price per item and quantity ');
      readln (price, quant);
      cost := price * quant;
      sum := sum + cost;
      writeln (lst, quant, ' ', item, ' $', cost:6:2);

      _____

      _____

    end; {while}
  writeln (lst, 'Total bill $', sum:7:2)
end.
```

Answer

```
writeln ('enter item name or xyz to stop ');
readln (item)
```
      • • •

REMARK   Note the splitting up of the two pairs of `write-readln` combinations within the body of the loop—one `write-readln` is at the bottom of the loop body, and the rest are at the beginning of the loop body. This is the case whenever information for each item cannot be read in with a single `readln` statement.   • • •

A general form for type C data sentinel loop is

```
write-readln (to get first part of first data group)
while data <> sentinel
  begin
    get rest of current data group
    process current data group
    write-readln {get first part of next group}
               {usually same write-readln as before loop}
  end;
```

Comparisons of the Types Type A loops have the simplest logic and provide the user with the clearest instructions. However, type A loops do require more data entry by the user than does either type B or C. Type C loops are superior to type B loops because although both of these types make identical demands on the user, type C loops are more efficient. (Type C needs only one sentinel test for each item, whereas type B needs two tests.)

7.3 MORE GENERAL TASK-CONTROLLED LOOPS

• •

In some situations when the condition for the completion of the task is not a count or a data sentinel, it is useful to think of a loop in terms of its task as follows:

```
while {task not completed} do        repeat
    {loop body}                          {loop body}
                                     until {task completed}
```

General Guidelines for Constructing the Loop

Let us apply the problem-solving guidelines of Section 4.4, focusing on issues that are important in loops.

1. **Understand the Problem**   What do you want the loop to accomplish? What do you want to be true by the end of the loop?

2. **Develop the Looping Algorithm**
    (a) Do you need a variable that goes up or down by a fixed step? Do you need other variables? What variable(s) will be needed in the exit condition?

    (b) Each execution of the loop body should make some progress toward achieving completion of the task, such as, processing a next term. For such a loop, how is the next term generated, and how is it processed?

    (c) Write a top down outline or pseudocode, including any needed initialization.

3. **Write the Complete Code for the Loop**

4. **Test the Loop**   Check that it does what it was supposed to. Pay particular attention to the first and last execution of the loop.

• • • • • • • • •
Example   The sum of the squares $1^2 + 2^2 + 3^2 + \cdots$ eventually goes over 1,000. Write a program to find the integer whose square first puts the sum over 1,000. The output should be of the form

```
Sum first goes over 1000 when you add __ squared
Sum is __
```

Variables   We need a variable n to go up by steps of 1 to generate 1^2, 2^2, 3^2, and so on. We also need a variable, sum, to keep track of the sum of the squares. The exit condition is obviously

```
while sum <= 1000
```

Pseudocode   Here is the pseudocode.

```
initialize n and sum
while sum <= 1000 do
    begin
        increase n by 1
        add n² to sum
    end
print the results
```

Here is the while version.

```
program over1000;
{finds first square to put sum over 1000}
var n, sum: integer;

begin
  n := 0;
  sum := 0;
  while sum <= 1000 do
    begin
      n := n + 1;
      sum := sum + (n * n)
    end; {while}
  writeln ('Sum first goes over 1000 when you add ', n, ' squared');
  writeln ('Sum is ', sum)
end.
```

• • •

REMARK   Note that this loop is not fixed step-controlled because the variable, n, that goes up by a fixed step is not the variable in the exit condition.

• • •

Here is a `repeat-until` version of `program over1000`.

```
program over1000;
{finds first square to put the sum over 1000}
var n, sum: integer;

begin
  n := 0;
  sum := 0;
  repeat
    n := n + 1;
    sum := sum + (n * n)
  until sum > 1000;
  writeln ('Sum first goes over 1000 when you add ', n, ' squared');
  writeln ('Sum is ', sum)
end.
```

REMARK   Note that the `repeat` and `while` versions of these two programs are identical except for the loop keywords and the exit conditions.

The condition . . . `until sum > 1000`

is the negation of . . . `while sum <= 1000 do`   • • •

Problem   (Ulam's Conjecture)   The following conjecture is known as Ulam's conjecture after the mathematician S. Ulam:

Start with any positive integer.

If it is even, divide it by 2; if it is odd, multiply it by 3 and add 1.

Obtain successive integers by repeating the process as long as the current integer is not 1.

Eventually, you will obtain the number 1 regardless of the starting integer. For example, when 26 is the starting integer, the sequence will be

26   13   40   20   10   5   16   8   4   2   1

Variables   Let us use a single variable n to run through all the values in the Ulam sequence. Thus, n will start at the number that we want the Ulam sequence for, and then each execution of the loop body should calculate and print the next number in the Ulam sequence.

Let us use a `repeat-until` loop. We want the loop to stop when n becomes 1 and we have output this value of n.

Pseudocode   Here is the pseudocode.

```
get starting value for n
output it
repeat
    find next number, n, in Ulam sequence
    output it
until n = 1
```

Write a program based on this pseudocode. *Hint:* Use a test of the form

```
if n mod 2 = 0
    then ...
    else ...
```

Answer

```
program Ulam;
{prints Ulam sequence for an input integer}
var n: integer;
begin
  write ('enter an integer over 1 ');
  readln (n);
  writeln ('Ulam sequence for ', n, ':');
  write (n);
  repeat
    if n mod 2 = 0
       then n := n div 2
       else n := 3 * n + 1;
    write (' ', n)
  until n = 1;
  writeln
end.
```

(while Loop version of Ulam)   A `while` loop version of this program would be the same except it would have exit condition `while n <> 1 do` instead of `repeat-until n = 1`, and its loop body would need `begin-end` markers.

• • •

Example   **(Compound Interest)**   If $500 is invested at 6 percent compounded annually, the balance at the end of the first year will be $530.00 ($500 + $30 interest). The balance at the end of the second year will be $561.80 ($530 + $31.80 interest).

The following program will determine the first year in which the ending balance exceeds $1,000:

```
program CompoundInt;
{finds when $500 at 6% first exceeds $1,000}
var balance: real;
    year: integer;
begin
  balance := 500;
  year := 0;
  while balance <= 1000 do
    begin
      balance := balance + 0.06 * balance;
      year := year + 1
    end; {while}
  writeln ('Balance over $1,000 at end of year ', year);
  writeln ('Balance was $', balance:7:2)
end.
```

The output will be

```
Balance over $1,000 at end of year 12
Balance was $1006.10
```

• • •

REMARK   In many loops, it matters whether a statement to increment a variable (like `year := year + 1`) appears at the top or the bottom of the loop body. In the previous program, *however,* note that the two statements in the loop body could have had their order switched since the variable, `year`, does not appear in the assignment statement for `balance`.   • • •

Guidelines for Selecting a Loop   When `for` loops can be used (whenever the number of iterations is known in advance), they are usually the simplest to construct. When `for` loops are not appropriate, use the following guidelines for deciding between `while` and `repeat`:

1. Ask yourself whether there are certain circumstances under which you would *not* want the loop body to be executed even once. If so, use a `while` loop.

2. If you know that you definitely want the loop to be executed at least once, choose whichever loop construct seems to better reflect the nature of the task. You should decide whether the algorithm is better expressed as "repeat the loop body until the task is completed" or as "while the task is not completed, do the loop body."

7.4 AVOIDING PITFALLS

• •

Pitfall: Infinite Loop

An infinite loop is a loop that keeps on being executed over and over again without end because the loop exit condition is never satisfied. For example

```
n := 0;
while n <> 15 do
   begin
      n := n + 2;
      write (n, ' ')
   end;
writeln ('so long');
```

The computer will stay in this loop indefinitely because n will take on only even values and hence will always be unequal to 15. The output will be

```
2  4  6  8  10  12  14  16  18  ...
```

The computer will never reach the statement writeln ('so long').

CAUTION   Testing for inequality in a while loop or equality in a repeat–until loop can be risky. It will lead to an infinite loop if the variable in the exit condition jumps over the stopping value without landing on it.

• • •

Stopping an Infinite Loop   Use CTRL-BREAK to stop the running of a program that is in an infinite loop. Note that when you stop an infinite loop this way, Turbo Pascal puts you into the debugger mode. If you wish to get out of the debugger mode and get rid of the blue highlighting, you should press CTRL-F2.

Silent Infinite Loop   If you were to run a program containing the preceding infinite loop, it would be obvious from the rapid-fire printing that there was an infinite loop. A more difficult situation to diagnose is one in which the computer is trapped in an infinite loop that does not produce any output. Such an infinite loop is called *silent*. The following program fragment would produce a silent infinite loop:

```
n := 0;
while n <> 15 do
   n := n + 2;
writeln ('so long');
```

If the computer is not responding to keyboard entries when you think that a program run is finished, you should suspect a silent loop.

Pitfall: Don't Forget to Initialize   In any kind of loop, failure to initialize a summing or counting variable will produce an error if the garbage initial value of that variable is different from the desired initial value.

Pitfall: Off-by-One Iteration or Out-of-Sync Error   A common error in a `while` or `repeat-until` loop is that the body might be executed one time too many or too few, or for the wrong starting value or final value of a variable.

Question   Each of the following loops is intended to produce the output

```
1 3  5 7 9
```

What will their outputs actually be?

(a)
```
n := 1;
while n < 9 do
   begin
      write (n, ' ');
      n := n + 2;
   end;
```

(b)
```
n := 1;
while n <= 9 do
   begin
      n := n + 2;
      write (n, ' ');
   end;
```

Answer   (a) 1 3 5 7   (b) 3 5 7 9 11   • • •

Protecting Against Off-by-One Errors   Quick and dirty check: Check what the situation will be after the first execution of the loop body and also after the final execution since these are the most common trouble spots. Note that the positioning of the statement to increment a variable can make a difference; so can whether < or <= is used.

Two common schemes for a loop body are

(a)   process current `n`
      increment `n`

(b)   increment `n`
      process current `n`

Sometimes it is more natural to use scheme (a), and other times it is more natural to use scheme (b). When you use (a), you would initialize n to the first value you want to process, whereas when you use (b), you would initialize n to a value one step prior to the starting value.

Considerations in Avoiding Off-by-One Errors   There is no magic formula. There is no substitute for being aware of the factors and being able to analyze whether your loop will do what it was intended to do. The factors that must work together in a while or repeat-until are

- Order of incrementing or updating of a key variable in relation to the remainder of the loop processing

- Initialization (at starting value or prior to it)

- Relational operator in exit condition (such as < or <=)

- - - - - - - - - -
Example   (Hand Tracing)

Review the suggested memory table method (refer to Section 6.4), and then do a hand trace for the following loop:

```
n := 10;
repeat
  m := n - 1;
  prod := m * n;
  writeln ('n = ',n , ' m = ',m , ' prod = ', prod);
  n := n - 3
until n = 1;
writeln (m * n);
```

(Snapshot After One Execution of the Loop Body)

n	m	prod	*Output*
10			
7	9	90	

Output box: `n = 10   m = 9   prod = 90`

Note that the writeln statement was executed before n was updated (from 10 to 7). Thus the output for n has the value 10 as opposed to the value that n has by the end of that loop body execution.

Final Output

```
n = 10   m = 9   prod = 90
n = 7    m = 6   prod = 42
n = 4    m = 3   prod = 12
3
```

• • •

• • • • • • • • • ## EXERCISES

• •

1. Give the outputs for each of the following segments.

(a)
```
n := 1;
while n <= 9 do
begin
   n := n + 5;
   writeln (n)
end;
```

(b)
```
n := 1;
while n <= 10 do
   writeln (n);
   n := n + 1;
```

(c)
```
x := 0;
repeat
   x := x + 1;
   writeln (x)
until x <= 5
```

2. **(i)** Give the outputs for each of the following segments.

(a)
```
m := 5;
n := 9;
repeat
   writeln (m, ' ', n);
   m := m + 2;
   n := n + 1
until m > n;
writeln (m, ' ', n)
```

(b)
```
x := 0;
y := 0;
repeat
   x := x + 2;
   y := x - 2;
   writeln (x, ' ', y)
until y > 5;
writeln ('So Long');
```

(ii) Write an equivalent `while` loop that will produce the same output as segment (i).

3. If a `while` loop is reached, it is certain that the loop body will be executed at least once. True or false?

4. Give the outputs for each of the following segments.

(a)
```
k := 5;
while k > 2 do
  begin
    n := 2*k;
    writeln (n*k);
    if k mod 2 <> 0
      then writeln (k)
      else writeln (n);
    k := k - 1;
end; {while}
```

(b)
```
x := 50;
y := 2;
while x > 0 do
    begin
      x := x div y;
      if x < 5 then
        writeln ('x*y = ', x*y)
      else
        begin
          z := x + y;
          writeln ('z is ', z)
        end; {else}
      y := y + 1
    end; {while}
writeln ('y = ', y);
```

5. Give the output for the following segment.

(a)
```
x := 30;
y := 7;
repeat
  x := x - y;
  if x < y then
    begin
      x := x + 1;
      writeln (x, ' ', y)
    end
  else
    begin
      y := y + 1;
      writeln (y)
    end
until x < 10;
writeln ('x = ',x, 'y = ',y);
```

(b)
```
bal := 100;
rate := 0.4;
yrs := yrs + 1;
repeat
    int := bal * rate;
    bal := bal + int;
    yrs := yrs + 1;
until bal > 200;
writeln (yrs);
```

6. In `program over1000` of Section 7.3 the output is correct.

> Sum first goes over 1000 when you add 14 squared
>
> Sum is 1015

What would the output be if the program were written incorrectly, with the order of the two statements in the loop body reversed?

Longer Assignments

7. Write a program to print the following Fahrenheit and Celsius temperature table. (*Hint:* Celsius = (Fahr − 32) * ⅝.)

```
Fahrenheit     Celsius
        32        0.0
        34        1.1
        36        2.2
         .          .
         .          .
         .          .
       100       37.8
```

8. Write a payroll program using a `while` loop with a sentinel. For each employee, the program should read in the employee's name, gender, hours worked, and hourly rate. The first part of the printout on paper should give each employee's name, hours worked, pay rate, and wage. The second part should give the average female wage and the average male wage.

9. Write the program for Exercise 15 of Chapter 6 using a `while` loop with a sentinel. (Do not assume there are 10 employees.)

10. Write the program for Exercise 16 of Chapter 6 using a `while` loop with a sentinel. (Do not assume there are 10 students.)

11. The powers of 2 are 1, 2, 4, 8, 16, 32, 64, and so on. To get the next power of 2, you multiply the previous one by 2. Write a program that will print the first power of 2 that exceeds 1,000.

12. Write a program in which the user is asked repeatedly to input integers from 1 to 5. The program should inform the user when he or she enters an integer that puts the sum of the input integers over 21. In addition to printing the message OVER 21, the computer should print the sum and the last integer entered.

13. Write a program that will print the Ulam sequences for an input integer. Format the output so that it contains no more than 10 numbers per line. The output should also give the length of the sequence. Typical output

```
Enter integer greater than one   148
Ulam sequence of 148
148   74   37   112   56   28   14    7   22   11
 34   17   52    26   13   40   20   10    5   16
  8    4    2     1
Length was 24
```

14. Mexico's population in 1994 was 58 million and growing at the rate of 7 percent. If Mexico maintains its current rate of growth, what is the first year in which its population will be over 100 million?

15. Joe starts with a balance of $100,000 invested at a rate of 5 percent compounded annually. At the end of the year, just after that year's interest is added on, Joe will withdraw $12,000 in a lump sum. What is the first year at the end of which his balance will not permit such a withdrawal?

16. Mexico's population is 58 million and growing at the annual rate of 7 percent. The United States' current population is 260 million and growing at the annual rate of 2 percent. If these two countries were to maintain their current rates of growth, in how many years will Mexico's population be more than half that of the United States?

17. The radioactive substance strontium 90 has a decay rate constant of 2.4 percent. That is, each year the amount lost through radioactive decay is

   (.024) ∗ (amount at start of that year)

   (a) Suppose you start with 50 grams of strontium 90. Write a program to print how many grams of strontium 90 remains after each year over a 10-year period.

   (b) Write a program to find an estimate for the half-life of strontium 90 (that is, the number of years after which half the original amount of strontium 90 remains). Your output should be of the form

   ```
   strontium 90 half-life between m and n years
   ```

   where n is the smallest integer number of years after which there is less than half the original amount.

∗ 18. e^x can be represented as the infinite series

$$e^x = 1 + x + \frac{x^2}{2!} + \frac{x^3}{3!} + \cdots$$

If we consider 1 as the 0th term, x as the first term, $x^2/2!$ as the second term, $x^3/3!$ as the third term, and so on, then the nth term is the previous term multiplied by x/n. Run a program based on this series to find an approximation for $e^{2.5}$. The program should stop when the term just added is less than .0001. Rerun the program to find an approximation for e. Compare these results to the values returned by the built-in Pascal function exp ( ).

Lab Exercises   **DEBUGGING AND SYNTAX ERRORS**

Chapter

8

MORE ON LOOPS

• • • In this chapter, we consider the following specific types of applications of loops: (1) loops with multiple exit conditions, (2) error-trapping loops, (3) nested loops, (4) fixed step loops with `real` step and, (5) the uses of loop invariants. • • •

8.1 MULTIPLE REASONS FOR LOOP EXIT

In cases when there are two possible reasons for terminating a loop, it will be necessary to use a compound condition in the exit test. Usually, in such situations, it will also be necessary to include an `if-then-else` test after the loop to determine which condition caused the exit.

• • • • • • • • • •
Example   (Bounded Number of Tries)   Write a program in which the user is given a maximum of three tries to give the capital of Alaska. If the user fails to give the correct answer by the third try, he or she is then informed what the correct answer is. Format the program so that it could produce the following two sample runs:

```
Give capital of Alaska  Nome
Give capital of Alaska  Provo
Give capital of Alaska  Omaha
You did not get it in three tries
The correct answer is Juneau
```

```
Give capital of Alaska   Nome
Give capital of Alaska   Juneau
Nice work. You got it on try 2
```

Here is the program.

```
program StateCapital;
const
   state = 'Alaska';
   capital = 'Juneau';
var tries: integer;
    guess: string;
begin
  tries := 0;
  repeat
    tries := tries + 1;
    write ('Give capital of ', state, ' ');
    readln (guess)
  until (guess = capital) or (tries = 3);
  if guess = capital then
    writeln ('Nice work. You got it on try ', tries)
  else
    begin
      writeln ('You did not get it in three tries');
      writeln ('The correct answer is ', capital)
    end
end.
```

• • •

Pitfall   It would be incorrect to use the test

```
if tries = 3
```

since the user might have gotten the answer on the third try.

repeat versus while   Generally, a `repeat-until` loop with two different reasons for exiting will have an `until` condition of the form

`until {reason 1}` or `{reason 2}`;

By contrast the `while` version would have a `while` condition of the form

`while {not reason 1}` and `{not reason 2}` do

Thus, if `program StateCapital` were written with a `while` loop, the loop header would be

```
while (guess <> capital) and (tries < 3) do
```

8.2   ERROR TRAPPING AND ROBUSTNESS

A common cause of faulty program output is the entry of incorrect data. Although there is no way to ensure that the user will not make mistakes in entering data, there are techniques the programmer can use to gain some protection against such errors.

One technique is to include clear prompts so that the user knows the precise form for the inputs. A second technique is to include program code to detect and trap mistakes. A program that contains such safeguards is said to be *robust* since it is strong in the sense of being resistant to some forms of bad data. The `repeat-until` loop is commonly used in error trapping.

Examples   Look for a possible weakness in the following program fragment, which determines whether an input capital letter is in the first half (A–M) or the second half (N–Z) of the alphabet:

```
write ('enter capital letter ');
readln (letter);
if (letter >= 'A') and (letter <= 'M')
   then writeln (letter,' in first half of alphabet')
   else writeln (letter,' in second half of alphabet');
```

Here is a run of the fragment in which the user failed to heed the prompt to enter a *capital* letter.

```
enter capital letter d
d in second half of alphabet
```

In the following robust program fragment, note the use of a `repeat-until` loop to force the user to enter a capital letter. Execution does not get beyond the loop until the user enters an uppercase letter.

```
repeat
  write ('enter capital letter ');
  readln (letter)
until (letter >= 'A') and (letter <= 'Z');
if (letter >= 'A') and (letter <= 'M')
  then writeln (letter,' in first half of alphabet')
  else writeln (letter,' in second half of alphabet');
```

Here is a typical run of the preceding robust code.

```
enter capital letter d
enter capital letter D
D in first half of alphabet
```

Stronger Jolt (Optional) A minor drawback of the previous error trap is that the user (in typing d) might not realize that he or she entered an inappropriate value. Rather the user might think that the program is asking for a second letter. The following error trap with the bell gives the user more of a jolt.

```
write ('enter capital letter ');
readln (letter);
while (letter < 'A') or (letter > 'Z') do
  begin
    writeln (chr(7), '*** NOT a capital letter');
    write ('enter capital letter ');
    readln (letter)
  end;
```

REMARK You could have used the built-in function, `upcase`, to automatically convert to uppercase any letter inadvertently entered in lowercase. Of course, that approach wouldn't protect against the user typing in a nonalphabetic character. • • •

8.3 NESTED LOOPS

• •

When one loop is completely contained in the body of another, the loops are said to be ***nested.*** This section briefly introduces nested loops. For further discussion, see Section 18.1.

. . . .
Example   Consider the following program fragment, which will compute separate point totals for males and females. The user will keep inputting data pairs such as 24 m and 47 f, where the first item of the data pair is the point total and the second is the sex of the player who achieved it.

It allows the user to enter m, M, f, or F for the sex.

```
MaleSum := 0;
FemSum := 0;
repeat
  write ('enter number of points ');
  readln (points);
  repeat
    write ('enter sex (m or f) ');
    readln (sex);
    SexCap := upcase (sex)
  until (SexCap = 'M') or (SexCap = 'F');
  if SexCap = 'M'
     then MaleSum := MaleSum + points
     else FemSum := FemSum + points;
  write ('Type y to continue, n to stop ');
  readln (ans)
until upcase (ans) = 'N';
```

REMARK   Note the use of the inner loop to error trap, allowing the input for sex to be lowercase or uppercase, even though the prompt said (m or f).

. . .

Nested for Loops   In nested `for` loops, the entire outer loop body is executed for each of the values of the outer loop control variable. Thus, for each value of the outer loop control variable, the inner `for` loop will run through *all* of its values.

. . . .
Question   What will be printed by the following program fragment?

```
for n := 2 to 4 do
  begin
    for i := 6 to 7 do
      writeln (n, ' ', i);
    writeln ('hello')
  end; {for n}
```

Answer

```
2 6
2 7        } ← printed when n = 2
hello
3 6
3 7        } ← printed when n = 3
hello
4 6
4 7        } ← printed when n = 4
hello
```

• • •

Nested Loops of Different Types   The outer and inner loops do not have to be of the same type.

• • • • • • • •
Question   What will be printed by the following program segment?

```
for n := 5 to 7 do
  begin
    sum := 0;
    while sum < 20 do
      sum := sum + n;
    writeln (sum, ' ', n)
  end; {for}
```

Answer

```
20 5
24 6
21 7
```

Note that for each n, sum is reset to 0.   • • •

Row-by-Row Processing   An important application of nested loops is in using an outer loop to process a number of rows, where the processing for each row also requires a loop. (This topic may also be covered later in the course in connection with two-dimensional arrays.)

• • • • • • • •
Example   Write a program segment to generate a right triangle with NumRows rows of asterisks, such that the first row has one asterisk, the second row has two asterisks, the third row has three asterisks, and so on, and where the

rightmost asterisks from each row are vertically aligned. For example, when NumRows = 5, the segment should generate the output

```
    *
   **
  ***
 ****
*****
```

Here is the pseudocode.

> **assign a value to** NumRows
> for n := 1 to NumRows do
>   begin
>   indent the appropriate number of spaces (loop needed)
>   print n asterisks (loop needed)
>   drop the cursor to the next line
>   end;

Note that the number of spaces you indent keeps decreasing by 1, as n increases by 1. Thus, with a little inspiration, you might realize that in the nth row, you must indent NumRows - n spaces, which can be done with a for loop that prints NumRows - n blanks.

Here is the actual code.

```
NumRows := 5;
for n := 1 to NumRows do
  begin
    for i := 1 to (NumRows - n) do      {print blanks}
      write (' ');
    for k := 1 to n do                  {print asterisks}
      write ('*');
    writeln
  end; {for n}
```

8.4 FIXED STEP LOOPS—WITH real STEP

Numerical Inaccuracy in Real Calculations   Fractions or decimals (like 1/3 or 0.1) can cause trouble because they do not have exact representations in base 2. For example, in some computer implementations

$$1/3 + 1/3 + 1/3$$

will not be exactly equal to 1, but rather to 0.999999999. Generally, you can protect against this sort of danger by employing the following rule:

Avoid using programming code that contains a test for exact equality or inequality of two real values.

Infinite Loop If there were no difficulty with the inexactness of real values, you would expect the following program to output the values

0, 1/3, 2/3

in decimal form and then stop.

```
program trouble;
{don't use <> or = in a real while test}
var x: real;

begin
  x := 0;
  while x <> 1 do
    begin
      writeln (x);
      x := x + 1/3
    end
end.
```

Unfortunately, for some implementations of Turbo Pascal, this program will produce an infinite loop because x will never be exactly equal to 1. For example, x might go directly from 0.999999999 to 1.333333333.

Off-by-One Danger When you write a fixed step loop with a real step, you must make sure that the loop body is executed the right number of times. For example, the exit condition

while x <= *final value* do

runs the risk of having the loop body not executed for the final value (if the calculated value of x should be exactly equal to the final value but is a very tiny bit above it because of numeric inaccuracy).

• • • • • • • • • •
Problem Write a program to produce the output.

```
1.0 squared is 1.00
1.2 squared is 1.44
1.4 squared is 1.96
1.6 squared is 2.56
1.8 squared is 3.24
2.0 squared is 4.00
```

Note that instead of using the `while` condition

```
while x <= 2 do
```

we use the `while` condition

```
while x <= 2 + 0.001 do
```

to protect against the possibility of numeric inaccuracy causing an off-by-one execution error.

Fill in the blanks in the following program:

```
program SafeLoop;
{protects against numeric inaccuracy}
var _____
begin
  x := ____;
  while x <= 2 + 0.001 do
    begin
      writeln (x:0:1, ' squared is ', x*x:0:2);
      x := _____
    end
end.
```

Answer   Since the starting value is `x` = 1 and the step is 0.2, we have

```
x := 1;
x := x + 0.2
```

Note also that x must be declared of type `real`.   • • •

8.5 LOOP INVARIANTS (Optional)

The issue of the extent to which you can *prove* that a program is correct is a difficult, theoretical topic and beyond the scope of this book. We will, however, introduce briefly the concept of a loop invariant, which can be used as a theoretical tool to help verify that a loop does what it is intended to do.

Using a Loop Invariant to Check a Loop

A *loop invariant* is an assertion that is true before the loop body is executed a first time and also true after each execution of the loop body. A loop can have many different loop invariants; the name of the game, however, is to find a well-chosen loop invariant(s) that is closely connected to what the loop is intended to accomplish. Usually, a well-chosen loop invariant is an assertion that involves the value(s) of key variable(s) and possibly the count for how many executions of the loop body have been completed so far.

Loop Invariant for over1000

In `program over1000` of Section 7.4, which finds the smallest n so that the sum $1*1 + 2*2 + \cdots + n*n$ goes over 1,000, a useful loop invariant is the assertion

```
sum = 1*1 + 2*2 + · · · + n*n
```

This assertion is true trivially before the loop since `sum = 0` and there are no terms yet. It is true after each execution of the loop body since

after the first execution, n = 1 and `sum = 1*1`

after the second execution, n = 2 and `sum = 1*1 + 2*2`

and so on since each next execution adds the square of the next integer to `sum`

Thus, on completion of the loop, `sum` will still equal

```
1*1 + 2*2 + · · · + n*n
```

Postcondition   A postcondition is a comment given after the loop that describes what the loop is supposed to have accomplished. Here is the loop for `over1000` with both the loop invariant and the postcondition given as documentation.

```
n := 0;
sum := 0;
while sum <= 1000 do
  begin
    n := n + 1;
    sum := sum + (n*n)
    {loop invariant-- sum = 1*1 + 2*2 + ... + n*n}
  end;
{postcondition--n is the smallest n to put the sum of the first}
{n squares over 1000}
```

Loop Invariant for Ulam

Sometimes a loop invariant is just a fancier way of saying, generate or process the next term. For `program Ulam` of Section 7.4, the loop invariant is a fancier way of saying that each execution of the loop body should print the next number in the Ulam sequence. This invariant could be worded as follows:

{*each execution of the loop body will output the next term in the Ulam sequence of the input number*}

Thus, if the computer exits from the loop after it has just printed a 1, it will have printed the full Ulam sequence.

Example (A Program to Divide by 4 Using Repeated Subtraction)

The following program will divide an input integer by 4 giving the quotient and remainder. For example, for input of 14, the output will be

```
4 goes into 14
3 times with remainder of 2
```

Here is the program.

```
program DivisionBy4;
var n, q, r: integer;
begin
   write ('enter a positive integer ');
   readln (n);
   r := n;
   q := 0;
   while r >= 4 do
      begin
         r := r - 4;
         q := q + 1
      end;
   writeln ('4 goes into ', n);
   writeln (q, ' times with a remainder of ', r)
end.
```

Possible Loop Invariant   Let us try the following equation, which we hope is satisfied by the end of the loop:

```
n = (4 * q) + r
```

(Before)   This equation holds before the loop since at that time $n = r$ and $q = 0$.

(After each execution)   After each execution of the loop body, this equation still holds. Here is why. The left side obviously stays fixed (n is not changed). On the right side, increasing q by 1 adds 4 to the right, which is balanced by subtracting 4 from r; thus, the net effect is no change on the right side either.

Thus, it is a loop invariant, and then since on exit from the loop the remainder r will be less than 4, the values of q and r will give the quotient and remainder, respectively.

EXERCISES

• •

1. Give the outputs for the following fragments.

(a)
```
k := 1;
m := 2;
while (k<6) and (m<50) do
   begin
      m := m * 2;
      writeln (k, ' ',m);
      m := m + 1;
      k := k + 2
   end; {while}
writeln (k, ' ',m)
```

(b)
```
p := 1;
m := 9;
n := 1;
repeat
   p := m * n;
   m := m - 1;
   n := n + 1;
   writeln ('p = ', p)
until (m<0) or (m=n);
writeln (m, ' ',n);
```

2. Give the outputs for the following fragments.

(a)
```
for n := 1 to 3 do
   for i := 5 to 7 do
      write (n, ' ', i, ' ');
```

(b)
```
for n := 1 to 3 do
   begin
      for i := 5 to 7 do
         write (n, ' ', i, ' ');
      writeln
   end;
```

(c)
```
c := 0;
for n := 1 to 3 do
   begin
      d := 0;
      for p := 5 to 7 do
         begin
            c := c + 1;
            d := d + 1
         end;
      writeln (n, ' ', c, ' ', d)
   end;
```

Longer Assignments

3. Write a `repeat-until` loop that will accomplish the same thing as the `while-loop` "stronger jolt" from Section 8.6.

4. A `repeat-until` loop is often used to edit input. Write a program that asks the user to enter a nonzero integer and then prints its reciprocal. Use a `repeat-until` loop to force the user to reenter the value if he or she enters 0 by mistake.

5. Write a program in which the user is asked to input 10 *odd* integers to be summed. Construct your program so that it will not be ruined if the user enters some *even* integers. The program should exit the loop and print the sum only after 10 odd integers have been entered.

6. An applicant for a secretarial job will be given a maximum of five typing tests. The applicant will be hired as soon as he or she scores over 50 words per minute on two tests. Write a program that allows a supervisor to enter each typing test score on completion of each test.
The program should print `Hire` as soon as the applicant qualifies without asking for further tests. If after five test scores have been entered the typist still hasn't qualified, the program should print `Reject`.
Here are two sample outputs.

```
enter score 52          enter score 41
enter score 47          enter score 48
enter score 54          enter score 52
Hire                    enter score 49
                        enter score 48
                        Reject
```

7. Write an interactive program that allows the user up to four tries to name the capital of California. Here is a typical run.

```
What is the capital of California? Los Angeles
Wrong, try again. San Francisco
Wrong, try again. Sacramento
Correct. You got it on try 3
```

If the user does not get the capital in four tries, your program should tell the user the correct answer.

8. Write a program that will print the full Ulam sequence for an input integer if the length of the full sequence is at most 10. Otherwise, the program should print just the first 10 numbers in the sequence. (See Section 7.4 for information on Ulam sequences.) Run your program several times.

9. Write a program that will evaluate the function $y = 4x^2 - 16x + 15$, with x going from 1 to 2 in steps of .1. For each x, the output should give the value of y and either the message POSITIVE or the message NOT POSITIVE. Format the output in the form

```
x value  y value
    1.0     3.00  POSITIVE
    1.1     2.24  POSITIVE
     .        .
     .        .
     .        .
    2.0    -1.00  NOT POSITIVE
```

10. (a) Give the output for the following loop if start has the value 2, NumValues has the value 9, and step has the value 0.5.

```
x := start;
for i := 1 to NumValues do
   begin
      write (x, ' ');
      x := x + step
   end;
```

(b) Give a for loop to output the values 5.0, 5.1, 5.2, . . . 8.0, that is, from 5.0 to 8.0, going up by steps of 0.1.

11. Write a program to produce each of the following outputs.

(a)
```
enter number of rows 4

*
**
***
****
```

(b)
```
enter number of rows 4

   *
  ***
 *****
*******
```

12. Newton's method for finding $\sqrt{x}$ is as follows.

(a) Start with $r_0 = x/2$ as an initial approximation.

(b) Compute successive approximations $r_1, r_2, r_3 \ldots$ as follows:

$$r_i = \tfrac{1}{2}(r_{i-1} + x/r_{i-1})$$

By this method, $\sqrt{8}$ would be approximated as follows ($x = 8$):

$$r_0 = 4$$
$$r_1 = \tfrac{1}{2}(4 + \tfrac{8}{4}) = 3$$

$$r_2 = \tfrac{1}{2}(3 + \tfrac{8}{3}) = \tfrac{17}{6} = 2.8333$$

etc.

Write a program to print approximations for the square root of an input number x (from 1 to 100) so that the program stops when

$$|x - (\text{approx})^2| < 0.001$$

* *13.* Write a program that uses a loop to count the number of digits in an input integer from 1 to 32,000. Typical output

```
5837 has 4 digits
```

* *14.* This exercise assumes that the reader is already somewhat familiar with the base 2 representation of numbers. For example, the base 2 number 1101 is equal to 13 in ordinary base 10 notation because the rightmost bit gives the number of 1s, the next bit gives the number of 2s, the next the number of 4s, the next the number of 8s, and so on. Thus, 1101 equals 1*1 + 0*2 + 1*4 + 1*8 = 13.

Complete the following loop to convert a base 2 number, like 1101, into its ordinary decimal representation, 13.

```
write ('enter number in base 2 ');
readln (base2);
n := base2;
dec := 0;
power := 1;
while n > 0 do
  begin
    bit := n mod 10;                {extract rightmost bit}
    dec := dec + bit * _____;     {add contribution to dec}
    power := _____;         {update power}
    n := n div 10                   {remove bit just processed}
  end;
writeln ('The binary number ', base2);
writeln ('is equal to ', dec, ' in base 10')
```

Lab Exercises **DEBUGGING AND SYNTAX ERRORS**

Lab8-1.pas   Finding Factorials
Lab8-2.pas   Numeric Inaccuracy

Chapter

9

TEXT FILES

• • • So far, in all the programs we have considered, any data has been entered interactively—that is, typed in during the running of the program. With this method, if the same data is needed later for another program, the user has to retype it. Clearly, this method is undesirable when large amounts of data are needed. For example, it would be extremely time consuming for a large company to retype all employee data each time a program was to put this information to a particular use.

Files provide an efficient means for storing data so that it can later be used by any number of programs. A file is a collection of related data items that is stored on an external storage device (such as a diskette or a hard drive) and given an external file name for reference. In this chapter, we will consider *text files.* In later chapters, we will look at other kinds of external files.

• • •

9.1 CREATING A TEXT FILE

You can create text files in Turbo Pascal just as you would create a program. The name that you give to a text file is called the file's ***external name***, and it is this name that will be used by any program that needs the file.

Suppose you wished to create the following file containing payroll information (name, hours worked, and hourly rate) for employees Foy, Day, and Lee and save it with the file name `wages.dat`.

Foy
45 6
Day
50 7
Lee
42 6

You begin the same as you would to type in a new program. First, you press **F3** and then type in the file name `wages.dat` and press the **ENTER** key. Then instead of typing program code, you type the file data; finally, when you are finished, you press **F2** to save the file.

9.2 USING AN EXISTING FILE

●●●

Assigning a File's Name to a Variable   The disk operating system recognizes a file by its external name—the name that you give to a file when you create it (see Section 9.1). In order for a program to have access to information in a file, the program has to assign the file's external name to a variable within the program. The statement used to make such an assignment is an **assign** statement.

Suppose an external file `wages.dat` was stored (saved) on the disk in drive B. The following statement would allow us to refer to the file as `WageFile` within the program:

```
assign (WageFile, 'b:wages.dat');
```

The variable `WageFile` would be declared in the `var` section as type `text`.

```
var WageFile: text;
```

REMARK   The drive prefix may be omitted from an `assign` statement when the file to be read is in the current directory.   ●●●

Opening a File for Reading   In order for a program to read information from a file, the program must contain both an `assign` and a **reset** statement, as in

```
assign (WageFile, 'wages.dat');
reset (WageFile);
```

The `assign` statement opens the file—that is, establishes the linkage between the file's external name and the file variable. The `reset` statement prepares the file for reading by the program. When a `reset` statement is executed, the file position pointer, which points to the next item to be read, is reset to the beginning of the data file.

eof Function The **eof** (end-of-file) function is a built-in boolean valued function used to test for the end of a file. When a file is created, the computer automatically places an end-of-file marker in the file after the last piece of data. The value of eof (WageFile) is true only if the file pointer is at the end-of-file marker (all the data items have been read). Thus, a loop with header

```
while not eof (WageFile) do
```

will continue to be entered so long as there is still more data to be read.

Closing a File After a program has finished reading information from a file, the file should be closed by a **close** statement. For example, to close the file whose file variable name is WageFile, use the statement

```
close (WageFile);
```

• • • • • • • • • •

Example In the following program, it is assumed that the external file wages.dat (as given in Section 9.1) has been saved on the disk in the logged drive.

```
program testfile;
uses printer;
var name: string;
    hours, rate, pay: integer;
    WageFile: text;

begin
  assign (WageFile, 'wages.dat');
  reset (WageFile);
  while not eof (WageFile) do
    begin
      readln (WageFile, name);
      readln (WageFile, hours, rate);
      pay := hours * rate;
      writeln ( lst, name, ' $', pay)
    end;
  close (WageFile)
end.
```

Program testfile will produce the following output on paper:

```
Foy $270
Day $350
Lee $252
```

REMARK

1. Note that the file variable `WageFile` must be declared to be type `text` in the variable declaration section.

2. Before a file may be read by a program, it must be opened by the `assign` and `reset` statements.

3. The `readln` statements that are used to read from the file are slightly different from the interactive `readln` statements we have seen. The name of the file variable must be given as the first item in parentheses. Naturally, no prompts are needed.

4. Note that we did not need to prime the pump by reading in any of the file's data before the `while` loop since the loop exit condition is not a particular data value as sentinel. As we will see later, the loop exit is controlled by the position of the file pointer—`eof (WageFile)` becomes true when the pointer is at the end of the file. Note also that the statement `reset (WageFile)` initializes the file pointer to the beginning of the file.   • • •

Question   The following program reads students' names and test scores from an external file called `scores.dat`. Each data group consists of a student's name followed by two scores on the next line. The program prints each student's name and whether she or he passed or failed, where passing is an average of at least 60. It also counts the numbers of students who pass and fail. Fill in the blanks.

```
program grades;
{reads in test scores from external file}
{prints pass or fail where passing is at least 60}
{and counts passing and failing grades}

uses printer;
var passcount, failcount, score1, score2: integer;
    average: real;
    StudFile: text;
    name: string;

begin
  assign (_____);

  _____
  passcount := 0;
  failcount := 0;
  while _____ do
    begin
      readln (_____, name);
```

```
        readln (_____);
        average := (score1 + score2) / 2;
        if average >= 60 then
          begin
            writeln (1st, name, ' Passed');
            passcount := passcount + 1
          end
        else
          begin
            writeln (1st, name, ' Failed');
            failcount := failcount + 1
          end
     end;
   close (StudFile);
   writeln (1st, passcount, ' students passed');
   writeln (1st, failcount, ' students failed')
end.
```

Answer   Here are the completed lines.

```
assign (StudFile, 'scores.dat');
reset (StudFile);

while not eof (StudFile) do

   readln (StudFile, name);
   readln (StudFile, score1, score2);
```

• • •

9.3   HOW A TEXT FILE IS STORED

A file is stored as a sequence of characters, including control characters.

eoln and eof Markers   When you type a file from the edit mode, each time you press the ENTER key (↵) an end-of-line (**eoln**) marker is copied onto the file. The end-of-line marker actually consists of two separate control characters, CR (for carriage return with ASCII value 13) and LF (for line feed with ASCII value 10). We will denote these pictorially by

Carriage Return	*Line Feed*	*eoln Marker*
■	●	■●

When you save a file or press CTRL-Z, an end-of-file (eof) marker that we will denote pictorially by △ is placed as the last character in the file.

File Pointer When a program executes a reset statement, the pointer for that file (which we will denote by a vertical arrow ↑) is set to the first character in the file. Thus, if program testfile from Section 9.2 uses the wages.dat file from Section 9.1, after the statement reset (WageFile) is executed, the file and pointer would be as follows:

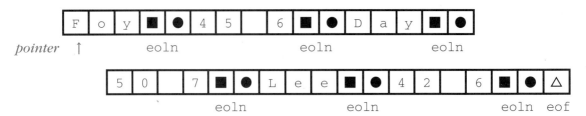

Whenever a readln statement is executed, the computer reads in values and then moves the file pointer past the next eoln marker. (This represents moving to the beginning of the next line, if there is one.)

• • • • • • • •
Question In program testfile, where would the file pointer be after the first execution of readln (WageFile, hours, rate)?

Answer It would be just past the eoln marker after 45 6.

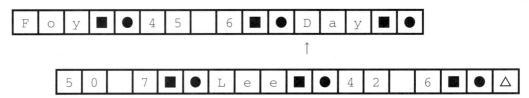

• • •

eof Function versus seekeof Function A potential danger of the eof function is that it has the value true only if the file pointer is at the eof marker. Thus, for example, if in typing a text file you press the ENTER key after typing the last item of data, an extra eoln marker would be included as part of the file. With such a file, there is a risk that a program using a while loop to read the file might enter the loop body an extra time (and produce garbage) because eof (WageFile) will not be true immediately after the last item of intended data is read.

seekeof In Turbo 4.0 and higher, the boolean valued **seekeof** is available. The seekeof function is safer than eof because it skips over blanks and control characters in checking whether the last data item has been read. That is, `seekeof (WageFile)` will be true not only if the file pointer is at the actual `eof` marker, but also if the only remaining characters before the `eof` marker are blanks or control characters such as end-of-line markers. Thus, `seekeof (WageFile)` will be true if all actual data has been read. For example, for the file shown here if the file pointer is positioned as indicated

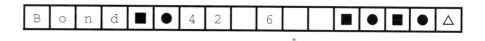

seekeof would have the value `true`, but `eof` won't have the value `true` until the pointer is at the `eof` marker.

Henceforth, we will use `seekeof` instead of `eof` in headers of `while` loops that read in the contents of a text file.

9.4 ENTERING THE EXTERNAL NAME INTERACTIVELY

• •

A user might want to run the same program a number of times for different files without having to edit the program for each run (changing the name of the file in the `assign` statement). This next example shows how a `string` variable can be used to store the external file name.

```
program drill;
var filename: string;
    WageFile: text;

begin
  write ('Please enter file name ');
  readln (filename);
  assign (WageFile, filename);
  reset (WageFile);
  .
  .
  .
```

If the user typed `WagesJan.dat` in response to the prompt, the preceding `assign` statement would have the same effect as

```
assign (WageFile, 'WagesJan.dat');
```

9.5   PROTECTING AGAINST BAD DATA

Suppose the file `scores.dat`, consisting of each student's name and test score (with 100 being the highest possible score), contains some bad data. For example, suppose it contains the data group

>   Smith
>   542

Obviously, Smith's score of 542 is incorrect.

When data is being read from an external file, we cannot use a `repeat-until` loop to force the input of an appropriate value. We can, however, use an `if-then-else` test to filter data so that good data is processed and certain bad data is rejected with a warning message. For example, we might use an `if-then-else` statement as follows:

```
while not seekeof (StudFile) do
  begin
    readln (StudFile, name);
    readln (StudFile, score);
    if (score >= 0) and (score <= 100) then
      .
      . {process data group}
      .
    else
      writeln ('BAD DATA', name, ' ', score);
```

REMARK   Note that this attempt to protect against bad data is limited in its effectiveness. For example, suppose that the person creating the file typed `48` when Smith's test score was actually 84. The `if-then` test would not detect this mistake. This simple form of error trapping will detect only data that is out of the expected range.   • • •

9.6   USING HEADERS

Recall from Chapter 6 that it is possible to have the user enter a number that tells how many data groups a `for` loop will have to read. Similarly, it is possible to include such a number in an external file. In an external file, this number is called a **header.** In order for a header to be included in an external file, the person who creates the data file must know how many data groups are to be processed.

• • • • • • • • • •
Example   Suppose we want to write a program that will find the average of a number of test scores that are read from an external file, where the first number in the file is a header. Here is a typical file, with 6 as the header value.

    6   85   92   100   81   79   95

Here is the program fragment that will find the average.

```
sum := 0;
read (StudFile, hdr);
for exam := 1 to hdr do
  begin
    read (fileA, score);
    sum := sum + score
  end;
average := sum/hdr;
```

                                                           • • •

REMARK   The same program could be used to find the average for a file containing eight scores. For example, it could process the file

    8   75   74   92   91   94   87   75   82   • • •

9.7   READ VERSUS READLN

For text files, the only difference between `read` and `readln` is the location of the file position pointer after execution. After a `readln` statement, the file position pointer is placed after the next `eoln` marker, whereas after a `read` statement, the file position pointer remains right after the value just read.

CAUTION   Strange things can happen if the computer attempts to execute a `read` or `readln` statement to read in values from a file *when the file pointer is at an* `eoln` *marker.* Empty `readln` statements should be used to avoid that situation.   • • •

Empty readln Statements   An empty `readln` statement containing the file name but no variable list like

      `readln (StudFile)`

can be used to move the file position pointer beyond the next `eoln` marker.

• • • • • • • • • •

Example   Suppose a text file containing each student's name and four quiz scores is formatted as follows:

     Jones
     10 8 7 8
     Smith
     8 7 9 6
        .
        .
        .

The following `while` loop will print each student's name and quiz sum.

```
while not seekeof (StudFile) do
  begin
    readln (StudFile, name);
    sum := 0;
    for quiz := 1 to 4 do
      begin
        read (StudFile, score);
        sum := sum + score
      end; {for}
    writeln (name, ' ', sum: 4: 1);
    readln (StudFile)
end; {while}
```

REMARK   Omitting `readln (StudFile)` from the previous program would have been bad style, but it would not have caused trouble since execution of `seekeof` advances the file pointer beyond an `eoln` marker. See Exercise 12 for a program that will crash if you omit `readln (StudFile)`.   • • •

9.8   SENDING OUTPUT TO A FILE
• •

So far we've directed program output to either the screen or the printer. There is also a third possibility—directing the output to a file on disk. In this way, program output can be stored for future printing or for use as input for another program. (Note that if program output is printed on paper and then later is needed as input for another program, it has to be typed in again by a person.)

Opening an Output File   You open and close an output file with the `assign` and `close` statements with which you are already familiar. To be able to write onto the file, you must use a `rewrite` statement instead of `reset`, as in

```
assign (fileB, 'data.out');
rewrite (fileB);
    .
    .
    .
close (fileB);
```

The `rewrite` command sets the file position pointer at the beginning of the data file and prepares the file for being written onto.

CAUTION   The `rewrite` statement will erase any prior contents of the file.   • • •

Updating a Text File   Suppose we want to add a $25 bonus to each employee's salary and save the new salaries. With text files, it is not possible to read from and write onto the same file. Thus, we must store the new list of salaries in a second file. We will read from the original salary file one data group at a time, update the salary, and then write the updated data group onto the second file. Here is a program that will accomplish this task.

```
program update;
{add $25 bonus to each wage}
var name: string;
    wage: integer;
    fileA, fileB: text;

begin
  assign (fileA, 'test.dat');
  assign (fileB, 'test2.dat');
  reset (fileA);
  rewrite (fileB);
  while not seekeof (fileA) do
    begin
      readln (fileA, name);
      readln (fileA, wage);
      wage := wage + 25;
      writeln (fileB, name);
      writeln (fileB, wage)
    end; {while}
  close (fileA);
  close (fileB)
end.
```

REMARK   In Exercise 11, you are asked to modify the previous program so that the original external file contains the updated information by the end of the run.   • • •

An Alternative to lst,

Pascal treats the printer and the console (the screen) as if they were files. Output can be sent to the printer by writing to the PRN file or to the screen by writing to the CON file.

Using these two files, you can write your program so that output goes to the screen during the testing stage, and then when you are satisfied with your program, you can run it again with the output printed on paper—*without having to insert* lst, *into any* writeln *statements.*

The following program illustrates this technique:

```
program drill;
var x: integer;
    fileA: text;
    filename: string;
begin
  writeln ('Where do you want to send the output?');
  write ('type PRN for printer or CON for screen ');
  readln (filename);
  assign (fileA, filename);
  rewrite (fileA);
  write ('enter a number ');
  readln (x);
  writeln (fileA, x, ' squared = ', x*x)
end.
```

Run 1   *Screen*   *Paper*

```
Where do you want to send the output?
type PRN for printer or CON for screen: con
enter number 5
5 squared = 25
```

Run 2   *Screen*   *Paper*

```
Where do you want to send the output?
type PRN for printer or CON for screen: prn
enter number 5
```

```
5 squared = 25
```

EXERCISES

● ●

1. **(a)** Does a `reset` statement use a file's external name or its associated file variable?

   (b) Does a file `readln` statement use a file's external name or its associated file variable?

   (c) What kind of statement uses both the file's external name and its associated file variable?

2. **(a)** Explain the difference between a `reset` statement and a `rewrite` statement.

   (b) What is a potential danger of a `rewrite` statement?

3. Assume you have a file with external file name `prog1.inp`. Write the syntax to open this file for reading and to open a second file `prog1.out` so that you may write output to it.

4. Must an `assign` statement always contain single quote marks for the external file name?

5. Fill in the blanks in program `honors` so that it will print the name of each student who had a test score of at least 90.

```
program honors;
var name: string;
    score: integer;
    StudFile _____

begin
   assign (StudFile, 'stud.dat');
   _____
   while _____ do
      begin
         _____
         readln (_____);
         if score >= 90 then writeln (name)
      end;
   _____
end.
```

Longer Assignments

6. Write a program to create a file that will contain all the divisors of an input integer. Each divisor should be on its own line.

7. Assume you have a text file named `stud.dat` on your disk. Each data group in the file contains a student's name and three test scores. Write a program to calculate and print each student's name and average.

8. Redo Exercise 7 assuming that there is a header in the file that specifies how many students are in the class.

9. Write a program to perform a yearly update on a salary file. Each data group in the file contains an employee's name, weekly wage, and number of years with the firm. At the end of the year, you must first increment the number of years with the firm by 1 and then give raises. If the employee has been with the firm for at least 10 years, he or she receives a weekly salary increase of $30; otherwise, the raise is only $15.

10. Each data group for the file `customer.dat` contains a customer's name, address, gender, and balance due on a store account. Write a program that will (1) create two separate files, `male.dat` and `female.dat`, with all the data for customers stored on the appropriate file, and (2) print out on paper the following information:

    total number of customers, number of males, number of females, average balance for males, and average balance for females

11. Modify the program in Section 9.8 so that the updated information is contained in the original external file (`test.dat`).

12. In the example of Section 9.7, suppose that the file is set up with each student's name on the line below his or her four scores (instead of above them). Write a program to find each student's sum. Note that this program will crash if you omit the `readln (fileA)` statement.

. . . .

Lab Exercises   **DEBUGGING AND SYNTAX ERRORS**

Lab9-1.pas   External File Name

Lab9-2.pas   Being in Sync

. . . .

Chapter

10

PROCEDURES WITH VALUE PARAMETERS

• • • In solving a complicated programming problem by the top-down approach, you start by breaking up the problem into smaller, more manageable subtasks. Pascal provides two kinds of special syntax for carrying out subtasks: *procedures* (introduced in Section 4.5) and *functions* (discussed in Chapter 13). Their use allows you to write a program with the main body acting as an outline that names the subtasks but with the details for performing the subtasks given elsewhere in the program. In this way, the overall organization of the program stands out more clearly.

The use of *subprograms* (procedures and functions) to carry out subtasks is known as *modularity.* Modularity makes it easier to write, debug, and revise a program since not only can the procedures be written and debugged fairly independently, but their use makes it easier to isolate just those parts that need modifying. Finally, for very large programs, modularity facilitates dividing up the work among a team of programmers—with each person responsible for a specific set of subprograms. As you will see, modularity provides protection against one person's subprograms disrupting what has been performed by someone else's.

Parameters may be used to communicate information between a program's main body and subprograms. In this chapter, we will discuss parameterless procedures and procedures with value parameters. (Variable parameters, functions, and nested subprograms will be considered in Chapters 11, 13, and 15, respectively.) • • •

10.1 PROCEDURES WITHOUT PARAMETERS

Procedures without parameters were introduced in Section 4.5. Recall that procedure declarations are positioned after the `var` section and before the main body of your program.

When a program is run, execution always begins with the first line of the main body of the program. When a statement consisting of the name of a procedure (a calling statement) is encountered, control is transferred to the procedure. After the body of the procedure is executed, control is returned to the statement immediately following the calling statement.

Here is a diagram for a program containing a procedure named `FINDTHIS`. Note the similarity between the structure of the main program and that of the procedure. Each contains a header, declarations, and a body enclosed in `begin-end` brackets.

```
program drill;
{procedure without parameters}
var . . . ; {global variables}

procedure FINDTHIS;
    var . . . ; {local variables}     } declaration of FINDTHIS
    begin
        .
        .
        .
    end; {FINDTHIS}

begin {main}
    .
    .
    .
    FINDTHIS;              ← calling statement
    .
    .
    .
end.
```

Example **(Personalized Campaign Letter)**

A politician wants a program to print up a "personalized" campaign letter based on the voter's age using the following outline:

- Input the voter's age.
- Same first paragraph for all voters, stressing eternal truths.

- Two different versions of paragraph two—the version for voters under 40, glorifying youth, and the other version for voters at least 40, stressing wisdom and maturity.

* * * * * * * * *

Question Note how similar the main body of the following program is to this outline. What will the output be if 46 is entered as the voter's age?

```
program CampaignLetter;
{personalized letter based on voter's age}
uses printer;
var age: integer;

procedure PARAG1;
  {same first paragraph for everybody}
  begin
    writeln (lst, 'Dear Citizen:');
    writeln (lst, '     More than ever this country');
    writeln (lst, 'needs honest and courageous leadership.')
  end; {PARAG1}

procedure YOUTHPARAG;
  {paragraph for younger voter}
  begin
    writeln (lst, '     I especially need the support');
    writeln (lst, 'of young voters.  I believe that');
    writeln (lst, 'the future of this country must be');
    writeln (lst, 'shaped by those with the greatest');
    writeln (lst, 'stake in the future -- namely young');
    writeln (lst, 'voters like yourself.')
  end; {YOUTHPARAG}

procedure OLDPARAG;
  {paragraph for older voter}
  begin
    writeln (lst, '     I especially need the support');
    writeln (lst, 'of mature voters.  I believe that');
    writeln (lst, 'the future of this country must be');
    writeln (lst, 'shaped by those with experience and');
    writeln (lst, 'wisdom -- namely mature voters like');
    writeln (lst, 'yourself.')
  end; {OLDPARAG}

begin {main}
  write ('enter age of voter ');
```

```
    readln (Age);
    PARAG1;
    if age < 40 then YOUTHPARAG
                else OLDPARAG
end.
```

Answer

```
Dear Citizen:
      More than ever this country
needs honest and courageous leadership.
      I especially need the support
of mature voters. I believe that
the future of this country must be
shaped by those with experience and
wisdom -- namely mature voters like
yourself.
```

• • •

REMARK Try to visualize what the main body of the program would look like if procedures had not been used. Since all the text for the letter would be included in the main body, the overall top down structure of the program would be somewhat obscured. • • •

10.2 **LOCAL AND GLOBAL VARIABLES**

A procedure is like a miniature program within a program, and as such, it can have its own declaration section. Any variable declared in a procedure's var section is known as a *local variable.* By contrast, any variable declared in the main program's declaration section, which is normally positioned before all the procedures, is known as a *global variable.* (Similarly, a constant declared in the procedure's declaration section is known as a local constant.)

Question The following program contains DRAWLINE, a procedure without parameters. Note that the main body calls this procedure twice. What will the output be?

```
program drill;
{no parameters}
var num: integer;

procedure DRAWLINE;
  {will draw a line of 10 asterisks}
  var i: integer;
  begin
    for i := 1 to 10 do
      write ('*');
    writeln
  end; {DRAWLINE}

begin {main body}
  num := 8;
  DRAWLINE;
  writeln (num, ' SQUARED ', num * num);
  DRAWLINE
end.
```

Answer

```
* * * * * * * * *
8 SQUARED 64
* * * * * * * * *
```

• • •

Memory   The memory cell for a global variable exists for the entire time that the program is running. By contrast, the memory cell for a local variable is more temporary—it is created anew each time the procedure is called and is erased when the computer finishes execution of a procedure call. Thus, a local variable cannot be accessed by a statement in the main body—any variable appearing in a statement of the main body of the program must have been declared as a global variable (that is, in the main `var` section). A similar distinction exists between local and global constants.

When to Use Local Variables   A variable should be declared as a local variable if it is needed by the procedure to carry out its subtask but is not needed by any statements outside the procedure. Typical uses of local variables include

1. Control variables of loops that are in the body of the procedure

2. Variables that keep track of intermediate results

It may be helpful for you to think of local variables as scratch work since once the procedure has completed its job, the memory cells for the procedure's local variables are erased. Not only does this free up memory, but as we shall see later, it also acts as a safety device.

Question   In the previous program, which variables were global and which were local?

Answer   Any variable appearing in the main body is a global variable and must be declared in the main body `var` section. Thus, the only global variable is `num`. The variable, `i`, is a local variable since it is declared in the procedure's `var` section.   • • •

10.3   VALUE PARAMETERS

Value parameters in a procedure allow a calling statement in the main body to communicate values to the procedure. In the version of program `drill` earlier in this chapter, a call to DRAWLINE always produced a line of 10 asterisks. Now we want to give DRAWLINE some flexibility.

If the calling statement is to specify the length of the line, we need to declare a value parameter that can be used by the procedure. Each value parameter must be declared in the procedure header. In the following program, `len` is declared as a value parameter in the header for DRAWLINE.

```
procedure DRAWLINE (len: integer);
```

Here is the revised version of program `drill`.

```
program drill;
var num: integer;

procedure DRAWLINE (len: integer);
  {will draw a line consisting of "len" asterisks}
  var i: integer;
  begin
    for i := 1 to len do
      write ('*');
    writeln
  end; {DRAWLINE}

begin
  num := 9;
  DRAWLINE (num);
  writeln ('hello');
  DRAWLINE (5);
  DRAWLINE (num + 2)
end.
```

• • • • • • • • •

Question   What will the output of program `drill` be?

Answer

```
* * * * * * * *
hello
* * * * *
* * * * * * * * * *
```

• • •

REMARK   A calling statement for procedure `DRAWLINE` must communicate what value `len` is to be given. Note that the call to `DRAWLINE` may do this by supplying an actual integer, as in `DRAWLINE (5)`; a variable of type `integer`, as in `DRAWLINE (num)`; or an expression, as in `DRAWLINE (num+2)`.

• • •

• • • • • • • • •

Question   In the previous program, classify each of the variables `len`, `num`, and `i` as either a global variable, a local variable, or a value parameter.

Answer   `len` is a value parameter of `DRAWLINE`—a value parameter is declared in a procedure header.

`i` is a local variable—a local variable is declared and used within a procedure's `var` section.

`num` is a global variable—each variable declared in the main body is a global variable.

• • •

Arguments and Parameters   A variable that is declared in the header of a procedure (within the parentheses) is known as a *parameter.* A value parameter is one kind of parameter. (The other kind, variable parameters, will be discussed in Chapter 11.)

The corresponding expression in the calling statement is known as an *argument.* The argument passes an initial value to the value parameter. Look again at program `drill`. In the calling statement

```
DRAWLINE (num);
```

the value 9 of the argument `num` is passed to the parameter `len`. The call `DRAWLINE (5)` passes `len` the value 5. The call `DRAWLINE (num+2)` passes `len` the value 11.

Note that an argument may be a variable or an expression, but a parameter must be a variable.

Alternative Terminology: Actual Parameters versus Formal Parameters   An "argument" is also known as an "actual parameter" since it provides an actual value to a parameter, whereas variables declared in a procedure header are also known as "formal parameters" since they act like place holders for values to be passed from the calling statement. We repeat: In some of the literature, the terms "actual parameter" and "formal parameter" mean the same thing as "argument" and "parameter," respectively. We will not further mention this alternative terminology.

Procedure Within a Loop   A common way to call a procedure a number of times is by placing the calling statement within the body of a loop.

Question   Suppose procedure DRAWLINE is defined as in program drill. What printout would be produced by the following main body?

```
begin {main}
   for num := 1 to 4 do
      DRAWLINE (num)
end.
```

Answer

```
*
**
***
****
```

Procedures with Several Value Parameters   If a procedure has several value parameters, they must all be declared in the header, as in the following version of DRAWLINE:

```
procedure DRAWLINE (len: integer; symbol: char);
{line length and symbol are specified in calling statement}
var i: integer;
   begin
     for i := 1 to len do
       write (symbol);
     writeln
   end; {DRAWLINE}
```

REMARK Note that a calling statement to this DRAWLINE would need to specify two values, one for each of the parameters. For example, DRAWLINE (8, 't') would draw

```
tttttttt
```

• • •

Argument and Parameter Matching Rules

1. There must be the same number of arguments and parameters.

2. Arguments must be given in the same order as the parameters to which they correspond since matching is done by order.

3. Each argument must be type-compatible with its corresponding parameter.

CAUTION Failure to use the same order could result in a type mismatch error. For example, for the previous procedure the call

```
DRAWLINE ('t', 8)
```

would cause a type mismatch error when the computer tries to assign the value 't' to the integer parameter len.

An even worse situation is when the calling statement uses the wrong order for two parameters of the same type. In that case, the computer would simply assign the wrong values and give an incorrect result with no warning.

• • •

More on Header Format When a procedure has parameters of different types, you may use a vertical stacking format in the procedure header to improve clarity. Recall that the compiler ignores extra blanks unless they are part of a literal string. Thus, for example

```
DRAWLINE (len: integer;
          symbol: char);
```

is equivalent to

```
DRAWLINE (len: integer; symbol: char);
```

• • • • • • • • •
Question

1. What would be output by the following program?

2. Why is cents declared as a local variable of FIND_TOTCENTS?

```
program NickelsDimes;
var dimes, nickels: integer;

procedure FIND_TOTCENTS (d, n: integer);
  var cents: integer;
  begin
    cents := (10 * d) + (5 * n);
    writeln (d, ' dimes and ', n, ' nickels = ', cents, ' cents')
  end; {FIND_TOTCENTS}

begin
  FIND_TOTCENTS (3, 4);
  dimes := 7;
  nickels := 2;
  FIND_TOTCENTS (dimes, nickels)
end.
```

Answer

1.
```
3 dimes and 4 nickels = 50 cents
7 dimes and 2 nickels = 80 cents
```

2. The value of cents is not passed to the procedure FIND_TOTCENTS. Instead, the value of cents is calculated within FIND_TOTCENTS.

• • •

Question Suppose the previous program contained the following additional statements at the bottom of the main body:

```
dimes := 9;
nickels := 2;
FIND_TOTCENTS (nickels, dimes)
```

What output would this call to FIND_TOTCENTS produce?

Answer Since matching is done by order, the value of nickels would be passed to the parameter d, and the value of dimes to the parameter n. Thus,

```
2 dimes and 9 nickels = 65 cents
```
• • •

10.4 MORE ON MEMORY

Safety Rule for Variables in Procedures As you will see in Chapter 11, the following safety rule helps protect against side effects—that is, one portion of a program accidentally interfering with work done by a different portion:

> Each variable in the body of a procedure should be declared by the procedure either as a parameter (in the header) or as a local variable.

• • • • • • • • •

Question Fill in the blanks in the following program that prints the sum of the digits for an input two-digit number. Here is a typical run

```
enter a 2 digit number 58
sum of its digits 13
```

```
program SumOfDigits;
{finds sum of digits of an input 2 digit number}
var numb: integer;

procedure DIGIT_SUM (n: integer);
  {finds sum of digits of n}
  var ones, tens: integer;
  begin
    ones := _____
    tens := _____
    writeln ('sum of its digits ', ones + tens)
  end; {DIGIT_SUM}

begin {main}
  write ('enter a 2 digit number ');
  readln (numb);
  DIGIT_SUM (numb)
end.
```

Answer By the safety rule, the body of the procedure should use the parameter n rather than the global variable numb. Thus, the lines with blanks should be

```
ones := n mod 10;
tens := n div 10;
```
• • •

Memory for Procedures Whenever a procedure is called, *temporary* memory cells are created for each of the procedure's value parameter(s) and local variable(s). Each value parameter's memory cell is then initialized with the value of the corresponding argument in the calling statement. After this initialization, the computer executes the body of the procedure.

The memory cells of the procedure can be thought of as temporary scratch space because when the computer exits from the procedure, these memory cells and their contents are erased.

Memory Snapshots   Suppose the user enters 58 for numb. Consider the following four snapshots of global and procedure memory. Global memory is given on the left side of the page and procedure memory on the right.

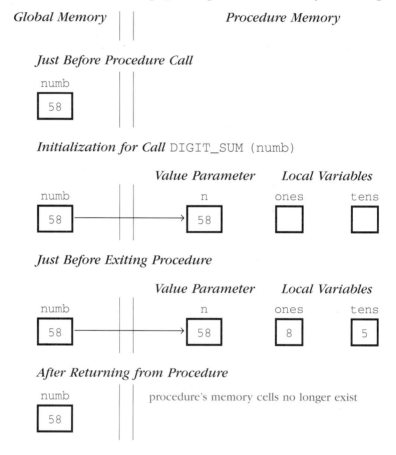

Global Memory   *Procedure Memory*

Just Before Procedure Call

numb

58

Initialization for Call DIGIT_SUM (numb)

	Value Parameter	*Local Variables*

numb   n   ones   tens

58 ───────────────→ 58

Just Before Exiting Procedure

	Value Parameter	*Local Variables*

numb   n   ones   tens

58 ───────────────→ 58   8   5

After Returning from Procedure

numb   procedure's memory cells no longer exist

58

REMARK   The assertion that *a procedure's memory cells no longer exist on exit from a procedure* is a simplified but useful way of depicting what is going on internally.   ● ● ●

Same Name Permissible   It is permissible, and in fact quite common, for a parameter and its corresponding global variable to have the same name. For example, suppose the previous program were revised so that numb was the name for both the global variable and the procedure's parameter. (To make this revision, you would replace n with numb throughout the procedure.) This revised program would be equivalent to the original program because whatever value is input for numb will be passed to the parameter numb.

Be aware that the global variable numb and the parameter numb would each have *its own memory cell.* If 58 were input for the global variable numb, DIGIT_SUM (numb) would pass the value 58 to the parameter numb.

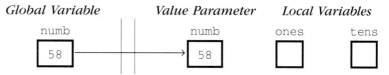

| *Global Variable* | *Value Parameter* | *Local Variables* |

REMARK On exit from the procedure call, the memory cell for the value parameter numb would be erased. ● ● ●

• • • • • • • • • •
Question Program ConvertDate uses the same variable names for global variables and the corresponding parameters. It converts an input date into standard slash form. Here is a typical run.

```
enter month day and year 12 6 1995
12/ 6/95
```

Fill in the blank lines.

```
program ConvertDate;
var _____ : integer;

procedure WRITE_DATE (_____ : integer);
  var _____ : integer;
  begin
    Last2Digits := year mod 100;
    writeln (month:2, '/', day:2, '/', Last2Digits:2)
  end; {WRITE_DATE}

begin {main}
  write ('enter month day and year ');
  readln (month, day, year);
  WRITE_DATE (month, day, year)
end.
```

Answer Note that the same variable names (month, day, and year) are used in the calling statement and as value parameters in the header. Last2Digits should be declared a local variable of WRITE_DATE since the value of Last2Digits is calculated within WRITE_DATE. The lines with blanks should be

```
var month, day, year: integer;

procedure WRITE_DATE (month, day, year: integer);
    var Last2Digits: integer;                          • • •
```

10.5 APPLICATIONS WITH LOOPS

• • • • • • • • •
Example   An employee receives 1.5 times his regular pay rate for each hour of overtime (each hour over 40 hours). Suppose that the employee data is on an external file. We will write a program to calculate and print on paper each employee's wage based on the following pseudocode:

```
open file
while not seekeof (Empfile) do
   begin
         get an employee's data
         FINDPAY—calculates the employee's pay and
                  then prints the employee's name and pay on paper
   end; (while)
```

Here is the program.

```
program payroll;
{finds and prints each employee's pay}
uses printer;
var  name    : string;
     hours   : integer;
     rate    : real;
     EmpFile : text;

procedure FINDPAY (name  : string;
                   hours : integer;
                   rate  : real);
   {finds and prints one employee's pay}
   var pay: real;
   begin
      if hours <= 40
         then pay := hours * rate
         else pay := 40 * rate + (hours - 40) * 1.5 * rate;
      writeln (1st, name, pay :8 :2)
   end; {FINDPAY}

begin {main}
```

```
    assign (EmpFile, 'employ.dat');
    reset (EmpFile);
    while not seekeof (EmpFile) do
       begin
           readln (EmpFile, name);
           readln (EmpFile, hours, rate);
           FINDPAY (name, hours, rate)
       end; {while}
    close(EmpFile)
end.
```

• • • • • • • • •

Problem   The ACME Company is seeking to hire more employees who are at least 40 years old. In giving job applicants a battery of two tests, ACME has decided to use the following curve:

> add five points to the applicant's raw average if the applicant is at least 40 years old, and add only two points to the raw average if the applicant is under 40

To be hired, an applicant needs a curved average of at least 75.0. Thus, an applicant with raw scores of 70 and 72 would have a curved average of either 76.0 or 73.0 depending on whether or not he was at least 40 years old.

Write a program to print on paper each applicant's name, scores, age, curved average, and whether or not he is hired.

File	*On Paper*
Smith	Smith 70 72 age 44
70 72 44	Curved Average 76.0 HIRE
Jones	Jones 73 72 age 21
73 72 21	Curved Average 74.5 REJECT
.	.
.	.
.	.

Pseudocode

open file
while not seekeof ( ) do
    begin
        get an applicant's raw data and print it
        DECIDE—procedure finds and prints an applicant's raw and curved
                average; also prints whether HIRE or REJECT
    end;

• • • • • • • • •

Question   Let DECIDE use the following variables in its body:

> score1, score2, RawAvg, CurvedAvg, age

    1. Which of these should be value parameters, and which should be local variables?

    2. Write the procedure DECIDE.

Answer   *1.* Note that RawAvg and CurvedAvg are not passed to DECIDE; instead, they are calculated within the body of DECIDE. Thus, they should be local variables.

    2. Here is the complete program.

```
program hiring;
{for each applicant decides whether to HIRE or REJECT}
{based on 2 test scores and age using a curving method}
uses printer;
var   name: string;
      score1, score2, age: integer;
      StudFile: text;

procedure DECIDE (score1, score2: integer;
                  age: integer);
   {decides for one applicant}
   var RawAvg, CurvedAvg: real;
   begin
      RawAvg := (score1 + score2) / 2;
      if age >= 40
         then CurvedAvg := RawAvg + 5
         else CurvedAvg := RawAvg + 2;
      write (lst, '   Curved Average ', CurvedAvg :7 :1);
      if CurvedAvg >= 75
         then writeln (lst, '   HIRE')
         else writeln (lst, '   REJECT')
   end; {DECIDE}

begin {main}
   assign (StudFile, 'score.dat');
   reset (StudFile);
   while not seekeof (StudFile) do
      begin
         readln (StudFile, name);
         readln (StudFile, score1, score2, age);
```

```
        writeln (lst, name, score1:4, score2:4, ' age', age:4);
        DECIDE (score1, score2, age)
    end; {while}
  close (StudFile)
end.
```

• • •

Why Bother with Parameters and Local Variables? Safety, clarity, and modularity are very important goals in programming. Parameters facilitate an orderly flow of information (the passing of specific values) between the main body and a procedure.

It is important that you learn good style right from the start. If you ignored the principles of good style, although many of your programs would still work, some others would produce incorrect results. For example, if you brazenly disregarded the safety rule and simply made all variables global with no parameters or local variables, your program could run a risk of *side effects*—one portion of your program accidentally interfering with the work done by another portion. (The case of the Get Well Like Flies Hospital of Section 11.4 provides a dramatic illustration of this danger.)

10.6 PROTECTION FEATURE
• •

Protection Feature of Value Parameters When you rent a movie from a video store, the video is protected against your recording over it or otherwise altering its contents. Value parameters provide a similar protection feature.

> When global variables are used in the calling statement, they communicate initial values for the corresponding value parameters. Any changes the procedure body makes to a value parameter will not affect the corresponding global variable, even if it has the same name.

Thus, when value parameters are used, data contained in corresponding global variables will remain intact. This protection feature results directly from the fact that a value parameter has its own memory cell.

• • • • • • • • •
Question What will be printed by the following program?

```
program drill;
var x: integer;

procedure JOB (x: integer);
  begin
    x := x + 5
  end; {JOB}

begin {main}
  x := 0;
  x := x + 1;
  JOB (x);
  writeln (x)
end.
```

Answer   The output will be 1 since when x has its value increased by 5 in the procedure body, this does not affect the value of the global variable x.   ● ● ●

● ● ● ● ● ● ● ● ●

Question   A store is offering a one-day discount. For just that day, the unit price of every item is to be reduced by 20 percent. What will be printed by the following program if the user inputs 4 for quantity and 2.50 for UnitPrice?

```
program OneDaySpecial;
var quantity: integer;
    UnitPrice: real;

procedure COST_TODAY (quantity: integer; UnitPrice: real);
  {just for today unit prices on all items is 20% off}
  begin
    UnitPrice := 0.80 * UnitPrice;
    writeln ('Cost of purchase today $', quantity * UnitPrice:6:2)
  end; {COST_TODAY}

begin {main}
  write ('enter quantity and Unit price ');
  readln (quantity, UnitPrice);
  COST_TODAY (quantity, UnitPrice);
  writeln ('Cost of purchase tomorrow $', quantity * UnitPrice:6:2)
end.
```

Answer

```
enter quantity and Unit Price 4 2.50
Cost of purchase today $  8.00
Cost of purchase tomorrow $ 10.00
```

• • •

REMARK   Because of the protection feature of value parameters, the change in the value of the parameter UnitPrice does not affect the global variable UnitPrice. (In fact, they have different memory cells.)   • • •

• • • • • • • • •

Question   We want to modify the payroll program of Section 10.5 so that it also prints the total amount paid in wages. What will be printed by the following incorrect program? (*Hint:* What effect does the procedure body statement

```
total := total + pay
```

have on the global variable total? Note that total is also a value parameter.)

```
program incorrect;
{want to print total payroll as well as each employee's pay}
uses printer;
var name: string;
    hours: integer;
    rate, total: real;
    EmpFile: text;

procedure FINDPAY (name: string;
                   hours: integer;
                   rate, total: real);
  {processes one employee}
  var  pay : real;
  begin
    if hours <= 40
      then pay := hours * rate
      else pay := 40 * rate + (hours - 40) * 1.5 * rate;
    writeln (lst, name, '  $', pay :7 :2);
    total := total + pay
  end; {FINDPAY}

begin {main}
  assign (EmpFile, 'employ.dat');
  reset (EmpFile);
```

```
  total := 0;
  while not seekeof (EmpFile) do
    begin
      readln (EmpFile, name);
      readln (EmpFile, hours, rate);
      FINDPAY (name, hours, rate, total)
    end;   {while}
  writeln (1st, 'Total payroll $', total :8 :2);
  close (EmpFile)
end.
```

Answer The total will be printed incorrectly as

```
        Total payroll $ 0.00
```

The mistake is caused by the fact that `total` is a value parameter. Thus, because of the protection feature, the procedure body statement

```
        total := total + pay;
```

affects only the value parameter `total`. It does not affect the global variable `total`, which remains at zero.   • • •

"Unsolvable" Problem? We wish to fix program `incorrect` so that it prints the actual total payroll. Try to find a way to do this that satisfies the following three requirements:

1. Modify just the procedure and not the main body.

2. Obey the safety rule of Section 10.4.

3. Use *only value parameters* as parameters.

If you can find such a solution, you are probably a genius.

Variable Parameters As you have just seen, the protection feature of value parameters is also a limitation since there are situations in which you want the procedure to be able to alter the value of a global variable. In Chapter 11, we will give a simple way to fix program `incorrect` by using variable parameters as opposed to value parameters.

• • • • • • • • • EXERCISES
               •

1. What will be output by

```
program drill;

procedure PRINT_AVG (name: string;
                     s1, s2: integer);
  var avg: real;
  begin
    avg := (s1 + s2)/2;
    writeln (name, avg:5:1)
  end; {PRINT_AVG}

begin {main}
  PRINT_AVG ('Smith', 80, 90);
  PRINT_AVG ('Jones', 70, 73)
end.
```

2. Find the error in

```
program drill;
var years: integer;

procedure HOW_LONG (yrs: integer);
  begin
    writeln (yrs, ' years');
  end; {HOW_LONG}

begin
  yrs := 20;
  HOW_LONG (yrs);
end.
```

3. Write a two-paragraph campaign letter program that receives as input the voter's name and sex. The first paragraph of the letter should not depend on the person's sex, whereas the second paragraph should. Use three procedures. Let procedure PARAG1 print the greeting with the person's name as well as the actual first paragraph.

4. Write a program in which the user inputs his or her height in feet and inches. The output should be his or her height in just inches. Use a procedure HEIGHT_IN_INCHES with two parameters. (*Hint:* Use a local variable InchTotal.)

5. Write a program in which the main body has the user input the number of dimes and quarters. The main body should call a procedure DOLLAR_AMT (with two parameters) that will calculate and output the total amount in dollars (like $3.45).

6. Write a program in which the main body has the user input his or her name and age. The main body then calls a procedure YOU_LOOK (with two parameters) that tells someone who is at least 25 that he or she looks much older by 10 years, and tells someone under 25 that he or she looks much younger by 5 years. Here is a typical run.

```
What is your name? Marge
How old are you Marge 29
Marge, you look much older.
I thought you were 39.
```

7. Give the output for each program.

(a)
```
program drill;
var x: integer;

procedure JOB (w: integer);
  begin
    w := w + 1;
    writeln (w)
  end; {JOB}

begin {main}
  x := 0;
  JOB (x);
  writeln (x)
end.
```

(b)
```
program drill;
var x: integer;

procedure JOB (x: integer);
  begin
    x := x + 1;
    writeln (x)
  end; {JOB}

begin {main}
  x := 0;
  JOB (x);
  writeln (x)
end.
```

8. (a) Describe in words what value gets assigned to total each time the statement

```
total := total + pay
```

is executed (in the procedure body) in program incorrect of Section 10.6.

(b) Use the built-in debugger to trace the values of total.

Longer Assignments

9. Two fractions can be added as follows

$$\frac{a}{b} + \frac{c}{d} = \frac{ad + bc}{bd}$$

Write a program containing a procedure ADD_FRACTIONS with parameters a, b, c, d, such that the main body calls

```
ADD_FRACTIONS (1,3,4,7);
ADD_FRACTIONS (1,2,1,4);
```

would produce output

```
1/3 + 4/7 = 19/21
1/2 + 1/4 = 6/8
```

10. **(a)** Write a procedure that is passed a value between 1 and 80 for its parameter n. The procedure should cause the cursor to drop down to the next line and print an asterisk in column n of that line.

   (b) Write a procedure that is passed two values, the first between 1 and 71 for its parameter n, and the second between 1 and 10 for its parameter p. The procedure should cause the cursor to drop down to the next line and then, starting in column n, print p asterisks.

11. The XYZ Supplies Company has an unusual wage formula for its employees. An employee's weekly wage is equal to

   $100 + $(employee's age) + $(1 + 2 + 3 · · · + years with XYZ)

   Thus, a 37-year-old employee who has been with XYZ for six years would earn a weekly wage of $158 (that is, 100 + 37 + 21). (The value 21 comes from 1 + 2 + 3 + 4 + 5 + 6.)

   (a) Write a program that will receive as input one employee's name, age, and years with XYZ and print on paper the employee's wage information. Use FINDPAY to calculate and print the employee's name and wage information.

   (b) Modify the program in part (a) so that it processes all the employees in a file.

12. **(a)** Write a program that receives an integer greater than 1 as input. The main body should call a procedure ULAM to print that integer's Ulam sequence and its length. (See Section 7.4 for a discussion of Ulam.)

   (b) A file contains a list of integers greater than 1. Modify the program in part (a) so that it processes the entire file.

13. Write a program that will read from a text file each employee's name, hours, rate, and number of dependents. The main body should call a procedure FIND_NET to calculate and print an employee's base pay, tax, and net pay. The base pay is simply hours times rate and the tax rate is either.

(a) 0.20 − (number of dependents * 0.01) if the number of dependents is three or less, or

(b) 0.16 if the number of dependents is four or more.

14. Each employee of a firm has been assigned a three-digit ID number with the property:

hundreds digit = tens digit + units digit

A text file contains a list of names of people and their alleged ID numbers. Write a program that prints each person's name along with an appropriate message (either SEEMS OKAY or INVALID ID) based on whether the ID number has the aforementioned property. The main body should call a procedure DECIDE to process each person. (*Hint:* The tens digit of a three-digit number can be obtained by first taking div 10 and then mod 10.)

15. Write a DRAWRECT procedure with two parameters, height and width. DRAWRECT should draw a *rectangle* with height rows of asterisks, where each row has width asterisks in it. Thus, the calling statement

```
DRAWRECT (3, 5)
```

should produce

```
* * * * *
* * * * *
* * * * *
```

Lab Exercises   **DEBUGGING AND SYNTAX ERRORS**

Lab10-1.pas   Syntax Errors

Lab10-2.pas   Correct Use of Variables

Chapter 11

VARIABLE PARAMETERS

• • • This chapter begins with a simple solution to `program incorrect` of Chapter 10, in which the total payroll was incorrectly output to be $0.00. The solution involves declaring `total` to be a ***variable parameter***—a second kind of parameter—that allows a procedure to alter the value of a global variable that appears in its calling statement. We then further modularize this program by using a `GETDATA` procedure.

Next, we discuss the use of ***structure chart*** diagrams to depict the overall organization and data flow of a program; they can be used not only as documentation but also as an aid in writing the program. We also provide practice at deciding whether to make something a value parameter, a variable parameter, or a local variable.

Finally, we take a detailed look at hand tracing of procedures so that you will be better able to avoid some of the pitfalls that can occur. The Get Well Like Flies example dramatically illustrates the danger of not obeying the safety rules for procedures. • • •

11.1 VARIABLE PARAMETERS

Under some circumstances, you may want a procedure to be able to change the value of a global variable. For a parameter to have the capacity to change the value of the calling statement variable, it must be declared as a variable parameter in the procedure header. A variable parameter is declared by using the keyword `var` in the header declaration for that parameter.

In the next example, `group` will be a value parameter and `salary` a variable parameter. Note the header.

```
procedure RAISE (group: integer; var salary: integer);
```

* * * * * * * * * *

Example   A company has subdivided its employees into two groups, Group 1 and Group 2. Each employee in Group 1 will receive a raise of $25 per week, whereas each employee in Group 2 will receive a raise of only $15 per week.

In `program payraise`, `salary` is declared as a variable parameter because we want a call to procedure `RAISE` to change the corresponding global variable `YourSalary`.

```
program payraise;
{prints new salary based on}
{input group and current salary}
var YourGroup, YourSalary: integer;

procedure RAISE (group: integer; var salary: integer);
  {finds new salary}
  begin
    if group = 1 then salary := salary + 25
                 else salary := salary + 15
  end; {RAISE}

begin {main}
  write ('Enter your group and current salary ');
  readln (YourGroup, YourSalary);
  RAISE (YourGroup, YourSalary);
  writeln ('Your new salary is $ ', YourSalary)
end.
```

Here is a typical run of the program.

```
Enter your group and current salary 2 280
Your new salary is $ 295
```

Value versus Variable Parameters—Memory Cells   When a procedure is called, a separate memory cell is created for each value parameter. By contrast, a variable parameter does not receive its own memory cell. Instead, a variable parameter uses the memory cell of the corresponding global variable in the calling statement. Thus, any change a procedure makes to a variable parameter will also affect the value of the corresponding global variable.

The following figure depicts the memory boxes during a call to RAISE with the values 2 and 280:

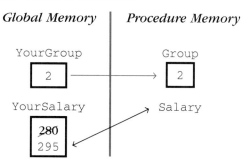

Global Memory | *Procedure Memory*

YourGroup | Group
2 | 2

YourSalary | Salary
~~280~~
295

Note that the value parameter group receives its own memory cell, whereas the variable parameter salary does not. (The blue arrow indicates receiving an initial value; the black double arrow indicates sharing a memory cell.) When the procedure is exited, the memory cell of the value parameter group and the pointer from salary to YourSalary are erased.

The following rule stems from the fact that a variable parameter uses the memory cell of the corresponding argument:

> An argument that corresponds to a variable (formal) parameter must be a variable. Moreover, both must be of the same type. (By contrast, an argument that corresponds to a value parameter may be either a variable, an expression, or a literal value and need only be of a compatible type.)

Payroll Total Solved   In the incorrect program payroll of Section 10.6, the incorrect printout gave $0.00 for the total payroll. The statement

```
total := total + pay
```

in the body of FINDPAY did not change the value of the global variable total since total was a value parameter of FINDPAY. Thus, the global variable total remained at zero.

To correct this program, simply change total to a variable parameter of FINDPAY by adding the keyword var before total in the procedure header.

```
procedure FINDPAY (name: string;
                    hours: integer;
                    rate: real;
                    var total: real);
  {processes one employee}
  var pay: real;
  begin
    if hours <= 40
      then pay := hours * rate
```

```
        else pay := 40 * rate + (hours - 40) * 1.5 * rate;
   writeln (lst, name, ' $ ', pay :7 :2);
   total := total + pay
 end; {FINDPAY}
```

· · · · · · · · · ·

Example   (GETDATA as a Procedure)   In the following version of `program payroll`, we have modularized further by using procedure `GETDATA` to get an employee's raw data.

```
program payroll3;
{prints the total payroll as well as each employee's pay}
uses printer;
var   name: string;
      hours: integer;
      rate, total: real;
      EmpFile: text;

procedure GETDATA (var EmpFile: text;
                   var name: string;
                   var hours: integer;
                   var rate: real);
  {gets one employee's data}
  begin
    readln (EmpFile, name);
    readln (EmpFile, hours, rate)
  end; {GETDATA}

  ┌─────────────────────────┐
  │ procedure FINDPAY       │
  │     goes here           │
  └─────────────────────────┘

begin {main}
  assign (EmpFile, 'employ.dat');
  reset (EmpFile);
  total := 0;
  while not seekeof (EmpFile) do
      begin
         GETDATA (EmpFile, name, hours, rate);
         FINDPAY (name, hours, rate, total)
      end; {while}
  writeln (lst, 'Total payroll $ ', total :8 :2);
  close (EmpFile)
end.
```

REMARK

1. Note that name, hours, and rate must be variable parameters in GETDATA since we want the values assigned to them in GETDATA to be available to the main body for the call to FINDPAY.

2. When a file variable is used as a parameter in a procedure, it *must* be declared a variable parameter. This is because a file variable not only links to a particular external file but it also keeps track of the current location of the file pointer (which will be advanced by any readln statements that are executed during a procedure call).

• • •

11.2 STRUCTURE CHARTS

A structure chart is a diagram depicting the overall top down structure of a program that includes an analysis of any data flow between the main body and procedures. It can be used not only as a form of documentation but also, if you wish, as a tool in writing the program.

Here is a structure chart for the previous program.

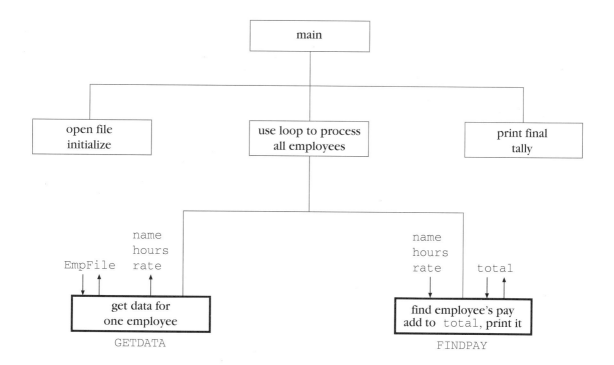

Structure Chart Conventions in This Book

1. Each box contains a description of what that program segment does. When a box is carried out by a procedure, the procedure's name is written underneath the box.

2. The following arrows are used in data flow (import and export):

(a) ↓ Import. Value imported by a procedure via value parameters.

(b) ↕ Import and export. Global variable that is updated based on its previous value.

(c) ↑ Export. Global variable that receives a new value not based on its previous value.

Both (b) and (c) use variable parameters.

• • • • • • • • •
Example In a certain course that is marked on a pass-fail basis (pass is an average score of 60 or better), each student has taken two tests. Write a program that prints each student's name, scores, average, and grade. It should also print how many students passed and the highest score on each test.

```
stud2.dat    Paper

Adams        Adams   60   70   65.0   Pass
60 70        Bond    75   40   57.5   Fail
Bond         Clark   70   82   76.0   Pass
75 40        2 students passed
Clark        Highest score on test 1:   75
70 82        Highest score on test 2:   82
```

Pseudocode

initialize `passcount` and `max1`, `max2`
for each student

GETDATA	Get a student name and two scores
FINDMARK	Find and print a student's average and mark; update `passcount` if necessary
UPDATE_MAXES	Update `max1`, `max2` when necessary
SUMMARIES	Print final summaries after the loop

• • • • • • • • •
Question Give a next level of pseudocode completing the calling statements using the parameters

```
StudFile, name, score1, score2, passcount, max1, max2
```

Put a check mark (√) over each argument in a calling statement that corresponds to a variable parameter.

Answer Here is a next refinement of the pseudocode.

```
passcount := 0;
max1 := -1;    max2 := -1;
while not seekeof (      ) do
   GETDATA (StudFile, name, score1, score2);
   FINDMARK (name, score1; score2, passcount);
   UPDATE_MAXES (score1, score2, max1, max2);
SUMMARIES (passcount, max1, max2);
```

• • •

REMARK SUMMARIES has no variable parameters. In general, any procedure call that is the last line of the main body will have no variable parameters since there is nothing farther along in the main body to pass information to.

• • •

This time let us give the structure chart before writing the program. Here is the structure chart based on the previous pseudocode.

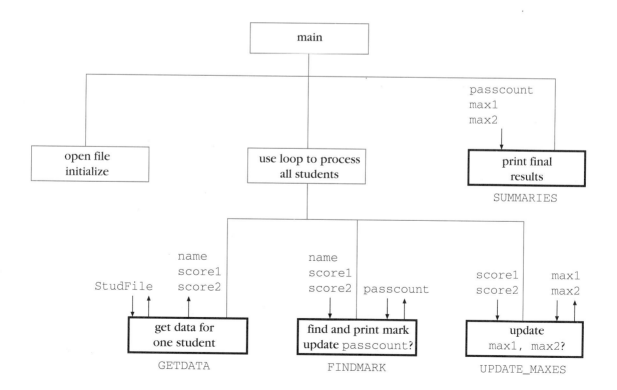

Here is the complete program.

```
program class;
{prints each student's grade, the high score, and pass count}
uses printer;
var  name: string;
     score1, score2, max1, max2, passcount: integer;
     StudFile: text;

procedure GETDATA (var StudFile: text;
                   var name: string;
                   var score1, score2: integer);
  begin
    readln (StudFile, name);
    readln (StudFile, score1, score2)
  end; {GETDATA}

procedure FINDMARK (name: string;
                    score1, score2: integer;
                    var passcount: integer);
  {finds a student's mark (Pass or Fail), updates passcount}
  var  avg: real;
  begin
    avg := (score1 + score2) / 2;
    write (lst, name, score1 :3, score2 :3, avg :5 :1);
    if avg >= 60 then
       begin
          writeln (lst, '  Pass');
          passcount := passcount + 1
       end
    else
       writeln (lst, '  Fail')
  end; {FINDMARK}

procedure UPDATE_MAXES (score1, score2: integer;
                        var max1, max2: integer);
  {updates highest score for test 1 or test 2 when necessary}
  begin
    if score1 > max1 then max1 := score1;
    if score2 > max2 then max2 := score2
  end; {UPDATE_MAXES}

procedure SUMMARIES (passcount, max1, max2: integer);
  {print how many passed and the highest score on each test}
  begin
    writeln (lst, passcount, ' students passed');
```

```
      writeln (lst, 'Highest score on test 1: ', max1);
      writeln (lst, 'Highest score on test 2: ', max2)
   end; {SUMMARIES}

begin {main}
   assign (StudFile, 'stud2.dat');
   reset (StudFile);
   passcount := 0;
   max1 := -1;
   max2 := -1;
   while not seekeof (StudFile) do
      begin
         GETDATA (StudFile, name, score1, score2);
         FINDMARK (name, score1, score2, passcount);
         UPDATE_MAXES (score1, score2, max1, max2)
      end;
   SUMMARIES (passcount, max1, max2);
   close (StudFile)
end.
```

REMARK   We used the shortcut method for initializing max1 and max2. If you wanted to use score1 and score2 for the initialization of max1 and max2, you would need to process the first student separately before the loop.

• • •

Divisors of an Integer

• • • • • • • • •
Question   What will be printed by the following fragment?

```
n := 12;
for d := 1 to n do
   if n mod d = 0 then
      write (d:3);
```

Answer

```
  1  2  3  4  6 12
```

• • •

• • • • • • • • •
Problem   Write a program that will print the divisors for each of the integers from 15 to 20, indicating which integers had more than four divisors. The program

should also print the count for how many had more than four divisors. Have the output formatted as follows:

```
15:    1   3   5 15
16:    1   2   4   8 16    More than 4 divisors
17:    1 17
18:    1   2   3   6   9 18    More than 4 divisors
19:    1 19
20:    1   2   4   5 10 20    More than 4 divisors

 3 of them had more than 4 divisors
```

Here are some program ideas.

Imitate code you've already seen.

You will need two separate counting variables—one for the number of divisors of an integer and one for how many integers have more than four divisors.

Use a `for` loop in the main body.

Pseudocode

```
over4 := 0;
for n := 15 to 20 do
    DIVISORS (  )
```

Print all the divisors of n. If n has more than four divisors, print a message and update `over4` counter.

print final count for `over4`

Before reading further, write the entire main body. Put a check mark over any variable in the calling statement `DIVISORS (   )` that is matched with a variable parameter. Here it is.

```
begin {main}
    over4 := 0;
    for n := 15 to 20 do
        DIVISORS (n, over4);
    writeln (over4, ' of them had more than 4 divisors')
end.
```

Writing the full program is Exercise 10.

11.3 HAND TRACING

Same Name Conflict Suppose that the same name that is used for a global variable is also used as either a local variable or a parameter of a procedure called by the main body. How does the computer determine which memory cell is being referred to when that variable appears in a statement? It does so by where the statement is located. If the statement is in the main body, then it is the global variable. If the statement is in the body of the procedure, then it is the local variable or parameter.

• • • • • • • • • •

Question   What will be printed by the following program? Note that the statement in the main body that contains x refers to the global variable x, whereas the statements in the procedure refer to the value parameter x. Also note that each call of JUNK initializes the value parameter x with the value of the corresponding calling statement variable—in this case, x.

```
program drill;
var x, y: integer;

procedure JUNK (x: integer; var y: integer);
  begin
    x := x + 2;
    y := y + 5;
    writeln (x, ' ', y)
  end; {JUNK}

begin {main}
  x := 4;
  y := 20;
  writeln (x, ' ', y);
  JUNK (x, y);
  writeln (x, ' ', y);
  JUNK (x, y);
  writeln (x, ' ', y)
end.
```

Answer   *Output*

```
4  20
6  25
4  25
6  30
4  30
```

• • •

Here is a hand trace for the previous program.

Global Memory | *Procedure Memory*

```
    x   y
    4   20  . . . . . . . . . . . . . . . . . . . . . . . . . . . . . . . .
        25                   JUNK (x,      y)      1st Call
                                    ↓        ‖
                          params  | x |     y
                                  |   |
                                  | 4 |
                                  | 6 |
  . . . . . . .  . . . . . . . . . . . . . . . . . . . . . . . . . . . . . .
        30                   JUNK (x,      y)      2nd Call
                                    ↓        ‖
                          params  | x |     y
                                  |   |
                                  | 4 |
                                  | 6 |
```

Hand Trace Format   Note that we

1. Used the left side of the page for the global memory cells and the right side for procedure memory cells.

2. Aligned each procedure parameter directly underneath the corresponding argument of the calling statement. The ↓ for a value parameter indicates that it receives the value of its corresponding argument. The ‖ for a variable parameter indicates that it uses the memory cell of the corresponding global variable.

3. Used dotted horizontal lines to separate different procedure calls.

• • • • • • • • •

Question   What will be printed by the following program?

```
program drill;
var a, b, w: integer;

procedure JOB (var x: integer;
               y: integer);
  var w: integer;
  begin
    w := 5;
    x := x + 1;
    y := w + 2;
    writeln (x, '   ', y, '   ', w)
  end; {JOB}

begin {main}
```

```
    a := 0;   b := 0;   w := 0;
    JOB (a, b);
    writeln (a, ' ', b, ' ', w);
    a := a + 20;
    w := w + 20;
    JOB (a, b);
    writeln (a, ' ', b, ' ', w)
end.
```

Here is the trace.

Global Memory   *Procedure Memory*

a	b	w
0	0	0
1		

JOB (a,   b)   1st call
      ‖   ↓   local var
      x | y | w |
           | 0 | 5 |
           | 7 | |

| 21 | | 20 |
| 22 | | |

JOB (a,   b)   2nd call
      ‖   ↓   local var
      x | y | w |
           | 0 | 5 |
           | 7 | |

Answer

```
 1  7  5
 1  0  0
22  7  5
22  0  20
```

11.4 TRACING WITH ORDER SWITCHED (OPTIONAL)

Question   What will be printed by the following program?

```
program drill;
var a, b, c: integer;

procedure BOB (var x, y: integer;
               z: integer);
  begin
    x := x + 1;
    y := y + 2;
    z := z + 3;
    writeln (x, ' ', y, ' ', z)
  end; {BOB}

begin {main}
  a := 10;    b := 20;    c := 30;
  BOB (b, c, a);    {note the unnatural order}
  writeln (a, ' ', b, ' ', c);
  BOB (c, a, b);    {note another unnatural
order}
  writeln (a, ' ', b, ' ', c)
end.
```

Global Memory   *Procedure Memory*

a	b	c
10	20	30
	21	32

BOB(b, c, a)   1st call
     ‖ ‖ ↓
     x y │ z │
          │10│
          │13│

a	b	c
12		33

BOB(c, a, b)   2nd call
     ‖ ‖ ↓
     x y │ z │
          │21│
          │24│

Answer

```
21 32 13
10 21 32
33 12 24
12 21 33
```

• • •

11.5 SIDE EFFECTS

• •

The primary goals of procedure handling in Pascal are safety and clarity. When a procedure changes the value of a global variable in an unexpected and therefore potentially dangerous way, a side effect is said to have occurred. Recall the safety rule of Chapter 10: *Each variable in the body of a procedure should be either a parameter or a local variable of the procedure.* Be aware that violation of this safety rule will not produce a syntax error; thus, the computer does not warn the programmer of any potential danger.

Sources of Side Effects   The main source of a side effect is a procedure that violates the safety rule. More specifically, the most common way in which you might cause a side effect is by *forgetting* to declare as a local variable each intermediate variable that a procedure uses to perform its task. This might disrupt the value of a global variable that coincidentally has the same name as the intermediate variable. The `program incorrect` illustrates this danger.

• • • • • • • • • •
Question   The Get Well Like Flies Hospital uses `program incorrect` to input a patient's temperature and two pulse readings taken five minutes apart, and then print the temperature and the status of the pulse. In the event that the patient's temperature is below 85, the life support system is to be shut off to conserve energy. Thus, for the input `98.6`, `71`, and `74`, the intended output is

```
Stable pulse
temperature 98.6
```

In `program incorrect`, the variable `temp` is used both by the main body for temperature and by the procedure as a *temporary* difference variable. Unfortunately for the patient, the programmer failed to declare `temp` as a local variable of `PULSE_STATUS`.

For the preceding input, what will the actual output of the program be?

```
program incorrect;
{illustrates side effects}
var temp: real;
    pulse1, pulse2: real;

procedure PULSE_STATUS (pulse1, pulse2: real);
  {determines stability of pulse}
```

```
    begin
      temp := pulse1 - pulse2;
      if abs (temp) > 10
        then writeln ('Irregular pulse')
        else writeln ('Stable pulse')
    end; {PULSE_STATUS}

begin {main}
  write ('enter temperature and 2 pulse rates ');
  readln (temp, pulse1, pulse2);
  PULSE_STATUS (pulse1, pulse2);
  writeln ('temperature ', temp:5:1);
  if temp < 85 then
    writeln ('Patient dead.  Shut off life support.')
end.
```

Answer

```
Stable pulse
temperature -3.0
Patient dead. Shut off life support.
```

• • •

This erroneous output resulted because the programmer used the variable `temp` in the main body and a variable by the same name within the body of the procedure but neglected to declare `temp` as a local variable within the procedure. If you fail to declare a local variable, a statement in the procedure body that was designed merely to carry out the work of the procedure may disrupt the value of the global variable with the same name. Hence, the program could be corrected by declaring `temp` as a local variable of PULSE_STATUS.

Exceptions   There are two situations in which you might intentionally disregard either the safety rule or the protection feature of value parameters.

1. **Object-oriented programming**   This topic, discussed in Chapter 30, uses a quite different approach to safety.

2. **Large data structures**   A large data structure such as an array (see Chapter 17) might be sent as a variable parameter as a way of conserving memory since a value parameter would in effect create a duplicate copy of that data structure during the call.

• • • • • • • • • •   EXERCISES

1. What will the outputs be for these programs?

(a)
```
program drill;
var c: integer;

procedure JUNK;
   begin
      c := c + 1
   end; {JUNK}

begin {main}
   c := 0;
   JUNK;
   JUNK;
   writeln (c)
end.
```

(b)
```
program drill;
var a, c: integer;

procedure JUNK (c: integer);
   begin
      c := 5
   end; {JUNK}

begin {main}
   a := 0;
   c := 0;
   JUNK (a);
   writeln (a, ' ', c)
end.
```

2. **(a)** Explain why a variable parameter can be matched only with a variable in the calling statement and not with a constant or an expression.

   (b) What is a main cause of side effects?

3. What will the output be?

```
program drill;
var x, y: integer;

procedure PROB (a, b: integer);
   begin
      if a = b
         then writeln ('sum ', a + b)
         else writeln ('prod ', a * b);
   end;

begin
   x := 3;
   y := 5;
   while (x >= 0) and (y >= 0) do
      begin
         PROB (x, y);
         y := y - 2;
         x := x - 1
      end
end.
```

4. **(a)** What will the output be for the following program?

```
program drill;
var a, b: integer;

procedure SILLY (var a: integer;
                     b: integer);
  begin
    a := a + 2 * b;
    b := a + 1;
    writeln (a, ' ', b)
  end; {SILLY}

begin {main}
  a := 1;
  b := 6;
  SILLY (a, b);
  writeln (a, ' ', b);
  SILLY (a, b);
  writeln (a, ' ', b)
end.
```

(b) Suppose in SILLY that a had been declared a value parameter and b a variable parameter. What would the output be?

(c) Use the built-in debugger to trace the program one line at a time.

5. What will the output be?

```
program drill;
var a, b, z, w: integer;

procedure HAT (x: integer; var y, z: integer);
  var w: integer;
  begin
    x := x + 1;
    y := y + 25;
    w := x;
    z := z + 10;
    writeln (x, ' ', y, ' ', z, ' ', w)
  end; {HAT}

begin {main}
  a := 5;   b := 5;   z := 5;   w := 5;
  HAT (a, b, z);
  writeln (a, ' ', b, ' ', z, ' ', w);
```

```
    HAT (a, b, z);
    writeln (a, ' ', b, ' ', z, ' ', w)
end.
```

* **6. (a)** What will the output be?

```
program drill;
var a, b, c: integer;

procedure MIX (var x, y: integer; z: integer);
   var t: integer;
   begin
     t := z + 1;
     z := y;
     y := x;
     x := t;
     writeln (x, ' ', y, ' ', z, ' ', t)
   end; {MIX}

begin {main}
   a := 2;
   b := 4;
   c := 6;
   MIX (a, b, c);
   MIX (b, c, a);
   writeln (a, ' ', b, ' ', c)
end.
```

(b) What additional two lines of output would be produced by inserting the following two statements at the bottom of the main body of the program in part a?

```
MIX (c,a,b);
writeln (a, ' ', b, ' ', c)
```

* **7.** What will be the output of the following program if the user enters the values <u>14</u>, <u>8</u>, <u>12</u>, and <u>−1</u>?

```
program side_effects;
{will give incorrect value for number of lines printed}
var i, n: integer;

procedure TROUBLE (n: integer);
```

```
    {print a line of asterisks; i should be local variable}
    begin
      for i := 1 to n do
        write ('*');
      writeln
    end; {TROUBLE}

begin {main}
  i := 0;
  write ('Enter n or -1 to stop ');
  readln (n);
  while n >= 0 do
    begin
      TROUBLE (n);
      i := i + 1;
      write ('Enter n or -1 to stop ');
      readln (n)
    end; {while}
  writeln ('You have printed ', i, ' lines')
end.
```

* **8.** When you use the same names for variables and parameters, you should have the same names correspond. That is not done here and can lead to confusion. What will the output be?

```
program drill;
var a, b: integer;

procedure BUB (var a: integer;
                   b: integer);
  begin
    a := b * b;
    writeln (a, ' ', b)
  end; {BUB}

begin {main}
  a := 5;
  b := 7;
  BUB (b, a);    {bad style}
  writeln (a, ' ', b)
end.
```

Longer Assignments

9. Modify `program class` of Section 11.2 so that the output also gives the name of the student who achieved the highest score on each test. (Your program may ignore the possibility of a tie.)

10. Write the program based on the pseudocode given in Section 11.2 to determine which integers from 15 to 20 have more than four divisors and count how many such integers there were.

11. Write a program that will do the payroll for all the employees at XYZ Supplies Company. (See Exercise 11 of Chapter 10 for the wage formula.) In addition to printing each employee's wage information, the program should print the total payroll and the count for the number of employees earning over $300.

12. Modify Exercise 14 of Chapter 10 so that the program also prints how many people had an invalid ID and how many seemed okay, and whether or not there were at least as many that seemed okay as not. Have the main body call procedures `DECIDE` and `PRINT_TALLIES`.

13. Modify Exercise 13 of Chapter 10 so that the program also prints the total amount of tax collected.

14. The Livelong Life Insurance Company offers insurance policies at low premiums because it insures only applicants who smoke fewer than 10 cigarettes per day and weigh under 180 pounds. Write a program that will process a list of applicants. Input for each applicant consists of name, number of cigarettes smoked daily, and weight. The printout should have

   • Each applicant's name, number of cigarettes smoked daily, and weight, along with a message stating whether the applicant has been `ACCEPTED` or `REJECTED`. If the applicant has been `REJECTED`, the reason(s) why should be printed.

   • The average number of cigarettes smoked daily and the average weight for those applicants who have been `ACCEPTED`.

15. The sum of the divisors of the number 15 is 24 (1 + 3 + 5 + 15). Write a program that will print the sum of the divisors for each of the integers from 100 to 110. The final line of the printout should state which integer had the largest sum. Format the output as follows:

```
100:    1  2  4  5  10  20  25  50  100
sum of divisors 217
 .
 .
 .
```

```
110:  1  2  5  10  11  22  55  110
sum of divisors ____
     ____ had maximum sum of divisors
```

Use procedures named FIND_DIVISOR_SUM and TESTMAX.

16. Some integers are larger than the length of their Ulam sequence; some are not. (See Section 7.3 for an explanation of Ulam's conjecture.) For example, 16 is larger than the length of its Ulam sequence, whereas 7 is not. Write a program that will print the Ulam sequence for each of the integers from 10 to 20. After each Ulam sequence, the program should print the appropriate message, LARGER THAN LENGTH OF ITS SEQ or NOT LARGER THAN LENGTH OF ITS SEQ. After all the Ulam sequences and messages, the output should give a count of how many numbers from 10 to 20 were larger than the length of their Ulam sequence. Have your program use two procedures, ULAM and TEST_IF_LARGER.

17. (a) Put 10 states and their capitals in a text file. Write an interactive program that will produce as its final output the number of states for which the user was able to guess the capital in four or fewer guesses. (See Section 8.1.) Have the main body call procedures GETDATA with two parameters and GUESS_CAPITAL with three parameters.

    (b) Modify the program so that its final output gives both the number of state capitals gotten in one guess and the number of state capitals gotten within four guesses.

* *

Lab Exercises   **DEBUGGING AND SYNTAX ERRORS**

Lab11-1.pas   Average of Even Numbers
Lab11-2.pas   Finding the Oldest
Lab11-3.pas   Summing a Block of Integers

* *

Chapter

12

MULTIWAY SELECTION

• • •   Chapter 4 discussed using the if-then-else statement to have the computer choose between two alternatives. In some cases, however, you may need to have the computer choose from more than two alternatives. At this point, the only technique you have seen for doing so is to use several separate if-then tests.

This chapter presents two other methods of multiway selection.

1. nested if statements

  (a) linear nested if

  (b) more general nested if

2. case statements   • • •

12.1 LINEAR NESTED if
• •

When the then or else branch of an if statement is itself an if statement, we call the entire construct a nested if statement.

• • • • • • • • • •

Question   In the following nested if, what will be output when

  (a) x = 5, y = 9   (b) x = 6, y = 4   (c) x = 8, y = 8

```
if x > y then
   writeln ('x bigger')
else if x < y then writeln ('x smaller')
               else writeln ('x and y equal');
```

Answer   (a)   Since the condition `x > y` is false, the computer will go to the main `else` branch test `if x < y`. Since this will be true, the computer will output

```
x smaller
```

(b)   Since the first condition `x > y` is true, the computer will output

```
x bigger
```

and exit without performing any additional tests.

(c)   It will output

```
x and y equal
```

• • •

• • • • • • • •

Question   What will be output by the following when x = 5 and y = 9?

```
if x > y then
   writeln ('x bigger')
else if x < y then
   writeln ('x smaller')
else
   writeln ('x and y equal');
```

Answer   Since we have changed only spacing and indentation, computer execution will not be affected by this new format. The output will be (as before)

```
x smaller
```

The advantage of this second format is that it is easier to read once you know the rule for its execution.

• • •

Linear Nested if   The statement in the previous question is known as a linear nested `if` statement. You can use linear nested `if` to select one alternative from a list of `if-then` tests. Here is a general format for linear nested `if`.

```
if {condition-1} then
    statement-1
else if {condition-2} then
```

```
        statement-2
else if {condition-3} then
        statement-3
            .
            .
            .

else {optional}
        statement-n;
```

REMARK

1. The first test is simply `if-then`. All the middle tests are `else-if`, whereas the optional last clause is simply `else`.

2. The computer will execute at most one branch—namely, the statement associated with the first test that is true—and then exit; if none of the tests is true, the computer will execute the final `else` branch when there is one or do nothing if there is not.

3. This entire construct is a single statement, and thus there are no semicolons separating the individual branches. A semicolon at the end of the entire multiway test may be needed, however, to separate the test from the statement that immediately follows it.

4. Any of the statements could be compound statements.   • • •

Question What will be output by the following segment for each of the given values of numb?

(a) numb = 7   (b) numb = 12   (c) numb = 3

Note that the computer will execute *only* the branch associated with the first condition that tests true, and the `else` branch if no condition is true.

```
if numb >= 8 then
   cost := numb * 10
else if numb >= 4 then
   cost := numb * 11
else
   cost := numb * 12;
writeln ('$', cost);
```

Answer (a) $77 because when numb = 7, the first condition that evaluates to true is if numb >= 4.

(b) $120 because the computer exits immediately after executing the branch associated with if numb >= 8.

(c) $36 because the final `else` branch is executed.   • • •

••••••••••
Question   Suppose that in the previous segment, `numb` is the number of team hats purchased. Describe the three-level pricing scheme that would be implemented by that linear nested `if`.

Answer   If at least eight hats are purchased, the price is $10 per hat.

If at least four but fewer than eight hats are purchased, the price is $11 per hat.

If fewer than four hats are purchased, the price is $12 per hat.   •••

••••••••••
Question   Write code to output the letter grade for a student and to increase the counter for the number of Cs by 1 if it was a C. Use the variables `score` and `Ccount`, where

A is 90 and over.

B is at least 80 but less than 90.

C is at least 70 but less than 80.

D is at least 60 but less than 70.

F is under 60.

Answer

```
if score >= 90 then
   writeln ('A')
else if score >= 80 then
   writeln ('B')
else if score >= 70 then
   begin
      writeln ('C');
      Ccount := Ccount + 1
   end
else if score >= 60 then
   writeln ('D')
else
   writeln ('F');
```

•••

••••••••••
Question   We could have used a compound condition for each `else-if` test. For example, the test for a `grade` of B could have been

```
else if (score >= 80) and (score < 90) then
   grade := 'B'
```

Why was this unnecessary?

Answer   The only way the computer could get to this test would be if the condition `score >= 90` was false (that is, `score` was less than 90).   • • •

Efficiency and a Pitfall   Observe that the order of the tests in the previous segment was important because of the overlapping conditions.

• • • • • • • • • •

Question   Suppose that a student is assigned a grade of Good, Fair, or Poor as follows:

Good for a score of at least 85.

Fair for a score under 85 but at least 70.

Poor for a score under 70.

Neither of the program segments given is well written—one is correct but inefficient; the other is incorrect. Explain what is wrong with each.

(a)
```
if score >= 70 then
    grade := 'Fair'
else if score >= 85 then
    grade := 'Good'
else
    grade := 'Poor';
```

(b)
```
if score >= 85 then grade := 'Good';
if (score >= 70) and (score < 85) then grade := 'Fair';
if score < 70 then grade := 'Poor';
```

Answer   (a)   A score of 85 or above would be incorrectly assigned a grade of `Fair`.

(b)   Using separate `if-then` tests is *inefficient*. For example, when `score = 90`, the computer will correctly assign a grade of `Good` but will continue to perform all the other tests on `score`.   • • •

12.2   GENERAL NESTED if
• •

In a linear nested `if` statement of pure form, none of the `then` branches contain further testing within them; it is only the `else` branches that contain tests within them. (Take another look at the format given in the previous section.) In a general nested `if`, we remove this restriction.

• • • • • • • • •
Example   An auto insurance agency assigns rates based on sex and age. Males below age 25 pay the highest premium, $1,000. Males 25 or older pay $700. Females below age 21 pay $800, whereas those 21 or older pay $500. Here is a nested `if` statement that will assign the appropriate rate.

```
if sex = 'm' then
   if age < 25 then rate := 1000      ⎫ main then branch
                else rate := 700      ⎬
else {sex = 'f'}                       ⎫ main else branch
   if age < 21 then rate := 800        ⎬
                else rate := 500;
```

• • •

REMARK   This is not a pure *linear* nested `if` statement because a `then` branch contains an `if` test within it.   • • •

Matching   As previously mentioned, you should use spacing and indentation to improve the clarity of your programs for the reader, but the computer ignores spacing and indentation. How, then, does the computer know how to interpret a nested `if` statement? More specifically, how does the computer know which `if-then` test an `else` branch belongs to? The computer follows this matching rule.

> Each `else` branch is matched with the closest free, unmatched `then` branch that precedes it.

Dangling else   When you format a nested `if` so that your intended logic is at odds with the matching rule, we say that there is a *dangling* `else`.

• • • • • • • • •
Question   Something is seriously wrong with the following program fragment. It is intended to hire candidates who pass the exam and are eligible, and to reject those who fail the test. Nothing should be printed for those who pass but are ineligible. What is the mistake? (*Hint:* Consider the matching rule.)

```
if score >= 90 then
   if status = 'eligible' then
      writeln ('Hire')
else
   writeln ('Reject');
```

Answer   The indentation used is at odds with the matching rule. The computer will pair the `else` branch with the `then` branch that immediately precedes it, not the main `then` branch as desired. Here is the indentation that corresponds to how the computer will interpret this code.

```
if score >= 90 then
   if status = 'eligible'
     then writeln ('Hire')
     else writeln ('Reject');
```

Thus, this code would incorrectly print nothing for a score under 90. (It was supposed to print `Reject` in that case.) There are various ways to correct this code. One way is to use `begin-end` markers so that the `then` branch from the `status` test is not *free* to be matched with an `else`, as follows:

```
if score >= 90 then
    begin
        if status = 'eligible' then writeln ('Hire')
    end
else
   writeln ('Reject');
```

• • •

When Dangling else Can Occur Dangling `else` is a possible danger whenever you wish to include a `then` branch containing an `if-then` test as opposed to an `if-then-else` test because Pascal will match that `then` branch with the next free `else` branch below it. Note that there was no danger of dangling `else` in the insurance example since the `then` branch contained an `if-then-else` test.

12.3 **THE case STATEMENT**
• •

Ordinal Types In an ***ordinal*** data type, each value (except the last) is followed by a unique successor and each value (except the first) is preceded by a unique predecessor. The ordinal types so far were `integer` types, `char`, and `boolean`. For example, 526 is followed by 527 and preceded by 525; c is followed by d and preceded by b.

The only other ordinal type in Turbo Pascal is the ***enumerated type*** (discussed in Chapter 16). Be aware that the data types `real` and `string` are not ordinal. For example, there is no next number that follows 2.83; 2.84 is not the next real number after 2.83 since both 2.835 and 2.831 follow it even more closely.

Double-Dot Notation for Subranges A list of consecutive ordinal values is known as a *subrange* and can be denoted by giving its starting value followed by two periods and its final value. For example, the notation

```
80..85
```

specifies the list 80, 81, 82, 83, 84, and 85.

case Statement Introduced Like the linear nested `if`, the **case** statement can be used to select one alternative from a list. It is generally simpler to use and debug than the nested `if` statement. As you will see, however, there are situations in which the `case` statement cannot be used.

Suppose we wish to write a statement that will print either 30 days, 31 days, or 28 or 29 days based on the value (1 through 12) of month. We could use a `case` statement, as follows:

```
case month of
   2                     : writeln ('28 or 29 days');
   4, 6, 9, 11           : writeln ('30 days');
   1, 3, 5, 7, 8, 10, 12 : writeln ('31 days')
end;
```

REMARK Note that the `case` statement terminates with the word `end` but has no corresponding `begin`. Also note the semicolon at the end of each statement in the `case`, except the one preceding the word `end`. The variable month is called the *selector* of the preceding `case` statement because its value is used to select among the three alternative lists. A `case` statement may also contain an `else` alternative. • • •

General Syntax

```
case selector of
    altern. list₁ : statement₁;
    altern. list₂ : statement₂;
                  .
                  .
                  .
    altern.listₙ : statementₙ
    else {optional} statementₑ
end;
```

REMARK

1. The selector must be an expression of *ordinal* type. Thus, it cannot be of type `real` or `string`. If the value of the selector is in any one

of the alternative lists, then that alternative's statement is executed and control is passed to the first statement after the case end.

2. else *optional:* If the value of the selector is not on any of the alternative lists and there is an else statement, then the else statement is executed. (If there is no else statement, then no action is taken when the selector is not on any of the alternative lists.)

3. It is bad style to have any overlap in the alternative lists. In the event that the selector value does occur in more than one alternative list, just the statement associated with the first alternative list containing it is executed.

4. Subranges are permitted in the alternative list. For example

```
case numb of
   1..5, 7 : writeln ('x');
   6, 8..10 : writeln ('y')
end; (case)
```
• • •

Two Uses of else

1. **Error trapping**   The else alternative can be used to catch a selector value outside the intended range.

```
case month of
   2                     : writeln ('28 or 29 days');
   4, 6, 9, 11           : writeln ('30 days');
   1, 3, 5, 7, 8, 10, 12 : writeln ('31 days');
   else                    writeln ('invalid value of month')
end;
```

2. **Omitting longest alternative list**   If you are quite certain that the value of month will be in the intended range (1 to 12) you could use

```
case month of
   2           : writeln ('28 or 29 days');
   4, 6, 9, 11 : writeln ('30 days');
   else          writeln ('31 days')
end;
```

CAUTION   No colon is used in the else alternative following the word else.   • • •

case Statement versus Linear Nested if   Let's redo the error trapping version of the case statement for the number of days in a month using linear nested if.

```
if month = 2 then
   writeln ('28 or 29 days')
else if (month=4) or (month=6) or (month=9) or (month=11) then
   writeln ('30 days')
else if (month=1) or (month=3) or (month=5) or (month=7)
      or (month=8) or (month=10) or (month=12) then
   writeln ('31 days')
else
   writeln ('invalid value of month');
```

This construct is quite hard to decipher. Generally, when its use is permitted, the case statement results in much more readable code than the nested if does. However, if the selection from a list of alternatives depends on the value of a nonordinal variable (such as a value of type real or string) or on a comparison of two expressions, the nested if must be used.

More on Error Trapping   Good prompts for input values should be used to make clear what type of input is intended.

Question   What would be output by the following case statement for each of the following values of letter:

(a) letter = 'X'   (b) letter = 'R'   (c) letter = 'r'

```
program drill;
var letter: char;
begin
  write ('enter a capital letter ');
  readln (letter);
  case letter of
    'C','O','S','U','Q'     : writeln ('All curves');
    'B','D','G','J','P','R' : writeln ('Curves and straight lines');
    else                      writeln ('All straight lines')
  end {case}
end.
```

Answer

(a)

> All straight lines

(b)

> Curves and straight lines

(c)

> All straight lines

This undesired printout resulted from the fact that `'r'` was a lowercase letter.

• • •

A First Look at Sets   A *set* is a collection of values of an ordinal type. One way to define it is by listing its elements within square brackets. You can test to see whether a value is a member of a set by using the reserved word *in*. Thus,

```
if ch in ['a', 'e', 'i', 'o', 'u'] then . . .
```

is equivalent to the more cumbersome

```
if (ch = 'a') or (ch = 'e') or (ch = 'i')
   or (ch = 'o') or (ch = 'u') then . . .
```

Similarly, the subrange `['a'..'m']` could be used to specify the set consisting of the first half of the alphabet in lowercase.

• • • • • • • • • •

Question   Using set notation, rewrite the condition

```
until (letter >= 'A') and (letter <= 'Z')
```

Answer

```
until letter in ['A'..'Z']
```

Chapter 27 gives a fuller treatment of set syntax and its uses.   • • •

Compound Statements Within case   Any of the statements associated with the alternative lists may be compound statements. It could also be a subprogram call.

• • • • • • • • • •

Question   A student has taken two tests and his grade (A, B, C, D, or F) is assigned in the usual way (A for an average of at least 90, and so on.) The following `case` statement could be used to assign a grade and to update a counter for the number of students receiving an A. Fill in the value for the selector. (*Hint:* It cannot be of type `real`.)

```
avg := (score1 + score2) / 2;
case _____ of
  90..100 : begin
              grade := 'A';
              Acount := Acount + 1
            end;
  80..89 : grade := 'B';
  70..79 : grade := 'C';
  60..69 : grade := 'D';
  else     grade := 'F'
end;
```

Answer   `trunc (avg)`   • • •

• • • • • • • • •

Example   (Grade Point Average)   The external file `grades.dat` contains the grade and number of credits for each of the courses taken by John Doe. Assume it is formatted as follows:

```
A 3
C 4
  .
  .
  .
B 3
```

We wish to write a program to calculate John Doe's grade point average (GPA), where an A is worth 4 points, a B worth 3, a C worth 2, a D worth 1, and an F worth 0. Thus, the contribution of an A in a three-credit course is $4 * 3 = 12$, whereas the contribution of a C in a four-credit course is $2 * 4 = 8$.

To find the GPA, you must divide the total worth (that is, the sum of all the contributions) by the total number of credits.

```
program GPA;
{calculates a student's GPA}
var grade: char;
    credits, CreditTot, WorthTot: integer;
    GradeFile: text;

procedure UPDATE (grade: char;
                  credits: integer;
                  var CreditTot, WorthTot: integer);
  {updates the values of CreditTot and WorthTot}
  var value: integer;
```

```
    begin
      CreditTot := CreditTot + credits;
      case grade of
        'A' :   value := 4;
        'B' :   value := 3;
        'C' :   value := 2;
        'D' :   value := 1;
        'F' :   value := 0
      end; {case}
      WorthTot := WorthTot + value * credits
    end; {UPDATE}

begin {main}
  assign (GradeFile, 'grades.dat');
  reset (GradeFile);
  CreditTot := 0;
  WorthTot := 0;
  while not seekeof (GradeFile) do
    begin
      readln (GradeFile, grade, credits);
      UPDATE (grade, credits, CreditTot, WorthTot)
    end;
  if CreditTot > 0
    then writeln ('GPA is ', WorthTot / CreditTot: 5: 2)
    else writeln ('No courses taken');
  close (GradeFile)
end.
```

• • •

Menu-Driven Programs   A *menu* is a list of possible options for the user to choose from. In the next program, a `case` statement within a `repeat-until` loop allows the user to keep selecting from the menu until he or she wishes to quit. The actual work of each of the choices is farmed out to procedures.

```
program convert;
{allows user to convert from Fahrenheit to Celsius}
{or from Celsius to Fahrenheit}
var choice: integer;

procedure PRINTMENU;
  begin
```

```
    writeln ('MENU OF CHOICES');
    writeln ('  1) Convert Celsius to Fahrenheit');
    writeln ('  2) Convert Fahrenheit to Celsius');
    writeln ('  3) Quit -- No more conversions')
  end; {PRINTMENU}

procedure CONVERT_TO_FAHR;
  {converts input Celsius temperature to Fahrenheit}
  var Cels: integer;
      Fahr: real;
  begin
    write ('enter degrees Celsius ');
    readln (Cels);
    Fahr := (Cels * 9/5) + 32;
    writeln (Cels, ' Celsius = ', Fahr:4:1, ' Fahrenheit')
  end; {CONVERT_TO_FAHR}

procedure CONVERT_TO_CELS;
  {converts input Fahrenheit temperature to Celsius}
  var Fahr: integer;
      Cels: real;
  begin
    write ('enter degrees Fahrenheit ');
    readln (Fahr);
    Cels := (Fahr - 32) * 5/9;
    writeln (Fahr, ' Fahrenheit = ', Cels:4:1, ' Celsius')
  end; {CONVERT_TO_CELS}

begin {main}
  repeat
    PRINTMENU;
    write ('enter choice ');
    readln (choice);
    case choice of
      1 : CONVERT_TO_FAHR;
      2 : CONVERT_TO_CELS;
      3 : {quit the loop}
      else writeln ('invalid choice -- choose again')
    end; {case}
    writeln
  until choice = 3
end.
```

Here is a typical run of this program.

```
MENU OF CHOICES
   1)  Convert Celsius to Fahrenheit
   2)  Convert Fahrenheit to Celsius
   3)  Quit -- No more conversions
enter choice 1
enter degrees Celsius 30
30 Celsius = 86.0 Fahrenheit

MENU OF CHOICES
   1)  Convert Celsius to Fahrenheit
   2)  Convert Fahrenheit to Celsius
   3)  Quit -- No more conversions
enter choice 3
```

REMARK

1. The `else` branch of the previous `case` statement provides robustness.

2. When `choice` = 3, no action is taken by the `case` statement. The `until` condition, however, causes loop exit. • • •

• • • • • • • • • EXERCISES

• •

1. What will the output be for the following segment when the values for the variables are as given?

```
if (age > 20) and (weight > 150) then
   if sex = 'f' then writeln ('Ha')
                else writeln ('Hi')
else
   writeln ('Ho');
```

(a) age = 25, weight = 160, sex = 'm'

(b) age = 30, weight = 140, sex = 'f'

(c) age = 21, weight = 170, sex = 'f'

(d) age = 18, weight = 150, sex = 'm'

2. What will the output be for the following program segment?

```
letter := 'A';
for ch := 'a' to 'f' do
  begin
    case ch of
      'a', 'c': letter := upcase (ch);
      'b', 'd': letter := ch;
      else      writeln ('else')
    end; {case}
    writeln (ch, ' ', letter)
  end; {for}
```

3. Write a procedure that determines and prints what sort of honors a person graduates with, based on his or her GPA and the following scheme:

   GPA of at least 3.75 receives a Summa.

   GPA of at least 3.50 but under 3.75 receives a Magna.

   GPA of at least 3.25 but under 3.50 receives a Cum.

   GPA of under 3.25 receives No Honors.

4. Which of the following data types cannot be used as a selector in a case statement: integer, real, string, char?

5. Find the two syntax errors in the following case statement:

```
case selector of
  begin
     1,2  : writeln ('A');
     3,4  : writeln ('B');
     else : writeln ('C')
  end;
```

6. Write a program that will print each of the 26 capital letters of the alphabet with its classification—All curves, Curves and straight lines, or All straight lines—along side of it.

7. Write a procedure that converts a date given numerically into a date with the month written out and then prints the result. Thus, if the procedure received the values 5, 30, and 76, it should print

```
May 30, 1976
```

8. For a year to be a leap year, it must be divisible by 4. However, this by itself does not guarantee that the year is a leap year because some years

that are divisible by 4 are not leap years. (For example, the year 2100 is not a leap year.) The complete rule is:

> For a year to be a leap year it must be (divisible by 4) and (either (not divisible by 100) or (divisible by 400)).

Write code to determine whether a year is a leap year. (Do you need to use multiway selection?)

Longer Assignments

9. (a) Write a procedure that receives as parameters an employee's hourly rate (`real`) and hours worked (`integer`) and then calculates and prints the employee's salary for the week. An employee receives the regular rate for the first 40 hours, 1.5 times the regular rate (time and a half) for each hour over 40 hours (but not over 50), and 2 times the regular rate (double overtime) for each hour over 50 hours. For example, an employee working 51 hours at a rate of $10/hr would earn $570.

   (b) Modify the procedure so that it returns the salary earned to the main program.

10. Write a program that does the following 10 times:

    (a) Asks the user to enter a capital letter. (The program should not continue until the user obeys.)

    (b) Calls a procedure to determine and output whether the letter is a `vowel` (a, e, i, o, u), `sometimes a vowel` (y), or a `nonvowel`.

11. (a) A text file contains the name and three test scores for each student in a class. Write a program that prints each student's name, letter grade, and average, according to the scheme in the letter grade example in Section 12.1.

    (b) Rewrite the program using a `case` statement to determine a student's letter grade.

    (c) Drop the lowest score when determining the student's average.

12. Write a program that asks the user to enter an integer from ~~20 to 99~~ 0 to 100 in numeric form. The program should output the equivalent number in words; for example, an input of `58` would result in an output of `fifty-eight`. [*Hint:* Generate each of the two words separately to avoid 80 alternatives in a `case` statement. (The code to convert a number into words can be written in fewer than 30 lines.)]

13. Write a program to determine an applicant's eligibility for a loan. Assume an external file contains the following data for each applicant: name, credit history (`'good'` or `'bad'`), amount of loan requested, annual salary, and the value of other property owned. The bank will consider

only applicants with a good credit rating. From those, it will accept only applicants with a total of at least six points. Points are earned as follows:

5 points if salary is at least 50 percent of loan.

3 points if salary is at least 25 percent but under 50 percent of loan.

1 point if salary is at least 10 percent but under 25 percent of loan.

5 points if other property value is at least twice the loan amount.

3 points if other property value is at least equal to but less than twice the loan amount.

14. A job applicant takes five different tests. (The maximum possible score on each test is 10.) An applicant is classified as follows:

Hired if at least two of the test scores are at least 9.

Put on File if not Hired but all test scores are at least 7.

Rejected otherwise.

Write an interactive program that receives as input each applicant's name and five scores and then prints the name and classification for each applicant, as well as the total number of applicants classified as Hired.

* 15. The quadratic equation $ax^2 + bx + c = 0$ has three possible cases for its roots depending on the discriminant d, where $d = b^2 - 4ac$. Recall the quadratic formula

$$r = (-b \pm \sqrt{d}) / (2a)$$

Write an interactive program in which the user inputs the values of the coefficients a, b, and c. The output should first give one of the following three messages: HAS TWO REAL ROOTS, HAS ONE REAL ROOT, or HAS TWO IMAGINARY ROOTS; the output should then give what the root(s) are. Here are two typical outputs (for the equations $2x^2 - 7x + 3 = 0$ and $x^2 + x + 2 = 0$, respectively).

```
a = 2 b = 7 c = 3
HAS TWO REAL ROOTS
r1 = 3.00
r2 = 0.50
```

```
a = 1 b = 1 c = 2
HAS TWO IMAGINARY ROOTS
r1 = -0.50 + 1.32 * i
r2 = -0.50 - 1.32 * i
```

Hint: Have the main body calculate the discriminant, and then determine which of three possible procedures to call to complete the job.

16. Write a program that receives as input the lengths of the three sides of a triangle. The output should be either EQUILATERAL, ISOSCELES, or SCALENE. Do not assume that the lengths are in any particular order. Run your program using the inputs 222, 232, 223, 233, 234, 423.

17. Write a menu-driven program that allows the user to choose to find the area of either a circle, a rectangle, or a triangle or to quit. Have the menu redisplayed each time until the user chooses the quit option.
Hint:

Area of a circle $= \pi r^2$, where r is the radius.

Area of a rectangle $=$ width $\cdot$ height.

Area of a triangle in terms of its three sides is given by
$$\text{area} = \sqrt{s(s - a)(s - b)(s - c)}$$
where, a, b, and c are the lengths of the three sides and $s = (1/2)(a + b + c)$. Make sure you understand this formula by testing it by hand on the *right* triangle with sides 5, 12, and 13, which we know has area 30.

18. Write a menu-driven automatic teller program in which the user's bank balance is initialized to $1,000. The user should be allowed to perform as many transactions as he or she wishes from the menu

```
1. Deposit
2. Withdrawal
3. See balance
4. Quit
```

For the withdrawal option, the user should be prompted to select from the choices $50, $100, $200, and $500. (Do not allow the user to over-draw.) After each transaction, the program should print the current balance. On exiting, the program should print a courteous message.

19. In the two-person game of Rock-Scissors-Paper, each player selects either 'R', 'S', or 'P'. The winner is determined as follows: Rock breaks Scissors, Scissors cut Paper, Paper covers Rock. The game is a tie if both players select the same choice. Write a program that processes 10 games. (You may enter the players' inputs either interactively or using a file.) The first part of the output should give the results of each game. A typical result might be

```
S R Rock breaks Scissors. Player 2 wins
```

The second part of the output should say how many games were won by each player.

Lab Exercises   **DEBUGGING AND SYNTAX ERRORS**

Lab12-1.pas   Double Bonus
Lab12-2.pas   Triangle Classification

Chapter

13

FUNCTIONS

• • •   A function computes and returns a single result based on the value or values passed to it. We already considered a number of built-in Pascal functions such as `sqr`, `sqrt`, `abs`, and `round` in Chapter 5. In Pascal, to meet the particular needs of a given problem, you may also define your own functions as subprograms.

Programmer-defined functions, like procedures, enable the main body to farm out subtasks. The subtask should compute and return one value, nothing else. To create a programmer-defined function, you include a block of lines that gives the name of the function and the code defining what it does. This block is a declaration and is positioned after the `var` section.

After an introduction to functions, this chapter discusses the differences in syntax between functions and procedures and then gives some guidelines for deciding which to use in a given situation.   • • •

13.1 INTRODUCTION TO FUNCTIONS

Function Header   The header of a function must begin with the keyword `function`, followed by the name of the function and a parameter list in parentheses. Because the name of the function acts as a variable in which the function result is stored, the function type (the data type of the result of the function) must also be declared.

For example, if we were writing a cubing function called FINDCUBE, we could use the header

```
function FINDCUBE (n: longint): longint;
```

Notice that this header contains two declarations. First the value parameter n is declared to be of type longint. Second, the function FINDCUBE itself is also declared to be of type longint.

Here is a complete program using FINDCUBE.

```
program cubing;
{uses a programmer-defined cubing function}
var num, cube: longint;

function FINDCUBE (n: longint): longint;
   begin
      FINDCUBE := n * n * n
   end; {FINDCUBE}

begin {main}
   write ('enter an integer ');
   readln (num);
   cube := FINDCUBE (num);
   writeln (num, ' cubed is ', cube)
end.
```

Typical run.

```
enter an integer 12
12 cubed is 1728
```

Local Variables   In addition to value parameters, a function can have local variables and local constants. Memory for local variables and value parameters works exactly the same way in functions as it does in procedures.

Function Body   The body of a function should calculate the result and assign that result to the name of the function.

General Format of a Function

```
function fname (parameter list): ftype;   {function header}
   local declaration section
   begin
      calculate result                     {function}
      and assign it to fname               {body}
   end;
```

Function Calls   A function calculates and returns a single value. Unlike a procedure call, a function call cannot stand alone. Instead, a function call must be part of a statement that does something with the returned value. *Accordingly, a function call may appear wherever it is legal to use an expression.*

Three common uses of a function call are

1. On the right side of an assignment statement. For example, the main body of `program cubing` contains the call

```
cube := FINDCUBE (num);
```

2. As an item within a `writeln` statement. For example, the last two statements of the main body of `program cubing` could be replaced by

```
writeln (num, ' cubed is ', FINDCUBE (num));
```

3. As part of a boolean condition. For example, see Section 13.4.

13.2 RESTRICTION ON USE OF FUNCTION NAME

Within the function body, it is only under special circumstances that the name of a function will appear on the right side of an assignment statement. For example, the statement

```
FINDSUM := FINDSUM + i;
```

could not be used in the body of the following function FINDSUM. Until we discuss recursive functions in Chapter 25, you must *avoid using the function name on the right side of assignment statements in the function body.*

Example   In function FINDSUM, we declare a local variable `sum`, which is used to calculate the result. Then we assign the final value of `sum` to the function name, which is FINDSUM.

```
program drill;
var n: integer;

function FINDSUM (numb: integer): integer;
  {finds sum of first numb integers}
  var i, sum: integer;
  begin
    sum := 0;
```

```
      for i := 1 to numb do
         sum := sum + i;
      FINDSUM := sum
   end; {FINDSUM}

begin {main}
   writeln ('Will find the sum of the first n integers');
   write ('enter a value for n ');
   readln (n);
   writeln ('sum of first ', n, ' integers: ', FINDSUM(n))
end.
```

Power Function   In ordinary notation

$$3^4 = 3 * 3 * 3 * 3 = 81$$

Unfortunately, Turbo Pascal does not have a built-in exponentiation operator or power function.

We want to define a function POWER so that the call

```
   result := POWER (3, 4);
```

will return to result the value 81 (3^4).

• • • • • • • • •
Question   Fill in the blank so that POWER will calculate x^n for n positive.

```
function POWER (x: real; n: integer): real;
   {finds x to the n for n a positive integer}
   var i: integer;
       prod: real;
   begin
     prod := 1;
     for i := 1 to n do
       prod := _____;
   _____
   end;
```

Answer   Each time through the loop we want to multiply prod by x. (This will give n factors of x.) Further, we must assign the final value of prod to POWER. Thus, the lines with blanks should be

```
      prod := prod * x;
   POWER := prod
```

In Exercise 4, you are asked to write a revised `power` function that works for negative as well as positive powers.   • • •

13.3 FUNCTIONS VERSUS PROCEDURES

A common application of functions is to calculate a value by multiway selection. Accordingly, the body of a function might contain a `case` statement or a nested `if` statement.

Question

Suppose team jackets are priced at three different levels depending on the number purchased: $40 each for at least 10, $42 each for at least 5 but fewer than 10, and $44 each for fewer than 5.

`Program jackets` defines the function FINDCOST. Recall that the declaration of the function comes after the `var` section of the main body. Fill in the blanks.

```
program jackets;
{uses a function to find the cost of n jackets}
var n, cost: integer;

function FINDCOST (n: integer): integer;
   {finds cost of n jackets}
   begin
     if n >= 10 then
        FINDCOST := n * 40
     else if n >= 5 then

        _____

        else

        _____

   end; {FINDCOST}

begin {main}
   write ('enter number of jackets ');
   readln (n);
   _____;
   writeln (n, ' jackets cost $', cost)
end.
```

Answer   The three lines with missing parts are

```
FINDCOST := n * 42
FINDCOST := n * 44
cost := FINDCOST (n);
```
• • •

Function or Procedure?

There are some situations in which you can use either a function or a procedure. For example, `program jackets` could be done in two different ways.

It is instructive to contrast `program jackets` with a program that uses a procedure named `FINDCOST`. In the procedure version, the cost could be printed in the body of procedure `FINDCOST`. In this version, `cost` would be a local variable of the procedure, and the main body would contain the call

```
FINDCOST (n);
```

Note that in the procedure version, the calling statement stands alone, whereas in the function version, the function call is part of another statement, namely,

```
cost := FINDCOST (n);
```

More generally, if you want to compute and print a single value, you often have a choice. You could (1) compute and print the value in the body of the procedure or (2) use a function to compute the value and then pass the result to the main body for printing.

Style Rule for Functions

A function should be used only when the sole purpose of the subprogram is to return a single value. The body of a function should not read in any values or print anything (except during the debugging stage). The function header should not contain any variable parameters.

Thus, someone reading a program written in good Pascal style may assume that any function will do just one thing—calculate and return a single value.

• • • • • • • • • •
Example   In the following program, a person enters the month and day of his or her birthday. The output is the person's birth season—fall, winter, spring, or summer. The four solstices, September 21, December 21, March 21, and June 21, are used as the boundaries for the seasons. A typical run is

```
enter birth month and day numerically 12 19
You were born in fall
```

```
program birthseason;
{prints the birth season from an input birth month and day}
var month, day: integer;
    season: string;

function FINDSEASON (month, day: integer): string;
  {finds the season based on month and day}
  begin
    case month of
       1,2    : FINDSEASON := 'winter';
       4,5    : FINDSEASON := 'spring';
       7,8    : FINDSEASON := 'summer';
       10,11  : FINDSEASON := 'fall';
       3      : if day < 21 then FINDSEASON := 'winter'
                            else FINDSEASON := 'spring';
       6      : if day < 21 then FINDSEASON := 'spring'
                            else FINDSEASON := 'summer';
       9      : if day < 21 then FINDSEASON := 'summer'
                            else FINDSEASON := 'fall';
       12     : if day < 21 then FINDSEASON := 'fall'
                            else FINDSEASON := 'winter'
    end {case}
  end; {FINDSEASON}

begin {main}
  write ('enter birth month and day numerically ');
  readln (month, day);
  season := FINDSEASON (month, day);
  writeln ('You were born in ', season)
end.
```

REMARK   In Exercise 8, you are asked to write function FINDSEASON using a linear nested if statement with just four alternatives.   • • •

One Subprogram Calling Another   In general, the declaration of an identifier must precede its use. Accordingly, when one subprogram calls another we have the following rule:

> If subprogram A is to be called from within the body of subprogram B, then the declaration of subprogram A must precede the declaration of subprogram B.

In the next example, the value returned by FINDSEASON is needed as part of an updating task. Thus, it makes sense to return the calculated season to the body of a procedure instead of to the main body.

Example Effect of birth season on IQ. Given a data file where each line contains a person's birth month, day of birth, and IQ, we wish to calculate separately the average IQ for those people born in a warm season (spring or summer) and those born in a cold season (fall or winter). We will use the variables wsum and wcount for warm stats and csum and ccount for cold stats.

```
program IQ_Correlation;
{average IQ for people born in warm season vs cold season}
var  wsum, wcount, csum, ccount: integer;
     month, day, IQ: integer;
     season: string;
     BirthFile: text;

     function FINDSEASON
        as before - goes here

procedure UPDATE_STATS (IQ: integer;
                            var wsum, wcount: integer;
                            var csum, ccount: integer);
   {updates appropriate summing and counting variables}
   var season: string;
   begin
     season := FINDSEASON (month, day);
     if (season = 'spring') or (season = 'summer') then
        begin
           wsum := wsum + IQ;
           wcount := wcount + 1
        end {then}
     else
        begin
           csum := csum + IQ;
           ccount := ccount + 1
        end {else}
   end; {UPDATE_STATS}

begin {main}
   assign (BirthFile, 'birth.dat');
   reset (BirthFile);
   wsum := 0;   wcount := 0;   csum := 0;   ccount := 0;
   while not seekeof (BirthFile) do
      begin
         readln (BirthFile, month, day, IQ);
         UPDATE_STATS (IQ, wsum, wcount, csum, ccount)
      end; {while}
```

```
   if wcount > 0
      then writeln ('Warm IQ average ', wsum / wcount:6:1)
      else writeln ('No warm statistics');
   if ccount > 0
      then writeln ('Cold IQ average ', csum / ccount:6:1)
      else writeln ('No cold statistics');
   close (Birthfile)
end.
```

Structure Chart for Program IQ_Correlation

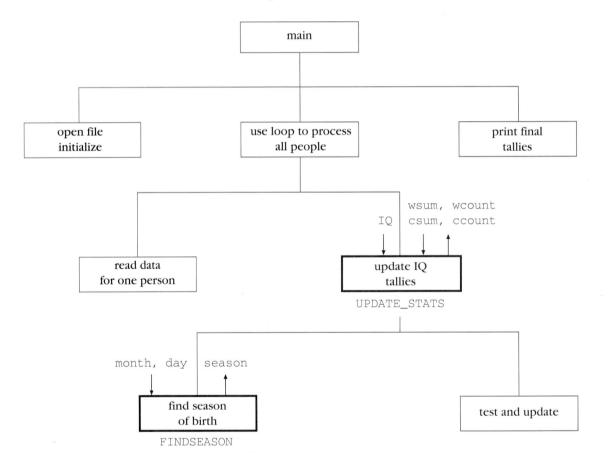

REMARK Note how we treat the function FINDSEASON in this structure chart. The variable, season, that receives FINDSEASON's calculated value gets just an up arrow. • • •

• • • • • • • • • •

Question

1. Look at the body of the previous program. Could the function FIND-SEASON have been replaced by an equivalent procedure? If so, would season have been a parameter? If so, what kind of parameter?

2. Could procedure UPDATE_STATS be replaced by an equivalent function?

Answer

1. A function can always be replaced with a procedure. Note that since season is needed further along in the main body (by UPDATE_STATS), a procedure version of FINDSEASON would require that season be a *variable* parameter.

2. No. Since UPDATE_STATS does not return a single value (it returns four updated values), UPDATE_STATS should be done as a procedure and not as a function. • • •

REMARK

1. We didn't really need the full strength of FINDSEASON. We could have written the program by devising a new function to return the value warm or cold. There is, however, an advantage to reusing code that has already been written and tested—it can save time and trouble.

2. Chapter 23 discusses *units,* which allow you to save a block of code so that it can be called by any program. Units enable you to build up a library of "external subprograms." • • •

Approximate Area (Engineering Application) The area under a curve $y = f(x)$ over the interval $[a,b]$ can be approximated by subdividing the interval $[a,b]$ into n equal subintervals and then constructing a rectangle over each subinterval (with the rectangle's base equal to the subinterval width and its height equal to the value of $f(x)$ at the midpoint of the subinterval). The sum of the areas of these n rectangles is an approximation of the area under the curve.

The following figure shows the exact area and the approximate area when $f(x) = x^2 + 1$ over the interval $[0,1]$ with $n = 3$.

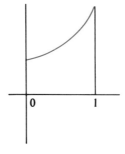
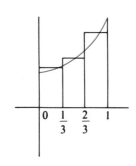

In program ApproxArea, the width of each rectangle is calculated by dividing the length of the interval by the number of rectangles to be constructed, that is,

```
width := (b - a) / n;
```

the height is equal to the value of function F at the midpoint of the rectangle.

```
program ApproxArea;
{finds the approximate area under the curve y = x * x + 1.}
{user specifies endpoints and number of rectangles}
{to change the function, the user must modify the program.}
var   area: real;
      a, b, n: integer;

function F (x: real): real;
  {defines the function x * x + 1}
  begin
    F := (x * x) + 1
  end; {F}

function FINDAREA (a, b, n: integer): real;
  {finds approximate area using n rectangles}
  var   i: integer;
        width, midpoint, height, Asum: real;
  begin
    width := (b - a) / n;
    Asum := 0;
    midpoint := a + width / 2;    {midpt of first subinterval}
    for i := 1 to n do
      begin
        height := F(midpoint);
        Asum := Asum + height * width;
        midpoint := midpoint + width    {next midpoint}
      end; {for}
    FINDAREA := Asum
  end; {FINDAREA}

begin {main}
  write ('enter endpts for interval and number of rectangles ');
  readln (a, b, n);
  area := FINDAREA (a, b, n);
  writeln ('Approximate area is ', area: 7: 4)
end.
```

REMARK   Note that function FINDAREA called function F.   • • •

13.4 BOOLEAN VARIABLES AND BOOLEAN-VALUED FUNCTIONS

The data type `boolean` has two values: `true` and `false`. In program `BooleanDrill`, note that `OfAge` is declared to be a variable of type `boolean` by

```
var OfAge: boolean;
```

```
program BooleanDrill;
{drill program on boolean variables}
var OfAge: boolean;
    score, age: integer;

begin
  write ('enter your score and age ');
  readln (score, age);
  if age >= 18
    then OfAge := true
    else OfAge := false;
  if (score > 90) and (OfAge)
    then writeln ('Hire')
    else writeln ('Reject')
end.
```

REMARK   No single apostrophes are used in a boolean assignment such as

```
OfAge := true;
```

because `true` is not a string value—it is a boolean value.   • • •

Second Method for Assigning a Boolean Value   In the preceding program, an `if-then-else` test was used to assign a value to `OfAge`. There is an alternative method that is shorter but slightly harder to read. The single assignment test on the left is equivalent to the `if-then-else` test on the right.

```
OfAge := age >= 18;
```

```
if age >= 18
  then OfAge := TRUE
  else OfAge := FALSE;
```

In this case, the expression `age >= 18` is evaluated, and its value (`TRUE` or `FALSE`) is assigned to `OfAge`.

The general format for this boolean assignment method is

{boolean variable} := *{boolean expression}*

Boolean-Valued Functions   It can be useful to create boolean-valued functions.

• • • • • • • • • •

Example   Suppose that each employee of a firm has been given a three-digit ID number and that each ID number has the following property:

hundreds digit = tens digit + ones digit

Our program will ask each person seeking entrance to the firm's grounds for his or her ID number. After checking whether this number has the required property, the program either should allow the person to enter or, if the ID number is invalid, should sound an alarm and call for the person's arrest. Here is the top down design using the boolean-valued function TESTS_OK.

```
get IDnumber
if TESTS_OK (IDnumber)
   then writeln ('You may enter')
   else writeln (chr (7), 'You are under arrest')
```

```
program IDtest;
{uses a function to test for valid ID number}
var IDnumber: integer;

function TESTS_OK (number: integer): boolean;
  {for 3 digit number: returns the
     value true if hundreds digit = ones + tens}
  var ones, tens, hundreds: integer;
  begin
    ones := number mod 10;
    tens := (number div 10) mod 10;
    hundreds := number div 100;
    if hundreds = ones + tens
      then TESTS_OK := true
      else TESTS_OK := false
  end; {TESTS_OK}

begin {main}
  write ('enter your 3 digit ID number ');
  readln (IDnumber);
  if TESTS_OK (IDnumber)
    then writeln ('You may enter')
    else writeln (chr(7), 'You are under arrest')
end.
```

• • •

Prime Numbers   An integer greater than 1 is called *prime* if its only positive divisors are 1 and itself. Thus, for example, the numbers 2, 3, 5, 7, and 11 are primes; 4 is not a prime because it is divisible by 2. Number theory tells us that if an integer n has no integer divisors between 2 and $\sqrt{n}$, then we can conclude that n is prime. Thus, to test whether 67 is prime, it is sufficient to check for a divisor between 2 and `round (sqrt (67))` (that is, between 2 and 8).

Example   (All Primes Between 100 and 200)   We want to write a program to produce as output

```
The primes between 100 and 200 are
101 103 107 113 127 .  .  .
```

The hard part is determining whether an odd integer is prime. We will use a *boolean-valued function* IS_ODDPRIME to determine whether or not an odd integer $n >= 3$ is prime. Note that we also use a *boolean local variable*, FoundDivisor.

Here is the pseudocode for function IS_ODDPRIME.

We want to keep testing possible odd divisors, d, between 3 and $\sqrt{n}$ until we either find a divisor or d exceeds $\sqrt{n}$. We will use a `repeat-until` loop.

```
FoundDivisor := false {initialize}
d := 1;
repeat
 d := d + 2; {3 is first possible divisor}
 if d divides n then FoundDivisor := true
until (FoundDivisor) or (d > √n);
if-then-else test to assign value to IS_ODDPRIME
```

Here is the complete program.

```
program primes;
{prints all the prime numbers between 100 and 200}
var n: integer;

function IS_ODDPRIME (n: integer): boolean;
  {will test whether an odd integer 3 or greater is prime}
  var d, upper: integer;
      FoundDivisor: boolean;
  begin
    upper := round (sqrt(n));
    FoundDivisor := false;
    d := 1;
```

```
      repeat
         d := d + 2;
         if n mod d = 0 then FoundDivisor := true
      until (FoundDivisor) or (d >= upper);
      if FoundDivisor
         then IS_ODDPRIME := false
         else IS_ODDPRIME := true
   end; {IS_ODDPRIME}

begin {main}
   writeln ('The primes between 100 and 200 are ');
   n := 101;
   while n <= 200 do
      begin
         if IS_ODDPRIME (n) then write (n, ' ');
         n := n + 2
      end;
   writeln
end.
```

In Exercise 9, you are asked to rewrite this program so that, after 10 primes have been output on a line, the output drops to the next one.

EXERCISES

1. What is the error in the following program fragment from the main body of a program that uses a function FINDSUM?

```
write ('enter an integer ');
readln (n);
FINDSUM (n);
```

2. **(a)** Would it be advisable to have the following statement in the body of a function FINDPROD? Explain.

```
FINDPROD := FINDPROD * i;
```

(b) Is it merely bad style to have a writeln or readln statement in the body of a function, or is it an actual syntax error?

3. What will the output be for the following programs?

(a)

```
program drill;
  var i: integer;

function TEST (n: integer): integer;
  var a, b: integer;
  begin
    a := n;
    b := n * n - 1;
    if (a > b) and (a <= 2)
        then TEST := 1
        else TEST := 2
  end; {TEST}

begin {main}
  for i := 1 to 3 do
    begin
      writeln ('i equals ', i);
      if TEST (i) = 1
        then writeln ('one')
        else writeln ('two');
      writeln ('three')
    end; {for}
  writeln ('four')
end.
```

(b)

```
program func;
var a, b, c: integer;

function JOB (x, y: integer): integer;
  var w, i: integer;
  begin
    w := 1;
    for i := 1 to y do
      w := w * x;
    JOB := w
  end; {JOB}

begin {main}
  a := 3;
  b := 4;
  c := JOB (a, b);
  writeln (a, ' ', b, ' ', c);
  b := JOB (b, a);
  writeln (a, ' ', b, ' ', c);
```

```
  a := JOB (a, a);
  writeln (a, ' ', b, ' ', c)
end.
```

(c)
```
program drill;

function WHAT (a, b: integer): integer;
  var sum: integer;
  begin
    sum := 0;
    while sum <= b do
      sum := sum + a;
    WHAT := b - sum + a
  end; {WHAT}

begin
  writeln ( WHAT(4, 15) );
  writeln ( WHAT(7, 40) );
  writeln ( WHAT(40, 7) );
  writeln ( WHAT(9, 184) );
end.
```

4. Modify the function POWER from Section 13.2 so that it can handle positive and negative numbers as well as zero.

* 5. (a) The precalculus fact $b^x = e^{x \log b}$ can be used as an alternative method of raising a base to a power. Use this fact to assign 5^n to an integer variable.

(b) What complications arise when the base is negative (for example, $(-5)^n$)?

6. (a) Write a function that will receive two integer parameters m and n, with m < n. The function should return the sum

$$\frac{1}{m} + \frac{1}{m+1} + \frac{1}{m+2} + \cdots + \frac{1}{n}$$

(b) Write a calling statement for the preceding function that will have the computer print the result of the sum

$$\frac{1}{101} + \frac{1}{102} + \cdots + \frac{1}{500}$$

to four decimal places.

7. Write a function that will receive three integer values representing scores.

The function should return the string value 'Good' for an average of at least 85, 'Fair' for an average of at least 70 but under 85, or 'Poor' for an average under 70.

8. Rewrite the function FINDSEASON from Section 13.3 so that it uses a linear nested if statement with four alternatives instead of a case statement.

9. Modify program primes, which prints the primes between 100 and 200, so that the printing carriage drops to the next line after 10 primes have been printed on a line. (See Section 13.4 for program primes.)

Longer Assignments

10. The following scheme is used to compute the monthly sales commission earned by an employee of Houses-R-Us Realtors:

Sales Total	Commission
Up to $100,000	1% of sales total
$100,000–$200,000	1% of first $100,000 plus 2% of anything over $100,000
Over $200,000	1% of first $100,000 plus 2% of next $100,000 plus 3% of anything over $300,000

(a) Write a function that computes a salesperson's monthly commission based on his or her sales total.

(b) Write a program that uses this function to process a group of employees.

(c) Write the program so that it will keep track of how many employees earned a commission of at least $2,000.

11. Write a function that calculates and returns a person's age in years based on his or her birthdate and the current date. The function should have six integer parameters: the month, day, and year of the person's birthdate and the current month, day, and year. For example, a person born 5/30/68 would be 21 years old on 5/27/90.

* 12. An external file contains the name, date of birth, and amount of commission for each of the employees of ARCO in the following form:

```
Smith
8   15   1964     200.00
```

Write a program that will first print each employee's name, age, and commission, and then print the commission totals for those employees who are under 30 years old and those employees who are at least 30 years old. Have the *user input the current date.*

Design your program so that the loop processing an employee contains a call to (a) a procedure GETDATA; (b) a function FINDAGE; and (c) a procedure UPDATE to update commission totals.

13. Write an interactive program to operate a horoscope booth at a carnival. Each time the mystic seer types in a customer's date of birth (for example, 12 5 1972), the computer will echo print on paper the date of birth followed by a horoscope based on the following scheme:

> If the birth year is divisible by four the horoscope number is 1. Otherwise, the horoscope number depends on the quarter of the year in which the person was born. For the first and third quarters, the horoscope number is year mod 3 + 1 and for the second and fourth quarters, the horoscope number is year mod 3 + 2.

Horoscope 1 is:

> The recent full moon has created tensions. Do not undertake any new projects this week.

You make up horoscopes for 2, 3, and 4.

Write the program so that when the mystic seer enters 0 0 0 at the end of the day, the computer prints how many times each horoscope was issued. Design your program so that it uses a function FIND_NUM to calculate a person's horoscope number and a procedure PRINT_HOR to print a horoscope and update the appropriate counter.

* 14. (a) Modify program ApproxArea of Section 13.3 so that it also prints a second calculation for the approximate area over each subinterval. Make the rectangle's height the average of F at the left and right endpoints of the subinterval.

   (b) Further revise your program so that if these two approximations differ by more than .005, then the number of subintervals will be doubled and two new approximations calculated. This process should be repeated until the two approximations differ by .005 or less.

* 15. $x^2 - x + 41$ is a famous prime-generating formula. For $x = 1$, the formula gives 41, which is prime; $x = 2$ gives 43; $x = 3$ gives 47. Write a program to find the smallest positive integer x for which the formula fails to give a prime. The program should print a factorization for the number generated by that x.

* 16. An integer n is called *perfect* if n is equal to the sum of all its divisors other than itself. For example, 6 is perfect since $6 = 1 + 2 + 3$. Write a program that will print the first three perfect numbers. Design your program so that the main body contains a repeat-until loop within which a boolean-valued function IS_PERFECT is called.

* *17.* An integer *n* is called *abundant* if *n* is less than the sum of its divisors other than itself. For example, 12 is abundant since 12 < 1 + 2 + 3 + 4 + 6. Odd abundant numbers are scarce. Write a program that will find and print all odd abundant numbers less than 1000. (This program may take a few minutes to run.)

* *

Lab Exercises   **DEBUGGING AND SYNTAX ERRORS**

Lab13-1.pas   Syntax Errors
Lab13-2.pas   Factorial Function
Lab13-3.pas   Finding Number of Minutes

* *

Chapter

14

SIMULATION

• • • Simulation involves attempting to produce a serviceable *imitation* of real events. Using simulation to get an estimate for some quantity, such as a probability of some event or an area under a curve, is called using ***Monte Carlo*** methods.

For example, when a coin is flipped 100 times, what is the probability that there will be at least one streak of five or more consecutive heads? Do you think it is more than 20 percent? You can get a very good estimate for this probability by performing 5,000 times the experiment of flipping a coin 100 times, and then taking the ratio of successes (the number of experiments in which you got at least 5 consecutive heads) divided by 5,000. Note that doing this involves 500,000 coin flips (5,000 × 100). Actually, flipping a coin that many times would take you several months of flipping. A much better idea is to have the computer simulate the 500,000 flips, which can be done in a matter of seconds.

In business and industry, computer simulation is used for more serious purposes, ranging from various types of forecasting to the testing of specifications for new industrial designs. Obviously, it is much quicker, less expensive, and generally more desirable to find out through computer simulation that a new design for an airplane wing is faulty than to build planes and have them crash.

The key to computer simulation in Turbo Pascal is the `random` function. With `random`, we can cause simulated events to occur with approximately the same frequencies as they would in the real world. • • •

14.1 THE FUNCTION RANDOM

There are two ways of using the function `random` in simulation programs.

1. Using `random` without an argument generates a random decimal between 0 and 1. This method can be used to simulate an event that has a decimal probability.

2. Using `random` with an argument generates a random integer from a list of integers. For example, `random (10)` returns a random integer from the list 0, 1, 2, . . . , 9. This method can be used to simulate an event in which there are a certain number of equally likely outcomes.

14.2   RANDOM WITHOUT AN ARGUMENT

Each time the function `random` is called in a program, the function returns a new random decimal greater than or equal to 0 and less than 1.

Example   Consider the following `for` loop:

```
for i := 1 to 4 do
   writeln (random:12:10);
```

A typical output *might* be

```
0.0000000002
0.0313799395
0.8610484672
0.2025809651
```

Note that three of these four decimals are less than .5. Only the decimal beginning with .8 is bigger than .5.   • • •

Procedure randomize   On some systems, every time you boot up, the first value to be assigned to `random` is reset to the same fixed value, called the ***standard seed***. Because each subsequent value for `random` is calculated from the previous value, different runs of a program will then produce exactly the same output if each run takes place immediately after booting up. In order to ensure that a different sequence of random decimals is used in different runs of a program that includes the `random` function, you should include a call to the built-in procedure **randomize** at the beginning of your program body with the statement

```
randomize;
```

This statement will assign the seed a value based on the computer's internal clock. Henceforth, the beginning of any program using `random` will contain this statement.

• • • • • • • • •

Example   The following program will simulate flipping a coin 10 times, displaying the result of each flip, and then counting the number of heads (H) and tails (T). For example, a typical output *might* be

```
THHTTHTHHH
There were 6 heads and 4 tails.
```

In order to simulate a single flip of the coin, we use the test

```
if random < 0.5 then {heads}...
```

because there is a 50 percent chance that the outcome will be a head.
    Here is the program.

```
program coin;
{flips coin 10 times, counts heads and tails}
var heads, tails, flip: integer;
begin
  randomize;
  heads := 0;
  tails := 0;
  for flip := 1 to 10 do
    if random < 0.5 then {heads}
      begin
        write ('H');
        heads := heads + 1
      end
    else {tails}
      begin
        write ('T');
        tails := tails + 1
      end; {loop body was if-then-else}
  writeln;
  write ('There were ', heads, ' heads');
  writeln (' and ', tails, ' tails.')
end.
```

• • •

REMARK   Note that the empty `writeln` statement after the `for` loop sends the cursor to the beginning of the next line.   • • •

• • • • • • • • •

Problem   In straight-11 ping-pong, the first player to reach 11 points wins; the player need not be ahead by 2. Suppose that when Moe plays Curly, Moe has a .56

probability of winning any given point. We want to write a program that simulates one game between Moe and Curly, with the printout displaying a running score of the game. For example, a typical output might be

```
Moe Curly
  1    0
  2    0
  2    1
  .    .
  .    .
  .    .
 11    8
Moe won 11 - 8
```

Here is the pseudocode.

```
initialize counters
print table headers
repeat
    play a point
    output a current score
until the game is over
find out who won and print the final score
```

Here is the program for straight-11 ping-pong. Fill in the blanks.

```
program pingpong;
{play game of ping-pong, Moe vs. Curly}
var Mpts, Cpts: integer;

begin
  randomize;
  Mpts := 0;
  Cpts := 0;
  writeln ('Moe':3, 'Curly':8);
  repeat
    if _____
      then Mpts := Mpts + 1
      else Cpts := Cpts + 1;
    writeln (Mpts:3, Cpts:8)
  until (_____) or (_____);
  if Mpts = 11 then
    writeln ('Moe won ', Mpts, ' - ', Cpts)
  else {Cpts = 11}
    writeln ('Curly won ', Cpts, ' - ', Mpts)
end.
```

Answer The `if` condition should be

```
if random < 0.56
```

because Moe has a .56 probability of winning a point.
The `until` condition should be

```
until (Mpts = 11) or (Cpts = 11);
```

because the game is over if either Moe or Curly has 11 points.   • • •

14.3 RANDOM WITH AN ARGUMENT

Each time the function **random(n)** is called, where n is a positive integer, the computer randomly chooses one value from the list of integers 0, 1, 2, . . . , $n - 1$.

Example In the following program, the user is given 10 multiplication questions. For each question, the computer randomly chooses two factors from the list 0, 1, 2, . . . , 12. The program also displays the number of questions (out of 10) that the user answers correctly. Note that `random(13)` is used to generate a random number from the list of 13 possible choices (0 through 12).

Here is the program.

```
program MathTeacher;
{gives 10 multiplication questions}
{counts number answered correctly}
var factor1, factor2: integer;
    YourAns, CorrectAns: integer;
    count, question: integer;

begin
  randomize;
  count := 0;
  for question := 1 to 10 do
    begin
      factor1 := random(13);
      factor2 := random(13);
      write (factor1, ' x ', factor2, ' = ');
      readln (YourAns);
      CorrectAns := factor1 * factor2;
      if YourAns = CorrectAns then
```

```
      begin
        writeln ('You are right, Good Work!');
        count := count + 1
      end {then}
    else
      begin
        writeln ('Sorry, you are wrong.');
        writeln ('Correct answer is ', CorrectAns)
      end {else}
  end; {for}
  writeln ('You scored ', count, ' correct out of 10')
end.
```

Dice Rolling   Suppose we want to simulate rolling one six-sided die. We
need to generate an integer from the list 1, 2, 3, 4, 5, 6. The function
random(7) will not work because it will generate from the list 0, 1, 2, 3, 4,
5, 6. The expression to use to simulate rolling a single die is

```
random(6) + 1
```

random(6) will contribute an integer value from 0 to 5, and by adding on
1 we will get a value from the list 1 to 6.

If you wished to roll a pair of dice, noting what you got on each individual
die as well as the sum, you could use

```
die1 := random(6) + 1;
die2 := random(6) + 1;
dsum := die1 + die2;
```

If you were interested only in the sum of the two dice, you could use the
shorter code

```
dsum := random(6) + 1 + random(6) + 1;
```

or the even shorter code

```
dsum := random(6) + random(6) + 2;
```

• • • • • • • • •

Example   Program rolling will keep rolling a pair of dice until an 11 is rolled. The
output will give each individual roll, the roll in which the first 11 occurs, and
how many 7s have been rolled by that time. A typical output might be

```
6 8 7 4 10 7 9 7 11
First 11 was on roll 9
There were 3 sevens.
```

```
program rolling;
{keeps rolling until first 11, prints roll count}
{and number of sevens}
var dsum, rolls, sevens: integer;

begin
  randomize;
  rolls := 0;
  sevens := 0;
  repeat
    dsum := random(6) + 1 + random(6) + 1;
    rolls := rolls + 1;
    write (dsum, ' ');
    if dsum = 7 then sevens := sevens + 1
  until dsum = 11;
  writeln;
  writeln ('First 11 was on roll ', rolls);
  writeln ('There were ', sevens, ' sevens.')
end.
```

• • •

Lists Starting with Any Integer

```
random(n) + s
```

will generate from a list starting with the integer s and containing n numbers altogether. Thus, `random(5) + 50` will generate from the list starting with 50 and containing 5 numbers—that is, the list 50, 51, 52, 53, 54.

14.4   APPLICATIONS WITH PROCEDURES

• •

Five Hundred Games of Ping-Pong   Let us reconsider Moe and Curly's games of straight-11 ping-pong, where Moe has a .56 probability of winning any given point. What do you think is the probability that Moe will win a game? (It is not .56.)

One way to get an estimate for the probability that Moe will win a game is to simulate playing a large number of games and then see what fraction are won by Moe. We could take the program to play one game and run it 500 times, keeping track by hand of how many games Moe wins. A much better idea, however, is to write a program that will play 500 games on a single run. The format for the output should be

```
Moe won __ games
Curly won __ games
Estimate for Moe probability __
```

Here is the pseudocode. The counters MoeGames and CurGames will keep track of how many games are won by Moe and Curly, respectively. The procedure PLAYGAME will play one game.

```
initialize counters—MoeGames, CurGames
for game := 1 to 500 do
  PLAYGAME (MoeGames, CurGames)
output final values of MoeGames, CurGames
output fraction of games won by Moe
```

Here is the program.

```
program ping500;
{Play 500 games of ping pong between Moe and Curly}
var game, MoeGames, CurGames: integer;
    probability: real;

    ┌─────────────────────────────────────┐
    │ procedure PLAYGAME goes here         │
    └─────────────────────────────────────┘

begin {main}
  randomize;
  MoeGames := 0;
  CurGames := 0;
  for game := 1 to 500 do
    PLAYGAME (MoeGames, CurGames);
  writeln ('Moe won ', MoeGames, ' games');
  writeln ('Curly won ', CurGames, ' games');
  probability := MoeGames/500;
  writeln ('Estimate for Moe probability ', probability:4:2)
end.
```

Question The procedure PLAYGAME should play a game and then, depending on who wins it, add 1 to either MoeGames or CurGames. Thus, MoeGames and CurGames must be variable parameters. Before reading on, write procedure PLAYGAME. Pay particular attention to what local variables will be needed by this procedure.

Answer

```
procedure PLAYGAME (var MoeGames, CurGames: integer);
  {simulates a game of Ping-pong}
  var Mpts, Cpts: integer;
  begin
    Mpts := 0;
```

```
    Cpts := 0;
    repeat
      if random < 0.56
        then Mpts := Mpts + 1
        else Cpts := Cpts + 1
    until (Mpts = 11) or (Cpts = 11);
    if Mpts = 11
      then MoeGames := MoeGames + 1
      else CurGames := CurGames + 1
end; {PLAYGAME}
```

• • •

Example

(Craps) In the dice game craps, the rules are as follows:

1. If your first roll is 7 or 11, you win outright.

2. If your first roll is 2, 3, or 12, you lose outright.

3. If your first roll is any other number, that number becomes your point number and you keep rolling until you either roll a 7 or roll your point number again. If you roll your point number first, you win; if you roll a 7 first, you lose.

Here are four typical results for a program that simulates a game of craps.

```
8
Your point number is 8
3 9 12 5 8
You won
```

```
7
You won
```

```
9
Your point number is 9
5 8 3 4 12 7
You lost
```

```
3
You lost
```

Here is the program.

```
program craps;
{plays one game of craps}
var pointnum: integer;
    outcome: string;
```

```
procedure FIRSTROLL (var pointnum: integer;
                      var outcome: string);
  {simulates first roll}
  begin
    pointnum := random(6) + 1 + random(6) + 1;
    writeln (pointnum);
    case pointnum of
      7, 11    : outcome := 'won';
      2, 3, 12 : outcome := 'lost'
      else       outcome := 'continue'
    end {case}
  end; {FIRSTROLL}

procedure FINISHGAME (pointnum: integer;
                       var outcome: string);
  {keep rolling until game is over}
  var dsum: integer;
  begin
    writeln ('Your point number is ', pointnum);
    repeat
      dsum := random(6) + 1 + random(6) + 1;
      write (dsum, ' ');
      if dsum = 7 then outcome := 'lost';
      if dsum = pointnum then outcome := 'won'
    until outcome <> 'continue';
    writeln
  end; {FINISHGAME}

begin {main}
  randomize;
  FIRSTROLL (pointnum, outcome);
  if outcome = 'continue' then
    FINISHGAME (pointnum, outcome);
  writeln ('You ', outcome)
end.
```

• • •

• • • • • • • • • •   EXERCISES

• •

1. Approximately how many times would you expect the integer 4 to be output by the following loop?

```
for i := 1 to 100 do
   writeln (random(5) + 1);
```

2. Write a program that will simulate rolling a pair of dice 100 times and then count the number of times the sum is 8, 9, or at least 10. The output should be of the form

```
8 was rolled ____ times
9 was rolled ____ times
Sum was at least 10 ____ times
```

3. Modify program pingpong of Section 14.2 so that to win a player not only must have at least 11 points but also must be ahead by at least 2 points.

Longer Assignments

4. Write a program to simulate flipping a coin 100 times. The output should first give the final tallies for the numbers of heads and tails, respectively. Then it should give one of the following three messages: More Heads Than Tails, More Tails Than Heads, or Same Number of Heads and Tails.

5. Write a program that will keep rolling a pair of dice until the third 7 is rolled. In addition to each individual roll, the printout should give the roll on which the third 7 occurs and how many 8s have been rolled by then.

6. Write a program that will perform the following experiment 1,000 times:

> Flip a coin 10 times, and then check whether there were exactly 5 heads.

The program should output the final tally for the number of experiments in which exactly 5 heads were flipped. The program should then output an estimate of the probability of getting exactly 5 heads in 10 flips. **Do not print any Hs and Ts.**

7. (a) Write a program that will simulate 100 coin flips, outputting the individual Hs and Ts, and then will state whether there was at least one streak of five or consecutive heads.
   (*Caution:* On some printers to avoid overwriting, you may need to include a program statement like

   ```
   if flip mod 40 = 0 then writeln(lst);
   ```

   (b) Write a program to estimate the probability of getting at least one streak of five or more heads in 100 coin flips. Have your program repeat the experiment of 100 flips 1,000 times. **Do not print any Hs and Ts in part (b).**

8. Suppose that the Bulls and the Knicks are to compete in a playoff series—

the first team to win four games wins the series. Assuming that the Bulls have a .72 probability of winning any given game, write a program to simulate the playing of *one* such series.

* 9. Suppose that the Celtics and the Lakers are about to play in a championship series—the first team to win four games wins the series. As you probably know, playing at home is a big advantage. Let us suppose that the Celtics and the Lakers are evenly matched in that the home team has a 75 percent chance of winning any given game. Let us further suppose that games 1 and 2 are to be played in Boston; games 3, 4, and 5 (if necessary) are to be played in Los Angeles; games 6 and 7 (if necessary) are to be played in Boston. Write a program to simulate the playing of *one* championship series between these two teams.

* 10. Write a program to play 2,000 championship series between the Celtics and the Lakers, where the situation is as described in Exercise 9. The output should just give how many series were won by each team.

11. Write a program to generate a three-digit number in which all three digits are distinct.

* 12. In the game of Mastermind, the computer selects a three-digit number in which all three digits are distinct. (See Exercise 11.) The task of the human player is to keep making guesses until he or she guesses all three digits in proper order. Each time the human makes a guess, the computer tells the human

How many *hits* the player had, where one hit means getting one correct digit in its correct position

How many matches the player had, where one match means getting one correct digit in the wrong position

Thus, if the computer's number was 586 and the human guessed 856, the computer would respond with

```
1 hit(s)
2 match(es)
```

Write a program to play Mastermind. After the human finally gets the number, the computer should print the total number of guesses.

13. Write a program to simulate playing craps for $1 per game, where you start with $5 and keep playing until either you have doubled your money ($10) or you have nothing left. The final line of the output should state whether you have doubled your money or are broke.

* 14. (a) On a certain ACME Airlines flight, the seating capacity is 100 passengers. Since statistics have shown that each person with a ticket has a 20 percent probability of canceling at the last minute, the airline overbooks this flight by selling tickets for 120 seats. Assume that

ACME Airlines breaks even on that flight if the flight has exactly 95 passengers, loses $300 for each unfilled seat under 95, and makes $300 for each passenger over 95. Assume further that the airline loses $600 (the cost of a hotel room and damage to the airline's reputation) for each ticket holder who must be bumped. Write a program to simulate the bottom line for one such flight.

(b) Modify the program so that it computes the average bottom line for the simulation of 200 such flights (use a procedure ONE_FLIGHT). (*Optional:* Have this program also count how many of those flights bumped at least one ticket holder.)

(c) The airline wants to have a better idea of the best number of advance tickets to sell. (It might not be 120.) Write a program that will simulate 200 flights for each of the possible values for advance tickets sold (from 100 to 140) and determine which number gives the best average bottom line. (Section 18.1 might be helpful.)

15. Write a program that will find an approximation to three decimal places for the shaded area under the curve $y = x^2$ from $x = 0$ to $x = 1$. (See the figure.) The program should randomly generate (but not print) 5,000 points inside the square, counting how many of those points lie in the shaded area. The ratio of such points to 5,000 will give an approximation to the shaded area since that ratio should approximate the ratio of the shaded area to the area of the square (which is 1). (*Hint:* Use x := random; y := random; to generate a random point in the square. What inequality must x and y satisfy for (x,y) to be in the shaded area?)

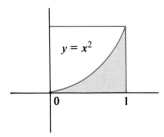

Lab Exercises   **DEBUGGING**

Lab14-1.pas   Rolling Pair of Dice 10 Times
Lab14-2.pas   Subtle Error
Lab14-3.pas   1,000 Games of Ping-Pong
Lab14-4.pas   1,000 Games of Crazy Eights

To get the real benefit of 14-3, try to do the debugging without comparing that program with the correct program from the chapter.

15

NESTED SUBPROGRAMS

• • • It is permissible for a subprogram to have subprograms contained within it. Such subprograms are called *nested subprograms.* • • •

15.1 ONE SUBPROGRAM CALLING ANOTHER

A general rule of Turbo Pascal is that an identifier must be declared prior to its use.

Nonnested Method In Chapter 13, you saw one method (without nesting) for subprogram A to call subprogram B. In that method, the declaration for subprogram B was given before that of subprogram A.

Nested Method A second method is to declare subprogram B within subprogram A—between the var section of A and the body of A. The nested method can be used when subprogram B is called only by subprogram A and not by any other part of the program.

• • • • • • • • •
Example At Christmas, an employee receives his or her usual wage (based on hours and pay rate, including a 50 percent higher rate for hours over 40), plus a bonus of $100, $50, or $25 (depending on whether the employee has worked at least 10 years, at least 5, or under 5). The following program uses nested subprograms to compute an employee's pay for the week before Christmas. Notice that procedure FINDPAY contains nested within it function BONUS.

```
program Xmas;
{finds an employee's pay}
var years, hours: integer;
    rate: real;

   procedure FINDPAY (years, hours: integer;
                         rate: real);
      {calculates base pay plus Xmas bonus}
      var basepay, Xmaspay: real;

      function BONUS (years: integer): integer;
         {finds bonus depending on years with the firm}
         begin {BONUS}
            if years >= 10 then
               BONUS := 100
            else if years >= 5 then
               BONUS := 50
            else {years < 5}
               BONUS := 25
         end; {BONUS}

      begin {FINDPAY}
         if hours <= 40 then
            basepay := hours * rate
         else
            basepay := (40 * rate) + (1.5 * rate) * (hours - 40);
         Xmaspay := basepay + BONUS (years);
         writeln ('$', Xmaspay:6:2)
      end; {FINDPAY}

begin {main}
   write ('enter years, hours, and rate ');
   readln (years, hours, rate);
   FINDPAY (years, hours, rate)
end.
```

• • •

REMARK Note that years is declared as a parameter of both FINDPAY
and BONUS, even though its value is used only in the body of BONUS. A value
for years should be passed to FINDPAY because FINDPAY, which was given
the task of finding the Christmas pay, should pass on to its subprogram BONUS
whatever information BONUS needs.   • • •

Nonlocal Variables Suppose that a subprogram named INNER is nested
within the subprogram OUTER. Any variable that is neither a local variable

nor a formal parameter of INNER is said to be **nonlocal** to INNER. A global variable is one kind of variable that is nonlocal to a subprogram. When there are nested subprograms, there may be other kinds as well.

• • • • • • • • • •

Question   In program Xmas, which variables are not global and yet are nonlocal to BONUS?

Answer   Both basepay and Xmaspay. They are local variables of FINDPAY and yet nonlocal to BONUS.   • • •

15.2 SCOPE OF AN IDENTIFIER
• •

The **scope** of an identifier means where it can be used (the portion of the program in which that identifier can be accessed). In Chapter 11, scope was discussed in the special case of when there is no nesting of subprograms.

Recall from Chapter 11 that the scope of a global identifier is the entire program except where same-name conflicts exist. For example, suppose that sum is declared both as a global variable and as a local variable of the subprogram SUB. In this case, the scope of the global variable sum is not the entire program because references to sum within SUB will refer to the local variable.

Recall also from Chapter 11 that a variable declared in subprogram P (either a local variable or a parameter) has as its scope just P. Since such a variable ceases to exist on exit from a call to subprogram P, it is an error to attempt to use that variable outside P.

The following general scope rule applies to any identifier regardless of whether there is nesting of subprograms:

> The scope of an identifier declared in the declaration section of program block B is all program block B, including any subprograms nested within B. This scope may be reduced as a result of same-name conflicts.

REMARK

1. By *subprograms nested within program block B* we mean not only subprograms of program block B but also subprograms nested within subprograms of block B.

2. An identifier declared in program block B is not accessible outside B. Attempting to use that identifier outside B will result in an error.

• • •

Scope Pictorially   To help determine the scope of identifiers, we draw a box around each of the subprograms. For nested subprograms, there will be boxes within boxes within boxes. The scope of an identifier in a declaration is the box in which that identifier is declared with the exception of any smaller "subboxes" in which an identifier with that same name is declared.

• • • • • • • • • •
Question   In the following program:

(a)   What is the scope of the variable y?

(b)   What is the scope of the global variable x?

(c)   What is the scope of the variable x declared in SUBJOB?

```
program scope;
var x: integer;

   procedure JOB (x: integer);
      var y: integer;

         procedure SUBJOB;
            var x: integer;
            begin {SUBJOB}
               x := 4;
               y := 4; {side effect}
               writeln (x, ' ', y)
            end; {SUBJOB}

      begin {JOB}
         x := 2;
         y := 2;
         SUBJOB;
         writeln (x, ' ', y)
      end; {JOB}

   procedure WORK;
      var x:integer;
      begin
         x := 100;
         writeln ('x in WORK - ', x)
      end; {WORK}

begin {main}
   x := 0;
   JOB (x);
   WORK;
   writeln (x)
end.
```

Answer

(a) Pictorially, the scope of y is the box around subprogram JOB. Thus, y can be used in the body of JOB *and* in the body of SUBJOB.

(b) The scope of the global variable x is not the entire box because of same-name conflicts—the scope of the global variable x is limited to just the main body since x is a parameter of JOB and a local variable of WORK.

(c) The scope of the variable x declared in SUBJOB is limited to SUBJOB itself. • • •

15.3 TRACING

When determining the scope of an identifier, we worked from the outside in. That is, we drew a box around the program block in which the identifier was declared, and this box included all smaller boxes contained within it. By contrast, you will see that when hand tracing a program for output, we tend to work from the inside out because of the way in which same-name conflicts are resolved.

Resolving Same-Name Conflicts To resolve same-name conflicts, the computer uses the innermost declaration that is applicable. For example, suppose the identifier sum is used in the body of subprogram B and sum is declared in at least two different places. To determine which declaration applies for the use of sum in subprogram B (which memory cell is being referred to), the compiler will first look for a declaration for sum within B. If it finds one, that is the declaration that applies. If not, it will look in the next smallest block properly containing subprogram B. If it finds a declaration of sum there, that is the one that applies. If not, the compiler will continue its search, moving up one level at a time through the nesting until the first occurrence of a declaration of sum.

Question What will be the output of program scope in Section 15.2?

Answer

```
4 4
2 4
x in WORK = 100
0
```

• • •

Side Effects Recall that a variable that is declared outside subprogram B and its nested subprograms is said to be nonlocal to subprogram B. A side effect is said to occur if a statement from subprogram B alters the value of a variable nonlocal to subprogram B. Just as we saw in Chapter 11, side effects are legal but dangerous because they can interfere with work done somewhere else in the program. (The safe way for subprogram B to communicate with variables nonlocal to it is through the use of parameters.)

REMARK   The statement in the body of SUBJOB

```
y := 4;
```

in the previous program was a side effect because it altered the value of a variable nonlocal to SUBJOB.   • • •

CAUTION   To avoid side effects, you should refrain from making free use of the scope rule. You should not include in the body of a nested subprogram any variables that are nonlocal to that subprogram.   • • •

15.4 GUESS THE COMPUTER'S NUMBER GAME

• • • • • • • • • •
Example   In a game of Guess the Computer's Number, the computer will randomly select an integer from 1 to 64. After each guess by the user, the computer will print either Too High, Too Low, or Correct. We want to write a program in which the user plays five games with the computer. After the fifth game, the program prints the average number of guesses the user needed to get the computer's number.

The pseudocode for the main body is

```
guesstotal = 0;
for game := 1 to 5 do
  writeln ('Game ', game);
    PLAYGAME will play a game
              and then increase guesstotal
              by however many guesses it took
find average number of guesses
writeln ('You averaged ', avg:4:1, ' guesses')
```

PLAYGAME includes a nested subprogram PROCESS_GUESS. Here is the pseudocode for PLAYGAME.

```
guesscount := 0 guesscount keeps track of the number
                    of guesses in this game
computer selects a mystery number
found := false found is a boolean variable
repeat
```

ask user for `guess`;
increase `guesscount` **by** 1
`PROCESS_GUESS` compares `guess` with mystery number and
                    prints appropriate message; changes
                    the value of `found` to `true` when human gets number
`until found`
write number of guesses it took

Here is the entire program.

```
program NumberGuessing;
{plays 5 games of Guess the Number}
{prints average number of guesses per game}
var game, guesstotal: integer;
    avg: real;

procedure PLAYGAME (var guesstotal: integer);
   {plays one game, updates guesstotal}
   var MysteryNum, guess, guesscount: integer;
       found: boolean;
   procedure PROCESS_GUESS (MysteryNum, guess: integer;
                                var found: boolean);
     begin {PROCESS_GUESS}
       if guess = MysteryNum then
         begin
           writeln ('You have found it');
           found := true
         end {then}
       else if guess > MysteryNum then
         writeln ('Your guess was too high')
       else {guess < MysteryNum}
         writeln ('Your guess was too low');
       writeln
     end; {PROCESS_GUESS}

   begin {PLAYGAME}
     guesscount := 0;
     MysteryNum := random (64) + 1;
     writeln ('The computer has picked a');
     writeln ('number from 1 to 64');
     found := false;
     repeat
       write ('What is your guess? ');
       readln (guess);
       guesscount := guesscount + 1;
       PROCESS_GUESS (MysteryNum, guess, found)
```

```
      until found;
      guesstotal := guesstotal + guesscount;
      writeln ('You got it in ', guesscount, ' guesses');
      writeln
   end; {PLAYGAME}

begin {main}
   randomize;
   guesstotal := 0;
   for game := 1 to 5 do
      begin
         writeln ('Game ', game, ':');
         PLAYGAME (guesstotal)
      end;
   avg := guesstotal / 5;
   writeln ('You averaged ', avg:4:1, ' guesses')
end.
```

• • •

• • • • • • • • • • **EXERCISES**

• •

1. Under what circumstances would you have a nonlocal variable that was not a global variable?

2. Suppose that a statement in the defining body of procedure A calls procedure B, but the procedures are not nested. Does it matter in which order the two procedures are declared?

3. Suppose that in program scope of Section 15.2, the declaration of x as a local variable of procedure SUBJOB were eliminated. What would the program output be?

4. Suppose that in program scope of Section 15.2, the extra statement y := 99; were inserted as the last line of the body of procedure WORK. What would the program output be?

5. Suppose that in program scope of Section 15.2, every occurrence of x in procedure WORK were replaced by y, including in the var section. What would the program output be?

6. Suppose that program A contains no procedure calls other than those shown in the diagram. Give the order in which the procedures will be called.

```
program A;

   procedure B;

      procedure C;
      ..

      begin
         C;
         ...
      end;

   procedure D;
      begin
         ...
         B;
         ...
      end;

   begin
      B;
      D;
   end.
```

Longer Assignments

7. Write a program for SDB Television Company. The program will ask the user to input how many TV sets are needed. The procedure FIND_COST will then be called. TV sets are sold to the retailer for $250. If the retailer buys more than 1,000 units, each additional set is discounted 10 percent. For each set over 5,000, the discount is 20 percent. If the retailer orders 5,500 TV sets, he pays full price for the first 1,000, gets a 10 percent discount on the next 4,000, and a 20 percent discount on the next 500. The nested function FIND_DISCOUNT will return the amount of money the retailer saves on discounts. FIND_COST will print the number of sets ordered, the cost not including discounts, the amount of the discount, and the final discounted cost.

8. A file contains information on students taking Computers 188. Each data group contains a student's name, exam average in Computers 188, and major. For example, a typical data group might contain

   Smith, John   88.3   COMPUTERS

Write a program to recommend the next computer course to be taken by each student based on the following:

Grade	Major	Next Course
A	Computers	Computers 212
B	Computers	Computers 201
at least B	not Computers	Computers 199
under B	any major	English 205

Have the main body call a procedure NEXT_COURSE, which contains the nested subprogram FINDGRADE where the grades A, B, C, D, and F are assigned as usual. (*Hint:* The table for recommending the next course contains four mutually exclusive conditions.)

9. Assume that you have a file containing each employee's name, hours worked, hourly rate, and number of dependents. Write a program that calls procedures GETDATA and SALARY. Procedure GETDATA should read the file; procedure SALARY should calculate gross pay and then should calculate net pay by calling the nested function TAX. TAX must use the following formulas:

Taxable income Grosspay reduced by $20 for each dependent.

Tax is 10 percent of taxable income if taxable income $<= 300$; otherwise, it is $30 + 20 percent of taxable income over $300.

Lab Exercises   **DEBUGGING AND SYNTAX ERRORS**

Lab15-1.pas   Syntax Error

Lab15-2.pas   Surprising Output

16

PROGRAMMER-DEFINED DATA TYPES

• • • Turbo Pascal allows the programmer to declare identifier names for constructed data types in a **type** section. Three common uses of this feature are (1) complying with a technical restriction on procedure parameter declarations, (2) declaring subrange types, and (3) declaring enumerated types. • • •

16.1 TYPE SECTION AND A PROCEDURE TECHNICALITY

Note the following technical restriction on procedure parameter declarations:

> Within a procedure header, each data type name must be a legal identifier. (Recall that legal identifiers may contain only letters, digits, and the underbar, and must start with a letter.)

Question   Which procedure header is illegal?

```
(a)  procedure HELLO (name: string[15]; sex: char);
(b)  procedure HELLO (name: string; sex: char);
```

Answer   The header in (a) is illegal since `string[15]` is not a legal identifier.

• • •

A Type Declaration Section   How then can we use a variable of type `string[15]` as a parameter? The correct way is to define a new global data type identifier and then to use that identifier in the procedure header.

A global type identifier must be defined in a `type` section that is positioned before the main `var` section and after the `const` section. An equal sign (=) is always used instead of a colon (:) for defining identifiers in the `type` section. For example, if we wished to declare a procedure parameter of type `string[15]` for the procedure HELLO, we could have

```
program drill;
type
  namestr = string[15];
var
  name: namestr;

procedure HELLO (name: namestr; sex: char);
 .
 .
 .
```

16.2 SUBRANGE TYPES

It is possible to declare variables with a specific ordinal subrange directly in the `var` section by using the double-dot notation (introduced in Section 12.3). For example,

```
var score: 0..100;
    CapLet: 'A'..'Z';
```

These variables could also be declared by first defining the type identifiers.

```
type
  ScoreRange = 0..100;
  CapLetters = 'A'..'Z';
var
  score: ScoreRange;
  CapLet: CapLetters;
```

REMARK   Defining a type identifier in a `type` section would be mandatory if you needed to declare a parameter with a subrange type.   • • •

Reasons for Making Subrange Declarations

1. Subranges help clarify the purpose of certain variables.

2. Subranges permit the computer to detect an out-of-range error when an assignment statement is used to assign to a variable a value that is unreasonable (that is, a value outside a defined range). See the discussion on {$R+}.

***The Directive {$R+}*** You can increase the capacity of Turbo Pascal to detect out-of-range errors by placing the compiler directive **{$R+}** above the program header. This will cause the computer to terminate the program run with a run-time error message for certain kinds of out-of-range errors. For example,

```
{$R+}
program drill;
var score: 0..100;
begin
  score := 99;
  score := score + 5;
  .
  .
```

The {$R+} would terminate this program run with the run-time error message

```
Error 201: Range check error
```

Without the {$R+}, assigning score the value 104 by score := score + 5 would not cause an error.

Further Features of Range Checking

1. Including {$R+} will not detect most kinds of out-of-range errors in readln statements. For example, if the user were to enter 105 for

   ```
   readln (score)
   ```

   this would *not* produce an error.

2. Including the directive {$R+} will cause a program to run more slowly. Thus, {$R+} is often included during the testing stage of a program and then removed after determining that there will not be any out-of-range errors.

16.3 ENUMERATED TYPES

• •

The ordinal types presented so far, integer, char, and boolean, are all built-in data types. Turbo Pascal also allows ***enumerated types,*** which are programmer-defined ordinal types. Enumerated types permit self-documenting code that increases the readability of a program.

Suppose, for example, that the price of theater tickets depends on the day of the week. The statement

```
case day of
     2, 3, 5, 6 : price := 6.00;
     1, 4, 7    : price := 8.00
end; {case}
```

is difficult to read because it is not obvious how much a ticket for a performance on, say, Wednesday costs. It would be easier to read if we were permitted to write the $8.00 alternative list as

```
'Sun', 'Wed', 'Sat' : price := 8.00    {illegal}
```

but unfortunately, it is illegal to use string values as case alternatives.

It is permissible, however, to use enumerated type values in case alternatives. If we declared an appropriate enumerated type and a variable day of that type, then we could use the more readable code

```
case day of
     Mon, Tue, Thu, Fri : price := 6.00;
     Sun, Wed, Sat      : price := 8.00
end; {case}
```

Syntax for Declaring Enumerated Types   An enumerated type is declared by listing its permissible values within parentheses. These values *should not be enclosed in quote marks* since they are not string values. For example, here are declarations for the enumerated types days and coins.

```
type days = (Sun, Mon, Tue, Wed, Thu, Fri, Sat);
     coins = (penny, nickel, dime, quarter);
var day1, day2, dayoff: days;
    coin: coins;
```

The variables day1, day2, and dayoff can be assigned values of type days. Thus, we could have

```
day1 := Wed;
day2 := Fri;
```

The ord Function   When the **ord** function is applied to an enumerated type value, it gives the position that the value occupies in the defining list, beginning with the value 0.

CAUTION   The first value in the defining list is considered to occupy position 0, the second value on the list position 1, and so on. Thus, with days defined as before,

```
ord (Sun) is 0
ord (Wed) is 3
```

• • •

Advantages of Enumerated Types   Since enumerated types are ordinal, they can be used

1. To provide additional documentation in

(a) `case` statements

(b) `for` loops; for example,

```
for day := Sun to Sat do
```

(c) array subscripts (see Chapter 17)

2. To perform arithmetic calculations on the positions of the values in the defining list. Thus, some coding tasks that are very tedious if strings are used can be performed easily with enumerated types. For example, suppose that `daystr1` and `daystr2` are string variables, and each has been assigned a value from the list of weekdays

```
'Mon', 'Tue', 'Wed', 'Thu', 'Fri'
```

Consider how tedious it would be to write a test to determine whether the value of `daystr2` is the day immediately following `daystr1`. We would need to use a test like

```
if   ((daystr1 = 'Mon') and (daystr2 = 'Tue'))
  or ((daystr1 = 'Tue') and (daystr2 = 'Wed'))
  or ((daystr1 = 'Wed') and (daystr2 = 'Thu'))
  or ((daystr1 = 'Thu') and (daystr2 = 'Fri'))
        then writeln ('It is the following day');
```

Using an enumerated type, we could have written

```
if ord (day2) - ord (day1) = 1 then
  writeln ('It is the following day');
```

Drawback of Enumerated Types Values of enumerated type variables cannot be output, nor can they be read in. Thus, the following statements are illegal:

```
writeln (day1);      {illegal}
readln (dayoff);     {illegal}
```

Because of these limitations, some programmers use enumerated types sparingly. If you need to output an enumerated type value, you must translate the value into a string. You might use a translation function like the one shown here.

```
function TRANSLATE (day: days): str3;
{translates an enumerated type value into string value}
begin
  case day of
    Sun : TRANSLATE := 'Sunday';
```

```
      Mon : TRANSLATE := 'Monday';
      Tue : TRANSLATE := 'Tuesday';
      Wed : TRANSLATE := 'Wednesday';
      Thu : TRANSLATE := 'Thursday';
      Fri : TRANSLATE := 'Friday';
      Sat : TRANSLATE := 'Saturday'
    end  {case}
end;  {TRANSLATE}
```

A call to function TRANSLATE might be

```
day1 := Tue;
writeln (TRANSLATE (day1));
```

This fragment would produce the output

```
Tuesday
```

REMARK   If you want to translate a string value into an enumerated type value, you cannot use a case statement because strings are not ordinal. Instead, you could use multiway selection with nested if-then-else.   • • •

• • • • • • • • •
Example   Program value uses a procedure COIN_STRING to convert an enumerated type value into a string and outputs the string. The program determines the total value in cents of the input coins. A typical output might be

Screen

```
Enter number of pennies 3
Enter number of nickels 2
Enter number of dimes 5
Enter number of quarters 6
Total value is $  2.13
```

```
program value;
{converts quantities of different coin types to dollar total}
type coins = (penny, nickel, dime, quarter);
var quant, sum: integer;
    coin: coins;

function FINDVALUE (coin: coins): integer;
```

```
  {returns integer value of enumerated type coin}
  begin
    case coin of
      penny   : FINDVALUE := 1;
      nickel  : FINDVALUE := 5;
      dime    : FINDVALUE := 10;
      quarter : FINDVALUE := 25
    end  {case}
  end;  {FINDVALUE}

function COIN_STRING (coin: coins): string;
  {returns description of enumerated type coin}
  begin
    case coin of
      penny   : COIN_STRING := 'pennies';
      nickel  : COIN_STRING := 'nickels';
      dime    : COIN_STRING := 'dimes';
      quarter : COIN_STRING := 'quarters'
    end  {case}
  end;  {COIN_STRING}

begin  {main}
  sum := 0;
  for coin := penny to quarter do
    begin
      write ('Enter number of ');
      write (COIN_STRING (coin), ' ');
      readln (quant);
      sum := sum + (FINDVALUE (coin) * quant)
    end;
  writeln ('Total value is $ ', sum/100 :6:2)
end.
```

• • •

The Functions succ and pred These two built-in functions can be used only with ordinal data types. The ***successor*** function, succ, when applied to an ordinal argument, returns the value immediately following the argument. The ***predecessor*** function, pred, returns the value preceding its argument.

• • • • • • • • •

Question Suppose that ch1, ch2, and ch3 are of type char, and coin1 and coin2 are of type coins (as defined in the previous program). What values will ch2, ch3, and coin2 have after the following fragment is executed?

```
ch1 := 'D';
ch2 := succ (ch1);
ch3 := pred (ch1);
coin1 := nickel;
coin2 := succ (coin1);
```

Answer   The values of ch2, ch3, and coin2 will be 'E', 'C', and dime, respectively.

• • •

16.4 RETYPING

• •

Retyping is the conversion of the value of one ordinal type into a value of another ordinal type. If type identifier is an ordinal type and argument is an ordinal value, then

type identifier (argument)

converts argument into the type identifier value that has the same position as argument.

Converting Input into Enumerated Type Value   A common application of retyping converts an integer into an enumerated type value. This is particularly useful since enumerated type values may not be read in directly. Suppose we have the declarations

```
type days = (Sun, Mon, Tue, Wed, Thu, Fri, Sat);
var day: days;
```

then

```
day := days (3)
```

would assign the value Wed to day.

Question   Suppose DayCode is of type integer and day is of type days. Fill in the blank of the following fragment so that it prints the appropriate message:

```
writeln (' 0   1   2   3   4   5   6 ');
writeln ('Sun Mon Tue Wed Thu Fri Sat');
write ('Enter code number for day ');
readln (DayCode);
_____

if (day = Sat) or (day = Sun)
  then writeln ('Weekend')
  else writeln ('Workday');
```

Answer   `day := days (DayCode);`   • • •

REMARK   If the user were to enter the day of the week as a string, it would be necessary to use a linear nested `if` to convert it to the corresponding enumerated type. (See Exercise 4.)   • • •

• • • • • • • • • • # EXERCISES

• •

1. Explain how to use the `type` declaration section to get around a technical restriction on procedure parameter declarations.

2. Suppose `day1` and `day2` are of type `days = (Sun, Mon, Tue, Wed, Thu, Fri, Sat);`. Write a program fragment to determine whether `day1` and `day2` are adjacent—that is, if either `day1` follows `day2` or `day2` follows `day1`. Design your code so that `Sat` and `Sun` are considered adjacent days.

3. Write a function that when given a variable or enumerated type value of type `days` will return the day of the week that is two days later. For example, `TWO_DAYS_LATER (Sat)` should return `Mon`.

4. Write a function that will convert a string value for the day of the week into a value of type `days`. For example, `STR_INTO_ENUM('Tuesday')` should return the value `Tue`.

Chapter

17

ONE-DIMENSIONAL ARRAYS

• • • An array provides a convenient structure for storing data items of the same data type. As you will see, arrays allow for both easy reading of the data into memory and efficient accessing of the data for processing.

In this chapter, we will consider two standard types of situations in which arrays are useful: (1) when a data list must be processed *more than once* and (2) when a large number of closely related summing or counting variables are needed. • • •

17.1 ARRAY SYNTAX

So far, all the variables that we have considered have been of simple type. A variable of **simple type** consists of a single memory cell that can hold only one value at a time. By contrast, a variable of **structured data type** consists of a collection of memory cells.

An **array**, the most elementary kind of data structure, consists of a collection of memory cells for storing a list of values that are all of the *same* type—for example, a list of integers, a list of `real` numbers, a list of strings of the same declared length, or a list of `boolean` values. The entire list is given a name.

An array can be compared to an apartment building. The name of the array represents the name of the building. The **elements** of the array represent the building's apartments, each of which has a **subscript** or **index**, which corresponds to an apartment number. Just as Riser[4] could be used to specify apartment 4 in a building called Riser, the notation `scores[4]` refers to the fourth memory cell of the array `scores`.

```
         Riser
   [1]  ┌──────────┐
        │          │
   [2]  ├──────────┤
        │          │
   [3]  ├──────────┤
        │          │
   [4]  ├──────────┤
        │          │
        └──────────┘
```

In order to specify an individual element of an array, you must give *both* the name of the array and the subscript. For example, for an array called scores, the statement

```
scores[4] := 86;
```

assigns the value 86 to the memory cell scores[4]. Similarly,

```
writeln (scores[6]);
```

outputs the contents of the memory cell scores[6].

● ● ● ● ● ● ● ● ● ●
Example   The following program assigns values to be stored in an array's elements, or memory boxes:

```
program drill;
var x: array[1..4] of integer;
begin
  x[1] := 83;
  x[2] := 59;
  x[3] := 88;
  x[4] := 72;
  writeln (x[4]);
  writeln (x[2]);
  writeln (x[2 + 1]);
  writeln (x[2] + 1)
end.
```

The **subscript range** [1..4] in the declaration of the array x tells the compiler to set aside four memory cells x[1], x[2], x[3], and x[4]. By the time the four assignment statements have been executed, four numbers will be stored in array x, which can be depicted as

```
 x[1]  x[2]  x[3]  x[4]
┌─────┬─────┬─────┬─────┐
│ 83  │ 59  │ 88  │ 72  │
└─────┴─────┴─────┴─────┘
```

An array can be depicted vertically or horizontally. This time we depict it horizontally.

The output will be

```
72
59
88
60
```

Declaring the Array   You can declare a variable of nonsimple data type in either of two ways: (1) by declaring the variable entirely in the var section or (2) by defining a type identifier in the type section and then declaring the variable to be of that type. The following fragments illustrate how the array x could be declared by each of these methods:

Method 1

```
var x: array[1..5] of integer;
```

Method 2

```
type numarray = array[1..5] of integer;
var x: numarray;
```

(*Note:* If you want to use the array x as a parameter for a subprogram, you must use the second method. Can you see why?)

The general form for defining an array entirely within the var section is

var {*arrayname*}: **array**[{*subscript range*}] of {*datatype*};

The form for declaring an array type is similar, except that an equal sign is used instead of a colon.

Using a for Loop   The numbers 83, 59, 88, and 72 could be assigned interactively to the array x using a for loop.

```
for i := 1 to 4 do
  begin
    write ('enter element ');
    readln (x[i])
  end; {for i}
```

**Subscript Range Checking {$R+}**   The execution of a program statement with an array subscript out of the declared range is potentially dangerous. (See Exercise 3 for an example of what can go wrong.) Including the compiler directive {$R+} at the top of a program will cause a program run to be terminated with an error message when this kind of trouble is encountered.

Remember, it is usually better to have a program terminate with an error message than to run to completion and produce unreliable results.

17.2 PROCESSING DATA MORE THAN ONCE

• •

An important use of arrays is in processing a data list more than once.

Example Suppose an external file `num.dat` contains a list of up to 25 numbers. For example, `num.dat` might contain

```
41
68
32
74
55
```

The following program will print the numbers in their original order and then in reverse order. The printout will be

```
original order 41 68 32 74 55
reverse order 55 74 32 68 41
```

```
{$R+}
program reverse;
{prints numbers in original and reverse order}
var i, size: integer;
    numbs: array[1..25] of integer;
    NumFile: text;
begin
  assign (NumFile, 'num.dat');
  reset (NumFile);
  write ('original order ');

  {read all the numbers from the file into the array}
  size := 0;
  while not seekeof (NumFile) do
    begin
      size := size + 1;
      readln (NumFile, numbs[size]);
      write (numbs[size], ' ')
    end; {while}
  writeln;
```

```
    write ('reverse order ');

    {second time through array}
    for i := size downto 1 do
      write (numbs[i], ' ');
    close (NumFile);
    writeln
end.
```

REMARK

1. The numbs array was declared to hold up to 25 integers. In the while loop that reads values into the numbs array, size is used as the array subscript. Note that the final value of size by the end of the while loop is the number of array cells actually used. (For the preceding file, size would have a final value of 5.)

2. In the for loop that takes a second look at the array, size is not a subscript but rather the upper limit of the loop. • • •

• • • • • • • • •

Question   What would happen in program reverse, which contains the {$R+} directive, if num.dat contained 34 numbers? *Hint:* With {$R+}, all subscripts out of range errors will be detected.

Answer   The program run would terminate during the while loop. After the program had read in and printed the first 25 file numbers in their original order, the next execution of the while loop would set size equal to 26 and the statement

```
    readln (NumFile, numbs[size]);
```

would produce a run-time error. To rectify matters, you would have to revise the program's array declaration, making the array large enough to store the file's contents. • • •

Using a Header   If the file numhdr.dat were set up with a header, we would use a modified version of program reverse to print the numbers in their original and reverse orders. We would replace the main body of program reverse by

```
begin {main}
  assign (NumFile, 'numhdr.dat');
  reset (NumFile);
  write ('original order ');
```

```
    readln (NumFile, size);
    for i := 1 to size do
       begin
          readln (NumFile, numbs[i]);
          write (numbs[i], ' ')
       end;
    writeln;
    write ('reverse order ');
    for i := size downto 1 do
       write (numbs[i], ' ');
    close (NumFile);
    writeln
end.
```

• • • • • • • • •

Problem   The file `grade.dat` contains the scores on an exam for each of the students in a class of at most 40 students. We want to write a program that first finds and prints the class average and then prints each of the scores that are above the class average. For example, if the file `grade.dat` contained the scores

```
70 80 71 58 79 92
```

(with one score per line), the output would be

```
Class average 75.0
Scores above average 80 79 92
```

An array is needed because the data must be processed twice—first to find the average and then to determine which scores are above the average. Let us call this array `scores`.

Here is a first draft in pseudocode.

read all the data from the file into the array `scores`
use a function to find class average
print the average
process `scores` a second time to determine which are above the class average and print them

Here is a refinement.

```
GETDATA (     )     file will also be opened and closed here
avg := FINDAVG (     )
writeln ('class average ', avg:5:1)
PRINTABOVE (     )
```

Before reading on, fill in the global variables in the calling statements, and put a check mark over those that correspond to variable parameters.

Here is the main body of the program.

```
{$R+}
program scoresabove_avg;
const maxsize = 40;
type scorestype = array[1..maxsize] of integer;
var scores: scorestype;
    size: integer;
    avg: real;

    ┌──────────────────────────────────────────────┐
    │ procedure GETDATA, function FINDAVG, and      │
    │ procedure PRINTABOVE go here.                 │
    └──────────────────────────────────────────────┘

begin {main}
  GETDATA (scores, size);
  avg := FINDAVG (scores, size);
  writeln ('class average ', avg:5:1);
  PRINTABOVE (scores, size, avg)
end.
```

Note the use of the constant `maxsize` in the declarations

```
const maxsize = 40;
type scorestype = array[1..maxsize] of integer;
```

As you will see later, in a program containing multiple references to the maximum size of an array, it is easier and safer to change a constant declaration of `maxsize`, should the need arise, than to change every reference to the array's maximum size.

Now let us consider the subprograms. Note that `size` is used as an array subscript only in the `GETDATA` procedure. In the other subprograms, `size` is the upper limit of the `for` loop.

```
procedure GETDATA (var scores: scorestype;
                   var size: integer);
  {reads data from text file into the array scores}
  var ScoreFile: text;
  begin
    assign (ScoreFile, 'grade.dat');
    reset (ScoreFile);
```

```
      size := 0;
      while not seekeof (ScoreFile) do
        begin
          size := size + 1;
          readln (ScoreFile, scores[size])
        end;
      close (ScoreFile)
  end; {GETDATA}
```

Question   When a *single* call of a procedure reads the *entire* contents of an external file into an array, it is quite customary to put all the file statements in that procedure. Thus, GETDATA contains the assign, reset, and close statements. Further, ScoreFile is declared as a *local variable* of the procedure.

Fill in the blank lines of FINDAVG and PRINTABOVE.

```
function FINDAVG (scores: scorestype;
                  size: integer): real;
  {calculates average of numbers in an array}
  var sum : integer;
      i: integer;
  begin
    sum := 0;
    for i := 1 to size do

      _____

    _____

  end; {FINDAVG}

procedure PRINTABOVE (scores: scorestype;
                      size: integer;
                      avg: real);
  var i: integer;
  begin
    write ('scores above the average ');

    _____

      if scores[i] > avg then
        write (_____)
  end; {PRINTABOVE}
```

Answer   The missing lines in FINDAVG are

```
        sum := sum + scores[i];
      FINDAVG := sum/size
```

The completed lines for PRINTABOVE are

```
for i := 1 to size do

    write (scores[i], ' ')
```

● ● ●

17.3 PARALLEL ARRAYS

●●

Suppose an external file contains the names of students in a class and each student's grade:

```
Smith
70
Jones
92
Johnson
88
Cohen
92
```

We want to write a program to find the highest grade achieved and then print the names of everyone who earned it. There might be one such person, or there might be more than one. For the preceding file, the printout would be

```
Highest grade 92
Achieved by:
Jones
Cohen
```

Notice that the list of scores will have to be processed twice. A first pass will determine what the highest score is, and a second pass will print the names of those who share it.

The program will use the ***parallel arrays*** names and scores. In the parallel arrays, a given student's name and score will be contained in memory boxes with the same subscript. That is, the element scores[i] will contain the score of the student whose name is in names[i].

Here is how the parallel arrays will be set up for the preceding data.

	names		scores
[1]	Smith	[1]	70
[2]	Jones	[2]	92
[3]	Johnson	[3]	88
[4]	Cohen	[4]	92

Question   Here is the program to find the highest grade and those who achieved it. Fill in the blanks.

```
{$R+}
program HighScorers;
{prints names of students with highest score}
const maxsize = 30;
type str_array = array [1..maxsize] of string;
     scorerange = 0..100;
     num_array = array [1..maxsize] of scorerange;
var scores: num_array;
    names: str_array;
    size: integer;
    maxscore: scorerange;

procedure GETDATA (var scores: num_array;
                   var names: str_array;
                   var size: integer);
  {reads all the data into parallel arrays}
  var GradeFile: text;
  begin
    assign (GradeFile, 'scores.dat');
    reset (GradeFile);
    size := 0;
    while not seekeof (GradeFile) do
      begin
        _____;
        readln (GradeFile, _____);
        readln (GradeFile, _____)
      end;
    close (GradeFile)
  end; {GETDATA}

function FINDMAX (scores: num_array;
                  size: integer): scorerange;
  {finds the highest score}
  var i: integer;
      maxsofar: scorerange;
  begin
    maxsofar := scores[1];
    for i := 2 to size do
      if scores[i] > maxsofar then
        maxsofar := scores[i];
    FINDMAX := maxsofar
```

```
  end; {FINDMAX}

procedure PRINTACHIEVERS (maxscore: scorerange;
                          scores: num_array;
                          names: str_array;
                          size: integer);
  {prints names of those achieving the highest score}
  var i: integer;
  begin
    for i := 1 to size do
      if _____ then
        writeln (_____)
  end; {PRINTACHIEVERS}

begin  {main}
  GETDATA (scores, names, size);
  maxscore := FINDMAX (scores, size);
  writeln ('Highest grade ', maxscore);
  writeln ('Achieved by: ');
  PRINTACHIEVERS (maxscore, scores, names, size)
end.
```

Answer

```
size := size + 1;
readln (GradeFile, names[size]);
readln (GradeFile, scores[size]);

if scores[i] = maxscore then
  writeln (names[i])
```
• • •

REMARK

1. A type must be defined prior to its use. Thus, note that `scorerange` was defined prior to its use in naming `num_array`.

2. Note that in `function FINDMAX`, `maxsofar` was initialized with the first element of the array.
• • •

Records as an Alternative to Parallel Arrays

A major weakness of parallel arrays is that the stored information for one particular individual (or item) is distributed over two or more data structures. This separation becomes a serious disadvantage when you need to shift the order of array contents—as, for example, in sorting. A superior data structure, that of records (to be discussed in Chapter 21), has the advantage of keeping together all the information for a particular individual (or item).

17.4 ARRAYS OF COUNTING VARIABLES

Arrays are particularly useful when you are tallying a number of related quantities. By using the array index, you can directly increment the appropriate counter instead of performing a tedious multiway selection.

Example (Vote Counting) Suppose that in a recently held election, there were four candidates 1, 2, 3, and 4. Suppose further that `vote.dat` is a file containing the votes cast in that election, in which 1 represents a vote for candidate 1, 2 a vote for candidate 2, 3 a vote for candidate 3, and 4 a vote for candidate 4. That is, `vote.dat` consists of a list like

    1 3 1 4 2 1 2 3   etc.

We wish to write a program to process the file `vote.dat`. The printout should be of the form

    CANDIDATE NO. OF VOTES
        1   17
        2   38
        3   24
        4   32

We will use the array of `votecnts` to keep track of the votes for each of the four candidates. By the time all the votes have been counted, `votecnts` will have the following values:

```
           votecnts
      [1]    17
      [2]    38
      [3]    24
      [4]    32
```

At the start of the program, the four memory boxes of `votecnts` should be initialized to 0.

Here is the pseudocode.

initialize `votecnts` to all zeros
PROCESS (`votecnts`) this procedure will use a loop to read in and process
                     each of the votes; for example, a vote of 3 will increase
                     `votecnts[3]` by 1

PRINTRESULTS (votecnts) this procedure will use a `for` loop to print the final values for each of the memory boxes of votecnts

Question   What kind of parameter should votecnts be in `procedure PROCESS`? In `procedure PRINTRESULTS`?

Answer   Because we want PROCESS to change the value of votecnts from all zeros to the final tallies for the candidates, votecnts should be a variable parameter in that procedure. By contrast, votecnts will be a value parameter in PRINTRESULTS.   • • •

Processing a Single Vote   Let us focus on a very important detail of PROCESS—how to process a vote just read in. The statement

```
readln (votefile, vote)
```

will read in a vote from the external file. The variable vote will have the value 1, 2, 3, or 4. An *inefficient* way to increase the appropriate candidate's counter by 1 is to use the `case` statement

```
case vote of
   1 : votecnts[1] := votecnts[1] + 1;
   2 : votecnts[2] := votecnts[2] + 1;
   3 : votecnts[3] := votecnts[3] + 1;
   4 : votecnts[4] := votecnts[4] + 1
end; {case}
```

Question   There is a much simpler way to accomplish what the `case` statement does. The entire `case` statement can be replaced by a single line. Fill in the blanks.

_____ := _____ + 1;

Answer   The value of vote (1, 2, 3, or 4) gives the subscript for the element of votecnts that should be increased by 1. Thus, the appropriate statement is

```
votecnts[vote] := votecnts[vote] + 1;
```

Here is the complete program.

```
program voting;
{processes the vote.dat file and prints each candidate's tally}
type voterange = 1..4;
     cntstype = array[voterange] of integer;
var votecnts: cntstype;


procedure INITIALIZE (var votecnts: cntstype);
```

```
    var i: voterange;
    begin
      for i := 1 to 4 do
        votecnts[i] := 0;
    end;  {INITIALIZE}

procedure PROCESS (var votecnts: cntstype);
    {reads in each individual vote from the external file}
    {and updates appropriate counter}
    var vote: voterange;
        votefile: text;
    begin
      assign (votefile, 'vote.dat');
      reset (votefile);
      while not seekeof (votefile) do
        begin
          readln (votefile, vote);
          if (vote >= 1) and (vote <=4)
            then votecnts[vote] := votecnts[vote] + 1
            else writeln(' Invalid vote ')
        end; {while}
      close (votefile)
    end; {PROCESS}

procedure PRINTRESULTS (votecnts: cntstype);
    {prints the number of votes for each candidate}
    var i: voterange;
    begin
      writeln ('CANDIDATE':9, 'NO. OF VOTES':16);
      for i := 1 to 4 do
        writeln (i:5, votecnts[i]:15)
    end; {PRINTRESULTS}

begin {main}
  INITIALIZE (votecnts);
  PROCESS (votecnts);
  PRINTRESULTS (votecnts)
end.
```

• • •

Arrays with Nonnumeric Subscripts

The subscripts for an array can be of any ordinal type. In the next application, the array subscripts will be of type `char`.

Suppose that we want to write a program that will keep track of students' marks. The user will interactively enter marks (A, B, C, D, or F) for 100 students.

The array `markcnts` will keep count of how many of each mark there are. For example, if there were 18 As, 32 Bs, 30 Cs, 12 Ds, and 10 Fs, after all the marks had been entered, `markcnts` would contain

```
                markcnts
  ['A']    [  18  ]
  ['B']    [  32  ]
  ['C']    [  30  ]
  ['D']    [  12  ]
  ['E']    [   0  ]
  ['F']    [  10  ]
```

If `markcnts` were defined entirely in the `var` section, the declaration would be

```
var markcnts: array ['A'..'F'] of integer;
```

Question Fill in the blanks in the following program fragment to produce the output:

```
Mark    Number of Students
 A              18
 B              32
 C              30
 D              12
 F              10
```

```
{initialize}
for mark := 'A' to 'F' do
  markcnts[mark] := 0;

{process grades}
for student := 1 to 100 do
  begin
    write ('enter student grade ');
    readln (mark);
    _____ := _____ + 1
  end;

{print results}
```

```
writeln ('Mark', 'Number of Students':23);
for _____ do
   if mark <> 'E' then
      writeln (_____);
```

Answer The three completed lines are

```
markcnts[mark] := markcnts[mark] + 1
for mark := 'A' to 'F' do
writeln (mark:3, markcnts[mark]:16);
```

• • •

17.5 DEBUGGING AND ERROR TRAPPING

Reporting First Sign of Trouble Debugging is easier when an error message flags the initial point of transgression rather than a place later on where the error may have been disguised or compounded. Let us reconsider program reverse of Section 17.2. Note that if the file contained more than 25 numbers, the computer would report the error occurring in the while loop statement

```
readln (NumFile, numbs[size]);
```

The error message would be even more informative if it flagged the earliest trouble spot—namely, the statement

```
size := size + 1;
```

Let us redo the declarations for program reverse, adding a type declaration of SubscriptType. Although declaring a subscript type requires more overhead, it can lead to easier detection of errors caused by a subscript that is out of the declared range.

```
{$R+}
program reverse;
const maxsize = 25;
type SubscriptType = 0..maxsize;
var i, size: SubscriptType;
   numbs: array[SubscriptType] of integer;
   NumFile: text;
```

Now, if the file is too large, the error message will flag the statement

```
size := size + 1;
```

Error Trapping   As was already mentioned, it is better for a program to crash (that is, terminate its run prematurely with an error message) than to produce unreliable results. It is better yet for the programmer to include statements that error trap. There are two approaches to error trapping. When an error is detected, the computer may be instructed to (1) discontinue execution after providing the user with the programmer's own meaningful explanation of the error or (2) continue execution after alerting the user to each occurrence of an error. The second method was used in program `voting`.

17.6 HAND TRACING WITH ARRAYS

Question   Suppose `arr` is of type `array [1..6] of integer`. What will the contents of array `arr` be by the end of the following?

```
for n := 1 to 6 do
   arr[n] := (5 * n) + 2;
```

Answer   7 12 17 22 27 32

This trace is quite easy since during each execution of the loop body, just one memory box of the array is involved—namely, when the control variable has the value n, just the nth box.   • • •

Question   (More Difficult)

The main complication in this next trace is that the action during each loop body execution involves not one but three array boxes. Suppose x is of type `array[1..6] of integer` and its starting contents are 35 18 10 24 47 55. What will the contents of x be after the following loop?

```
for n := 1 to 4 do
   if x[n] > x[n+1]
      then x[n+2] := x[n]
      else x[n+2] := n;
```

Answer   Here is a suggested method that you should use in some form in order to do a reliable trace.

For each execution of the loop body, you should keep track of

(a) The current value of the control variable
(b) Which array box(es) are being referenced
(c) The actual value(s) within those boxes
(d) Whatever actions are specified in the program, updating the array as needed

Here is the method applied.

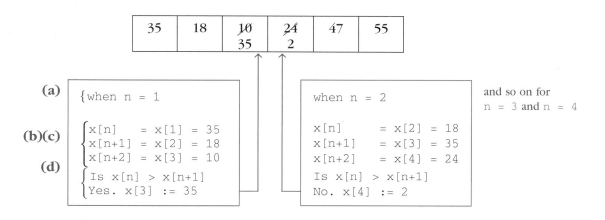

Final answer:

```
35 18 35 2 35 4
```

• • •

17.7 COMPARING ADJACENT CELLS
(Useful Applications)

• •

Some array manipulations can be handled by using a `for` loop to compare each of the pairs of adjacent cells—*one* execution of the loop body will compare the contents of *one* pair of adjacent cells and then take any further action that might be necessary.

Suppose that x is of type `array[1..maxsize] of integer` and that the integers that x contains are in *increasing* order. For example,

```
x[1] x[2]                                    x[size]
 14   14   22   25   25   25   25   38   38
```

Problem 1   Print all the distinct values contained in the ordered array. For example, if x has the preceding values, the output would be

```
14 22 25 38
```

Here is the code to solve Problem 1.

```
write (x[1]);
for i := 2 to size do
  if x[i] <> x[i-1] then write (x[i] :3);
```

First and Last Cells Are Special   Frequently, the first cell, last cell, or both cells of an array may require special consideration. (The middle cells should be handled entirely by the `for` loop.) The first cell may require extra code before the loop as a kind of initialization, whereas the last cell may require extra code after the loop.

In the solution to Problem 1, the first cell was handled in the part before the loop. Do you see what would have been printed without the `write` statement before the loop?

Problem 2   For an *ordered* array, print each distinct value and how many times it occurs. For x containing the same values as before, the output would be

```
14    2 occurrence(s)
22    1 occurrence(s)
25    4 occurrence(s)
38    2 occurrence(s)
```

This is more difficult than Problem 1 because each time we get a value that is different from the previous value (like the first 25), we won't know yet how many times this new value will occur.

The pseudocode to handle the middle boxes would be

```
if x[i] = x[i-1] then
    increase count for length of current streak
else
    print contents of x[i-1] and its length
    reset streak count at 1
```

This pseudocode is essentially the body of the `for` loop. Before reading on, see if you can write the entire solution to Problem 2—not simply the `for` loop but also any statements needed before or after the loop to handle the first or last boxes. Note that the last cell requires some attention after the loop.

Here is a solution to Problem 2.

```
count := 1;
for i := 2 to size do
  if x[i] = x[i-1] then
      count := count + 1
  else
      begin
         writeln (x[i-1], count:4, ' occurrence(s)');
         count := 1
      end; {else}
writeln (x[size], count:4, ' occurrence(s)');
```

17.8 ENUMERATED TYPE AS ARRAY SUBSCRIPTS

Assume that the text file `carsale.dat` is of the form

```
3 1 2 1 4 1 2
2 1 4 1 3 1 4
.
.
.
```

where 1 represents a sale of a Chevrolet, 2 a Buick, 3 an Oldsmobile, and 4 a Cadillac.

The following program uses an array of counters with enumerated type subscripts to print a table giving the number of cars of each type that were sold. Note that retyping is used (instead of multiway selection) to convert a car code number 1, 2, 3, or 4 into an enumerated type value.

```
program CarSales;
{uses an array of counters with enumerated type subscripts}
type cars = (Chevy, Buick, Olds, Cadillac);
     CountsType = array[cars] of integer;
     StringsType = array[cars] of string[20];

var CarCounts: CountsType;
```

```pascal
    CarStrings: StringsType;

procedure INITIALIZE (var CarCount: countsType;
                      var CarStrings: StringsType);
  {sets counters = 0 and puts car names in array}
  var car: cars;
  begin
    for car := Chevy to Cadillac do
      CarCounts[car] := 0;
    CarStrings[Chevy] := 'Chevrolet';
    CarStrings[Buick] := 'Buick';
    CarStrings[Olds] := 'Oldsmobile';
    CarStrings[Cadillac] := 'Cadillac'
  end;

procedure PROCESS (var CarCounts: CountsType);
  {processes the car sales file}
  var CarFile: text;
      CarCode: integer;
      car: cars;
  begin
    assign (CarFile,'carsale.dat');
    reset (CarFile);
    while not seekeof (CarFile) do
      begin
        read (CarFile, CarCode);
        if (CarCode < 1) or (CarCode > 4) then
          writeln ( 'Invalid entry ', CarCode)
        else
          begin
            car := cars (CarCode - 1);
            CarCounts[car] := CarCounts[car] + 1
          end
      end;
    close (CarFile)
  end; {PROCESS}

procedure RESULTS (CarCounts: CountsType;
                   CarStrings: StringsType);
  {print final results}
  var car: cars;
  begin
    writeln ('Number of each kind sold');
    for car := Chevy to Cadillac do
      writeln (CarStrings[car], ' ',CarCounts[car])
  end;  {RESULTS}
```

```
begin  {main}
  INITIALIZE (CarCounts, CarStrings);
  PROCESS (CarCounts);
  RESULTS (CarCounts, CarStrings)
end.
```

• • • • • • • • • • EXERCISES
• •

1. Show what will be output by the program fragment for the data

     5 12 8 4 23 19

if nums is of type array[1..6] of integer.

```
for i := 1 to 6 do
  read (nums[i]);
for i := 1 to 5 do
  if nums[i] > nums[i + 1]
    then nums[i] := 0
    else nums[i] := nums[i] + 5;
for i := 1 to 6 do
  write (nums[i], ' ');
```

2. Which compiler directive should be activated to catch subscript and out-of-range errors?

3. **(a)** If {$R+} is included at the top of the following program, what will happen when it is run?

   (b) If range checking is not activated, something very strange will happen. Try running the program without {$R+}.

```
program SubscriptTrouble;
var scores: array [1..3] of integer;
    age, n: integer;

begin
  age := 20;
  n := 4;
  scores [n] := 99;
  writeln ('age = ', age)
end.
```

4. Assume that the array B has been declared as

```
var B: array[1..10] of integer;
```

and filled with values. What is wrong with the following fragment?

```
for i:= 1 to 10 do
   B[i] := B[i + 1];
```

5. Suppose b is of type `array[1..6] of integer`. What will be output by each of the following:

(a)
```
for i := 1 to 6 do
   b[i] := 6 * i;
for i := 1 to 6 do
   b[i] := b[7 - i];
for i := 1 to 6 do
   write (b[i], ' ');
```

(b)
```
for n := 1 to 6 do
   b[n] := 7 * n;
for n := 1 to 5 do
   b[n + 1] := b[n];
for n := 1 to 6 do
   write (b[n], ' ');
```

6. Suppose x is of type `array[1..6] of integer` and its starting contents are 44 15 10 29 47 55. What will the contents of x[ ] be after the following loop?

```
for n := 1 to 4 do
   if x[n] > x[n + 1]
      then x[n + 2] := x[n]
      else x[n + 2] := x[n + 1];
```

7. Show what will be printed by the following program fragments.

(a)
```
for i := 1 to 6 do
   a[i] := 1;
for i := 1 to 5 do
   a[i] := i * a[i + 1];
for i := 1 to 6 do
   write (a[i], ' ');
```

(b)
```
for i := 1 to 6 do
   a[i] := i;
for i := 1 to 5 do
   a[i + 1] := i * a[i];
for i := 1 to 6 do
   write (a[i], ' ');
```

8. What will the following fragment print if `infile` contains the values

```
2 2 3 2 1
```

```
for i := 1 to 6 do
   x[i] := 0;
```

```
for i := 1 to 5 do
   begin
      read (infile,n);
      x[n+1] := x[n] + 1
   end; (for)
for i := 1 to 6 do
   writeln (x[i]);
```

9. Suppose that the parallel arrays names, IQs, and sex (m or f) contain information on a class of size students. Write a program fragment that will print the names of all females with IQs over 120.

10. (a) Write a subprogram that receives two five-element integer arrays and returns a 10-element array that consists of the elements of the first array followed by the elements of the second array.

    (b) Modify the subprogram to return an array in which the elements are intertwined (the first element of the first array, followed by the first element of the second array, followed by the second element of the first array, and so on).

Longer Assignments

11. File scores.dat contains each student's name and raw test score for a class of up to 30 students. The teacher has an unusual method of curving the scores. If there are fewer than five scores of 90 or above, each student has 8 points added to the raw score; otherwise, each student has only 4 points added to the raw score. (No student should receive a score greater than 100.) Using file scores.dat, write a program that will first print a list with each student's name and raw score, and then print a list with each student's name and curved score.

12. File scores.dat contains each student's name and raw test score for a class of up to 30 students. Write a program that will read this information into parallel arrays. The program should first compute the class average and then compute the standard deviation from the class average.

    The method for computing standard deviation is as follows. First the difference between the class average and a student's mark is computed for each student. Then the standard deviation is

    $$\sqrt{(\text{sum of squares of these differences})/(\text{class size})}$$

    For example, if the grades were 70, 74, 80, 82, 68, and 76, the average would be 75.0, and the standard deviation (sd) would be

    $$\sqrt{\frac{(70 - 75)^2 + (74 - 75)^2 + (80 - 75)^2 + \cdots + (76 - 75)^2}{6}}$$

Once these computations have been completed, the program should assign letter grades as follows:

A for a grade that is at least one sd above the average.

B for a grade that is at least one-third of an sd above the average, but less than one sd above the average.

C for a grade that is within one-third of an sd of the average.

D for a grade that is below the average by at least one-third of an sd, but less than one sd below the average.

F for a grade that is below the average by at least a full sd.

For example, for the list of grades given earlier, since the sd is $\sqrt{150/6} = 5.0$, a score of at least 80 would be needed for an A.

The output on paper should contain (1) a list with each student's name, numerical grade, and letter grade; (2) the class average and standard deviation; and (3) a table telling how many students received each letter grade.

13. Write a program that will simulate rolling a pair of dice 100 times and then print a list giving the number of times each outcome occurred. Format the output as follows:

```
2 was rolled _ TIMES
3 was rolled _ TIMES
.
.
.
12 was rolled _ TIMES
```

14. The ACME Specialty Store sells five items, with ID numbers 101, 102, 103, 104, and 105, respectively. A text file contains the following data pairs:

```
102 5    104 9    102 7    105 8    101 2    104 9
103 9    105 4    101 8    101 5    104 8    103 2
```

You may assume that there is one data pair to a line, with each pair representing the sale of an item. The first number gives the item's ID number, and the second tells how many units were sold. Thus, `102 5` means that 5 units of item number 102 were sold. Write a program that will print a table giving the ID numbers 101 to 105 and how many units of each were sold.

15. The first 10 positive Fibonacci numbers are 1, 1, 2, 3, 5, 8, 13, 21, 34, and 55. Each Fibonacci number greater than 1 is the sum of the two

previous Fibonacci numbers. Write a program to store the first 25 Fibonacci numbers in an array and then print them.

16. To test its freezer, a company is recording the freezer temperature (in Centigrade) once a day for the month of May. Suppose these 31 values are stored in an array. (Note that these values will all be *negative*.) Write a procedure that will receive this array as a parameter. The procedure should calculate and print the highest temperature and the day on which it occurred. (*Hint:* In finding the maximum, or minimum, values of the elements of an array, you should initialize the variable keeping track of the maximum, or minimum, with the *first element* and not with an arbitrary value.)

17. A consumer's research organization has a data file containing the names of stores and the price they charge for a particular VCR. Write a program to determine the lowest price charged for that VCR and then print two lists.

> List 1: The names of all stores charging the lowest price
>
> List 2: The names and prices for all stores whose price does not exceed the minimum by more than $15

18. Write a program to simulate a lottery drawing. Six different numbers from 1 to 54 should be selected at random. A typical output might be

```
the six numbers are 47 3 18 24 10 51
```

(*Hint:* Use an array of type `array[1..54] of integer`. Initialize this array with all zeros. A 0 will indicate that a number has not been selected yet, and a 1 will indicate that it has been selected. Alternatively, you could use an array of boolean values.)

* 19. (a) At the No-Wait Medical Center, each data group in an external file contains a doctor's name, specialty (such as cardiology or pediatrics), and availability status (0 for available and 1 for busy). Write a program that assigns one patient to a doctor as follows:

> The patient's name and preference for specialty are input. First, an attempt is made to assign the patient to a doctor whose specialty is as requested. If some doctors with the requested specialty are available, then the patient is assigned to one of those doctors *at random (not simply to the first available doctor with that specialty)*. Otherwise, a doctor is assigned *at random* from all the doctors who are available.

(b) Revise your program so that it can handle an input list of patients.

When a doctor is assigned to a patient, he or she is no longer available. (Your program may assume that doctors who are busy remain busy.)

* 20. An external file contains names of customers and amounts of purchases. There may be several entries for some customers, but they are grouped together because the list is alphabetical.

```
Adams
12
Adams
10
Bond
25
```

Write a program that calls GETDATA to read in all the data and then calls PRINT_REPORT to print each customer's name and purchase total. For the given data, the first line of this report would be

```
Adams $22
```

* 21. Revise the program from Exercise 20 so that it also prints the name(s) of the customer(s) with the largest purchase total.

* 22. A text file contains anywhere from 20 to 30 integers. *Without using an array,* write a program that will print those integers in the reverse of the original order (printing the last integer first.) (*Hint:* Use nested loops. See Sections 8.1 and 19.1.)

* 23. (a) In Turbo 7.0, the maximum size for an integer value is 32,767. Thus, no integer value can have more than five digits. Without using the data type real or longint, write a program that will find and print the sum of two input integers, where each integer may have up to eight digits. Your program should have the user enter the integers one digit at a time. The two integers should be read into the parallel arrays num1 and num2 and then added element by element. The result should be stored in a third array before it is printed.
    Caution: You must pad input integers that have fewer than eight digits with leading zeros. Don't forget to provide for carries when adding. Here are two typical outputs.

```
00050371 + 00670193 equals 00720564
```

```
74360418 + 52140327 equals 126500745
```

(b) Modify your program so that the leading zeros will not be printed in the output.

Lab Exercises   **DEBUGGING**

Lab17-1.pas	Pos, Neg, Zero
Lab17-2.pas	Counting Sevens
Lab17-3.pas	Finding Smallest
Lab17-4.pas	Counting Occurrences
Lab17-5.pas	Inserting

Chapter

18

MULTIDIMENSIONAL ARRAYS AND NESTED LOOPS

• • • So far, all the arrays we have considered have been one dimensional; thus, only one subscript has been needed to specify the desired element. When information fits naturally into a rectangular table, however, it is often advantageous to store it in a ***two-dimensional array,*** also called a ***matrix.*** Two subscripts are necessary to specify an element in a matrix—a row subscript and a column subscript. We begin this chapter by considering nested loops, which will be used extensively in working with matrices.

• • •

18.1   NESTED FOR LOOPS

Before considering two-dimensional arrays, we will take a look at a more complicated example of nested `for` loops.

Example   In this example, the body of the `for n` loop (marked by the brace) will be executed three times—first with n fixed at 2, then with n fixed at 3, and finally with n fixed at 4.

```
for n := 2 to 4 do
  begin
    for i := 6 to 8 do
      writeln (n, ' ', i);
    writeln ('hello')
  end; {for n}
```

The output will be

```
2 6
2 7          printed when n = 2
2 8
hello
3 6
3 7          printed when n = 3
3 8
hello
4 6
4 7          printed when n = 4
4 8
hello
```

• • •

• • • • • • • • •

Question Give the output for

```
count := 0;
for n := 2 to 4 do
  begin
    writeln ('n is ', n);
    sum := 0;
    for i := 6 to 8 do
      begin
        sum := sum + i;
        count := count + 1
      end; {for i}
    writeln ('sum is ', sum)
  end; {for n}
writeln ('count is ', count);
```

Answer

```
n is 2
sum is 21
n is 3
sum is 21
n is 4
sum is 21
count is 9
```

Note that sum was reset at 0 for each new value of n, whereas count was set at 0 just once before the nested loops. Here is a hand trace for the program.

n	i	sum	count
			0
2		0	
	6	6	1
	7	13	2
	8	21	3
3		0	
	6	6	4
	7	13	5
	8	21	6
4		0	
	6	6	7
	7	13	8
	8	21	9

• • •

18.2 TWO-DIMENSIONAL ARRAYS

The arrays that have been discussed so far have been lists of elements. Often, the data being processed can be organized as a table with several rows and columns. Such an array is called a two-dimensional array or a matrix.

Suppose sales is an array containing five-day sales figures for the 18 employees of SALES-R-US. The first row gives the week's sales figures for salesperson 1, the second row gives the figures for salesperson 2, and so on. For the moment, we will not concern ourselves with how these values were placed into this array.

sales

	1	2	3	4	5
1	25	31	29	40	30
2	41	39	38	42	33
3	48	58	62	47	40
.					
.					
.					
18	30	30	32	34	28

In order to access a particular cell from this array, we must specify the name of the array followed by the row and column of the desired cell. Thus writeln (sales[2,3]); would cause the computer to output 38—that is, the contents of the cell in row 2 and column 3.

•••••••••
Question   For the preceding sales array, what would be the effect of each of the following statements?

(a) writeln (sales[1,3]);   (b) sales[2,4] :=0;

Answer   (a) It would cause the computer to output

```
29
```

(b) It would cause a zero to be placed in the cell in row 2, column 4.

•••

Declaring a Two-Dimensional Array   Suppose we wish to declare sales as an array that can store five-day figures for up to 30 salespeople. We could declare sales without declaring an array type as follows:

```
const  maxsize = 30;
var    sales: array[1..maxsize,1..5] of integer;
```

Alternatively, we could first make the type declaration salestype and then declare sales to be of type salestype as follows:

```
const  maxsize = 30;
type   salestype = array[1..maxsize,1..5] of integer;
var    sales: salestype;
```

Finding Each Row Sum   Let us write a program fragment that will use the contents of the array sales to output a table giving each individual salesperson's weekly total. Here is the printout.

Salesperson	5-day total
1	155
2	193
.	.
.	.
.	.
18	154

We will assume that the number of salespeople is stored by the variable `size`. Here is the pseudocode.

```
print table heading
for salesperson :=1 to size do
    find saleperson's weekly total
    print it
```

Here is the code.

```
writeln ('Salesperson', '5-day total':15);
for salesperson := 1 to size do
  begin
    sum := 0;
    for day := 1 to 5 do
      sum := sum + sales[salesperson, day];
    writeln (salesperson:8, sum:15)
  end; {for salesperson}
```

Reading Data into a Two-Dimensional Array   Suppose that the external file `sales.dat` contains a header and sales figures for 18 salespeople.

```
    sales.dat
18
25 31 29 40 30
41 39 38 42 33
.
.
.
30 30 32 34 28
```

In the following procedure, note the use of the `read` statement to read across a line of the file and `readln (SalesFile)` to advance to the next line of the file.

```
procedure GETDATA (var sales: salestype;
                   var size: integer);
  {reads data from external file into array}
  var  salesman: 1..maxsize;
       day: 1..5;
       SalesFile: text;

  begin
    assign (SalesFile, 'sales.dat');
    reset (SalesFile);
    readln (SalesFile, size);
```

```
      for salesperson := 1 to size do
        begin
          for day := 1 to 5 do
            read (SalesFile, sales[salesperson, day]);
          readln (SalesFile)
        end;   {for salesperson}
      close (SalesFile)
    end; {GETDATA}
```

REMARK   If `sales.dat` had been a file without a header, then GETDATA would have used a `while` loop as the outer loop. Also there would *not* have been a need for the local variable `salesperson` (size would replace that subscript). The body of GETDATA would have been

```
assign (SalesFile, 'sales.dat');
reset (SalesFile);
size := 0;
while not seekeof (SalesFile) do
    begin
        size := size + 1;
        for day := 1 to 5 do
            read (SalesFile, sales[size,day]);
        readln (SalesFile)
    end; {while}
close (SalesFile)
```

• • •

Question   Fill in the blanks so that the following code will output the contents of `sales` in a matrix format:

```
for salesperson := 1 to size do
  begin
    for day := 1 to 5 do
          _____;

      _____
  end; {for salesperson}
```

Answer

```
        write (sales[salesperson, day]:4);
      writeln
```

• • •

Example   (Dropping the Lowest Score)   Professor Fairchild gives four exams and then determines each student's letter mark by taking the average of the student's three best scores. An A is at least 90, a B is at least 80 but under 90, a C is at least 70 but under 80, a D is at least 60 but under 70, and an F is under 60.

Suppose `scores.dat` is a file containing each student's name and four exam scores.

scores.dat

```
14
Smith
80 70 79 83
Jones
90 92 80 91
 .
 .
 .
Mills
70 75 66 70
```

Output on Paper

```
14 students
Smith 80 70 79 83
Jones 90 92 80 91
 .
 .
 .
Mills 70 75 66 70
Grades
Smith B
Jones A
 .
 .
 .
Mills C
```

In preparation for dropping each student's lowest score, we will find each student's lowest score and store it in an array called `lows`. For each student, the sum of the three top scores can be computed as

(sum of all four scores) − (lowest score)

In this program, we will use the following parallel data structures:

	names	scores				lows	best3avgs
1	Smith	80	70	79	83	70	80.67
2							
	.	.				.	.
	.	.				.	.
	.	.				.	.
size							

Here is the pseudocode.

`GETDATA` reads all the data from the external file into `names` and `scores`
`FINDLOWS` finds each student's low grade and stores these low grades in `lows`
`FINDBEST3AVGS` finds each student's average for the best three grades
`PRINTMARKS` prints each student's letter grade

Before reading on, try to complete the main body, based on this pseudo-code. You need to determine what variables should appear in each of the calling statements. Note, for example, that FINDLOWS does not need to know the names of the students.

Here is the main body.

```
{$R+}
program lettergrade;
{drops lowest grade in computing students' marks}
uses printer;
const maxsize = 30;
type
   namestype = array[1..maxsize] of string[15];
   scorestype = array[1..maxsize, 1..4] of integer;
   lowstype = array[1..maxsize] of integer;
   avgtype = array[1..maxsize] of real;
var
   names: namestype;
   scores: scorestype;
   lows: lowstype;
   best3avgs: avgtype;
   size: integer;

   The procedures GETDATA, FINDLOWS, FINDBEST3AVGS,
   and PRINTMARKS go here.

begin {main}
   GETDATA (names, scores, size);
   FINDLOWS (scores, size, lows);
   FINDBEST3AVGS (scores, size, lows, best3avgs);
   PRINTMARKS (names, size, best3avgs)
end.
```

Now let us consider the procedures.

```
procedure GETDATA (var names: namestype;
                   var scores: scorestype;
                   var size: integer);
  {will read data from file and echo it on paper}
  var StudFile: text;
      stud: 1..maxsize;
      exam: 1..4;
  begin
```

```
      assign (StudFile, 'scores.dat');
      reset (StudFile);
      readln (StudFile, size);
      writeln (1st, size, ' students');
      for stud := 1 to size do
        begin
          read (StudFile, names[stud]);
          write (1st, names[stud], ' ');
          for exam := 1 to 4 do
            begin
              read (StudFile, scores[stud, exam]);
              write (1st, scores[stud, exam], ' ')
            end; {for exam}
          writeln (1st);
          readln (StudFile)
        end; {for stud}
      close (StudFile);
      writeln (1st)
   end; {GETDATA}
```

Question   Complete the blank line in procedure FINDLOWS.

```
procedure FINDLOWS (scores: scorestype;
                    size: integer;
                    var lows: lowstype);
   {finds each low grade and stores it in an array}
   var stud: 1..maxsize;
       exam: 1..4;
       studmin: integer;
   begin
     for stud := 1 to size do
       begin
         studmin := scores[stud, 1];
         for exam := 2 to 4 do
           if scores[stud, exam] < studmin
             then _____
           lows[stud] := studmin
       end {for stud}
   end; {FINDLOWS}
```

Answer

```
   then studmin := scores[stud, exam];
```

Note that studmin is initialized with the student's first score.   • • •

• • • • • • • • •

Question   Procedure FINDBEST3AVGS **drops the lowest score. Fill in the blank.**

```
procedure FINDBEST3AVGS (scores: scorestype;
                         size: integer;
                         lows: lowstype;
                         var best3avgs: avgtype);
   {finds average of each student's 3 highest scores}
   var stud: 1..maxsize;
       exam: 1..4;
       sum: integer;
   begin
     for stud := 1 to size do
       begin
         sum := 0;
         for exam := 1 to 4 do
           sum := sum + scores[stud, exam];
         _____ := (sum - lows[stud])/3
       end {for stud}
   end; {FINDBEST3AVGS}
```

Answer   **The blank in** FINDBEST3AVGS **should be filled with** best3avgs[stud].
Here is PRINTMARKS.

```
procedure PRINTMARKS (names: namestype;
                      size: integer;
                      best3avgs: avgtype);
   {assigns a letter grade to each student and prints it}
   var stud: 1..maxsize;
       intscore: integer;
       mark: char;
   begin
     writeln (lst, 'Grades');
     for stud := 1 to size do
       begin
         intscore := trunc (best3avgs[stud]);
         case intscore of
           90..100 : mark := 'A';
           80..89  : mark := 'B';
           70..79  : mark := 'C';
           60..69  : mark := 'D';
           else      mark := 'F'
         end; {case}
```

```
        writeln (1st, names[stud], ' ', mark)
    end {for stud}
end; {PRINTMARKS}
```

· · ·

18.3 MATRIX OPERATIONS (For Students Familiar with Matrices)

In mathematics, a two-dimensional array with *m* rows and *n* columns is known as an $m \times n$ matrix.

Matrix Addition   If *A* and *B* are both $m \times n$ matrices, then the sum $A + B$ is defined by adding corresponding elements. For example,

$$\begin{bmatrix} 3 & 1 \\ 5 & 7 \end{bmatrix} + \begin{bmatrix} 6 & 0 \\ -2 & 1 \end{bmatrix} = \begin{bmatrix} 9 & 1 \\ 3 & 8 \end{bmatrix}$$

Here is a program fragment to find the matrix sum $C = A + B$, where *A* and *B* are both $m \times n$ matrices.

```
for row := 1 to m do
  for col := 1 to n do
    C[row,col] := A[row,col] + B[row,col];
```

Matrix Multiplication   The definition of matrix multiplication is considerably more complicated than that of addition. Be aware that the product of two matrices is defined only when the number of columns of the matrix on the left equals the number of rows of the matrix on the right. If *A* is $m \times n$ and *B* is $n \times p$, then the product matrix $C = AB$ is an $m \times p$ matrix, where $C[i,j] := \sum_{k=1}^{n} A[i,k] * B[k,j]$. Thus, the *i,j*th element *C* is calculated by taking the dot product of the *i*th row of *A* with the *j*th column of *B*. For example,

$$\begin{bmatrix} 2 & 3 \\ 5 & 1 \\ 6 & -1 \end{bmatrix} \begin{bmatrix} -1 & 5 & 2 & 1 \\ 3 & 1 & 0 & 1 \end{bmatrix} = \begin{bmatrix} 7 & 13 & 4 & 5 \\ -2 & 26 & 10 & 6 \\ -9 & 29 & 12 & 5 \end{bmatrix}$$

Note that `c[1,2]` = 13 since $2\cdot 5 + 3\cdot 1 = 13$.

· · · · · · · · · ·
Question   Assume that the main declaration section of a program contains the declarations

```
const maxrows = 10;
      maxcols = 10;
```

```
type MatType = array [1..maxrows,1..maxcols] of integer;
```

Fill in the blanks in procedure PROD_MAT so that if it is sent an n × p matrix B, it will return the product matrix C = AB.

```
procedure PROD-MAT (A,B: MatType;
                         var C: MatType;
                         m,n,p: integer);
{finds product AB where A is m by n and B is n by p}
var k, sum, row, col: integer;
begin
  for row := 1 to m do
    for col := 1 to p do
      begin
        sum := 0;
        for k := 1 to n do

        _____

      _____

      end {for col}
end; {PROD-MAT}
```

Answer   The completed lines with blanks are

```
    sum := sum + A[row,k] * B[k, col];
  C[row,col] := sum
```

In Exercise 21, you are asked to write a program that allows the user to input two matrices A and B. The output on paper should give (1) each of the input matrices and (2) either the product matrix or a message that the product matrix does not exist.   ● ● ●

Higher-Dimensional Arrays   It is sometimes useful to use arrays of more than two dimensions. In the next example, we show how to declare and make use of a ***three-dimensional array.***

Example   Suppose a chain of car dealerships has three different dealers and each dealer sells Chevrolets, Buicks, Oldsmobiles, and Cadillacs. The breakdown of how many cars of each brand were sold by each dealer on Sunday could be put into a two-dimensional array.

		Chevy	Buick	Olds	Caddy
Sunday	1	2	0	1	2
	2	1	0	3	0
	3	4	2	1	4

Suppose we want to store such information for each of the seven days of the week. Instead of using seven separate two-dimensional arrays, we could use a single three-dimensional array with the declarations

```
type
    days = (Sun, Mon, Tue, Wed, Thu, Fri, Sat);
    cars = (Chevy, Buick, Olds, Caddy);
    salestype = array[1..3, cars, days];
var
    sales: salestype;
```

Although memory is in fact linear, it helps us to keep track of what is going on by picturing it as a three-dimensional rectangular solid that is composed of layers of memory cells arranged as two-dimensional arrays.

From the illustration, we see that sales[2, Buick, Mon] has the value 4. Thus, dealer number 2 sold four Buicks on Monday.

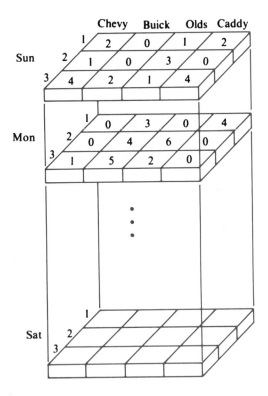

• • •

• • • • • • • • •
Question   What will be output by the following program fragment?

```
total := 0;
for dealer := 1 to 3 do
  for car := Chevy to Caddy do
    total := total + sales[dealer,car,Mon];
writeln (total);
```

Answer   The day is fixed at Mon. This finds the sum of all the elements with Mon as the third subscript. The value of total would be 25.   • • •

• • • • • • • • • •

Question   We can "slice" the "rectangular solid" in another direction. Write a loop to find and print the total number of Buicks sold.

Answer   Now we keep the second subscript fixed at Buick.

```
total := 0;
for dealer := 1 to 3 do
  for day := Sun to Sat do
    total := total + sales[dealer, Buick, day];
writeln (total);
```

• • •

• • • • • • • • • •

EXERCISES

• •

1. Give the output for

```
for i := 1 to 4 do
  begin
    sum := 0;
    for j := 1 to 3 do
      begin
        sum := sum + 10;
        if i > j then b[i,j] := 4
                 else b[i,j] := sum + j
      end {for j}
  end; {for i}
```

2. Give the output if the contents of array x are as indicated.

```
count := 0;
for m := 1 to 4 do
    begin
        myst := x[m,4];
        for k := 1 to 3 do
            if x[m,k] > myst then
                begin
                    write (x[m,k], ' ');
                    count := count + 1
                end;
        writeln (count);
    end;
```

43	55	32	77
18	55	22	11
44	33	20	27
50	60	70	63

3. Draw a picture of the current contents of the array in question as indicated.

(a)
```
for r := 1 to 3 do
    for c := 1 to 3 do
        x[r,c] := 10*c + 5*r;
{Draw a picture of x here}

for r := 1 to 3 do
    for c := 1 to 2 do
        x[r,c+1] := x[r,c] + 1;
{Draw a picture of x here}
```

(b)
```
for r := 1 to 3 do
    for c := 1 to 3 do
        y[r,c] := 10*r + 4*c;
{Draw a picture of y here}

for r := 1 to 3 do
    for c := 1 to 3 do
        y[r,c] := y[c,r];
{Draw a picture of y here}
```

4. Suppose that boxes is a square array with n rows and n columns.

(a) Write a program fragment to find the sum of the elements down the main diagonal of boxes (starting in the upper left corner and moving down to the lower right corner). For example, for the 3 × 3 array

5	1	1
12	7	9
10	3	2

the sum of the elements in the main diagonal would be 14 (5 + 7 + 2).

(b) Write a program fragment to find the sum of the elements in the other diagonal. For the given array, it would be 18 (10 + 7 + 1). (The fragment should be for an *n* by *n* array.)

5. Write a program fragment to print the contents of an array with m rows and n columns so that each row's contents appears on its own line.

6. Suppose `mat` is of type `array [1..5,1..4] of integer`.

   (a) Write a program fragment to print across one line the contents of *column* 3 of `mat`.

   (b) Write a program fragment to print each *column's* contents on its own line. The first line should give the first column's contents, the second line should give the second column's contents, and so on.

Longer Assignments

7. A basketball team with six players has played four games. A file contains the raw data with a typical data group like

```
Smith
12 14 7 10
```

   giving a player's name and points scored in each of the four games. Write a program that will first print the raw data in a nicely formatted table form, then print each player's scoring average, and finally print the number of points scored by the team game by game.

8. Write a program for the previous exercise so that all the output is contained in a single table.

9. You have on file the closing prices of several stocks for each weekday of last week. Write a program that will read the names and prices into two parallel arrays. For each stock, the program should print the maximum and minimum price and the day it was achieved. (Make a neat table under suitable headings.) Finally, it should print the maximum and minimum prices for the entire portfolio.

10. Suppose that a 3 × 3 array contains Xs, Os, and possibly blanks, representing a game of tic-tac-toe. Write a procedure that will determine and print the outcome of the game. For example, for

O	O	X
	X	X
X		O

    the output should be

    ```
    Player X won
    ```

(You may assume that all moves are legal.)

11. (a) A magic square is an $n \times n$ array such that the sum of every row, column, and diagonal is the same. Write a program that reads in the values for a 3×3 array and tests whether it is a magic square.

  * (b) Design your program so that the computer does not continue to find sums if it has already found two sums that are not equal.

12. Write a procedure that receives two $m \times n$ matrices and returns a third matrix whose values are the sum of the corresponding values in the other two matrices.

13. Write a program to produce a multiplication table for the integers 1 through 9. Format it as follows:

```
       1   2   3   4   5   6   7   8   9
   1   1   2   3   4   5   6   7   8   9
   2   2   4   6   8  10  12  14  16  18
   3   3   6   9  12  15  18  21  24  27
   .                                   .
   .                                   .
   .                                   .
   9   9  18  27  36  45  54  63  72  81
```

14. (a) A triple of positive integers a, b, c is called a *Pythagorean triple* if

$$c^2 = a^2 + b^2$$

For example, 3, 4, 5 is a Pythagorean triple. Write a program to print all Pythagorean triples with $c \leq 25$. (*Hint:* Use a nested loop with depth 3.)

  * (b) Modify the program so that you do not allow duplications of similar triangles. Thus 3, 4, 5 should appear on the list, but 6, 8, 10 should not. (Print only the reduced form.)

15. Write a program for use by a ticket agency in selling seats in a theater that has rows labeled A to E and seats numbered 1 to 10 in each row. Before each seat request is made, the customer is told which seats are available or if the performance is sold out. If the performance is not sold out, the customer must then input his seat choice. If he picks a seat that has already been sold, he must choose again.

16. The XYZ Company has a chain of five stores, each of which sells the same three items. The stores are numbered 1 through 5, and the items are numbered 1 through 3. Write a program that will read in data from an external file. Each line of data will represent a single sale and will consist of a store number, item number, and sales amount. Use a two-dimensional

array (5 × 3) to keep track of the sales total for each store and item combination.

The output should consist of a neatly formatted table showing the gross sales for each store and item combination. If any element has a sales total of $0.00, print a blank space instead of 0.00.

When creating your data file (of at least 25 sales), be sure to include some store and item combinations with more than one sale and some with no sales.

* **17.** Modify the program in Exercise 15 so that when the customer requests a particular row

(a) you offer him the first available seat in that row.

(b) you offer him the available seat closest to the middle of that row.

* **18.** Write a program that will allow a teacher to use a computer to grade her students' responses to a multiple-choice exam consisting of 10 questions. The data file will contain two lines for each student: The first will have the student's name, and the second will have the student's responses to the 10 questions. You can assume that all the answers will be in the range of 1 to 5. The 10 questions are lettered A to J.

The output of your program should consist of the following:

The name and test score for each student.

A classwide summary of the number of correct responses to each question, along with the letter of each question.

The average score for the class.

Use the following answer key to do the grading:

2 5 3 3 4 1 2 5 4 1

The answer key will be the first line of the data file. Following is an example of the data for one student:

```
John Doe
2 5 4 3 3 1 1 2 4 4
```

19. For the three-dimensional array given in Section 18.3, write a program fragment to find the total number of Chevys sold by dealer 2.

* **20.** Write an interactive program that will allow two people to play tic-tac-toe on the computer. Store the current state of the board in a global 3 × 3 array. Each element can be X, O, or a blank. Include the following:

A procedure to print the current state of the board.

A procedure to request the next move of the appropriate player and to check that the move is legal—that the space is on the board and that it is unoccupied. (You may assume that X always goes first.)

A procedure to determine whether the game is over and why.

(*Optional:* After you are sure that the program works, modify it so that a running record of the game is created on an external file.)

  * *21.* Write the matrix multiplication program that is discussed in Section 18.3.

* *

Lab Exercises   **DEBUGGING**

Lab18-1.pas   Plus, Minus Summation
Lab18-2.pas   Same Bonus for Each Row
Lab18-3.pas   Column by Column

* *

Chapter

19

SORTING AND SEARCHING

• • • Arranging a list of values in order is known as **sorting**. For example, we might sort a list of numerical values in increasing order or a list of names in alphabetical order. Locating a particular item in a list is known as **searching**. Searching a sorted list is generally much faster than searching an unsorted list. Consider, for example, looking up someone's telephone number in an alphabetical directory versus a nonalphabetical one. This is not to imply, however, that you should always sort a list before searching it because sorting can be quite time consuming. The decision whether to sort a list before searching it depends to some degree on how many times the list will be searched.

In this chapter, we discuss two searching algorithms: (1) the **linear search,** which can be used on any list, and (2) the **binary search,** which is more efficient but should be used only on a *sorted* list.

We also discuss three elementary sorting algorithms: (1) the **selection sort,** (2) the **bubble sort,** and (3) the **insertion sort.** For a small array of 100 or fewer items, each of these sorts is quite satisfactory since the sorting time will be less than a second whichever is used. However, to sort a really large array, the amount of computer time needed to perform the sort becomes an important consideration, and it makes sense to use an advanced sort such as the quick sort discussed in Chapter 28.   • • •

19.1 LINEAR SEARCH

In a linear search (also called a *sequential search*) of an array, we start with the first cell of the array and look at one cell after another until we either find the searched-for item or have looked at all the cells without finding it. The following `LINSEARCH` function returns either the location of the desired item or, if the item was not on the list, the value zero.

The linear search is another example of a Bounded Number of Tries (introduced in Section 8.1). Here we give one of the most common ways to code the linear search of an array. Note (1) the use of the boolean variable `found` and (2) `index` is initialized to 1 (not 0) before the loop—this causes the loop to be skipped if the array is empty.

```
function LINSEARCH (want: str15;
                    names: namestype;
                    size: integer): integer;
{returns the subscript of the box containing}
{the wanted item or returns 0 if not in array}
var found: boolean;
    index: integer;
begin
  found := false;
  index := 1;
  while (not found) and (index <= size) do
    if names[index] = want
        then found := true
        else index := index + 1;

  {determine cause of loop exit}
  if found then LINSEARCH := index
           else LINSEARCH := 0
end; {LINSEARCH}
```

• • • • • • • • •

Question   Suppose that `names` and `salaries` are parallel arrays. We want to write a program that asks the user to enter the name of an employee. The printout will be either that employee's salary or the message that he or she is not on the list. The procedure `GETDATA` will read the data from an external file into the parallel arrays.

Fill in the blank in the following program fragment, which uses `LINSEARCH`:

```
begin {main}
  GETDATA (names, salaries, size);
  write ('enter name of employee ');
  readln (want);
  spot := LINSEARCH (want, names, size);
```

```
    if spot = 0
        then writeln (want, ' not on payroll')
        else writeln (want, ' salary is $ ', _____:8:2)
    end.
```

Answer   Since the arrays `names` and `salaries` are parallel, the desired subscript is `spot`. Thus, the blank should be filled with `salaries[spot]`.   ● ● ●

CAUTION   Recall that two string values must be identical to be equal. Thus,

```
    'Jones' = 'Jones '
```

has the value `false`. This fact could cause a problem if the person creating a list types `Jones` with trailing blanks (for example, by hitting the spacebar before pressing the ENTER key) and the user enters the searched-for name as `Jones` without trailing blanks. Under these circumstances, `LINSEARCH` would incorrectly conclude that Jones is not on the list.

In Section 20.5, we will define a `TRIM` function that can be used to remove trailing blanks from a string. For now, however, be careful not to include trailing blanks when entering `string` values.   ● ● ●

19.2   BINARY SEARCH (OF A SORTED ARRAY)

A linear search works well enough for a fairly short list. If you wanted to look up the telephone number for William Phillipson in the Manhattan directory, however, it would be foolish to start with the very first name and continue searching one name at a time. A more efficient method would take advantage of the alphabetical ordering of the names to jump immediately to a place in the second half of the book.

The binary search is akin to the method you would automatically use to look up a phone number. In the binary search, you keep narrowing the search by repeatedly eliminating half the remaining list. Of course, in order to perform a binary search, you must have a list that is sorted.

Example   Suppose we want to search for the number 57 in the following array:

start of
array   middle
 ↓   ↓
x[1]   x[2]   x[3]   x[4]   x[5]   x[6]   x[7]   x[8]   x[9]   x[10] x[11] x[12] x[13]

23	35	40	48	57	62	64	75	78	84	87	92	95

First, we compare the searched-for number, 57, to the contents of the middle box, x[7]. Since 57 is less than 64, we can conclude that if 57 is in the array at all, it must be in the left half—that is, among cells x[1] through x[6].

middle
↓

	x[1]	x[2]	x[3]	x[4]	x[5]	x[6]
Segment still under consideration	23	35	40	48	57	62

Next, we compare the searched-for number, 57, to the contents of the current middle box, x[3]. *When there are an even number of boxes, we take the middle cell to be that cell just to the left of the midline.* Since 57 is greater than 40, we can narrow the search to the remaining right half—that is, the cells x[4] through x[6].

middle
↓

	x[4]	x[5]	x[6]
Segment still under consideration	48	57	62

This time the searched-for number, 57, is equal to the contents of the middle box. Thus, it has been located in cell x[5].   • • •

Binary Search Function

We want the function BINARYSEARCH to return either the subscript of the cell containing the wanted item or 0 if the item is not in the array. The variables first, last, and mid will keep track of the subscripts of the first, last, and middle cells of the segment still under consideration.

The key test, one that occurs repeatedly, in a binary search compares the wanted item with the contents of the current middle cell. If they are equal, the wanted item has been found. If the wanted item is less than the contents of the middle cell, then the segment under consideration should be changed to the half segment to the left of the middle cell, shaded in gray.

Note that the segment under consideration can be changed to the left half by assigning last a new value, namely,

```
      last := mid - 1
```

• • • • • • • • • •

Question In function BINARYSEARCH, fill in the blank that adjusts the segment to be considered when wanted is bigger than the contents of x[mid].

```
function BINARYSEARCH (wanted: integer;
                       nums: numstype;
                       size: integer): integer;
  var first, last, mid: integer;
      found: boolean;
  begin
    first := 1;
    last := size;
    found := false;
    repeat
      mid := (first + last) div 2;
      if wanted = nums[mid] then
        found := true
      else if wanted < nums[mid] then
        last := mid - 1
      else
      _____

    until (found) or (last < first);
    if found then BINARYSEARCH := mid
              else BINARYSEARCH := 0
  end; {BINARYSEARCH}
```

Answer When wanted > nums[mid], we want to search the segment to the right of the middle. Thus, the else alternative is

```
      else first := mid + 1
```
• • •

Hand Traces

We already did one trace of the binary search before we gave the code. Let us do two more traces using the same array as before.

x[1]	x[2]	x[3]	x[4]	x[5]	x[6]	x[7]	x[8]	x[9]	x[10]	x[11]	x[12]	x[13]
23	35	40	48	57	62	64	75	78	84	87	92	95

Trace When wanted = 48 Note that the values of first and last at the bottom of an execution of the loop body are given by the subscripts of the current subarray. Thus, after the first execution of the loop body, the subarray `x[1..6]` means that `first = 1` and `last = 6`.

Exec. of Loop Body	Action
1	`mid = 7`, subarray becomes left half—`x[1..6]`
2	`mid = 3`, subarray becomes right half—`x[4..6]`
3	`mid = 5`, subarray becomes left half—`x[4]`
4	`mid = 4`, found **since** `wanted = x[mid]`

Trace When `wanted = 82` (Not in the Array)

Exec. of Loop Body	Action
1	`mid = 7`, subarray becomes right half—`x[8..13]`
2	`mid = 10`, subarray becomes left half—`x[8..9]`
3	`mid = 8`, subarray becomes right half—`x[9]`
4	`mid = 9`, `first` becomes 10, `last` stays 9 Thus `first > last` causes loop exit

When wanted Is Not in the Array   In general, do you see why `function BINARYSEARCH` will correctly return the value 0 when `wanted` is not in the array? Obviously, `wanted` won't be found, but why couldn't the `repeat-until` loop be an infinite loop? The answer is that when `wanted` is not in the array, eventually

`first > last`

because each execution of the loop body either increases the value of `first` or decreases the value of `last`. Thus, after finitely many executions, we will have `first > last`.

Efficiency: Binary versus Linear Search   For a linear search on a list of size *N*,

1. If the item is on the list, an average of *N*/2 comparisons will be required to locate its position.

2. If the item is not on the list, *exactly N* comparisons will always be required.

For a binary search on a list of size *N*, at most $(\log_2 N + 1)$ comparisons will be required, whether or not the item is on the list. Thus, for a list of size 128, ascertaining that an item was not on the list would take 128 comparisons by the linear search method. The same task would take at most 8 executions of the loop by the binary search method. (Each time the loop body is executed, the current segment is cut in half.)

The GetTime Procedure   The built-in procedure `GetTime`, contained in the DOS unit, returns the current time according to the computer's internal 24-hour clock. For example, when the current time is 9:54 and 2.73 seconds, the call

```
GetTime (hr, min, sec, sec100);
```

would return the values of 9, 54, 2, and 73 to the variables `hr`, `min`, `sec`, and `sec100`, respectively. The current time can be converted into a current total number of seconds by

```
TotSeconds := (hr * 3600) + (min * 60) + sec + sec100/100;
```

To time how long it takes to execute a segment of a program, you can place calls to `GetTime` before and after that segment and then calculate the number of seconds elapsed. Note that the DOS unit is declared by

```
uses DOS;
```

Note also that the parameters of

```
GetTime:
```

hr, min, sec, and sec100 *must be* declared of type `word`.

REMARK   `GetTime` can be used to study the efficiency of various algorithms (for example, see Exercise 9). Be aware, however, that in some microcomputers, the `sec100` reading may be accurate to only one-fourth of a second.

• • •

19.3 **THE SWITCH PROCEDURE**
• •

Suppose x has the value 5 and y has the value 9. We want to write code to switch the values of x and y—so that x becomes 9 and y becomes 5. Note that the code

```
x := y;
y := x;
```

will *not* work because the first statement erases the starting value of x. After the preceding two statements were executed, x and y would both be equal to the starting value of y. Thus, x and y would both be equal to 9.

The correct way to switch the values of x and y is to use another variable named `temp` to *temporarily* store the starting value of x before assigning the value of y to x. Here is the correct code.

```
temp := x;
x := y;
y := temp;
```

There is a mnemonic device for remembering this code. Note that `temp` appears on the *left* side of the first statement and on the *right* side of the last statement. Also note that one of the two diagonals has x and the other has y.

Consider the following analogy for introducing the variable `temp`: If you had a cup of coffee and a cup of tea and you wanted to switch the contents of the two cups, you would need some form of temporary storage, such as a third cup.

• • • • • • • • •

Question   For the following program, what will be printed

(a)   if 23 and 19 are input

(b)   if 35 and 38 are input

```
program drill;
var a, b: integer;

procedure SWITCH (var x, y: integer);
  {switches the values of x and y}
  var temp: integer;
  begin
    temp := x;
    x := y;
    y := temp
  end; {SWITCH}

begin {main}
  write ('enter 2 integers: ');
  readln (a, b);
  if a > b
    then SWITCH (a, b)
    else writeln ('No switch');
  writeln (a, ' ', b)
end.
```

Answer

(a)
```
19  23
```

(b)
```
No switch
35 38
```

• • •

19.4 **SELECTION SORT**

• •

We begin our discussion of sorting with the selection sort, which is the easiest sort to understand. The selection sort is similar to what the average person might actually do if asked to sort a list of 40 numbers (or alphabetize a list of 40 names). Its basic idea is to first find the smallest number and put it in position 1; then restricting attention to the remaining numbers, find the next smallest number and put it in position 2. Continuing in this fashion, once the smallest 39 numbers have been put in position, the remaining number is the largest and belongs at the end, and the list is sorted.

Let us illustrate the selection sort for the following array:

| 53 | 44 | 39 | 12 | 56 | 30 | 48 |

A pass is a trip through the entire array (or a remaining portion of the array) that makes some progress toward sorting the array.

During pass 1, you go through the entire array locating the smallest number and then *switch* the positions of the number in position 1 with the smallest number. Thus after pass 1, the array will be

| 12 | 44 | 39 | 53 | 56 | 30 | 48 |

During pass 2, you go through the subarray $x[2]$, . . . , $x[7]$, locating its smallest number, which is 30, and then switch the positions of 44 and 30; that is, switch the contents of $x[2]$ and $x[6]$.

During pass 3, you go through the subarray $x[3]$, . . . , $x[7]$, locating its smallest number, which is 39, and then since 39 is already in its proper position, there is no need to do a switch.

After six passes, this array will be sorted since when the six smallest numbers are in their proper positions, the remaining number, which is the largest, will be in $x[7]$.

Now let us consider an array with size numbers and describe what happens during pass p, with an eye to writing the computer code.

| $x[1]$ | | | $x[p-1]$ | $x[p]$ | | $x[size]$ |

At the start of pass p, the smallest $p - 1$ numbers are in their proper position—thus, we can restrict our attention to $x[p]$, . . . , $x[size]$.

We need to go through the subarray $x[p]$, . . . , $x[size]$ to find the location (call it SmIndex) of the smallest element of that subarray, and then if the smallest is not already in cell p, we will switch the contents of $x[p]$ and $x[SmIndex]$.

In the pseudocode, note that we need only `size - 1` passes. For example, if the array had seven elements, then after six passes (`size - 1` passes), the six smallest elements would be in their proper place, and so the remaining element, the largest, would be in position 7.

Here is the pseudocode.

```
for p := 1 to size - 1 do
   begin {perform pass p}
      use an inner for loop to find SmIndex, which points to the
         location of the smallest element of x[p], . . . , x[size]
      after the inner loop, if necessary, switch x[p] and x[SmIndex]
   end; {for p}
```

Here is the actual code.

```
procedure SELECT_SORT (var x: ArrayType;   size: integer);
   {sorts an array of up to 100 integers}
   var p, i, SmIndex: integer;
      smallest, temp: integer;   {since integer array}
   begin
      for p := 1 to size - 1 do
         begin
            {find SmIndex and smallest}
            SmIndex := p;
            smallest := x[p];
            for i := p + 1 to size do
               if x[i] < smallest then
                  begin
                     smallest := x[i];
                     SmIndex := i
                  end;

            {if necessary switch x[p] and x[SmIndex]}
            if x[p] <> x[SmIndex] then
               begin
                  temp := x[p];
                  x[p] := x[SmIndex];
                  x[SmIndex] := temp
               end
         end {for p}
   end;   {SELECT_SORT}
```

Note that for pass p, the body of the outer `for` loop processes the subarray `x[p], x[p + 1], . . . , x[size]`, finding its smallest element and then putting it in `x[p]`.

Do you see why the inner `for` loop header can start at p + 1 rather than p? Answer: Since `smallest` is initialized with `x[p]`.

A Complete Program Calling Procedure SELECT_SORT

```
program NumbSort;
{reads a list of integers from a file into an array, sorts the
 array, and then prints the sorted list}
type
  ArrayType = array[1..100] of integer;
var
  ArrayToSort: ArrayType;
  i, size: integer;

  ┌─────────────────────────────────────────────────────┐
  │ procedure GETDATA and procedure SELECT_SORT         │
  │ go here.                                            │
  └─────────────────────────────────────────────────────┘

begin {main}
  GETDATA (ArrayToSort, size);
  SELECT_SORT (ArrayToSort, size);
  for i := 1 to size do
    writeln (ArrayToSort[i])
end.
```

Modifications Required for Sorting Names

Essentially, the same program can be used to sort a list of names (as opposed to numbers). The modifications that must be made are to change the `type` declaration in the main program to an array of strings

```
type
  ArrayType = array[1..100] of string[20];
```

and to change the declaration of the local variables `temp` and `smallest` in procedure `SELECT_SORT` to

```
temp,smallest: string[20];
```

19.5 BUBBLE SORT
• •

Each pass in the bubble sort consists of a trip through a remaining (potentially still out-of-order) subarray. During a pass, the contents of each successive pair of adjacent boxes of that subarray are compared and then switched if they are out of order.

First Pass of the Bubble Sort   Suppose that four numbers are stored in an array with memory cells x[1] through x[4]. We wish to sort those numbers in increasing order. The first pass of the bubble sort would do the following:

Compare the contents of x[1] and x[2]; if x[1] contains the larger number, switch their contents.

Compare the *current* contents of x[2] with that of x[3]; switch if necessary.

Compare the *current* contents of x[3] with that of x[4]; switch if necessary.

At the end of the first pass, the largest number will be in x[4].

The following figure illustrates the first pass when x[1] through x[4] contain 34, 28, 43, and 15, respectively.

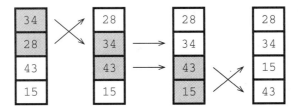

Notice that for the first pass the number of comparisons is size - 1. In this example of an array of four elements, there are three comparisons during the first pass.

Pass 2 of Bubble Sort   Since the largest number is necessarily in x[4], pass 2 is performed on the subarray x[1],x[2],x[3].

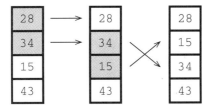

Pass 3 of Bubble Sort   Since the two largest numbers are in their proper place, pass 3 is performed on subarray x[1],x[2].

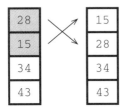

The array is now sorted. Note that for an array with `size` elements, the array is ensured of being sorted after `size - 1` passes.

• • • • • • • • •

Question   This array of six elements will be sorted in fewer than five (`size - 1`) passes. What will the contents of this array be after pass 1, after pass 2, and after pass 3?

36	25	49	21	52	38

Answer

After pass 1:	25	36	21	49	38	52
After pass 2:	25	21	36	38	49	52
After pass 3:	21	25	36	38	49	52

Note that the array is sorted after pass 3.   • • •

REMARK   The bubble sort is so named because (viewing the array vertically) the smaller numbers "bubble" to the top as the larger ones are put in place at the bottom. Each pass is guaranteed to put *at least one* more next largest number in its proper place. In the previous example, the first pass put only the largest number, 52, in its place. The second pass, however, put 49, 38, and 36 in place.   • • •

Two Versions of Bubble Sort   Next, we present two versions of the bubble sort. In version 1, the computer makes `size - 1` passes even if the array is sorted in fewer passes. In version 2, the computer stops making passes as soon as it has made a pass in which no switches were made since this implies the array is already sorted.

Version 1 of Bubble Sort   Here is the pseudocode.

```
for pass := 1 to size-1 do
  for i := 1 to size - pass do
    if x[i] > x[i+1] then
        switch the contents of x[i] and x[i+1]
```

Let us check the correctness of the upper limit in the inner loop

```
for i := 1 to size - pass
```

The upper limit is the number of comparisons made during that pass.

When `pass = 1`, the inner loop does what it is supposed to since its header will be `for i := 1 to size - 1`, and thus it will make `size - 1` comparisons (as it should).

For each succeeding pass, the upper limit of the inner loop decreases by 1 since `pass` increases by 1. Thus, for each successive pass, the number of comparisons will be decreased by 1.

Version 2 of Bubble Sort (Early Exit)   If an array is sorted in fewer than size - 1 passes, we would like the computer to stop making passes. How will the computer know when the array is already sorted? Answer: If it makes a pass in which no switches were made, then the array is already sorted.

In the code for version 2 below, note the use of the boolean variable NoSwitches.

Here is the pseudocode for version 2.

```
pass := 0;
repeat
  pass := pass + 1;
  perform pass over remaining subarray
until perform a pass that made no switches
```

Here is the actual code for version 2.

Note the use of the boolean variable NoSwitches. Before each pass, NoSwitches is initialized to true. If there is a switch during the pass, then NoSwitches is assigned the value false. But if no switches were made during a pass, then NoSwitches will still have the value true by the end of that pass.

```
procedure BUBBLESORT (var x: ArrayType; size: integer);
  {improved version to sort an array of integers}
  var NoSwitches: boolean;
      i, pass: integer;
      temp: integer;          {since array of integers}
  begin
    pass := 0;
    repeat
      pass := pass + 1;
      NoSwitches := true;
      for i := 1 to size - pass do
        if x[i] > x[i + 1] then
          begin
            NoSwitches := false;
            temp := x[i];
            x[i] := x[i + 1];
            x[i + 1] := temp
          end {then}
    until NoSwitches
  end; {BUBBLESORT}
```

The same complete program used for SELECT_SORT from Section 19.4 can be used by merely replacing all references to SELECT_SORT with BUBBLESORT.

19.6 INSERTING INTO A SORTED ARRAY

• •

Suppose one new entry is to be added to a sorted array and we want the enlarged array to end up sorted. An inefficient method would be to first put the new entry at the end of the array (in the cell with the subscript size + 1) and then use the bubble sort on this new array. A much better method, which takes advantage of the fact that the starting array is sorted already, is to follow these three steps:

1. Search the array to locate the cell in which the new element should be inserted. Let spot be the subscript of that cell.

2. For each of the cells with subscripts spot through size, shift the contents of that cell one cell to the right. (Before you can put the new entry in the cell with subscript spot, you must make room for it.)

3. Put the new entry in the cell with the subscript spot.

Example   Suppose the new entry 55 is to be inserted into the following array:

First we search the array to locate the cell in which 55 should be inserted, and we let spot become 4. Next we make room for the new entry. After the shifting we have

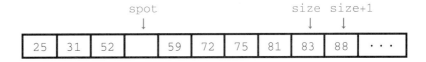

Actually, the box with subscript spot will not be empty, as indicated in the diagram, but will still contain the old value 59, which we will overwrite.

Finally, we put 55 in the cell with subscript spot and update size.

Here is procedure INSERTING, based on the method just described.

Each element of the array is of type `EntryType`. (In the array used to demonstrate insertion, `EntryType` was of type `integer`.)

```
procedure INSERTING (entry: EntryType;
                          var list: listtype;
                          var size: integer);
   {inserts into a sorted array}
   {resulting array is still sorted}
   var i, spot: integer;
       SpotFound: boolean;
   begin
     {locate spot}
     SpotFound := false;
     spot := 1;
     while (not SpotFound) and (spot <= size) do
       if entry <= list[spot]
          then SpotFound := true
          else spot := spot + 1;

     {shift to make room for new entry}
     for i := size downto spot do
       list[i + 1] := list[i];

     size := size + 1; {update size}
     {put new entry into list[spot]}
     list[spot] := entry
   end;   {INSERTING}
```

Question   Note that a `downto` loop is used to shift. What would be wrong with using the following loop instead?

```
for i := spot to size do
  list[i + 1] := list[i];
```

Answer   The initial value in `list[spot]` would be propagated throughout the rest of the array. For the preceding example, in which we inserted 55, the result of a procedure with this incorrect `for` loop would be

25	31	52	55	59	59	59	59	59	59

• • •

Question   Suppose that the new entry to be inserted into the array in the previous example was 95.

(a)   What would `spot` equal in terms of `size`?

(b)   What would happen during the `downto` loop?

Answer (a) `spot` would equal `size + 1`

(b) The `downto` loop with header

```
for i := size downto spot do
```

would be skipped since `size < spot`. This is exactly what we want since we don't need any shifting in this case.

• • • • • • • • • •

Example Now let us consider a complete program that uses the INSERTING procedure. The program will first read in an alphabetized list of names from an external file. Then it will allow the user to add names to the list, one at a time. Finally, it will print the new list in alphabetical order.

```
{$R+}
program ReadAndInsert;
{reads in alphabetized list}
{adds input name and prints sorted list}
uses printer;
const maxsize = 50;
type EntryType = string[15];
     listtype = array[1..maxsize] of EntryType;
var  i, size: integer;
     name: EntryType;
     list: listtype;

procedure GETFILE (var list: listtype;
                   var size: integer);
  {reads contents of file into an array}
  var NameFile: text;
  begin
    assign (NameFile, 'info.dat');
    reset (NameFile);
    size := 0;
    while not seekeof (NameFile) do
      begin
        size := size + 1;
        readln (NameFile, list[size])
      end; {while}
    close (NameFile)
  end; {GETFILE}


  procedure INSERTING goes here.
```

```
begin {main}
  GETFILE (list, size);
  write ('Enter name or xyz to quit ');
  readln (name);
  while (name <> 'xyz') and (size < maxsize) do
    begin
      INSERTING (name, list, size);
      write ('Enter name or xyz to quit ');
      readln (name)
    end; {while}
  if name <> 'xyz' then
    writeln ('Array full. Cannot add ', name);

  {print final list}
  writeln (lst, 'Final List');
  for i := 1 to size do
    writeln (lst, list[i])
end.
```

REMARK   Note that `program ReadAndInsert` does not test if a name is already on the list—duplicate names will be added to the list. In Exercise 14(a), you are asked to modify `procedure INSERTING` so that it doesn't add duplicates to the list. In Exercises 14(b) and (c), you are asked to use a binary search for `INSERTING`.   • • •

• • • • • • • • •   EXERCISES
• •

1. **(a)** Suppose the array b contains the numbers

14 26 18 25 40 32 12 6 49

What will be the contents of that array after the following for loop is executed?

```
for i := 1 to 7 do
  if b[i] > b[i + 1] then
    begin
      temp := b[i + 2];
      b[i + 2] := b[i + 1];
      b[i + 1] := temp
    end; {then}
```

(b) Suppose that x is an array of type array[1..5] of integer. **What will be printed by the following fragment?**

```
for i := 1 to 5 do
   x[i] := i * 5;
for i := 1 to 5 do
   begin
      if x[i] <> 10 then
         begin
            here := x[i];
            x[i] := x[6-i];
            x[6-i] := here
         end;   {then}
      writeln (i, ' ', x[i]);
   end;   {for i}
for i := 1 to 5 do
   write (x[i}, ' ');
```

2. Suppose that an array contains

    4 23 11 45 2 16 44 9 33 29

What will the contents of the array be after three passes of the

(a) selection sort?

(b) bubble sort?

3. Give an example of an array of 100 elements in which at most two elements are out of position, and yet version 2 of the bubble sort will require 100 passes.

4. Suppose that the binary search is applied to an array containing

    4 8 12 20 25 33 35 40 50 60 65 72 77 82 88

(a) When wanted = 8, how many times will the loop body be executed? In answering this question, trace the values of first and last by the bottom of each execution of the loop body.

(b) Same question for wanted = 65.

(c) When wanted = 27, what values will first and last have when the loop is exited?

Longer Assignments

5. Write a subprogram to sort an array of n numbers. In addition to printing a sorted list, the program should determine whether there was a tie for the largest number. If there was a tie, the subprogram should print how many numbers were tied for largest.

6. The median of a sorted array of numbers can be defined as follows:

> For an odd number of numbers, it is the number in the middle box. For an even number of numbers, it is the average of the numbers in the two boxes closest to the middle.

Thus, the median of a sorted array of 25 numbers is the number in the 13th box, whereas for an array of 24 numbers it is the average of the numbers in the 12th and 13th boxes. Write a procedure to find the median for a *sorted* array.

7. A file contains the name and IQ for each student in a class of up to 50 students. The names are not in alphabetical order. Write a program that will print an alphabetical list containing the names of the students and their IQs. Be sure that each name has the correct IQ printed with it and not someone else's.

8. A file contains the name and score for each student in a class of up to 50 students. The names are not in alphabetical order. Letter grades are assigned as follows:

> A for at least 90.
>
> B for at least 80 but under 90.
>
> C for at least 70 but under 80.
>
> D for at least 60 but under 70.
>
> F for under 60.

Write a program that will print an alphabetized list containing each student's name, score, and letter grade.

9. (a) Write a procedure that could be used to compare the efficiency of the original and improved versions of the bubble sort on an array of integers. First the procedure should perform the original version of the sort. In doing so, the procedure should keep track of and print the total number of comparisons and the total number of switches. Then the procedure should perform the improved bubble sort on the same array. In doing so, the procedure should keep track of and print the total number of comparisons, the total number of switches, and the number of times `pass := pass + 1` was executed.

   (b) Using the procedure in part (a), write a program that will generate and store 1,000 random integers from 1 to 5,000, print the unsorted list, and sort the list first by means of the bubble sort and then by means of the improved bubble sort. The printout should give the number of comparisons and the number of switches made, first for the bubble sort and then for the improved bubble sort.

   (c) Use the `GetTime` procedure to compare the average execution time for the two sorting methods, where the experiment of sorting 1,000 random integers in the range of 0 to 5,000 is repeated five times.

* *10.* The *mode* of a list of numbers is defined as the number having the largest number of occurrences in the list. For example, the list

        72, 72, 72, 75, 75, 78, 82, 82, 82, 82, 85, 85, 85, 89

has mode 82. Write a procedure that will determine the mode for a *sorted* array of integers.

11. Write a procedure `PRINT_ALL` that has four parameters: the unsorted parallel arrays `first` and `last`, `size`, and `WantedLast`. The procedure should either print the first names of all the people with `WantedLast` as last names or the message `NONE` if there aren't any.
For example,

        PRINT_ALL (first, last, size, 'Jones');

might cause the computer to print

```
Jones Bill
Jones Mary
```

* *12.* Modify the procedure in Exercise 11 as follows:
  (a) First sort the arrays by last name.
  (b) Use a binary search to find one occurrence of `WantedLast` (if it exists).
  (c) Print the first and last names of *all* the people with `WantedLast` as a last name. Once you have found one, you still must print *all* the others.

* *13.* Write a telephone directory program that reads names and phone numbers into two parallel arrays and sorts both arrays by name. When the user enters a name in response to a prompt, the program should see if the name is already in the directory. (Use a binary search.) If so, it should print the phone number. If not, it should prompt the user to enter the phone number, and then it should add the name and the number to the arrays using the insertion sort.

14. (a) Revise `program ReadAndInsert` (page 335) so that if an input name is already on the list, the name will not be added.
  (b) Same as part (a) but use a binary search.
  (c) Same as part (b) but have `procedure INSERTING` call a `BINSEARCH` procedure, where `BINSEARCH` has five parameters: `name`, `list`, `size`, `spot`, and `OnList`.

15. Write a program that uses an insertion sort to sort a nonalphabetized list of names contained in a file. That is, each time a name is read in, the name should be inserted into the array of names so that at each stage the array of names read in so far is sorted.

* *16.* The shaker sort is a variant of the bubble sort that tends to be slightly more efficient. Instead of always going from top to bottom on each pass, the shaker alternates—every other pass proceeds from bottom to top. Thus, the first pass moves the largest element to the bottom, the second pass moves the smallest element to the top, the third pass moves the next largest out-of-place element into position, and so on. Write a procedure for the shaker sort.

* *17.* Write a program that first reads in an alphabetized list of names from an external file and then repeatedly presents the user with the following menu of choices.

1. Add another name to the list
2. See a printout of the list so far
3. Delete a name from the list
4. Quit

When the user chooses to quit, the program should write the current list onto a new text file.

* *

Lab Exercises   **DEBUGGING**

Lab19-1.pas	Linear Search
Lab19-2.pas	Binary Search
Lab19-3.pas	Testing if Sorted
Lab19-4.pas	Selection Sort
Lab19-5.pas	Sorting and Then Using a Binary Search

* *

Chapter

20

STRING MANIPULATIONS

• • • Up to this point, we have worked with a string value as a whole. We are now ready to examine and manipulate parts of a string, either one character at a time or in larger chunks. This chapter presents several functions and procedures that can be used to manipulate strings and their components. • • •

20.1 ACCESSING INDIVIDUAL CHARACTERS

A string variable resembles an array of characters with some additional features.

Example Suppose name has been declared of type string. Then after the statement

```
name := 'John';
```

the current contents for name could be depicted as shown here.

```
                          name
        [0]    [1]    [2]    [3]    [4]    [5]            [255]
      ┌──────┬──────┬──────┬──────┬──────┬──────┬ ─ ─ ┬──────┐
      │      │  J   │  o   │  h   │  n   │      │ · · ·│      │
      └──────┴──────┴──────┴──────┴──────┴──────┴ ─ ─ ┴──────┘
```

REMARK   The memory box `name[0]` is used to store the length of the current value of `name`. It is stored in *character* form, however—that is, `name[0]` contains the character whose ordinal value is the length of name. Thus, when `name` has the value `'John'`, `name[0]` will store the character whose ASCII number is 4.   ● ● ●

We can access individual characters in a string as we would the elements of an array. Thus, with `name` as shown, the statement

```
writeln (name [3]);
```

would output the letter h.

● ● ● ● ● ● ● ● ●
Example   In `program drill`, the computer will examine a string character by character to count how many e's it contains.

```
program drill;
{count number of e's in a string}
var ecount, i: integer;
    word: string;

begin
  ecount := 0;
  write ('type a word in lowercase ');
  readln (word);
  for i := 1 to length (word) do
    if word[i] = 'e' then ecount := ecount + 1;
  writeln ('Number of e''s in ', word, ': ', ecount)
end.
```

   ● ● ●

Changing a Single Character   You may change any character in a string simply by assigning a new character to that position in the string.

● ● ● ● ● ● ● ● ●
Example   After the statements

```
str := 'word';
str[3] := 'o';
```

are executed, the contents of `str` will be `'wood'`.   ● ● ●

CAUTION   Be careful not to assign values to individual boxes that are beyond the length of the current value of the string variable. For example, the code

```
str := 'hand';
str[5] := 'y';
```

is *not* recommended. This assignment does not change the value stored in str[0]—the length of the current value of str. Thus, when str is accessed, the value 'hand' will be found. Consequently, the statement writeln (str) will still produce hand as its output—it will not output the y.   • • •

Question   The following program will replace all occurrences of the letter e in an input word with asterisks. For example, if Peter is entered, the output will be P*t*r. Fill in the blank.

```
program drill;
var str: string [15];
    i: integer;
begin
  write ('Enter a word ');
  readln (str);
  for i := 1 to length (str) do
    if str[i] = 'e' then _____;
  writeln (str)
end.
```

Answer   The blank should say

```
str[i] := '*';
```
   • • •

Compatibility   As with integers and reals, we have another instance of one-way compatibility. You may assign a character to a string variable but not a string (even of length 1) to a character variable. Thus, for declarations

```
var name: string;
    st: string[1];
    ch: char;
        .
        .
        .
    st := 'a';   {okay}
    st := ch;    {okay}
    ch := st;    {ILLEGAL}
```

```
ch := name[3];      {okay, since name[3] is a character value}
ch := '';           {ILLEGAL, since null string is not a character}
ch := ' ';          {okay, blank is a character}
st := '';           {okay to assign null string to st}
```

A First Look at the pos Function   The **pos** function may be used to determine whether a particular character appears in a string. Here is the syntax:

```
pos (ch, host)
```

returns either the position of the first occurrence of the character ch in the host string or the value 0 if there are no occurrences of ch.

Example   In the fragment

```
letter := 'm';
strg := 'pepper';
loc := pos ('e', strg);
spot := pos (letter, strg);
```

loc is assigned the value 2 since e first occurs at position 2, and spot becomes 0 since m cannot be found in the string.   • • •

20.2   CONCATENATING STRINGS

In Turbo Pascal, both the + operator and the **concat** function can be used to join strings.

+ Operator   Here is the syntax of the + operator.

```
str1 + str2 + . . . + strn
```

will return the string value consisting of those strings joined.
Thus, 'Good' + 'Day' will produce the value 'GoodDay'.

CAUTION   In the assignment result := str1 + . . . + strn, if the maximum length of result is not large enough to hold all the characters, then the excess will be truncated from the right end.   • • •

Example   Suppose that str1, str2, and str3 all have been declared of type string[12]. The fragment

```
str1 := 'Have a';
str2 := 'nice day';
str3 := str1 + str2;
writeln (str3);
```

will produce the output

```
Have anice d
```

• • •

concat Function   Here is the syntax:

```
concat (str1, str2, . . . , strn).
```

returns the same result as `str1 + str2 + . . . + strn`.

Null String versus One Blank   The **null string** (` ' '`) is typed as two consecutive single quotes, with *no* space between, and has length 0. The string consisting of one blank (` ' ' `), on the other hand, is typed as one blank between single quotes and has length 1.

• • • • • • • • • •
Question   What will be output by the following fragment?

```
word1 := '';
word2 := ' ';
word3 := 'dog' + word1 + 'house';
word4 := 'dog' + word2 + 'house';
writeln (word3);
writeln (word4);
```

Answer

```
doghouse
dog house
```

• • •

Building a String One Character at a Time   It is sometimes useful to *initialize* a string variable to the null string and add on to this string one character at a time.

• • • • • • • • • •
Question   Suppose the user enters the five names

      Charlie Joe Frank Oscar Peter

when the following program is run. What will the output be?

```
program drill;
const null = '';
var i: integer;
    name, result: string;

begin
  result := null;
  for i := 1 to 5 do
    begin
      write ('Type a name ');
      readln (name);
      result := result + name[2]
    end;
  writeln (result)
end.
```

Answer   Setting `result` equal to the null string before the loop is a form of initialization. During the loop, the second letter of each name is added to `result`. The output will be

```
horse
```

• • •

20.3 SOME EXAMPLES

• •

Substitution Encoding   In substitution encoding, each letter of the original message is replaced by the letter appearing beneath it in the following key.

    A B C D E F G H I J K L M N O P Q R S T U V W X Y Z
    J V K M L O N I B H D C R E F Z U P Y G X A S Q W T

Thus, the message

    JOHN, MEET ME AT ZOO.

would be encoded as

    HFIE, RLLG RL JG TFF.

The following program will ask the user to input a message and then will output the coded message. Note that for any given *capital* letter, the function TRANSLATE will return the letter that will replace it. If ch is not a capital letter, however, TRANSLATE (ch) will retain its old value.

• • • • • • • • •
Question Fill in the two blanks in the program. (*Hint:* In function TRANSLATE, treat alphabet and key as parallel arrays.)

```
program coding;
{will encode a message by substitution}
const null = '';
var i: integer;
    ch: char;
    OrigPhrase, CodedPhrase: string[80];

function TRANSLATE (ch: char): char;
  {returns substitute letter for upper case letter}
  {or original character otherwise}
  var loc: integer;
      alphabet, key: string[26];
  begin
    alphabet := 'ABCDEFGHIJKLMNOPQRSTUVWXYZ';
    key :=      'JVKMLONIBHDCREFZUPYGXASQWT';
    loc := pos (ch, alphabet);
    if loc > 0 then TRANSLATE := _____
               else TRANSLATE := ch
  end; {TRANSLATE}

begin {main}
  write ('Type a message in all caps ');
  readln (OrigPhrase);
  CodedPhrase := null;
  for i := 1 to length (OrigPhrase) do
    begin
      ch := OrigPhrase[i];

      _____

    end;
  writeln (CodedPhrase)
end.
```

Answer The blank in the function TRANSLATE should say

```
key[loc]
```

The blank line in the main body should say

```
CodedPhrase := CodedPhrase + TRANSLATE (ch)
```

• • •

REMARK   In Exercise 9, you are asked to encode the message using the previous key, but in a way that eliminates all spaces and punctuation. • • •

Playing Fortune Hangman   In `program hangman`, the user plays hangman with the computer. The computer selects a word at random from an external file containing 25 words. Then, for each turn, the computer simulates a spin of the wheel of fortune, returning a random multiple of $100 (up to $500). The user then guesses a letter. If the guess is correct, the human's potential earnings are increased by the random dollar amount times the number of occurrences of the letter in the mystery word. If the guess is incorrect, the total earnings are not changed; the incorrect letter is added to the string of incorrect guesses. The user wins if he or she guesses the word with no more than eight incorrect guesses. Here is a typical output.

```
Word so far:   -------
    Incorrect guesses:
    This guess is worth $300
    Pick a letter s

Word so far:   -------
    Incorrect guesses: s
    This guess is worth $200
    Pick a letter e

Word so far:   e-e----
    Incorrect guesses: s
    This guess is worth $400
    Pick a letter i

Word so far:   e-e----
    Incorrect guesses: si
    This guess is worth $100
    Pick a letter n
    .
    .
    .
Congratulations!  You won $1600
```

The variable `WordSoFar` will keep track of what the user has been able to fill in so far. If the word had a length of 7, `WordSoFar` would start as `-------`. Further along in the game `WordSoFar` might be `e-er---`.

Here is the pseudocode for the main body.

```
SELECTWORD at random
INITIALIZE initializes WordSoFar, WrongList, and counters
repeat
    GUESS_PROMPT tells user what has been guessed thus far and spinwheel
                 amount
```

PROCESS_GUESS tests whether guess is in word; updates various variables
accordingly
until (**8 wrong guesses**) or (WordSoFar = word)
output final message

Here is the program.

```
program hangman;
{plays one game of fortune hangman}
var WordSoFar, word, WrongList: string;
    earnings, SpinAmt : integer;


    Procedure SELECTWORD
    Procedure INITIALIZE
    Procedure GUESS_PROMPT
    Procedure PROCESS_GUESS go here


begin {main body}
  randomize;
  SELECTWORD (word);
  INITIALIZE (word, WordSoFar, WrongList, earnings);
  repeat
    GUESS_PROMPT (WordSoFar, WrongList, SpinAmt);
    PROCESS_GUESS (SpinAmt, word, WordSoFar, WrongList, earnings);
  until (length(WrongList) = 8) or (word = WordSoFar);
  if word = WordSoFar
    then writeln ('Congratulations!  You won $ ',earnings)
    else writeln ('Sorry, you lost.  The word was ',word)
end.
```

Following are the four procedures used in hangman:

```
procedure SELECTWORD (var word: string);
  {pick a word at random from file}
  var i, num: integer;
      WordFile: text;
  begin
    assign (WordFile, 'words.dat');
    reset (WordFile);
    num:= random(25) + 1;
    for i := 1 to num do
      readln (WordFile, word);
    close (WordFile)
  end; {SELECTWORD}
```

• • •

REMARK Alternatively, we could have read all 25 words into an array and then selected an array subscript at random. This approach would make sense if the program allowed the user to play many games on a single run. • • •

```
procedure INITIALIZE (word: string;
                      var WordSoFar, WrongList: string;
                      var earnings: integer);
  const null = '';
        dash = '-';
  var i: integer;
  begin
    WordSoFar := null;
    for i := 1 to length(word) do
      WordSoFar := WordSoFar + dash;
    WrongList := null;
    earnings := 0
  end; {INITIALIZE}

procedure GUESS_PROMPT (WordSoFar, WrongList: string;
                        var SpinAmt: integer);
  {print status of game and prompt for guesses}
  begin
    writeln;
    SpinAmt := 100 * (random(5) + 1);
    writeln ('Word so far:  ',WordSoFar);
    writeln ('   Incorrect guesses  ',WrongList);
    writeln ('   This guess is worth $ ',SpinAmt);
    write ('   Pick a letter ')
  end; {GUESS_PROMPT}

procedure PROCESS_GUESS (SpinAmt: integer;
                         word: string;
                         var WordSoFar, WrongList: string;
                         var earnings: integer);
  {read in a player's guess and process it}
  var i, count: integer;
      guess: char;
  begin
    readln (guess);
    count := 0;
    for i := 1 to length(word) do
      if word[i] = guess then
        begin
          WordSoFar[i] := guess;
          count := count + 1
        end;
```

```
    if count > 0
       then earnings := earnings + count * SpinAmt
       else WrongList := WrongList + guess
  end; {PROCESS_GUESS}
```

20.4 ACCESSING SUBSTRINGS

In most of our applications so far, we have manipulated a string one character at a time. To facilitate manipulation of larger chunks, Turbo Pascal provides the following four built-in subprograms.

Functions	*Procedures*
pos	insert
copy	delete

pos Function for Substring Search The **pos** function of Section 20.1 may also be used to determine whether a string appears as a substring within a host string. Here is its syntax.

```
pos (wanted, host)
```

returns either the starting position of the first occurrence of wanted in host or the value 0 if there are no occurrences.

Example This fragment will assign the value 3 to loc and the value 0 to spot.

```
str := 'enforce';
loc := pos ('for', str);
spot := pos ('fore', str);
```

The copy Function The **copy** function will return a substring of a given string. Here is the syntax of the copy function.

```
copy (strg, start, len)
```

returns the substring of strg that starts in position start and consists of len characters.

Thus, copy (strg, 5, 2) will return a string value consisting of the characters in the fifth and sixth positions of strg. If strg had the value 'enforce', copy (str, 5, 2) would return the value 'rc'.

Special cases: (1) If the value of start exceeds the length of strg, copy will return the null string. (2) If len is greater than the number of remaining characters, the function will copy only the remaining characters.

• • • • • • • • •
Question   What values will `str1` and `str2` have after this fragment is executed?

```
word := 'birthday';
phrase := 'good day';
str1 := copy (word, 3, 4);
str2 := copy (phrase, 4, 3);
```

Answer   `str1` will have the value `'rthd'` and `str2` will have the value `'d d'`. The variables `word` and `phrase` will retain their original values.   • • •

CAUTION   The `copy` function (even when used to copy a single character) always returns a string value. Thus, if `ch` is of type `char` and `strg` of type `string`, the following are illegal:

```
ch := copy (strg, 4, 1);        {type mismatch}
strg[3] := copy (strg, 4, 1);   {type mismatch}
```
    • • •

The insert Procedure   The **insert** procedure will insert a string into a specified location in a host string. Here is the syntax:

```
insert (strg, host, start)
```

will insert `strg` into host just before the character at position `start`. Note that `host` must be a string variable—it cannot be a literal.

Thus, if `strg` had the value `'Json'`, `insert ('ack', strg, 2)` would change the value of `strg` to `'Jackson'`.

Special cases: (1) If the maximum length of the host string is less than the new length after the insertion, truncation on the right will take place. (2) If the starting position for insertion is beyond the actual length of the host string, the insertion string will be concatenated to the end of the host.

The delete Procedure   The `delete` procedure is used to delete from a host string a portion of a specified length. Here is the syntax:

```
delete (host, start, len)
```

will delete from host the substring beginning at position start and of length, `len`. Note that host must be a *string* variable—it cannot be a literal.

Thus, `delete (host, 3, 5)` will delete from `host` the 3rd, 4th, 5th, 6th, and 7th characters.

Special cases: (1) If `start` is greater than the length of the host string, then no characters are deleted from the host string. (2) If `len` specifies more characters than remain starting at position `start`, then the remainder of the string is deleted.

Question   What will the output be for the following fragment?

```
host := 'shadings':
delete (host, 5, 3);
writeln (host);
```

Answer

```
shads
```

• • •

The str Procedure   `str` converts an `integer` or `real` value into a `string` value. Here is the form of `str` for `integer` values.

```
str (IntVal, st)
```

converts the `integer` value, IntVal, into a `string` and assigns it to the variable, st.

Thus, `str (476, st)` assigns st the value `'476'`. (See Section 29.4 for an application.)

20.5   DEFINING YOUR OWN STRING SUBPROGRAMS

In addition to using the built-in string manipulating functions and procedures, you may wish to define some of your own.

Example   (Trimming Blanks at the Right End)   Recall that if `name1 := 'Smith, Al'` and `name2 := 'Smith, Al     ';` with extra blanks at the end, then unfortunately

```
if name1 = name2 then . . .
```

will test as false. Accordingly, it is useful to have a function `TRIM_END` that can delete any blanks at the right end of a string.

```
function TRIM_END (strg: string): string;
  {deletes all blanks from the right end}
  const  blank = ' ';
```

```
var  n: integer;

begin
  n := length (strg);
  while strg[n] = blank do
    begin
      delete (strg, n, 1);
        n := n - 1
    end; {while}
  TRIM_END := strg
end; {TRIM_END}
```

REMARK   This is a good example of a situation in which a `while` loop should be used instead of a `repeat-until` loop.   ● ● ●

Example   **(A Replace Procedure)**   There is no built-in procedure in Turbo Pascal to replace one string with another. For example, suppose `strg` contains a personalized message to "Mr. Smith" in which the name "Mr. Smith" occurs several times. If we wanted to send the same personalized message to "Mrs. Peterson," we would need to change each occurrence of "Mr. Smith" to "Mrs. Peterson."

Now consider the following fragment. Would it change all occurrences of "Mr. Smith" to "Mrs. Peterson"?

```
loc := pos ('Mr. Smith', strg);
if loc > 0 then
  begin
    delete (strg, loc, length('Mr. Smith'));
    insert ('Mrs. Peterson', strg, loc)
  end;
```

No. It would just change the first occurrence of "Mr. Smith" to "Mrs. Peterson." To change all occurrences obviously would require a loop.

Question   Complete the code that will replace in `strg` all occurrences of substring `old` by `new`.

```
procedure REPLACE_ALL (var strg: string;
                          old, new: string);
  {replaces all occurrences of old with new}
  var loc: integer;
  begin
```

```
      loc := pos (old, strg);
      while loc > 0 do
        begin
          delete (strg, loc, _____);
          insert (new, strg, loc);

          _____
        end
    end; {REPLACE_ALL}
```

Answer   The lines with blanks should be

```
        delete (strg, loc, length(old));
        loc := pos (old, strg);
```
• • •

REMARK   This is another example in which a `while` loop should be used instead of `repeat-until` since if there are no occurrences of `old`, we would not want to enter the loop body even a first time.   • • •

• • • • • • • • •
Question   The preceding REPLACE_ALL has several possible pitfalls. Give one.

Answer   If `length (new)` is greater than `length (old)`, then there is the danger that `strg` will not be able to accommodate all the additional characters. In Exercise 10(a), you are asked to revise REPLACE_ALL so that the user is warned when this occurs. A second possible pitfall is explored in Exercise 10(b).   • • •

20.6   COMPARING ADJACENT CELLS (Optional)

Since a string is essentially an array of characters, certain string processing problems can be solved using a `for` loop to compare each of the pairs of adjacent characters (as was done in Section 17.7).

• • • • • • • • •
Example   (Counting the Number of Words)   Suppose the variable `strg` contains some text that we know *ends* with a punctuation mark. For example

I	F		Y	O	U		C	A	N	,		D	O		I	T	.	

	O	T	H	E	R	W	I	S	E	,		I		W	I	L	L	.

We can count the number of words by counting how many times the following occurs:

the current cell has a nonletter and the previous has a letter

Here is a program fragment to count how many words are in `strg`. The `boolean` variables `CurIsLet` and `PrevIsLet` keep track of whether the current cell and previous cell contain a letter. The declaration (see Chapter 27 for more details) needed for `LetterSet` is

```
var LetterSet: set of char;
```

```
{assumes that strg ends with a punctuation mark}
LetterSet := ['A'..'Z', 'a'..'z'];
wordcount := 0;
for i := 2 to length(strg) do
  begin
    PrevIsLet := strg[i - 1] in LetterSet;
    CurIsLet := strg[i] in LetterSet;
    if PrevIsLet and (not CurIsLet) then
      wordcount := wordcount + 1
  end; {for}
```

REMARK   It was not necessary to finish processing the last cell after the loop because it was specified that the string ended with a punctuation mark.

• • •

• • • • • • • • • EXERCISES

• •

1. Assuming `part1`, `str1`, and `str2` are all of type `string[20]`, what will be printed by the following fragment?

```
str1 := 'A STITCH';
str2 := 'IN TIME';
part1 := copy (str1, 2, 3);
writeln (part1, ' ', str1);
insert (part1, str2, 5);
part1 := copy (str1, 6, 2);
writeln (part1, '   ', str2);
```

2. **(a)** Assuming `part` and `str` are both of type `string[12]`, what will be printed by the following fragment?

```
str := 'computer';
delete (str, 2, 3);
writeln (str);
insert ('omm', str, 2);
writeln (str);
part := copy (str, 4, 3);
insert (str, part, 2);
writeln ('str = ', str, ' part = ', part)
```

(b) If `str` were of type `string[5]`, what would be printed by the fragment in part (a)?

3. What will be output by each of the following programs?

(a)
```
program drill;
const null = '';
var ch: char;
    s1, s2, s3, s4: string[20];
    i, spot: integer;
begin
  s1 := 'aeiou';
  s2 := 'beautiful';
  s3 := null;
  s4 := null;
  writeln (length(s2));
  for i := 1 to length(s2) do
    begin
      ch := s2[i];
      spot := pos (ch, s1);
      if spot > 0
        then s3 := s3 + ch
        else s4 := s4 + ch
    end; {for}
  writeln (s3);
  writeln (s4)
end.
```

(b)
```
program drill;
const null = '';
var k: integer;
    ch: char;
    state, strg, new1, new2: string;
begin
```

```
new1 := null;
new2 := null;
state := 'TENNESSEE';
strg :=  'THE MAN FROM';
for k := 1 to length (state) do
  begin
     ch := strg[k];
     if ch < state[k]
        then new1 := new1 + ch
        else new2 := new2 + ch
  end;
writeln (new1 + '**');
writeln (new2 + '**');
writeln (strg + ' ' + state)
end.
```

4. Write a procedure that receives as a value parameter a person's name, with the last name followed by a comma, one space, and then the first name. The procedure should print the person's first name followed by his or her last. For example, if the procedure receives the value

```
Smith, John
```

it should output

```
John Smith
```

5. (a) Modify `program hangman` in Section 20.3 so that it contains an error trap to prevent the user from cheating by picking a letter that he or she already knows is in the word.

   (b) Modify `hangman` so that the user can play as many games as he or she wishes on a single run.

Longer Assignments

6. Write a programmer-defined function named POS_FUNC that does exactly what the built-in `pos` function does. (Do not use `pos` in the defining body.)

7. Write a programmer-defined function named COPY_FUNC that does exactly what the built-in function `copy` does. COPY_FUNC should have three parameters. (Do not use `copy` in the defining body.)

8. A file contains a list of 20 words and their opposites (with one word to a line).

(a) Write a program that will output a list giving each word, its opposite, and those letters the two words have in common. If a letter appears more than once in both the word and its opposite, it should be listed just once. After the list, the pair with the most letters in common should be output. (You may disregard the possibility of a tie.) Format the output as follows:

```
Word                Opposite              Common
interesting         boring                inrg
fat                 skinny
happy               sad                   a
tallest             shortest              tes


Pair with most letters in common _____ , _____
```

(b) Change the program for part (a) so that, if a letter appears more than once in both words, it is listed the number of times it occurs in both words. Thus, "tallest" and "shortest" would have "test" in common.

9. Modify program coding in Section 20.3 so that the encoded message has all spaces and punctuation eliminated. Thus, JOHN MEET ME AT ZOO would be encoded as HFIERLLGRLJGTFF.

10. (a) Revise procedure REPLACE_ALL of Section 20.5 so that it replaces all occurrences of old with new and prints a warning if insertion causes strg to be truncated.

(b) Revise procedure REPLACE_ALL of Section 20.5 so that it will handle the case where the new string contains the old string. For the original version of REPLACE_ALL, replacing 'big' by 'bigger' will cause an infinite loop.

11. (a) Write a procedure that will print all the letters in a word in alphabetical order. If a letter is repeated, it should be printed as many times as it occurs. For example, ''defeated'' would become ''addeeeft''.

(b) Modify the procedure in part (a) so that letters are not printed more than once. For example, ''defeated'' would become ''adeft''.

12. The following system is used to encode and decode messages. Each letter of the alphabet is replaced by the letter that is three positions further along. Thus, A is replaced by D, B by E, and so on, with X replaced by A, Y by B, and Z by C. Write a program to encode a message of type string[80]. (*Hint:* Create a string that contains the alphabet. For each letter of the original message, find its position in the alphabet and add 3; if the result is greater than 26, you must wrap around. Alternatively, you could use ASCII numbers and the ord and chr functions.)

13. Write a procedure that receives two parameters, a message of type `string[80]` and an integer n from 1 to 25. The procedure should print an encoded message, using an n-shift. That is, each letter in the message is replaced by the letter n positions further along. The end of the alphabet wraps around to the beginning, as in Exercise 12.

14. Write a subprogram to implement the following coding scheme. The first letter of the message is replaced by its 1-shift replacement, the second letter of the message by its 2-shift replacement, the third letter by its 3-shift replacement, and so on. (See Exercise 12.) Nonletters are simply reproduced. Thus,

AT THE ZOO.

would become

BV WLJ FVW.

15. A message has been coded using one of the 25 possible shift codes. (See Exercises 12 and 13.) You may assume that every word in the message contains at least one vowel—thus, the message does not contain words such as "Mr." You do not know what the shift number n is. Any n that produces a decoding that includes some words with no vowels should be rejected. Write a program that gives as its output the decodings that were not rejected.

16. Redo Exercise 4 so that the input name may have leading blanks in front of the name and in front of and behind the comma. That is, the input could be

```
Smith         John
```

* *17.* (a) Suppose that `phrase` is a variable of type `string[80]`. Write a procedure that receives `phrase` as a value parameter and outputs each of the words in `phrase`, where a word is defined as a letter string that terminates in a nonletter. (You may assume that the last character in phrase is a punctuation mark.)

(b) Revise the procedure so that it works whether the last character is a letter or punctuation mark.

18. Write a program to delete excess blanks from an input string so that the revised string will not contain two consecutive blanks anywhere and no blanks at either the beginning or the end of the string. For example,

```
'      here      are    a    lot of spaces      '
```

will become

```
'here are a lot of spaces'
```

19. On a certain keyboard, the key for the letter t has a tendency to stick. Write a procedure that will receive a string message and reprint it so that the letter t never occurs more than twice consecutively in the message.

Then the procedure should output all the words in this revised message that have two consecutive t's.

20. A palindrome is a string that reads the same forward and backward. Two examples of palindromes are

    Madam I'm Adam

    Able was I ere I saw Elba

Write a program that will determine whether an input string is a palindrome. (You should consider uppercase and lowercase versions of the same letter to be equal and ignore nonalphabetical characters.)

* 21. Write a program that will convert Roman numerals into their decimal equivalents. Assume a maximum of 10 Roman numeral digits chosen from

    M—1,000   D—500   C—100   L—50
    X—10   V—5   I—1

Lab Exercises   **DEBUGGING**

    Lab20-1.pas   Replacing First Character
    Lab20-2.pas   Finding Common Letters

Chapter

21

RECORDS

• • • A *record,* like an array, is a data structure for storing related data items. In this chapter, we will see that one advantage of a record over an array is that the data items in a record need not all be of the same data type. This chapter also discusses arrays of records (a data structure that is superior to parallel arrays), nested records, and variant records.   • • •

21.1 INTRODUCTION TO RECORDS

Example   We could store three data items—an employee's name, social security number, and pay rate—

```
Jones, Al  252-47-1364  $6.50
```

in a record variable called `employee` containing three fields.

	name	socsec	payrate
employee	Jones, Al	252-47-1364	6.50

Accessing the Contents of a Record Variable   To access the contents of one of the cells of `employee`, we must specify both the name of the record variable and the particular field we want. A dot separates the name of the record variable from the name of the field. For example, if the record variable `employee` contained the preceding data, the statement

```
            writeln (employee.socsec);
```

would print

```
252-47-1364
```

Declaring a Record Variable   Usually a record variable is declared in two stages—first the record type is defined, and then the record variable is declared to be of that type. Here is a declaration for the `employee` record variable.

```
type
  EmployeeRec = record
    name: string[20];
    socsec: string[11];
    payrate: real
  end; {EmployeeRec}
var
  employee: EmployeeRec;
```

REMARK   Like the `case` statement, the declaration of a record contains an `end` with no matching `begin`.   • • •

• • • • • • • • • •

Question   By first defining a type identifier, give a declaration for the record variable `person` that could contain the following data:

name	phonenum	sex
Smith, Jane	212-495-7722	f

Answer

```
type
  personrec = record
    name: string[20];
    phonenum: string[12];
    sex: char
  end; {personrec}
var
  person: personrec;
```

                                                                        • • •

• • • • • • • • • •

Question   Suppose that the external text file `employ.dat` contains information on one employee—name, social security number, hours worked, and pay rate.

employ.dat

```
Smith, Jane
140-42-5975
40  6.00
```

Fill in the blank lines in the following program so that when it is run it produces the output

```
Smith, Jane  Soc Sec # 140-42-5975
wage $240.00
```

```pascal
program drill;
{reads employee data for one employee}
{from external file into record variable; then processes data}
type
  EmployeeRec = record
    name: string[20];
    socsec: string[11];
    hours: integer;
    rate: real
  end; {EmployeeRec}
var
  employee: EmployeeRec;
  wage: real;

  procedure READINTOREC (var employee: EmployeeRec);
    {reads from file into one record variable}
    var EmployFile: text;
    begin
      assign (EmployFile, 'employ.dat');
      reset (EmployFile);
      readln (EmployFile, employee.name);
      readln (_____);
      readln (EmployFile, employee.hours, employee.rate);
      close (EmployFile)
    end; {READINTOREC}

begin {main}
  READINTOREC (employee);
  wage := _____;
  writeln (employee.name, '  Soc Sec # ', employee.socsec);
  writeln ('wage $ ', _____)
end.
```

Answer   The completed lines should say

```
readln (EmployFile, employee.socsec);
wage := employee.hours * employee.rate;
writeln ('wage $ ', wage:6:2)
```
• • •

Using a with Statement

The `with` statement allows us to avoid tedious repetitions of the name of a record variable. Suppose that `birthdate` is a record variable with three fields: `month`, `day`, and `year`. The following assignment statements are equivalent.

```
birthdate.month := 5;
birthdate.day := 30;
birthdate.year := 1940;
```

```
with birthdate do
   begin
      month := 5;
      day := 30;
      year := 1940
   end; {with}
```

The general form of a `with` statement is

```
with {record variable} do
      {single statement or block enclosed in begin-end brackets}
```

Inside the body of the `with` statement, we give only the name(s) of the field(s), omitting the name of the record variable and the period.

• • • • • • • • •
Question   Redo the body of procedure `READINTOREC` for the previous program, using a `with` statement.

Answer

```
assign (EmployFile, 'employ.dat');
reset (EmployFile);
with employee do
   begin
      readln (EmployFile, name);
      readln (EmployFile, socsec);
      readln (EmployFile, hours, rate)
   end; {with}
close (EmployFile)
```
• • •

21.2 ARRAY OF RECORDS

An array of records can be used as an alternative to parallel arrays. For example, the array of records class might be loaded with data as follows:

	name	major	grade
class[1]	Adams, Jay	HIST	A
class[2]	Foy, Joe	CHEM	C
class[3]	Hunt, Al	MATH	B
class[4]	Kent, Judy	CHEM	A
	. . .	. . .	. . .

Declaring the Array   To declare an array of records, we may make *two* type declarations—a record type and an array type. Then we declare class to be of the declared array type.

```
type
   studentrec = record
     name: string[20];
     major: string[4];
     grade: char
   end; {studentrec}
   classtype = array[1..30] of studentrec;
var
   class: classtype;
```

Reading from a File into an Array of Records   Suppose that the text file class.dat contains the name, major, and grade for each student.

class.dat

```
Adams, Jay
HIST
A
Foy, Joe
CHEM
C
.
.
.
```

Question   Procedure GETDATA will be used to read data from file class.dat into an array of records. Fill in the blank in the procedure.

```
procedure GETDATA (var class: classtype;
                   var size: integer);
  {reads from file into array of records}
  var ClassFile: text;
  begin
    assign (ClassFile, 'class.dat');
    reset (ClassFile);
    size := 0;
    while not seekeof (ClassFile) do
      begin
        size := size + 1;

        _____

        begin
          readln (ClassFile, name);
          readln (ClassFile, major);
          readln (ClassFile, grade)
        end {with}
    end; {while}
    close (ClassFile)
  end; {GETDATA}
```

Answer   The array class is an array of records: class[1] is the first record, class[2] is the second record, and so on. For any given value of size, we want to read into the record class[size]. Thus, the line with the blank should say

```
with class[size] do                                        • • •
```

Example   In program SearchClass, the user is presented with a menu from which he or she is to select a choice—either to print the names and grades of all the students with an input major or to print the names and grades of all the students with an input grade. Here is the output for a typical run.

```
MENU OF CHOICES
  1.  All students with a given major
  2.  All students with a given grade
  3.  Quit
Enter choice 1
Enter first four letters (all capitals)
of desired major CHEM
```

```
    List of CHEM Majors
Foy, Joe   C
Kent, Judy   A
   .
   .
   .

Enter choice 2
Enter grade (for list of students with that grade) B
Jones, Al   HIST
   .
   .
   .

Enter choice 3
```

Here is the program.

```
program SearchClass;
{presents user with a menu from which to select}
{desired type of list}
const maxsize = 30;
type
  studentrec = record
     name: string[20];
     major: string[4];
     grade: char
  end; {studentrec}
  classtype = array [1..maxsize] of studentrec;
var
  class: classtype;
  size, choice: integer;


  ┌─────────────────────────────────────────┐
  │ procedure GETDATA goes here.             │
  └─────────────────────────────────────────┘

procedure PRINTMENU;
  begin
    writeln ('MENU OF CHOICES');
    writeln ('  1. All students with a given major');
    writeln ('  2. All students with a given grade');
    writeln ('  3. Quit')
  end; {PRINTMENU}

procedure HAVING_MAJOR (class: classtype;
                        size: integer);
  {User inputs a major.  Procedure prints list of all}
```

```
{students having that major}
var stud: integer;
    WantedMajor: string[4];
begin
  writeln ('Enter first four letters (all capitals)');
  write ('of desired major ');
  readln (WantedMajor);
  writeln ('  List of ', WantedMajor, ' Majors ');
  for stud := 1 to size do
    with class[stud] do
        if major = WantedMajor then
          writeln (name, '   ', grade)
end; {HAVING_MAJOR}
```

```
Procedure HAVING_GRADE goes here. It is
similar to HAVING_MAJOR. Writing it is Exercise 5.
```

```
begin {main}
  GETDATA (class, size);
  PRINTMENU;
  repeat
    write ('Enter choice ');
    readln (choice);
    case choice of
      1: HAVING_MAJOR (class, size);
      2: HAVING_GRADE (class, size);
      3: {quit the loop}
      else writeln ('invalid choice -- choose again')
    end; {case}
    writeln;
  until choice = 3
end.
```

REMARK The action in alternative 3 is a null statement. Its purpose is to have the computer do nothing in the event that 3 is chosen and to prevent the execution of the `else` action. • • •

21.3 SEARCHING AND SORTING AN ARRAY OF RECORDS

• •

A linear or binary search of an array of records is essentially the same as a linear or binary search of an ordinary array. The only complication in searching an array of records is that you must single out one of the record fields as the search field—this field is called the *record key* for the search.

• • • • • • • • •

Question   Suppose that `school` is an array of records with three fields: `name`, `socsec`, and `telephone`. Suppose further that the array of records is ordered alphabetically by name.

Following is a function that can be used to determine the name and telephone number of the student having a given social security number. This function will return either the subscript of the record with that social security number or the value 0 if none of the students has that number.

Note that we cannot take advantage of the alphabetical ordering of the records when we wish to search for a particular social security number. Thus, the search is linear, not binary. Fill in the blank lines.

```
function SEARCH_SOCSEC (school: schooltype;
                        size: indexrange;
                        WantedSocSec: str11): indexrange;
   {returns the subscript of record with WantedSocSec or 0}
   var index: indexrange;
       found: boolean;
   begin
     found := false;
     index := 1;
     repeat
       with school[index] do
         if _____ then
           begin
             found := true;
             SEARCH_SOCSEC := index
           end {then}
         else index := index + 1
     until (found) or (index > size);
     if not found then SEARCH_SOCSEC := 0
   end; {SEARCH_SOCSEC}
```

Answer   Since the key field is `socsec`, the line with a blank should say

```
if socsec = WantedSocSec then
```

If you wished to write the code without using a `with` statement, the `if` statement would be

```
if school[index].socsec = WantedSocSec then
```                                                    • • •

• • • • • • • • •

Question   The following program fragment contains a call to `SEARCH_SOCSEC`. The fragment will print either the name and the telephone number of the person with the input social security number or the message `not on list`. Fill in the blank.

```
write ('enter social security number ');
readln (WantedSocSec);
spot := SEARCH_SOCSEC (school, size, WantedSocSec);
if spot > 0
  then writeln (_____)
  else writeln (WantedSocSec, ' not on list'):
```

Answer `(school[spot].name. ' ', school[spot].telephone)` • • •

Assigning an Entire Record A single assignment statement can be used to assign the entire contents of one record variable to another record variable of precisely the same type. For example, if `student1` and `student2` are both record variables with fields `name`, `socsec`, and `grade`, the single statement on the left is equivalent to the *three* statements on the right.

```
student2 := student1;
```

```
student2.name := student1.name;
student2.socsec := student1.socsec;
student2.grade := student1.grade;
```

CAUTION You may *not* read in an entire record from a text file using a `readln` statement that makes no mention of the data fields. For example, the following statement is not allowed:

```
readln (fileA, class[i])   {illegal}
```
• • •

• • • • • • • • • •

Question Suppose that `class` is an array of student records, in which each student record has three fields: `name`, `socsec`, and `grade`. Here are the declarations.

```
type
  studentrec = record
    name: string[20];
    socsec: string[11];
    grade: char
  end; {studentrec}
  classtype = array[1..30] of studentrec;
var
  class: classtype;
```

Procedure BUBBLE will sort an array of these records alphabetically by name. Note that just three assignment statements are needed to switch the records class[i] and class[i + 1]. If these switches were done field by field, not three but *nine* assignment statements would be required.

Complete the declarations for the parameter class and the local variable temp. Also fill in the condition for the if-then statement.

```
procedure BUBBLE (var class: _____;
                  size: integer);
  {sorts an array of records alphabetically by name}
  {uses a bubble sort}
  var i: integer;
      NoSwitches: boolean;
      temp: _____;

begin
  repeat
    NoSwitches := true;
    for i := 1 to size - 1 do
      if _____ then
        begin
          temp := class[i];
          class[i] := class[i + 1];
          class[i + 1] := temp;
          NoSwitches := false
        end {then}
  until NoSwitches
end;   {BUBBLE}
```

Answer
```
var class: classtype;

temp: studentrec;

if class[i].name > class[i + 1].name then
```
• • •

21.4 NESTED RECORDS

It is permissible for a field of a record to be a record itself. Such records are said to be ***nested,*** or hierarchical. For example, IdRec is a nested record type (because at least one of its fields is a record).

```
type
  NameRec = record
    first: string[20];
    initial: char;
    last: string[20]
  end; {NameRec}
  AddressRec = record
    street: string[20];
    city: string[20];
    state: string[2];
    zip: string[5]
  end; {AddressRec}

  IdRec = record
    name: NameRec;
    address: AddressRec;
    spousename: NameRec
  end; IdRec
```

Figure 21.1 illustrates the hierarchy within a record variable ID that has been declared as type IdRec. Note that name, address, and spousename are at a higher level than are the fields that are nested inside them.

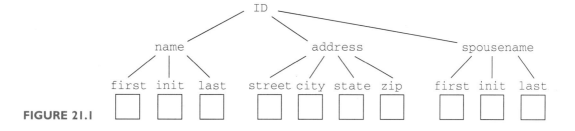

FIGURE 21.1

Accessing Data   Suppose IDs is declared as an array of records, with each record of the type IdRec declared earlier.

```
var IDs: array[1..50] of IdRec;
```

To access a particular memory cell of IDs, we must specify not only the element of the array but also its field and subfield—that is, we must specify a complete path to that cell. Thus, to print the zip code of the fourth person in the array, we would use the statement

```
writeln (IDs[4].address.zip);
```

REMARK

1. A period is needed before each field identifier.

2. The field identifier that is higher in the hierarchy is specified first.

• • •

Storing Data The diagram in Figure 21.1 is called a ***tree diagram,*** for obvious reasons. The joints of the tree, called ***nodes,*** may have any number of branches extending out from them. (In Figure 21.1, name, address, and spousename are nodes.) Those nodes that are at the end of a branch and have no branches extending from them are called ***terminal nodes*** or ***leaves.*** It is in these terminal nodes that all the data is stored. Hence, we may access information only through these terminal nodes. (The one exception to this rule is when we use an assignment statement to assign the entire contents of one record variable to another. See Section 21.3.)

Example To print the contents of the subrecord name in the fourth element of IDs, we could write

```
with IDs[4].name do
  writeln (first, ' ', init, '. ', last)
```

or we could write

```
writeln (IDs[4].name.first, ' ', IDs[4].name.init, ' ',
         IDs[4].name.last)
```

We cannot merely write

```
writeln (IDs[4].name)   {illegal}
```

Question Write a segment to print the full name, city, and state of the fourth element of the array IDs using nested with statements.

Answer

```
with IDs[4] do
  begin
    with name do
      writeln (first, ' ', init, '. ', last);
    with address do
      writeln (city, ' ', state)
  end; (with IDs [4])
```

• • •

21.5 VARIANT RECORDS

In the arrays of records considered so far, each record in the array has had exactly the same fields. There are situations, however, in which a single record format is not appropriate for all the items in the array. For example, a company might wish to store slightly different kinds of information on employees depending on whether they are currently working, retired, or resigned. Variant records provide such flexibility.

The first portion of a variant record declaration, called the fixed part, declares the data fields that are the same for all the records. The second portion, called the variant part, begins with the keyword case. The identifier immediately following case is called the *tag field identifier.*

Example

```
type
   emptype = (current, retired, resigned);
   emprec = record
     name: string[20];                             } fixed part
     TelNum: string[12];

     case class: emptype of
       current:      (department: string[15];
                      hourly_wage: real;
                      employ_id: integer);
                                                    } variant part
       retired:      (pension: real;
                      socsec: string[11]);

       resigned:     ( )
     end; {emprec}
   employeestype = array[1..50] of emprec;
var employees: employeestype;
```

Syntax for Variant Part

1. The variant part begins with the keyword case followed by the tag field's identifier, the type declaration (it must be ordinal), and the keyword of. Next is given a list of possible values of the tag field, each of which heads a field list enclosed in parentheses.

2. The variant part needs no begin–end brackets. It begins with the keyword case and is terminated by the end that terminates the record declaration.

3. Empty parentheses ( ) are used for any field list that has no additional fields (for example, resigned in the previous declaration).

. . . .
Example   Suppose `employees.dat` is a text file containing data on at most 100 employees of XYZ Company. It has every employee's name and annual salary followed by a code (`C, H, D`) for level of education. The data on college graduates includes the name of their college, their grade point average, and their major. Data on high school graduates includes the name of their high school, and data on dropouts includes the last grade completed.

employees.dat
```
Adams, Louis
19000
H
Brentwood High School
Baker, Herbert
38000
C
Yale College
3.5
Biology
Doe, John
21000
D
9
  .
  .
  .
  .
```

Program `salary_study` reads the data into an array of variant records. It allows the user to choose whether he or she wants to print a report on all employees or only those whose salary exceeds a certain input amount.

Here is a typical output on paper supposing the user selects option 2 and inputs `20000`.

```
Employees earning over $20000
Baker, Herbert   $38000
   Yale College   3.5 GPA   Biology
Doe, John   $21000
   Dropout   Completed through Grade 9
 .
 .
 .
```

```
program salary_study;
{allows the user to receive a report on all employees or}
{just those with salary above a certain input amount.}
uses printer;
const maxsize = 100;
type
  employeerec = record
    name: string[20];
    salary: real;
    case educode: char of
      'C': (college: string[20];
            GPA: real;
            major: string[20]);
      'H': (HighSchool: string[20]);
      'D': (LastGrade: integer)
  end; {employeerec}
  employee_array = array [1..maxsize] of employeerec;
var
  employees: employee_array;
  size, answer: integer;

procedure GETDATA (var employees: employee_array;
                   var size: integer);
  {reads file into an array of variant records.}
  var infile: text;
  begin
    assign (infile, 'employees.dat');
    reset (infile);
    size := 0;
    while not seekeof (infile) do
      begin
        size := size + 1;
        with employees[size] do
          begin
            readln (infile, name);
            readln (infile, salary);
            readln (infile, educode);
            case educode of
              'C': begin
                     readln (infile, college);
                     readln (infile, GPA);
                     readln (infile, major)
                   end;
                'H': readln (infile, HighSchool);
                'D': readln (infile, LastGrade)
```

```
          end {case}
      end {with}
    end; {while}
  close (infile)
end; {GETDATA}


procedure PRINT_ONE_REC (employee: employeerec);
  {prints the record of the employee.}
  {completing it is Exercise 13}


procedure PRINT_ALL (employees: employee_array;
                     size: integer);
  {prints the record of each employee in the array.}
  var i: integer;
  begin
    for i := 1 to size do
      PRINT_ONE_REC (employees [i]);
  end; {PRINT_ALL}

procedure ABOVE_SAL (employees: employee_array;
                     size: integer);
  {prints the record of each employee with a salary greater}
  {than the input salary.}
  {completing it is Exercise 13}


begin {main}
  GETDATA (employees, size);
  writeln ('Type  1) if you want all employee records');
  writeln ('Type  2) if you want those above certain salary');
  readln (answer);
  if answer = 1 then PRINT_ALL (employees, size)
              else ABOVE_SAL (employees, size)
end.
```

Note that writing procedures PRINT_ONE_REC and ABOVE_SAL is Exercise 13.

REMARK

1. Before we can assign values to variant fields, we must make sure that the tag field has been assigned a value. For example, in GETDATA, educode must be read in before the case statement.

2. Compare the syntax for the case that declares the variant part of a record with the syntax for the case statement in procedure GETDATA.

• • •

EXERCISES
• •

1. Information for all the employees of the ACME company is stored in the array of records variable named company. For example, company might contain

	name	sex	payrate
company[1]	Bond, Al	m	7.50
company[2]	Brock, Ann	f	8.25
company[3]	Doyle, Don	m	6.50
	.	.	.
	.	.	.
	.	.	.

Write a declaration for the array company.

2. Here is a declaration for a variable called employees, which will hold an array of records.

```
type
  employrec = record
    name: string [20];
    age: integer;
    salary: real
  end; {employrec}
  EmployeesType = array[1..30] of employrec;
var
  employees: EmployeesType;
```

Suppose that values have been read into this array. Write program fragments to

(a) print the name and age of the fourth employee in the array employees.

(b) print the names of all those employees earning over $25,000.

(c) change the salary of the third employee to $20,000.

3. Write the declaration for the record represented by the following diagram:

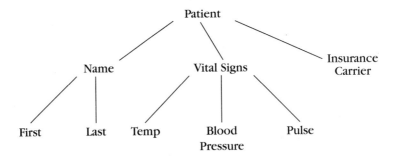

4. Declare a data structure to store the following kinds of information for up to 50 employees:

Name	Sex	Languages (maximum of 6)
Adams	m	French, Spanish
Brock	f	Spanish, German, Russian, Chinese
Doyle	m	French
.		
.		
.		

5. Write procedure `HAVING_GRADE` for program `SearchClass` in Section 21.2.

Longer Assignments

6. A text file contains depositor information. For each depositor, the file contains the depositor's name, account number, type of account (special or regular), and current balance. Write a program to print two tables, each containing all the data for each customer. The first table should be sorted by name and the second by account number.

7. A text file contains the name, age, and IQ for each student in a class. (The file is not sorted.) Write a program that will print three tables. The first should give the names, ages, and IQs ordered alphabetically by name. The second should give the names, ages, and IQs ordered by age, with the youngest listed first. The third should give the names, ages, and IQs ordered by IQ, with the highest IQ listed first.

8. A text file contains the name, age, and IQ for each student in a class of at most 50 students. The file is sorted alphabetically by name. Write a menu-driven program that allows the user to enter queries as many times as he or she wishes. The menu should offer the following options:

```
1. Get list of all students with input age.
2. Get list of all students with IQ above input IQ.
3. Print average IQ of all students.
4. Get data on a student.
5. Quit.
```

9. Rewrite the program in Exercise 8 of Chapter 19 using records instead of parallel arrays.

10. Rewrite the telephone directory program in Exercise 13 of Chapter 19 using records instead of parallel arrays.

* 11. A text file contains the preweekend win-loss records for each of the teams in a Little League. First the program should read the data into an array of records and print a table giving the preweekend standings. Then the program should allow the user to update the teams' records after the weekend. The user should be prompted to enter the winner and loser for each of the games played over the weekend. After the update session is over, a new table of the standings (ordered by winning percentage) should be printed on paper.

Set up the external file so that the standings before the weekend are

	Won	Lost	Pct
Cubs	7	3	.700
Bills	5	4	.556
Mets	5	5	.500
Lions	3	5	.375
Sharks	3	6	.333

For the update, enter the results of at least six games, making sure some of the results change the standings.

* 12. There are seven candidates in a mayoral election in which voters vote for their top three choices in order of preference. A first-place vote is worth 5 points, a second-place vote is worth 3 points, and a third-place vote is worth 1 point. The seven candidates—Cane, Hund, Wolff, Chien, Fideau, Perro, and Spaniel—are numbered 1 through 7. A text file contains the names of the seven candidates and then each of the individual ballots. For example, the text file might contain

```
Cane
Hund
.
.
.
Spaniel
```

```
2   7   4
6   7   2
    .
    .
    .
```

The first ballot 2 7 4 would give 5 points to Hund (candidate 2), 3 points to Spaniel (candidate 7), and 1 point to Chien (candidate 4).

Write a program that will process all the ballots and then print a table (ordered by point total) that gives each candidate's name; the number of first, second, and third place votes he or she received; and the candidate's point total.

13. Complete `program salary_study` in Section 21.5 by writing procedures `PRINT_ONE_REC` and `ABOVE_SAL`.

* 14. The college bookstore needs you to set up an array of records that can hold information on up to 100 different books. The following information is needed for each book: title, author, and price when new. A book can be either very old, old, or brand new. If a book is very old, a newer edition has been published, and the book is worthless to the bookstore. Therefore, the name of a library that will accept the book must be stored. If the book is old, the bookstore will be selling used copies, and a used price must be stored. If the book is brand new, no excess information is needed. Set up the `type` and `var` definitions for the bookstore.

* 15. Given the array of records in Exercise 14, sort the books in terms of brand new, old, and very old. Within each of these categories, sort the books in ascending order by price.

Chapter

22

BINARY FILES

So far, the only type of file we have considered has been the text file. There is a second general type of file called a binary file. A *binary file* consists of a sequence of items, each of which is of the same data type. For example, a binary file might contain a sequence of integers or a sequence of records. The data type of each of the items is called the *component* type of the file. The declaration of a binary file variable must specify the component type for the file.

Data in a binary file is stored in the form in which it is used internally by the compiler (that is, binary form). In a text file, the data is stored in character form. Records in a binary file can be accessed not only sequentially (like a text file) but also directly (like an array).

22.1 DECLARING FILE VARIABLES

Declaring an Integer File For a file that might contain the integer values

```
25  29  41  36  28  48  83  52
```

we would declare the file variable as follows:

```
var fileA: file of integer;
```

Declaring a Record File   For a file that might contain the records

name	telnum
Adams, Jay	491-2210
Baker, Al	491-2511
Brown, Joe	564-3722
. . .	. . .

we would make the following declarations:

```
type
   membertype = record
      name: string[20];
      telnum: string[8]
   end; {membertype}
var
   fileB: file of membertype;
```

REMARK   To pass `fileB` to a procedure as a parameter, you must make the additional type declaration

```
fileBtype = file of membertype;
```

and then declare `fileB` to be of type `fileBtype` both in the `var` section and in the procedure header.   • • •

22.2 ADVANTAGES OF BINARY FILES

A binary file has two major advantages over a text file.

1. A binary file is like an *array* in that it allows direct access to a particular record without having to access all the preceding records, as was the case for text files. (Unlike an array, however, a binary file does not occupy internal computer memory. This is important since for many applications, only a relatively small number of the file's records actually need to be read into internal memory.)

2. Processing time of binary files is shorter because data is already stored in the way that it is internally represented. In contrast, text files have data stored in character form, which then must be converted into computer-recognizable binary form.

As an example of the primary advantage of a file of records, consider an alphabetized list of 1,000 names and telephone numbers. To find the telephone number of the 998th person on the list, the computer could go directly to the 998th record, whereas with a text file, the 997 names and telephone numbers preceding the desired one would have to be accessed first.

22.3 CREATING A BINARY FILE

Binary Files versus Text Files Following are some important ways in which binary files differ from text files:

1. It is *not* possible to create a binary file from within the edit mode. A binary file can be created only by running a program.

2. The contents of an existing binary file can be accessed only through a Pascal program. If you list the file or if you load it and then look at it in the edit mode, what will appear will be unintelligible because of the form in which binary file data is stored.

3. Only `read` or `write` statements can be used in interfacing with a binary file—`readln` and `writeln` statements are not permissible.

4. `Seekeof` is not available for binary files.

Opening a Binary File for Creation A program to create a binary file must contain `assign` and `rewrite` statements, such as

```
assign (MembFile, 'member.dat');
rewrite (MembFile);
```

The `assign` statement establishes the link between the file's external name and the file variable. (Recall that the drive prefix may be omitted from an `assign` statement if the file in question is to be on the diskette in the logged drive. Henceforth, we will assume that this is the case.)

The `rewrite` statement then creates a blank file for writing onto.

CAUTION If an external file named `member.dat` already existed, then the previous `rewrite` statement would cause its contents to be erased. • • •

Writing a Record The statement

```
write (MembFile, member);
```

will cause the current contents of the record variable `member` to be written onto the file at the current position of the file pointer. When you have written onto a file, the file pointer is always positioned just beyond the record most recently written.

• • • • • • • • • •
Example Here is an interactive program to create a binary file of records.

```
program create;
{creates file of records from user input}
type
  membertype = record
    name: string[20];
    telnum: string[8]
  end; {membertype}
var
  MembFile: file of membertype;
  answer: char;
  member: membertype;

begin
  assign (MembFile, 'member.dat');
  rewrite (MembFile);
  answer := 'y';
  while answer <> 'n' do
    begin
      write ('enter name ');
      readln (member.name);
      write ('enter telephone number ');
      readln (member.telnum);
      write (MembFile, member);
      write ('type y to continue, n to stop ');
      readln (answer)
    end; {while}
  close (MembFile)
end.
```

Following is a typical run.

```
enter name Adams, Ed
enter telephone number 492-5799
type y to continue, n to stop y
enter name Baker, Joe
enter telephone number 492-5151
type y to continue, n to stop y
enter name Bond, Al
enter telephone number 357-6262
type y to continue, n to stop n
```

Here is the file created by that run. This program and the file will be used again in Section 22.6.

member.dat

name	telnum	
Adams, Ed	492-5799	← record position 0
Baker, Joe	492-5151	← record position 1
Bond, Al	357-6262	← record position 2

Record Position Numbers   As mentioned in Section 22.2, a binary file of records is similar to an array of records in that it allows direct access to any record. This direct access is made possible by the numbering of the records as they are written onto the file.

CAUTION   The first record written onto the file has position number 0.

• • •

Closing a File   Be sure to include a file closing statement (for example, `close (fileA)`) in any program that writes onto a file. Failure to do so may result in some data remaining in the file buffer (a temporary storage area) and not being written onto the file.

The computer does not actually write onto the file with each execution of a file writing statement. Instead, it stores this data in a file buffer that it outputs to the file periodically. The file closing statement will flush out whatever remains in the buffer.

The filesize Function   The `filesize` function (which applies to binary files only) returns the number of records contained in a file. Thus, if `fileA` is linked to the `member.dat` file created earlier, then the value of

```
filesize (fileA)
```

equals 3 because that file contains three records. Note, however, that the third and last record is in record position 2.

• • • • • • • • •

Question   Which of the following is the *record position number* for the last record in `fileB`?

(a) `filesize (fileB)`   **(b)** `filesize (fileB) — 1`

(c) `filesize (fileB) + 1`

Answer It is `filesize (fileB) − 1` because the record position number starts with 0.

● ● ●

22.4 ACCESSING AN EXISTING FILE

● ●

A binary file of records resembles an array of records in that the record number acts like an array subscript to provide direct access to a particular record.

The seek Procedure The predeclared procedure

```
seek (filename, recnumber)
```

positions the file pointer at the record whose record number is `recnumber`. For example, the statement

```
seek (MembFile, 5)
```

would move the pointer to the record whose record number is 5.
The statements

```
seek (MembFile, 5);
write (MembFile, member);
```

would write the contents of the record variable `member` onto record number 5 and advance the pointer to record number 6.

The read Procedure The `read` statement

```
read (filename, recvariable)
```

for binary files reads into `recvariable` the contents of the record currently pointed to and then positions the file pointer at the next record. Often `seek` and `read` are used in conjunction. For example

```
seek (MembFile, 5);
read (MembFile, member);
```

would read the record with record number 5 into `member`.

CAUTION After execution of either `read (MembFile, member)` or `write (MembFile, member)`, the file pointer advances to the next position.

● ● ●

Interrogation versus Updating Often we wish to read information stored in a binary file without modifying the file in any way. This process is called ***file interrogation.*** We can also modify the data stored in a binary file—this is called ***updating*** the file.

CAUTION For both interrogation and updating, the file in question should be opened with `reset` rather than `rewrite` since `rewrite` would erase the contents of the file. • • •

Whether Record Number Is Supplied or Calculated Interrogating or updating a binary file can be done in two different settings.

1. Where the record number is directly supplied by the user (discussed in Section 22.5) or by a file

2. Where the record number must be determined by a search (discussed in Section 22.6)

The filepos Function `filepos (filename)` returns the record number of the record currently being pointed to in `filename`. The statement

```
seek (filename, filepos(filename) - 1)
```

is used to move the file pointer back to the previous record.

22.5 RECORD NUMBER IS SUPPLIED
• •

In this section, we will assume that the following file of records exists for the ACME Hardware Store. Each item's `IDnum` will simply be its record position number.

IDnum	Name	Price
0	rake	7.00
1	shovel	20.00
2	stapler	6.00
3	drill	50.00
4	hammer	4.50
5	rasp	2.50

Interrogating the File As a first example, consider a program in which the user inputs the ID number and the quantity purchased for a certain item. The program then looks up the unit price of the item and prints the cost.

```
program bill;
{User supplies record number and quantity for purchase item}
```

```
type
   itemrec = record
      name: string;
      price: real
   end; {itemrec}
var
   StockFile: file of itemrec;
   item: itemrec;
   IDnum, quant: integer;
   cost: real;

begin
   assign (StockFile,'ACME.dat');
   reset (StockFile);
   write ('enter IDnum and Quantity ');
   readln (Idnum, quant);
   seek (StockFile, IDnum);
   read (StockFile, item);
   with item do
     begin
       cost := price * quant;
       writeln (quant, ' ', name, '(s) cost $: ', cost:5:2)
     end; {with}
   close (StockFile)
end.
```

REMARK Invalid ID numbers (out of the range 0..filesize(StockFile) − 1) could be screened for by inclusion of an `if-then` test or a `repeat-until` loop. • • •

Multiple Retrievals In Exercise 4, you are asked to modify `program bill` to allow the cashier to input several purchases. The output should be an itemized receipt that also includes the total. Also see Exercise 5.

Updating a Binary File Individual records in a binary file may be modified. Be aware that you must write an entire record to a binary file (not just some of its fields). Thus, to modify a file record, you should read the record into a record variable, modify the field(s) you wish to change, and then write the contents of the record variable back to the file.

Example (Updating One Record) We want to write a program that allows the store manager to change the price of an item in his stock file. For instance, if he wants to change the price of a drill to $53, the display on the screen would be

```
enter ID number of item for price change: 3
drill old price : $50
enter new price of drill : $53
```

• • •

• • • • • • • • • •

Question Here is the pseudocode for changing the price of an item whose ID number has already been entered (suppose it is 3).

```
seek (StockFile, IDnum)
read (StockFile, item)
modify price of item
_____
write (StockFile, item)
```

1. What would go wrong if the blank line remained blank? (*Hint:* Where is the file pointer positioned?)

2. Fill in the blank so that this is corrected.

Answer *1.* The `read` statement advances the file pointer to the next record after the one just read, so the `write` statement would overwrite the next record. (For example, an attempted update of the drill record would be overwritten onto the hammer record.)

2. `seek (StockFile, IDnum)` will reposition the file back to where you want to write. • • •

• • • • • • • • • •

Question Fill in the two blank lines in the following program to update the price of an item in the stock file

```
program ChangePrice;
{User enters IDnumber and new price}
type
  itemrec = record
    name: string;
    price: real
  end; { itemrec}
  stocktype = file of itemrec;
var
  IDnum : integer;
  StockFile : stocktype;

procedure REPLACE (var stock: stocktype;
                   IDnum: integer);
```

```
{Replaces old price with new one entered by user}
var  item: itemrec;
begin
  seek (StockFile, IDnum);
  read (StockFile, item);
  with item do
    begin
      write (name, ' old price : $ ' , price : 5:2);
      write ('enter new price of ', name, ':$');
      readln (price)
    end; {with}
  seek (_____);        {write revised record}
  write (_____)        {onto the file}
end; {REPLACE}

begin
  assign (StockFile, 'ACME.dat');
  reset (StockFile);
  write ('enter ID number of item for price change: ');
  readln (IDnum);
  if IDnum in  [0.. filesize (StockFile) - 1]
    then REPLACE (StockFile, IDnum)
    else writeln ('Invalid ID number');
  close (StockFile)
end.
```

Answer

```
seek (StockFile, IDnum);
write (StockFile, item);
```

The seek statement also could have been

```
seek (StockFile, filepos(stock)-1)
```                                            • • •

REMARK   Note that the program needed to use seek twice. The first use
of seek is to position the file pointer to the desired record and the second
seek is to move the file pointer back to that record since the read statement
advanced the file pointer.   • • •

Multiple Updates   In Exercise 6, you are asked to modify program
ChangePrice to allow several updates. Also see Exercise 7.

22.6   RECORD NUMBER NOT SUPPLIED

In some situations, the record number for a desired record is not known
initially but must be determined by a search.

. . . .
Example (Finding Someone's Telephone Number) Let us assume that member.dat contains the names and telephone numbers of 1,000 members of a club, in alphabetical order. When you call club information to find out a particular member's telephone number, you would not be expected to know the member's file record number. Instead, you would tell the club's operator the member's name.

The following program will find a desired telephone number using a form of the binary search:

```
program findnum;
{finds telephone numbers for names}
{entered by the user}
type
  nametype = string[20];
  membertype = record
    name: nametype;
    telnum: string[8]
  end; {membertype}
  Membtype = file of membertype;
var
  MembFile: Membtype;
  name: nametype;
  spot: integer;
  member: membertype;

function BINSEARCH (var MembFile: Membtype;
                    wanted: nametype): integer;
  {performs a binary search; returns the value of the record}
  {or -1 if wanted is not in the file}
  var first, last, mid: integer;
      member: membertype;
      found: boolean;
  begin
    last := filesize (MembFile) - 1;
    first := 0;
    found := false;
    repeat
      mid := (first + last) div 2;
      seek (MembFile, mid);
      read (MembFile, member);
      if wanted = member.name then
          found := true
      else if wanted < member.name then
          last := mid - 1
      else {wanted > member.name}
```

```
                    first := mid + 1
         until (found) or (last < first);
         if found then BINSEARCH := mid
                 else BINSEARCH := -1
     end; {BINSEARCH}

begin {main}
   assign (MembFile, 'member.dat');
   reset (MembFile);
   write ('enter name or xyz to stop ');
   readln (name);
   while name <> 'xyz' do
     begin
        spot := BINSEARCH (MembFile, name);
        if spot > -1 then
          begin
             seek (MembFile, spot);
             read (MembFile, member);
             writeln (member.name, '  ', member.telnum)
          end {then}
        else {spot = -1}
          writeln (name, ' not on list');
        write ('enter name or xyz to stop ');
        readln (name)
     end; {while}
   close (MembFile)
end.
```

REMARK

1. The function BINSEARCH returns the value -1 if the wanted name is not on the list. This value is used because the first record in the file has position 0.

2. Note that the seek procedure is used twice. First, it is called within BINSEARCH. Then it is called again in the main body to reset the file pointer to the record number spot because the statement

```
read (MembFile, member)
```

will have advanced the pointer so that it points to the record after the record just read.   ● ● ●

Updating a File   Updating a file when the record number is not directly supplied involves two steps. You must locate the desired record and then call a procedure like REPLACE (see Section 22.5) to replace the old record with the modified record.

In Exercise 8, you are asked to write an interactive program that allows a clerk to update the phone number for several members. See also Exercise 9.

Sorted Transaction File

Suppose there are a number of updates collected on a file (called a transaction file) and the transaction file is sorted on the same field as a master file.

If the transaction file contains only a few records, it would make sense to use a binary search for each item. If, however, the transaction file contains many updates, then it could be inefficient to start from scratch to locate the position of each update item in the master file. Instead, we can begin a linear search for the desired record at the location of the previous update.

REMARK   The master file must be a binary file (since we want to write directly to it), whereas the transaction file can be either a text or a binary file since it is read sequentially (without ever needing to back up) and never written to.   • • •

Example   The Lern Mawr College Alumni Association has a master file of graduates' names, occupations, and total contributions since graduation. A transaction file contains the names and this year's contributions for some of the graduates. Both of these files are sorted by name. Program contributions updates the master file by adding on this year's contributions.

(a)   Suppose you are guaranteed that every name on the transaction file actually appears on the master file. Here is a quite detailed pseudocode for an update program

```
open and reset files
read (mastfile, master)
while not eof(transfile) do
  read (transfile, trans)
  while master.name < trans.name do {locates position on master}
    read (mastfile, master)
  master.tot := master.tot + trans.amt
  seek (mastfile, filepos(mastfile) - 1) {moves pointer back}
  write (mastfile, master)
close files
```

(b)   Suppose that the previous guarantee is eliminated. The update program should print a message NOT FOUND for each bad name on the transaction file. Before reading further, you should consider what changes you would make in the pseudocode for situation (a).

Here is the complete program.

```
program contributions;
{Uses a transaction file to update a master.}
{Assumes master file is not empty.}
type
  masterrec = record
    name: string;
    occupation: string;
    tot: longint
  end; {masterrec}
  transrec = record
    name: string;
    amt: longint
  end; {transrec}
var mastfile: file of masterrec;
    transfile: file of transrec;
    master: masterrec;
    trans: transrec;

begin
  assign (mastfile, 'master.dat');
  reset (mastfile);
  assign (transfile, 'trans.dat');
  reset (transfile);
  read (mastfile, master);
  while not eof(transfile) do
    begin
      read (transfile, trans);
      while (master.name < trans.name) and (not eof(mastfile)) do
        read (mastfile, master);
      if master.name = trans.name then
        begin
          master.tot := master.tot + trans.amt;
          seek (mastfile, filepos(mastfile) - 1);
          write (mastfile, master)
        end {then}
      else
        writeln (trans.name, 'NOT FOUND')
    end; {while}
  close (mastfile);
  close (transfile)
end.
```

• • • • • • • • •

Question   Will the program work even if the name of a person on the master file appears several times on the transaction file?

Answer   Yes. If a person's transaction has just been processed and the next transaction involves that same person, the inner `while` loop will be skipped.   • • •

REMARK   In Exercise 11, you are asked to give an example to show why the `not eof` condition is needed in

```
while (master.name < trans.name) and (not eof (mastfile)) do
```
• • •

22.7   APPENDING, MERGING, AND SORTING

• •

Appending   Suppose that we have two files of records and we wish to create a file whose records consist of all the records in the first file followed by all the records in the second file. This process is known as ***appending***. Here is a program that will write the combined file as a third file.

```
program append;
{writes the combined file as a third file}
type
  membertype = record
    name: string[20];
    telnum: string[8]
  end; {membertype}
var
  i: integer;
  fileA, fileB, fileC: file of membertype;
  member: membertype;

begin
  assign (fileA, 'membA.dat');
  reset (fileA);
  assign (fileB, 'membB.dat');
  reset (fileB);
  assign (fileC, 'membC.dat');
  rewrite (fileC);
  for i := 0 to filesize (fileA) - 1 do
    begin
      read (fileA, member);
      write (fileC, member)
    end; {for}
  for i := 0 to filesize (fileB) - 1 do
    begin
```

```
      read (fileB, member);
      write (fileC, member)
    end; {for}
  close (fileA);
  close (fileB);
  close (fileC)
end.
```

REMARK   A more common type of append program would not use a third file. Instead it would write the contents of fileB directly to the end of fileA. In Exercise 13, you are asked to write such a program. It would use seek (fileA, filesize) to position the file pointer right after the last record in fileA.   • • •

Merging   Now let us consider the more difficult problem of merging two files. Two files of membertype are each ordered alphabetically by name. We wish to create a third file that contains all the records of both files, ordered alphabetically. Here is the pseudocode for such a merge.

```
open the three files
read (fileA, employA);
read (fileB, employB);
while not eof (fileA) and not eof (fileB) do
    use a test to
        write onto fileC whichever of the current two records has the name
            field that comes first
    read the next record from the file whose record was just written onto
        fileC
{The while loop will be terminated once one of the two files has been exhausted.
The last record of the exhausted file will be in memory. It still remains to write
this record and the rest of the nonexhausted file onto fileC.}
close the three files
```

Writing a program based on this pseudocode is Exercise 14.

EXERCISES

1. Give a type declaration for a file that contains member records for the John Doe Society. Each record has fields for name, sex, age, and occupation.

2. For the file in Exercise 1, write a program that will print on paper each of the records contained in the file.

3. What would happen if the following *incorrect* code were executed for the file in Exercise 1? The code is intended to update the current occupation of

James Clark, whose record is in record position 14, from plumber to surgeon.

```
seek (fileA, 14);
read (fileA, member);
member.occupation := 'surgeon';
write (fileA, member);
```

Longer Assignments

4. Modify `program bill` of Section 22.5 so that the cashier can input several purchases. The output should be an itemized receipt that also includes the total.

5. Suppose that student.dat is a file of records, with each record containing a student's name, ID number, number of credits completed, and grade point average. The file is sorted in ascending order by ID number. Write a program that gives the user the following choices:

> 1. List all data for the student whose ID number is input by the user.
>
> 2. List all data for those students whose grade point average is greater than or equal to that input by the user.
>
> 3. List all data for those students who have a grade point average greater than or equal to that input by the user and who also have completed less than a certain number of credits input by the user.

6. Modify `program ChangePrice` to allow several updates.

7. A binary file contains the name and yearly salary for each of the employees at ACE Company. Write a program that will increase each employee's salary by 10 percent and revise the file accordingly.

8. A binary file contains the name and telephone number for each of the members of a club in alphabetical order. Write an interactive program that allows a clerk for the club to update the file by entering a change of telephone number for each of several members. Your program should use the `BINSEARCH` procedure of Section 22.6.

9. Suppose that inventory.dat is a file of records containing information on the items sold by a hardware store. Each record consists of an ID number, item name, price, and quantity in stock. The records are ordered according to ID number. Write a program that gives the user the following choices and then updates the quantity in stock accordingly.

1. Sales transaction by ID number—the clerk inputs the ID number and the quantity sold.

2. Sales transaction by item name—the clerk enters the name of the item and the quantity sold.

3. Shipment transaction by ID number—the clerk inputs the ID number and the quantity received.

4. Quit.

10. (a) Write a program that will store in a file of integers all the odd integers between 100 and 200.

 (b) Write a program that will store in a file of integers all the prime numbers between 100 and 200.

11. In program contributions in Section 22.6, why is the following statement necessary?

```
while (master.name < trans.name) and (not eof (mastfile)) do
```

Give an example to illustrate your answer.

12. Write a procedure SWAP_REC that has as its parameters a file variable and the record position numbers of two records from the file. SWAP_REC should swap those two records in the file.

13. Write a program that will append the contents of fileB directly to the end of fileA. Do not use a third file. (See Section 22.7 for further details.)

* 14. Based on the pseudocode given in Section 22.7, write a program to merge two ordered files.

* 15. Write a program that will merge two ordered files, eliminating any duplicate records. That is, if some of the records occur in both of the files, they should be written only once onto the merged file.

Chapter

23

UNITS

• • • A ***unit*** is an external block of code that can be used by any program (or other block of code) that declares the unit. In addition to the built-in units that come with Turbo Pascal, you may create your own units and thus build up a library of procedures and functions. Not only is this much less work than starting from scratch for each new program, but it is also safer (since you will save blocks of code that have already been debugged and tested). Typically, a long, complicated program might be pieced together by using some units that already exist as well as new units written specially for the program. A further advantage of units is that they can reduce compilation time since they permit independent compilation. This chapter first reviews built-in units and then discusses how to write and use your own units. • • •

23.1 BUILT-IN UNITS

The following six built-in units, contained in the file `turbo.tp1`, are automatically loaded into memory when Turbo 4.0–7.0 is loaded.

 1. `system` contains all the standard and built-in procedures and functions of Turbo 4.0–7.0. This unit is always linked into every program.

 2. `crt` contains a set of declarations for input and output (such as `clrscr` to clear the screen).

 3. `printer` contains the declaration for `lst` that allows output to be sent to the printer.

4. graph3 contains the full set of graphics routines for Turbo 3.0. This unit maintains compatibility with programs created with Turbo 3.0.

5. DOS contains various Pascal equivalents of commonly used DOS calls.

6. turbo3 contains Turbo 3.0 keywords and subprograms that have not been included in Turbo 4.0–7.0.

In addition, the compiled file graph.tpu contains a full set of Turbo 4.0–7.0 graphics routines.

Declaration for a Built-in Unit
In order to use one or more units, you must include in your program an appropriate uses statement such as

```
uses printer;
```

or

```
uses printer, crt;
```

Normally, the uses statement immediately follows the program header.

REMARK   It is not necessary to declare the unit system because this unit is linked to every program.   • • •

The crt Unit
If the crt unit is declared, the following procedures (partial list) may be called:

1. clrscr will clear the output screen and position the cursor in the upper left corner of the screen.

2. gotoXY (a,b). The full output screen contains 80 columns and 25 rows (and thus 2,000 print positions). The gotoXY procedure takes two arguments, the column and row for the cursor position. That is,

```
gotoXY (a,b)
```

will move the cursor to column a and row b. Thus,

```
gotoXY (40,3);
write ('H');
```

would display an H in row 3, column 40.

Note that clrscr moves the cursor to print position (1,1).

3. delay (n) will produce a delay of approximately n milliseconds. Thus,

delay (100) would produce a delay of one-tenth of a second

delay (300) would produce a delay of three-tenths of a second

Example

```
program animation;
{will move a face, chr(2), across row 5 of the screen}
uses crt;
var i, r, c: integer;
begin
  clrscr;
  r := 5;
  c := 1;
  gotoXY (c,r);
  write (chr(2));   {prints a face}
  for i := 1 to 79 do
    begin
      gotoXY (c,r);
      write (' ');   {erases face}
      c := c + 1;
      gotoXY (c,r);
      write (chr(2));
      delay (300)
    end
end.
```

23.2 WRITING AND USING YOUR OWN UNITS

A unit is a kind of external program. To write and use your own units, you must learn

- The syntax for writing units
- How to write an application (or host) program that makes use of the units you've written
- How to compile units and run an application program

Special Form of Unit Syntax Here is a no-frills format for a unit. Later, we will mention two additional features (private declarations and an initialization section) that can be included.

```
unit {name};
interface
   {uses, const, type, or var declarations, if any}
   {procedures and function headers}
implementation
   {full declarations of procedures and functions}
end.
```

The unit header consists of the reserved word **unit** followed by the name given to the unit.

The interface section begins with the reserved word **interface.** The identifiers declared in the interface are public in that they can be referenced by any program (or unit) that declares this unit.

The implementation section begins with the reserved word **implementation** and is followed by the complete definitions of the subprograms with the header repeated. *The last subprogram must end with a semicolon.*

The unit declaration ends with the keyword end followed by a period, not a semicolon.

CAUTION   You should use the same identifier for both the unit name and the prefix of the Pascal file name to that unit's source code. For example, if the unit has the name ArrManip, the Pascal file name should be ArrManip. pas. (This is mandatory in Turbo Pascal 6.0-7.0 and suggested good style in Turbo Pascal 4.0-5.5.)   ● ● ●

● ● ● ● ● ● ● ● ●

Example   The unit ArrManip declared here contains two procedures for manipulating an array.

GET_DATA will read numbers from a text file into an array of integers.

PRINT_REVERSE will print on paper the numbers in the reverse of their original order.

```
unit ArrManip;
interface
 uses printer;
 const maxsize = 20;
 type ArrType = array[1..maxsize] of integer;
 procedure GET_DATA(filename: string;
                    var numbs: ArrType; var size: integer);
 procedure PRINT_REVERSE (numbs: ArrType; size: integer);

implementation
 procedure GET_DATA (filename: string;
                     var numbs: ArrType; var size: integer);
   var NumFile: text;
   begin
     assign(NumFile, filename);
     reset (NumFile);
     size := 0;
```

```
      while not seekeof(NumFile) do
        begin
          size := size + 1;
          read (NumFile, numbs[size])
        end;
      close (NumFile)
    end;

procedure PRINT_REVERSE (numbs: ArrType; size: integer);
  var i: integer;
  begin
    for i := size downto 1 do
      write(lst, numbs[i], ' ');
    writeln (lst)
  end;
end.
```

Program Using the ArrManip Unit   Suppose that the text file numb.dat contains the numbers

```
35 26 82 44 75
```

When the following host program UnitApplic is run, the output on paper will be

```
75 44 82 26 35
```

```
program UnitApplic;
uses ArrManip;

var   numbs: ArrType;
      size: integer;

begin
  GET_DATA ('numb.dat', numbs, size);
  PRINT_REVERSE (numbs, size)
end.
```

• • • • • • • • •

Question   Program UnitApplic did not directly contain the type declaration

```
type ArrType = array[1..maxsize] of integer
```

nor did it contain a declaration of the constant maxsize or the printer unit. Why wasn't this an error?

Answer   The declarations in the interface section of `ArrManip` are public; that is, they are accessible to any program (or block of code) that declares the unit `ArrManip`.   ● ● ●

Mechanics of Saving, Compiling, and Running

1. After you have written a unit, you should save it in two forms:

    (a) As a source file (that is, as a `.pas` file). The prefix of this file name should be the same as the unit's name.

    (b) In compiled form (known as a `.tpu` file, for Turbo Pascal Unit). To do so, you start with the unit's source file in memory. Then, compile (to disk) by pressing ALT-F9.[*]

2. Once each of the custom written unit(s) declared by the application program has been compiled (as a `.tpu` file) to the current default drive, you may compile and run the application program as you normally would.

Units Using Other Units   If you want unit A to use unit B, you can declare unit B in a `uses` declaration of unit A. You then must also be sure to compile the `tpu` file for unit B before compiling the `tpu` file for unit A.

Units from Other Directories   If you want a program to use a unit whose `tpu` file is contained in a directory other than the current directory, you should use the options submenu to inform the compiler where to look for `tpu` files besides the current directory. From the options submenu, select the `Directories` choice, and then in the dialog box, give path specifications for all needed `tpu` files.

Modifying Units and the Make and Build Options   Suppose that you compiled and ran a host program and then modified some of those units some time later. Now you want to run the host program again so that it uses the most current version of each of the units. If you are certain that you saved the most current version of each unit as a `.tpu` file, you can simply recompile and run the host program. Otherwise, you can choose one of the following methods:

1. With the host program in the editor, select the `make` option from the compile submenu. This automatically recompiles each unit whose `.pas` source files have a date and time later than that of the unit's `.tpu` file.

---

[*]In Turbo 4.0–5.5, from the compile submenu set the destination to "Disk" by pressing the letter D. Then compile by pressing ALT-F9. (Be aware that pressing D acts as a toggle. To set destination back to memory, you should press D again.)

2. With the host program in the editor, select the `build` option from the compile submenu. This will recompile all the unit source files into `.tpu` files. (You would use this if there are no `.tpu` files for some of the units.)

Other Features

1. The implementation section of a unit may contain private declarations (new identifiers that can only be accessed within the unit). Such declarations would not be accessible to portions of the application program when one of the unit's subprograms is not being executed.

2. A unit may also have an initialization section that could be used to assign initial values to any variables declared within the unit. The initialization section would begin with the reserved word `begin` and contain statements. The initialization section does not take an extra `end`—it is terminated by the `end.` for the unit.

• • • • • • • • •   EXERCISES

• •

1. Add the following two subprograms to `ArrManip`:

   function `FINDAVG`
   procedure `PRINT_ABOVE_AG`

   and run a modified application program to print the numbers in reverse order and then just those numbers above the average.

2. Write a unit that contains a procedure `GETDATA` and two functions, `ROW_SUM` and `COL_SUM`, for summing elements of an $m \times n$ array, where both m and $n \leq 8$. Each of the functions will have four parameters—the array, the values for m and n, and the row or column to be summed. Thus `COL_SUM (sales, 6, 7, 3)` would return the sum of the elements in the third column of the 6×7 array `sales`. Run an application program for this unit.

Chapter

24

GAME-PLAYING PROGRAMS
THAT LEARN

• • • One branch of computer research is devoted to the study of ***artificial intelligence***—programming the computer to perform tasks that would seem to require real "intelligence." In this chapter, we consider three versions of a game-playing program. The third version could be considered to involve artificial intelligence because the program endows the computer with the capacity to "learn" to play well. In fact, the computer can learn the optimal strategy even if the programmer does not know it. • • •

24.1 INTRODUCTION TO THE TEN-MATCH GAME

The rules for the 10-match game are as follows:

1. There are 10 matchsticks at the start.

2. A player may remove one or two matches on each turn.

3. The person who takes the last match is the loser.

This chapter considers three different types of programs in which the computer plays the 10-match game against a human opponent. In the first type of program, the computer moves at random, and the human opponent should win most of the time. In the second type of program, the computer plays perfectly on every attempt; the writing of such a program requires that the programmer know the perfect strategy. Writing such a program for the 10-match game is Exercise 3.

The third type of program is the most intriguing—the computer plays poorly at first but has the capability of learning to play well. Against a good player, it will learn quickly how to play a perfect game. Interestingly, this type of program can be written by a programmer who does *not* know how to play perfectly.

In all the match game programs of this chapter, the human will move first.

24.2 COMPUTER MOVING RANDOMLY

In `program RandomMatch`, the computer moves at random. Try playing against the computer using this program—you will find it easy to win. To play, just load the program into the computer and run it. The computer will tell you when it is your turn.

The following is a typical run.

```
Start game. There are 10 matches
Human goes first
How many matches do you leave?   8
     Computer leaves 6
How many matches do you leave?   5
     Computer leaves 4
How many matches do you leave?   3
     Computer leaves 2
How many matches do you leave?   1
     Computer leaves 0
*** Human won ***
```

Question Fill in the blank in `program RandomMatch`.

```
program RandomMatch;
{Human goes first.  Computer moves at random.}
type moverange = 0..10;
var left_by_human, left_by_comp: moverange;

function COMP_LEAVES (number: moverange): moverange;
```

```
      {selects how many matches the computer will leave}
      var take: 1..2;
      begin
        if number = 1 then
          COMP_LEAVES := 0
        else
          begin
            take := random(2) + 1;
            COMP_LEAVES := number - take
          end {else}
    end; {COMP_LEAVES}

  begin {main}
    randomize;
    writeln ('Start game.  There are 10 matches');
    writeln ('Human goes first');
    repeat
      write ('How many matches do you leave? ');
      readln (left_by_human);
      if left_by_human > 0 then
        begin
          left_by_comp := _____;
          writeln ('  Computer leaves ', left_by_comp)
        end;
    until (left_by_human <= 0) or (left_by_comp = 0);
    if left_by_comp = 0
      then writeln ('*** Human won ***')
      else writeln ('*** Computer won ***')
  end.
```

Answer   The number of matches the computer leaves is obtained by applying
COMP_LEAVES to the number just left by the human.

        left_by_comp := COMP_LEAVES (left_by_human);   • • •

REMARK   This program is vulnerable to human cheating. In Exercise 2, you
are asked to identify the two ways in which a human could cheat and then
add code to the program so that cheating is not allowed.   • • •

24.3 THE GETSMART PROGRAM

In the next program, GetSmart, the computer improves as it plays.
Opposing a good player, it learns how to play a perfect game very quickly.
We will refer to the number of matches the computer chooses to leave as

a *position.* The main principle of this program is that the computer keeps a record of the success of the various positions it left in previous games. On its turn, the computer moves so that it leaves the position that has previously been most successful. For example, suppose its human opponent has just left 7 matches. The computer has a choice between leaving 6 matches and leaving 5 matches. It will check which of these moves worked better in previous games. (If leaving 5 worked better in previous games, the computer will leave 5.)

Since the human goes first, the computer will never have a chance to leave 9 matches. Thus, it will use the memory boxes `values[8]`, `values[7]`, `values[6]`, `values[5]`, and so on to keep track of the desirability values of leaving 8, 7, 6, 5, and so on. At the start of the program (during the first game of a run), all positions will have desirability value 0. Whenever the computer wins a game, it will add 1 to the desirability values of those positions that it used during that game. For example, if the computer won a game in which it left positions 8, 4, and 1, it would add 1 to the contents of the memory boxes `values[8]`, `values[4]`, and `values[1]`. Whenever the computer loses a game, it will subtract 1 from the desirability values of the positions it left during that game.

Suppose the computer has already played several games during a run of the program and is now playing another game. The human opponent has just left 8, and the computer must decide whether to leave 7 or 6. The function `COMP_LEAVES` will compare `values[7]` with `values[6]` to see which has the greater desirability value. (In the event that the two positions have the same desirability value, the computer will leave the larger number of matches.)

An integer variable `count` is used to count how many moves the *computer* makes during a game. The number of matches the computer leaves on each move is stored in the array `moves`. If the computer leaves 7 on its first move of a game, `moves[1]` will have the value 7. If the computer leaves 5 on its second move, `moves[2]` will become 5, and so on.

At the end of a game, `procedure UPDATEVALUES` will adjust the desirability values of those positions that the computer left during that game.

Here is the pseudocode.

```
for i := 0 to 8 do    (initialize)
   values[i] := 0;
repeat
   PLAYGAME—passes on the winner, the count of the number of moves
           made by the computer, and the actual positions left by the
           computer
   UPDATE_VALUES—adjusts the desirability values of the positions left by the
           computer, adding or subtracting 1 to each
   write ('Shall we play again--y/n?')
   readln (answer)
until answer = 'n'
```

Here is the program.

```
program GetSmart;
{computer is supplied with a learning procedure}
type moverange = 0..10;
     valuestype = array[moverange] of integer;
     movestype = array[1..5] of moverange;
var winner: string;
    values: valuestype;
    moves: movestype;
    count, i: integer;
    answer: char;

procedure PLAYGAME (values: valuestype;
                    var winner: string;
                    var count: integer;
                    var moves: movestype);
  {plays one game}
  var  left_by_human, left_by_comp: moverange;

  function COMP_LEAVES (number: moverange;
                        values: valuestype): moverange;
    {used by computer to select its move}
    begin
      if number = 1 then
        COMP_LEAVES := 0
      else if values[number - 1] >= values[number - 2]
             then COMP_LEAVES := number - 1
             else COMP_LEAVES := number - 2
    end; {COMP_LEAVES}

  begin {PLAYGAME}
    writeln ('Start game. There are 10 matches.');
    count := 0;
    repeat
      write ('How many do you leave? ');
      readln (left_by_human);
      if left_by_human > 0 then
        begin
          left_by_comp := COMP_LEAVES (left_by_human, values);
          writeln ('  Computer leaves ', left_by_comp);
          count := count + 1;
          moves[count] := left_by_comp
        end {then}
    until (left_by_human = 0) or (left_by_comp = 0);
    if left_by_comp = 0
```

```
      then winner := 'human'
      else winner := 'computer';
    writeln (winner, ' won')
  end; {PLAYGAME}

procedure UPDATEVALUES (var values: valuestype;
                            winner: string;
                            count: integer;
                            moves: movestype);
  {updates the array values}
  var adjust, i: integer;
  begin
    if winner = 'computer' then adjust := 1
                           else adjust := -1;
    for i := 1 to count do
      values[moves[i]] := values[moves[i]] + adjust
  end; {UPDATEVALUES}

begin {main}
  for i := 0 to 8 do      {initialize}
    values[i] := 0;
  repeat
    PLAYGAME (values, winner, count, moves);
    UPDATEVALUES (values, winner, count, moves);
    write ('Shall we play again--y / n? ');
    readln (answer)
  until answer = 'n'
end.
```

Improving the GetSmart Program   There is a way to improve the preceding program so that the computer will learn to play well much more quickly. In updating the array `values`, program `GetSmart` considers only the positions left by the *computer* during the game just played. In Exercise 4, you are asked to modify this program so that it keeps track of the positions that were left both by the computer and by the human. Then at the end of a game, it adds 1 to the desirability values of those positions left by the winner and subtracts 1 from those left by the loser.

• • • • • • • • •   **EXERCISES**
• •

1. Suppose `program GetSmart` has just played the first game of a run and the game went as follows: Human 8, Computer 7, Human 6, Computer 5,

Human 4, Computer 3, Human 1, Computer loses. At the start of the second game, what positions will have desirability value -1?

2. A drawback of the RandomMatch and GetSmart programs is that they are vulnerable to human cheating.

    (a) Identify the ways in which a human could cheat.

    (b) Add code to the RandomMatch program to prevent cheating.

Longer Assignments

* 3. Write a program for the 10-match game that will allow the computer to play perfectly from the start. This program will be much simpler than GetSmart, but you *do* have to know the perfect strategy yourself.

* 4. Write an ImprovedSmart program for the 10-match game in which the computer updates the desirability values of the positions left by both players. The computer should add 1 to the desirability values of the winner's positions and subtract 1 from the desirability values of the loser's positions.

* 5. Write a program similar to GetSmart or ImprovedSmart to play a game in which there are 13 matches at the start and a player can take 1, 2, or 3 matches per turn. The loser is the person who takes the last match.

* 6. It is possible for a clever human to win at least 50 of 100 games played on a single run of program GetSmart. Explain a strategy the human could use.

Chapter

25

RECURSION

• • • We have already seen examples in which the body of a subprogram contains calls to *other* subprograms. In a ***recursive*** subprogram, however, the body of the subprogram contains a call to *itself.*

You might wonder how it could possibly be useful to define something in terms of itself. As you will see, recursion is used when the original task can be reduced to a simpler version of itself. The idea is that after a number of successive reductions, the reduced problem will eventually be simple enough to be solved directly, and its solution will be used to piece together a solution to the original problem.

As an illustration, recall that for n, a positive integer, n! is equal to the product of the first n integers. For example,

$$4! = 4 * 3 * 2 * 1 = 24$$
$$5! = 5 * 4 * 3 * 2 * 1 = 120$$

0! is defined as 1.

Note that for any positive n

$$n! = n * (n - 1)!$$

Thus, finding $n!$ can be reduced to the similar but simpler task of finding $(n - 1)!$. • • •

25.1 INTRODUCTION TO RECURSIVE SYNTAX

Remember that whenever a subprogram call has been completed, control is returned to the point at which the subprogram was called. The same rule applies to recursive calls.

Terminal Case   In order that successive recursive calls not continue indefinitely, the body of a recursive subprogram should include at least one terminal case—a case that contains no further calls to the recursive subprogram. (As you will see, terminal cases are similar to loop exit conditions.)

In the following example, note that the terminal case is $n = 1$.

• • • • • • • • • •
Example   (Recursive Factorial Function)

```
program drill;
{computes factorial using a recursive factorial function}
var numb: integer;
    result: longint;

function FACT (n: integer): longint;
  {recursive function that computes n!}
  begin
    if n = 1 then
      FACT := 1
    else
      FACT := n * FACT (n-1)
  end; {FACT}

begin {main}
  write ('enter a positive integer ');
  readln (numb);
  result := FACT (numb);
  writeln (numb, ' factorial is ', result)
end.
```

Here is the output to compute 4!.

```
enter a positive integer 4
4 factorial is 24
```

When this program is run to compute 4!, there will be four calls to the recursive function FACT. The first call is to FACT (4) from the main body. This call cannot be completed immediately since FACT (4) calls FACT (3), which calls FACT (2), which calls FACT (1). The call to FACT (1) is the first call that can be completed. Then the computer winds back up and assigns FACT the value 1. That value is sent to the place where FACT (1) was called. Then the call of FACT (2) is completed and the value 2 is sent to the place where FACT (2) was called. Then the call of FACT (3) is completed, and the value 6 is sent to the place where FACT (3) was called. Finally, the original call of FACT (4) is completed.

In the following diagram for FACT (4), the winding back up is indicated by the blue arrows, and the value returned is encircled in blue.

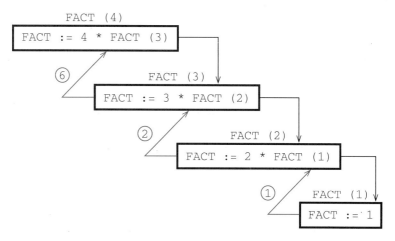

• • • • • • • • • •

Example (Recursion Procedure)   The following program will take a further look at "winding back up" to finish unfinished calls:

```
program RecurProced;

procedure JOB (n: integer);
  begin
    if n = 1 then    {terminal case}
       writeln ('n = 1  GO BACK')
    else             {recursive step}
       begin
         writeln (n, ' hi');
         JOB (n-1);
         writeln (n, ' bye')
       end {else}
  end; {JOB}

begin
  JOB (4)
end.
```

First, the call JOB (4) is started. The computer outputs 4 hi, and then JOB (3) is called. (Note that JOB (4) still has not been completed.) In starting JOB (3), the computer outputs 3 hi and then calls JOB (2), in which it first outputs 2 hi and then calls JOB (1). JOB (1) is a terminal case since its execution does not produce further calls to JOB—it outputs n = 1 GO BACK.

The computer must still *wind back up* and finish *all the unfinished calls.* (The unfinished part of each call is encircled.) It returns to the point in JOB (2) where JOB (1) was called and outputs 2 bye. Then it finishes JOB (3), outputting 3 bye, and JOB (4), outputting 4 bye.

The entire output will be

```
4 hi
3 hi
2 hi
n = 1 GO BACK
2 bye
3 bye
4 bye
```

Here is a trace diagram of program RecurProced.

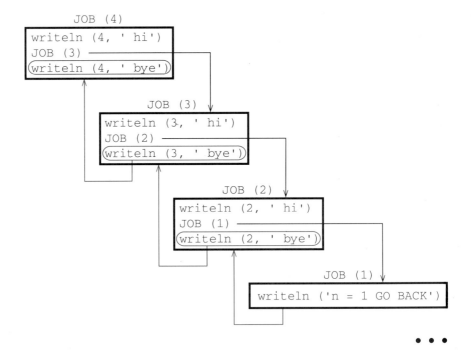

CAUTION   In recursive procedures and functions, beware of the possibility of infinite recursion. Even if you include a terminal case, there remains the possibility that it will never be reached.   • • •

25.2 STRATEGY FOR USING RECURSION

Recursive versus Iterative   A block of code that repeats a task without the use of recursion is called *iterative*. The purpose of the examples in this section is to familiarize you with the basics of recursion even though all these examples can be written more easily using iterative code.

Recursive Forms   In one common form of recursion, the recursive subprogram has n as a parameter and reduces the task in steps of one down to $n = 1$. That is, it has a terminal case of $n = 1$ and a recursive step containing a call with $n - 1$ as an argument.

In this section, we consider two examples that have this pattern and two examples that have a more general structure.

Example   **(BACKWARDS)**   Suppose that numbs is an array of integers and we want BACKWARDS to output the array's contents in reverse order. Thus, for numbs

64	29	44	81	37	58

the call BACKWARDS (numbs, 6) should produce the output

```
58 37 81 44 29 64
```

Here is the pseudocode.

```
if n = 1 then
    there is just one element, so write (numbs[1], ' ')
else
    Assume that BACKWARDS (numbs, n-1) solves the n-1 problem, that is,
    outputs elements 1 through n-1 in reverse order. The else branch must
    solve the full, size n, problem.
```

Question   Fill in the blank lines.

```
procedure BACKWARDS (numbs: numbstype;
                     n: integer);
  begin
    if n = 1 then
        write (numbs[1], ' ')
    else
```

```
        begin
        _____
        _____
        end {else}
    end; {BACKWARDS}
```

Answer   The else branch must give code to output the full, size *n,* array backwards. Thus, first output the *n*th element, and then output the elements 1 . . . *n* − 1 in reverse order. Thus,

```
write (numbs [n], ' ');
BACKWARDS (numbs, n-1)
```

• • •

• • • • • • • • • •

Example   (ORIGINAL)   This time we want to write a recursive subprogram, ORIGI-NAL, to output the array's contents in their original order.

Here is the pseudocode.

```
if n = 1 then
   write (numbs [1], ' ')
else
```
   Assume that ORIGINAL (numbs, n-1) solves the *n* − 1 problem, that is, outputs the elements 1 through *n* − 1 in their original order. The else branch must solve the *full,* size *n,* problem.

Writing procedure ORIGINAL is Exercise 4.

• • • • • • • • • •

Example   (ULAM)   In the following program, we use a recursive procedure, ULAM, to output the Ulam sequence of a positive integer (see Chapter 7). Note that the else branch of ULAM does *not* contain a call to ULAM(n-1). Nevertheless, the recursive step contains calls to a reduced Ulam sequence problem.

• • • • • • • • • •

Question   Fill in the blanks.

```
program UlamRecur;
var n: integer;

procedure ULAM (n:integer);
  begin
    write(n:3);
    if n = 1 then       {terminal case}
        {do nothing}
```

```
      else                    {recursive step}
        begin
          if n mod 2 = 0
            then _____
            else _____
        end
  end;


begin
  write ('enter a positive integer ');
  readln (n);
  ULAM (n)
end.
```

Answer

```
then ULAM (n div 2)
else ULAM (3 * n + 1)
```
• • •

REMARK

1. Finding the Ulam sequence of the next number in an Ulam sequence is a shorter problem than finding the original number's Ulam sequence. For example, the Ulam sequence of 22 is shorter than the Ulam sequence of 7.

2. The terminal case is the loop exit condition of the `repeat-until` version (see Chapter 8). Also note that you could have written the terminal case implicitly by replacing the main `if-then-else` with `if n <> 1 then`.   • • •

• • • • • • • • •

Example **(Recursive Binary Search)**   The algorithm for the recursive version of the binary search is essentially the same as that for the iterative version (see Section 25.3). Note, however, the following differences:

1. The recursive version requires that `first` and `last` be parameters because each recursive call to BINSEARCH must receive the values of `first` and `last` defining the new smaller segment to which the search should be restricted.

2. The loop exit conditions in the iterative version become the terminal cases in the recursive version. (Either you have found what you are looking for or the value of `first` exceeds the value of `last`.)

Question   Fill in the blank in function BINSEARCH.

```
function BINSEARCH (list: stringarr;
                    want: str20;
                    first, last: integer): integer;
{recursive binary search}
var mid: integer;
begin
  mid := (first + last) div 2;
  if first > last then
    BINSEARCH := 0
  else if want = list[mid] then
    BINSEARCH := mid
  else if want < list[mid] then
    BINSEARCH := BINSEARCH (list, want, first, mid - 1)
  else
    BINSEARCH := _____
end; {BINSEARCH}
```

Answer   BINSEARCH := BINSEARCH (list, want, mid + 1, last)

• • •

Potential Inefficiency of Recursion

Recursive code can be inefficient, in terms of processing speed and amount of memory needed, since there can be a great deal of duplication of effort and memory when there is deep nesting of recursive calls. For example, see the trace of FIB in Section 25.4.

When to Use Recursion

Despite its potential inefficiency in use of computer resources, recursion can be a very useful programming tool since some programs can be written much more easily using recursion (for example, the Towers-of-Hanoi problem discussed in Section 25.4 or the merge sort discussed in Chapter 28). This presents two possible strategies for using recursion.

1. For some algorithms, the recursive code is fine in terms of its efficiency.

2. For other algorithms, use recursion to point the way. That is, first write a recursive solution, and then try to rewrite the code iteratively.

25.3   RECURSION AND LOCAL VARIABLE STACKS

• •

A ***stack*** is a data structure in which new entries are added to the *top,* and entries are deleted from the *top* as well. It is useful to envision a stack as a pile of dishes—when you add a dish to the pile you put it on top, and when you remove a dish from the pile you remove it from the top.

As you will see, the computer uses a stack to internally implement a local variable of a recursive subprogram.

As already mentioned, a recursive subprogram's call to itself is essentially a nested subprogram call. In the following program, for each new call of REVERSE, ch is a new local variable.

Thus, when

```
readln (ch);
```

is executed in the else branch, the character previously read in is not erased—it is still stored so that it can be accessed when the computer is winding back up.

• • • • • • • • • •

Question   For program StackDrill, what will the output be if the user successively inputs A, B, C, and D?

```
program StackDrill;
{illustrates a local variable stack}

procedure REVERSE (n: integer);
   var ch: char;
   begin
     write ('type a letter ');
     readln (ch);
     if n = 1 then
       write (ch)
     else
       begin
         REVERSE (n-1);
         write (ch)
       end {else}
   end; {REVERSE}

begin
   REVERSE (4)
end.
```

Answer

```
type a letter A
type a letter B
type a letter C
type a letter D
DCBA
```

• • •

Stack for the local Variable ch   In procedure REVERSE, a stack is used to store the values of the successive local variables, all named ch. When $n = 4$, ch becomes A. Thus, we have

$$
\begin{array}{cc}
 & \text{ch} \\
n = 4 & \boxed{\text{A}}
\end{array}
$$

When $n = 3$, ch becomes B. Thus, we have

$$
\begin{array}{cc}
 & \text{ch} \\
n = 3 & \boxed{\text{B}} \\
n = 4 & \boxed{\text{A}}
\end{array}
$$

When $n = 2$, ch becomes C. Thus, we have

$$
\begin{array}{cc}
 & \text{ch} \\
n = 2 & \boxed{\text{C}} \\
n = 3 & \boxed{\text{B}} \\
n = 4 & \boxed{\text{A}}
\end{array}
$$

When $n = 1$, ch becomes D. Thus, by the time the computer reaches the terminal case $n = 1$, we have

$$
\begin{array}{cc}
 & \text{ch} \\
n = 1 & \boxed{\text{D}} \\
n = 2 & \boxed{\text{C}} \\
n = 3 & \boxed{\text{B}} \\
n = 4 & \boxed{\text{A}}
\end{array}
$$

Remember that the memory for a local variable exists until the computer completes the call of the subprogram in which it was declared. In winding back up to $n = 4$, the computer keeps completing unfinished calls. When it has completed the call with $n = 1$, the top value for ch, D, is printed, and then memory is released for that local variable. Then, when the computer has completed the call with $n = 2$, the current top value for ch, C, is printed and then deleted, and so on. Thus, a stack is exactly the data structure that is needed to implement the "different" local variables ch.

25.4 MULTIPLE CALLS

In the recursive subprograms considered so far, execution of the body of the subprogram has never involved more than one call to itself from statements in that body.

In the next examples, by contrast, one execution of the subprogram body can lead to several recursive calls. For example, the statement

```
FIB := FIB(n - 1) + FIB(n - 2)
```

makes two calls to FIB.

Fibonacci Numbers   The Fibonacci numbers are a famous sequence of numbers. The first and second positive Fibonacci numbers are both 1. Thereafter, each Fibonacci number is the sum of the previous two Fibonacci numbers. Here are the first 12 positive Fibonacci numbers.

$$1 \quad 1 \quad 2 \quad 3 \quad 5 \quad 8 \quad 13 \quad 21 \quad 34 \quad 55 \quad 89 \quad 144$$

If Fib_n is used to denote the nth Fibonacci number, the Fibonacci sequence is determined by the following three equations:

$$Fib_1 = 1$$

$$Fib_2 = 1$$

$$Fib_n = Fib_{n-1} + Fib_{n-2}$$

Example   (Fibonacci Recursively)   Note how naturally the determining equations fit the scheme for recursion. The terminal case is $(n = 1)$ or $(n = 2)$, and finding FIB (n) can be reduced to the simpler task of finding the value of FIB (n - 2) + FIB (n - 1).

Here is the recursive FIB function.

```
function FIB (n: integer): integer;
{recursive}
  begin
    if (n = 1) or (n = 2) then
      FIB := 1
    else
      FIB := FIB (n - 1) + FIB (n - 2)
  end; {FIB}
```

Tracing for Call FIB(5)   This trace is somewhat complicated. The call to FIB(5) leads to eight additional calls in the following order:

```
FIB(4), FIB(3), FIB(2), FIB(1), FIB(2), FIB(3), FIB(2),
FIB(1)
```

as indicated by the diagram.

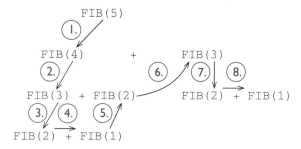

REMARK   Note the inefficiency of this recursive execution. For example, each time FIB(3) is executed (twice), the computer evaluates it from scratch. A call of FIB(6) would involve three calls to FIB(3) and two calls to FIB(4), each evaluated from scratch. By contrast, an iterative program would use an array to store previously calculated Fibonacci values. (See Exercise 9.)

• • •

Example   (Towers of Hanoi)   Finally, we present a problem that is much easier to solve recursively than iteratively.

There are three pegs, A, B, and C, and *n* rings all of different sizes. Initially, peg A contains all the rings in order of size (with the smallest on top). The object is to move the rings one at a time so that eventually all the rings are on peg C. All moves must obey the following two rules:

1. Only the top ring from a peg can be moved.

2. A larger ring must never be put on top of a smaller ring.

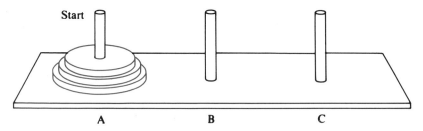

Towers of Hanoi when *n* = 3

Move smallest ring from A to C. Move next ring from A to B. Move ring from C to B. Move largest ring from A to C. At this point we will have

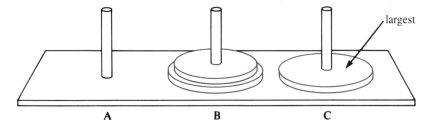

Hand Solution when *n* = 3

The problem has been reduced to a similar *n* − 1 problem—moving two rings from B to C. The hand solution to this would be: Move the smallest ring from B to A. Move remaining ring from B to C. Move the smallest ring from A to C.

Recursive *MOVE_PILE*   Let MOVE_PILE have four parameters.

```
procedure MOVE_PILE (n: integer;
                     peg1, peg2, ExtraPeg: char);
```

We want a call such as MOVE_PILE (5, 'A', 'C', 'B') to move the five rings from peg A to peg C. To write the else branch of this procedure, think of how you would solve the full-size *n* problem using *two* calls to MOVE_PILE with parameter *n* − 1.

The first call in the else branch should achieve

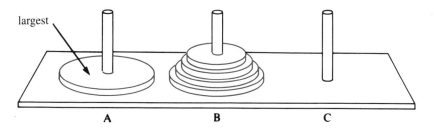

```
else {pseudocode}
   MOVE_PILE—to move n − 1 rings from peg A to peg B

   move largest ring from A to C
   MOVE_PILE—to move n − 1 rings from peg B to peg C
```

Filling in the blank line in the following procedure is Exercise 10.

```
procedure MOVE_PILE (n: integer;
                     peg1, peg2, ExtraPeg: char);
   begin
      if n = 1 then
```

```
        writeln ('Move smallest ring from ', peg1, ' to ', peg2)
    else
        begin
          MOVE_PILE (n-1, peg1, ExtraPeg, peg2);
          writeln ('Move ring from ', peg1, ' to ', peg2);
          MOVE_PILE (_____)
        end; {else}
end; {MOVE_PILE}
```

25.5   MUTUAL RECURSION

• •

Occasionally, it is desirable for procedure A to call procedure B and procedure B to call procedure A. Such calling back and forth is known as **mutual recursion.** This presents a potential problem since each procedure must be declared before it is called.

Mutual recursion is made possible by the command

```
forward;
```

To declare mutually recursive procedures, you first give *just the header* (including any parameter declarations) for one procedure, followed by the `forward` command. Then you give the full declaration of the other procedure. Finally, you give the declaration of the first procedure but without including its parameter declarations in its header. In this way, you ensure that the compiler sees a full header for each subprogram before it is called.

• • • • • • • • •

Example   The mutually recursive procedures, PROCESS and PRINT_TEST, are used in the following Ulam sequence program:

```
program drill;
{uses mutually recursive procedures}
{to print Ulam sequence of input integer}
var n: integer;

procedure PROCESS (var n: integer); forward;

procedure PRINT_TEST (var n: integer);
  begin
    write (n, ' ');
    if n <> 1 then PROCESS (n)
```

```
    end; {PRINT_TEST}

procedure PROCESS;
  begin
    if n mod 2 = 0
      then n := n div 2
      else n := 3 * n + 1;
    PRINT_TEST (n)
  end; {PROCESS}

begin {main}
  write ('enter positive integer ');
  readln (n);
  PRINT_TEST (n)
end.
```

REMARK   Note that the parameter declarations for PROCESS are given in the `forward` declaration of PROCESS but not in the subsequent declaration of PROCESS that introduces its body.   ● ● ●

● ● ● ● ● ● ● ● ● ●   EXERCISES
● ●

1. 0! is defined to be 1. Modify the recursive factorial function in Section 25.1 so that the call FACT (0) returns the value 1.

2. Turbo Pascal does not contain a built-in exponentiation function. Implement exponentiation using a recursive function POWER that receives a base x and an exponent n, where x is real and n is a nonnegative integer. Use the fact that

$$x^n = \begin{cases} x^{n-1} \cdot x & \text{if } x > 0 \\ 1 & \text{if } x = 0 \end{cases}$$

3. Write a recursive function to find the sum of a numerical array's contents.

4. Write recursive procedure ORIGINAL (of Section 25.2) to output an array's contents in their original order.

Longer Assignments

5. Write a recursive function to determine whether or not a string consisting of all uppercase letters is a palindrome. Note that 'FABBAF' and 'CEDEC' are palindromes, whereas 'GAEG' is not.

6. Write a recursive function to perform a linear search on an array of names. Let the function's parameters be `WantedName`, `names`, and `size`.

7. The following algorithm can be used to convert a number to base 2 representation: Divide the original number by 2—the first remainder will give the units digit. Divide the previous quotient by 2—this remainder will give the twos digit. Divide the previous quotient by 2—this remainder will give the fours digit. And so on. Finally, the quotient of 1 divided by 2 will give a quotient of 0 and a final remainder of 1. The base 2 representation will be the remainders written in reverse order.

   For example, to convert 14 to base 2, we divide as follows, starting from the bottom with $2\overline{)14}$:

   Remainders

0	1
$2\overline{)1}$	1
$2\overline{)3}$	1
$2\overline{)7}$	0
$2\overline{)14}$	

   Writing the remainders in the reverse order, we have that 14 in base 2 is 1110.

   (i) Use this algorithm to find the base 2 representations for

       (a) 26   (b) 38   (c) 43   (d) 79

   * (ii) Write a program that uses a recursive procedure based on the algorithm to print the base 2 representation of an input number. (*Hint:* The terminal case should be quotient $n = 1$. Note that the remainders are to be printed not as they occur, but in reverse order.)

* 8. Let the greatest common divisor of two positive integers x and y be denoted by gcd(x, y). The following number theory fact:

   $$\text{gcd}(x, y) = \text{gcd}(y, x \bmod y)$$

   can be applied repeatedly (until the second value divides the first) to find gcd(x, y). When this happens, the second value is the gcd. For example,

   $$\text{gcd}(36, 15) = \text{gcd}(15, 6) = \text{gcd}(6, 3) = 3$$

   Write a recursive program based on this method that will find the gcd of two input positive integers.

9. (a) For the recursive function `FIB` of Section 25.4, give a full trace of the call `FIB(6)`.

   (b) Write an iterative program using an array to find the nth Fibonacci number, where n is an input integer from 1 to 50.

10. Complete procedure `MOVE_PILE` of Section 25.4. Test it with $n = 5$, then with $n = 7$.

Chapter

26

POINTERS AND LINKED LISTS

• • • This chapter introduces the concept of *dynamic data structures* with a discussion of the pointer data type. Pointers have many applications in computer science, one of which is the creation of linked lists. • • •

26.1 INTRODUCTION TO LINKED LISTS

Static versus Dynamic Structures All the variables and data structures that we have considered so far have been static. With a *static* variable, the amount of memory space must be declared in advance and cannot be increased during the execution of the program if more memory space is needed.

An array of records is static since the precise amount of memory set aside for it is fixed by the declaration of the maximum size of the array. This lack of flexibility can be a significant disadvantage. If an array of records is declared to have maximum size of 1,000, the program will not work if more than 1,000 records must be stored in that array. On the other hand, if the maximum size declared for an array is much larger than the amount of memory space needed, the program will use memory very inefficiently, since the specified amount of memory will be set aside for the array, even if only a small portion of it is used.

Pointers permit the creation of *dynamic* data structures—structures that have the capacity to vary in size and that set aside only as much memory as they actually use. One such data structure is a linked list. A *linked list* consists of *nodes* that contain data and pointers linking the nodes. Figure 26.1 gives a rough depiction of a linked list. The implementation of linked lists is discussed in Sections 26.3–26.8.

FIGURE 26.1 Original List

Linked List versus Array   If we had an alphabetized list of 100 names, we could store it in an array names, with a declared maximum size of 200 names. The waste of memory space, however, would not be the only disadvantage of using an array rather than a linked list to store these names.

```
                    names
        [1]     Ames
        [2]     Ball
        [3]     Bond
        [4]     Brock
                      .
                      .
                      .
      [100]     Zerba
                      .
                (unused
                memory)
                      .
      [200]           .
```

Suppose we needed to add the name Beck to this array in its correct position. Not only would Beck have to be placed in cell names[3] but also the contents of 98 cells would have to be shifted—Bond would have to be moved to names[4], Brock to names[5], and so on, until Zerba had been moved to names [101].

By contrast, if the original 100 names had been stored in a linked list, as shown in Figure 26.1, the name Beck could be inserted much more easily.

In order to insert Beck into the list, we would merely have to do three things.

1. Create the memory box for Beck and read Beck into it.

2. Make the arrow from Beck point to the memory box for Bond.

3. Redirect the arrow from Ball so that it points to Beck instead of to Bond.

(See Figure 26.2.)

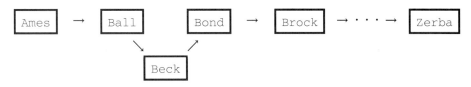

FIGURE 26.2 New List

26.2 POINTERS

• •

This section introduces the syntax of pointers. Do not be discouraged if you find pointers puzzling at first. They will make more sense to you when you see applications in Section 26.8.

If you refer to Figure 26.2, it should be apparent to you that it is desirable for Pascal to have variables with the capacity to "point to" other variables. The variables that point are called ***pointers***.

Declaring Pointers   There are two entities involved in pointing—the variables *doing the pointing* and the variables *being pointed to*. A ***pointer variable*** is a variable that does the pointing. In declaring a pointer variable, you name the pointer variable and then place a caret (^) before the type of the variable to which it will point. (This type must be given by a legal identifier.) For example,

```
type str20 = string[20];
var ptr: ^str20;
    q1, q2: ^real;
```

declares three pointer variables—`ptr` will point to a memory cell that can hold a string value, whereas `q1` and `q2` will point to memory cells that can hold real values. Note that the type definition of `str20` was necessary for the declaration of `ptr`.

Creating a Memory Cell   Merely declaring a pointer variable `ptr` does not create a memory cell for it to point to. The command `new` is used to create such a memory cell. Thus, the effect of

```
new (ptr)
```

is to create a memory cell to which `ptr` points and to store the address of this memory cell in `ptr`. You may envision the cell that `ptr` points to as being empty initially although more often it contains garbage.

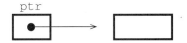

Accessing a Memory Cell That Is Pointed To The memory cell that a pointer points to can be accessed by placing a caret after the name of the pointer available. For example,

```
ptr^
```

refers to the memory cell pointed to by `ptr`. Consider the statements

```
new (ptr);
ptr^ := 'Smith';
```

The statement `new (ptr)` creates an unfilled memory cell that `ptr` points to. The second statement places the value `'Smith'` in that memory cell. We can depict memory as follows:

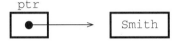

Internal Implementation Internally, pointers are implemented by having the memory cell of the pointer contain the address of the memory cell that is pointed to. Suppose, for example, that the address of `ptr` is `1015` and that the memory cell that `new (ptr)` creates has address `1242`. Then, the effect of

```
new (ptr);
ptr^ := 'Smith'
```

could be depicted at the memory address level as shown on the left or with the simpler diagram shown on the right.

Henceforth, we will use simpler diagrams of the kind given on the right.

REMARK Note that in a declaration of a pointer, the caret is placed to the *left* of its type, whereas in a statement that accesses the memory cell being pointed to, the caret appears on the *right*. • • •

Question What will be printed by the following program?

```
program drill;
var p, q: ^integer;
```

```
   x, y: integer;

begin
  new (p);
  p^ := 5;
  x := p^ + 1;
  y := p^;
  new (q);
  q^ := y + 3;
  writeln (x, ' ', y, ' ', p^, ' ', q^)
end.
```

Answer

```
6  5  5  8
```

Here is what memory will look like at the end.

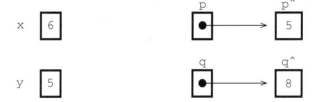

Assigning One Pointer to Another   Suppose p1 and p2 are both pointers of the same type. The effect of

```
p1 := p2;
```

will be to redirect p1 so that it points to the memory cell pointed to by p2. After the execution of p1 := p2, both pointers will point to the same box.

CAUTION   You *cannot* assign a pointer of one type to point to a pointer of a different type.   • • •

• • • • • • • • • •

Question   Suppose that p1 and p2 are both pointers of type integer. What will memory look like after execution of p1 := p2? What will be printed by the following fragment?

```
new (p1);
new (p2);
```

```
p1^ := 86;
p2^ := 45;
p1  := p2;
writeln (p1^, ' ', p2^);
```

Answer   Here is how memory will look after execution of p1 := p2.

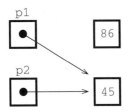

The output will be

```
45 45
```

• • •

REMARK   Observe that the value 86 can no longer be accessed. The value 45 can be accessed by either p1^ or p2^.   • • •

• • • • • • • • • •
Question   Suppose that p and q are both of type ^string. What will be printed by

```
new (p);
new (q);
p^ := 'Smith';
q^ := 'Jones';
q := p;
q^ := 'Adams';
writeln (p^);
writeln (q^);
```

Answer   Here is the trace of memory up to the time of the writeln statements.

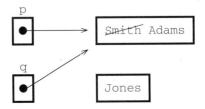

Thus, the output will be

```
Adams
Adams
```

Note that the memory cell containing Jones can no longer be accessed.

• • •

CAUTION There is a big difference between the statement

```
q := p;    {determines which memory cell q points to}
```

and the statement

```
q^ := p^;    {assigns a value to the memory cell pointed to by q}
```

• • •

• • • • • • • • • •

Question (a) What will be printed by the fragment in the previous question if the statement q := p is replaced by q^ := p^?

(b) What values would q^ have taken on during the run?

Answer (a)
```
Smith
Adams
```
(b) Jones, Smith, and Adams, in that order

• • •

Record Pointer A pointer may point to a record variable. For example, suppose ptr is declared as follows:

```
type
  StudentRec = record
    name: string[20];
    IQ: integer
  end; {record}
var ptr = ^StudentRec;
```

Then, after execution of

```
new (ptr);
ptr^.name := 'Smith';
ptr^.IQ := 105;
```

memory would contain

• • • • • • • •

Question   If memory is as shown, what pointer statement would output `Smith`?

Answer
```
writeln (ptr^.name);
```
• • •

Dynamic Nature of Pointers   The variables that are being pointed to are *not* declared. Only the variables doing the pointing are declared. As you will see, a statement like

```
new (p);
```

can be executed many times within a single program. Each time it is executed, a new memory cell will be created. Consequently, there is no declared limit to how many memory cells can be created within a program using a few pointers.

Arrays are said to be static because the maximum amount of memory space to be used must be declared and set aside in advance. Pointers are said to be dynamic because there is no such prior limit—memory space is created for them during the execution of the program.

• • • • • • • •

Question   (a)   What will be printed by the first seven lines of the following program fragment? Note the memory snapshots at various stages.

(b)   Can you fill in the blank line with a statement that will access the contents of the first memory cell and thus will print `Abe`?

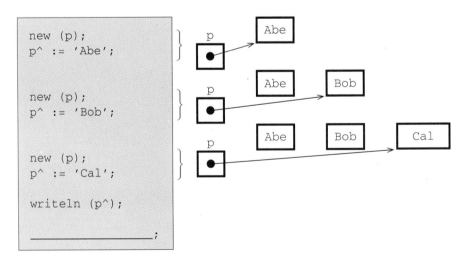

Answer   (a)

Cal

(b)   No. There is no way to access the contents of the memory cell containing Abe. When the computer executes `new (p)` a second time, it creates a new memory box whose address is then stored in p. The address of the memory box containing Abe is erased from p. In Section 26.3, you will see how to use linked lists to retain access to all the memory cells that have been created.   • • •

Releasing a Memory Cell   When we no longer need a value that is being pointed to, we can release the memory cell by using the `dispose` statement. For example, the statement

```
dispose (p)
```

will make the memory cell that p is pointing to available for other uses.

The nil Pointer   Pascal provides **nil**, a built-in pointer constant. The `nil` pointer does not point to any memory location. The assignment statement

```
p := nil;
```

will make p equal to the `nil` pointer. One use of the `nil` pointer is to mark the final record in a linked list. As you will see in the next section, the `nil` pointer serves as a ***sentinel.***

26.3   CREATING A LINKED LIST

For simplicity, let us create a linked list containing just three items called nodes. Each node will be a record with two fields: a name field and a pointer field. The data will be entered by using assignment statements. The linked list we will create is displayed in Figure 26.3.

Note that the last node in the list does not point to any other node. Instead, it contains the `nil` pointer. The `nil` pointer is being used here as an end-of-list sentinel, which will permit us to use a `while` loop to process an existing linked list.

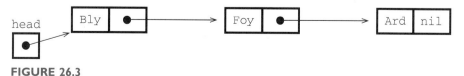

FIGURE 26.3

Note that the record being pointed to has two fields—a name field and a pointer field.

Declaring a Pointer Type   Note that in the following declaration of `ListPtr`, we have an exception to the rule that an identifier must be declared before it can be used—`NodeType` is used before it is declared.

```
type
  ListPtr = ^NodeType
  NodeType = record
    name: string[20];
    next: ListPtr
  end; {record}
var head, ptr: ListPtr;
```

In declaring a record pointer type, you first declare the pointer type identifier. (This declaration uses the *not yet declared* record type identifier.) Then you declare the record type identifier.

Accessing a Field of a Node

`ptr^.name` accesses the name field of the node pointed to by `ptr`.

`ptr^.next` accesses the pointer field of the node pointed to by `ptr`.

Thus, if we have `ptr` pointing to an unfilled node

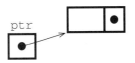

the statement

`ptr^.name := 'Bly'`

would result in

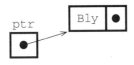

Example   We wish to write a program to create the linked list shown in the following figure.

- `head` will point to the first node in the list.
- `last` will keep being updated to point to the current last node of the list.

After the first three statements

```
new (head);
head^.name := 'Bly';
last := head;
```

memory will look like

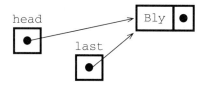

Here is the full program.

```
program create;
type
  ListPtr = ^NodeType;
  NodeType = record
    name: string[20];
    next: ListPtr
  end; {NodeType}
var head, last, extra: ListPtr;

begin
  new(head);                  {create first node}
  head^.name := 'Bly';        {fill it}
  last := head;               {update last}

  new(extra);                 {create new node}
  extra^.name := 'Foy';       {fill it}
  last^.next := extra;        {link it}
  last := extra;              {update last}

  new(extra);                 {same as}
  extra^.name := 'Ard';       {previous four lines}
  last^.next := extra;        {but with Ard}
  last := extra;

  last^.next := nil;          {sentinel}

  ┌─────────────────────────────────────────────────┐
  │ processing of this linked list would go here     │
  └─────────────────────────────────────────────────┘

end.
```

Question   Here is a snapshot of memory after the first five statements of the body are executed.

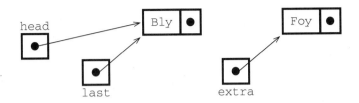

(a)   Draw a snapshot of memory after execution of the sixth statement

     `last^.next := extra;`

(b)   Draw a snapshot of memory after execution of the seventh statement

     `last := extra;`

Answer   (a)   The statement `last^.next := extra;` links the extra node to the list.

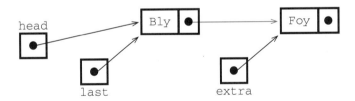

(b)   The statement `last := extra;` redirects `last` so that it points to the current last node.

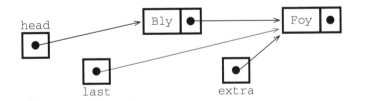

                                                        • • •

Question   (a)   Draw a snapshot of memory after execution of the next three statements (after `last^.next := extra;`).

(b)   What effect will the 11th statement (`last := extra`) have?

Answer (a)

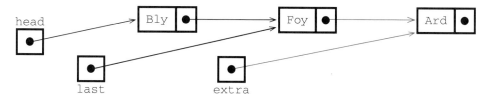

(b) It will redirect `last` so that it points to `Ard`'s node. **• • •**

Question What would be output if `ptr` were declared of type `ListPtr` and the following two lines were added to the bottom of program `create`?

```
ptr := head^.next;
writeln (ptr^.name);
```

Answer This would output `Foy` since

```
ptr := head^.next
```

would cause `ptr` to point to `Foy`'s node. **• • •**

26.4 TRAVERSING A LINKED LIST

Traversing a linked list means accessing each of the records in the list. In `procedure DISPLAY`, we will traverse a linked list of names, printing out each name on it.

Note that the procedure must be passed the pointer variable that holds the address of the first node on the list. Thus, the procedure is passed the pointer `head`. (`ListPtr` is as defined earlier.)

```
procedure DISPLAY (head: ListPtr);
{print each of the names on the list}
var ptr: ListPtr;

begin
  ptr := head;
  while ptr <> nil do
    begin
      writeln (ptr^.name);
      ptr := ptr^.next
    end
end; {DISPLAY}
```

Let us trace the values of ptr through this loop. Initially, ptr is assigned the value head so that it points to the first node on the list.

Each time through the loop, the last statement of the loop body,

```
ptr := ptr^.next;
```

makes ptr point to the next node. This is similar to incrementing a control variable using the statement i := i + 1. Finally, the loop is exited when ptr takes on the value nil—the sentinel nil is stored in the pointer field of the last node on the list.

REMARK   A call to DISPLAY might read

```
DISPLAY (head);
```

Obviously, if a program made use of two different linked lists, we could not use the same variable, head, to point to the beginning of each of the lists. Instead we would give the beginning-of-list pointers more specific names, such as nameshead or itemshead. Similarly, different pointer types would have to be given more specific names, such as NamesPtr.   • • •

26.5 CREATING A LIST USING A LOOP

Suppose that the *text* file name.dat contains the following names:

```
Bly
Foy
Ard
```

Question   Fill in the blank lines to create the linked list shown on page 443.

```
program create2;
{reads from a text file into a linked list}
type
  ListPtr = ^NodeType;
  NodeType = record
    name: string[20];
    next: ListPtr
  end; {record}

var head, last, extra: ListPtr;
    NameFile: text;
```

```
begin
  assign (NameFile, 'name.dat');
  reset (NameFile);
  head := nil;
  while not seekeof (NameFile) do
    if head = nil then  {create and fill first node}
      begin
        new (head);                         {create node}
        readln (NameFile, head^.name);  {fill it}
        last := head                        {update last}
      end  {then}
    else  {create, fill and link extra node}
      begin
        new (extra);                        {create node}
        readln (NameFile, extra^.name);  {fill it}
        _____            {link it}
        _____            {update last}
      end; {else}
  if head <> nil then _____
  close (NameFile)
end.
```

Answer

```
last^.next := extra;
last := extra;

if head <> nil then last^.next := nil;
```
• • •

REMARK

1. Note that if the file `name.dat` is empty, then the list created by

```
head := nil;
```

is called the null list and can be depicted as

head

2. In Exercise 5, you are asked to write an *interactive* program that uses a loop to create a linked list.

In Section 26.8, procedure MENU creates a linked list from a binary file of records.

• • •

26.6 ORDERED LINKED LISTS

In this section, we assume that we have an alphabetically ordered linked list of names. We give procedures for inserting a name to the list or deleting a name from the list.

Inserting Between Two Linked Nodes   Suppose that we wish to insert a node between two nodes of a linked list. For example, suppose `prev` and `curr` (for previous and current) point to two linked nodes, and `betw` points to an unattached node as shown.

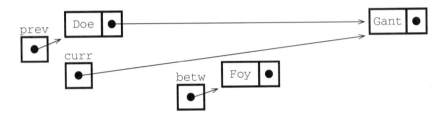

We wish to attach `betw` to the list so that it is between the `Doe` and `Gant` nodes.

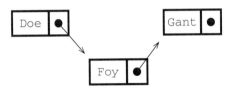

Question   Fill in the blank in the second statement so that the following two statements attach `betw` as depicted:

```
betw^.next := curr;   {attaches betw on its right}
prev _____ := _____;   {attaches betw on its left}
```

Answer   `prev^.next := betw;`   • • •

Locating Where the New Node Goes   In searching a linked list for where to insert a new name, we will use the pointers `prev` and `curr` (for previous and current). We will start `prev` and `curr` at the beginning of the list. By the end of the search, `prev` and `curr` should point to the two nodes between which the new name should be inserted.

An important step in searching the list is the shifting of both the `prev` and `curr` pointers one node to the right.

• • • • • • • • • •
Question   Suppose `prev` and `curr` are as depicted here. Which of the following pairs of statements will shift both `prev` and `curr` one node to the right (so that `prev` will point to the Kaye node and `curr` to the Mott node)?

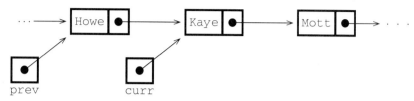

(a) `prev := curr;`
     `curr := curr^.next`

(b) `curr := curr^.next`
     `prev := curr`

Answer   Only (a) will work. Note that (b) would cause both `prev` and `curr` to point to the Mott node.   • • •

Special Case   (Searching When Guaranteed That KeyName Is Not Already on the List)

• • • • • • • • • •
Question   Suppose `KeyName` is guaranteed not to be on the list.

(a) Fill in the blanks so that `prev` and `curr` will point to the two nodes between which KeyName's node should be inserted.

(b) If KeyName goes at the beginning of the list, where will `curr` point to at the end of the code in (c)?

(c) If KeyName goes at the end of the list, where will `curr` point to by the end of the code?

```
curr := head;
done := false;
while (not done) and (curr <> nil) do
  if KeyName _____ curr^.name then
    begin
      prev := curr;          {shift}
      curr := curr^.next    {shift}
    end
  else
    done := true;
```

Answer   (a) `if KeyName > curr^.name`

(b) `curr` will point to the same node as `head`.

(c) `curr` will have the `nil` pointer.   • • •

General Case   In the general case, KeyName might be new or it might already be on the list. The general SEARCH procedure should have three variable parameters—`prev`, `curr`, and `OnList`. SEARCH should return the value `true` to `OnList` if KeyName is on the list and the value `false` if it is not.

```
procedure SEARCH (head: listPtr;
                  KeyName: str20;
                  var prev, curr: ListPtr;
                  var OnList: boolean);
  var done: boolean;

  begin
    curr := head;
    prev := nil;
    done := false;
    OnList := false;
    while (not done) and (curr <> nil) do
      if KeyName > curr^.name  then
        begin
          prev := curr;                          {shift}
          curr := curr^.next                     {shift}
        end
      else
        begin
          done := true;
          if KeyName = curr^.name then OnList := true
        end
  end; {SEARCH}
```

Question   (a)   If KeyName is on the list, which pointer will point to KeyName's node at the end, prev or curr?

(b)   If KeyName is the first name on the list, what values will prev and curr have?

Answer   (a)   curr will point to KeyName's node.

(b)   prev will be nil, and curr will point to the same node as head.

REMARK   If the user accidentally types an extra blank at the end of KeyName, SEARCH will not find a match even if it exists. Function TRIM_END, discussed in Chapter 20, could be used to protect against this danger.

INSERT Procedure   The INSERT procedure will receive the head pointer and the alleged new name as parameters. The first line of the body of INSERT will be a call to the SEARCH procedure. If NewName is already on the list, a message will be printed. If NewName is indeed new, then a node for it is created and this node, betw, is attached. Note that the code for attaching betw depends on whether or not betw goes at the beginning of the list.

```
procedure INSERT (var head: listPtr;
                     KeyName: str20);
   {Inserts keyname into ordered linked list if keyname is new}
   var prev, curr, betw: ListPtr;
       OnList: boolean;

   begin
     SEARCH (head, KeyName, prev, curr, OnList);
     if OnList then
       writeln (KeyName, ' is already on list')
     else
       begin
         new (betw);                        {create new node}
         betw^.name := KeyName;             {put KeyName in}
         if curr = head then
           begin                            {insert at head of list}
             betw^.next := head;            {attach betw on its right}
             head := betw                   {on its left}
           end {then}
         else
           begin                            {insert at middle or end}
             betw^.next := curr;            {attach betw on its right}
             prev^.next := betw             {on its left}
           end {else}
       end {main else}
   end; {INSERT}
```

• • • • • • • • •

Question   Why is `head` a `var` parameter?

Answer   Only because the `NewName` might be inserted at the beginning of the list. Only in this case would `INSERT` change the value of `head`.   • • •

• • • • • • • • •

Question   Why can inserting a name at the end of the list be handled using the same code as inserting to the middle, and yet inserting at the beginning requires separate code?

Answer   When `KeyName` goes at the head of the list, the insertion cannot be handled in terms of `prev` and `curr` since `prev` would have the value `nil` and `prev^.next` wouldn't exist. When `KeyName` goes at the end, `prev` will point to the last node and `curr` will be the `nil` pointer.   • • •

DELETE Procedure   To delete a node, we begin by calling the previous SEARCH procedure. If the name is on the list, SEARCH will have `curr` pointing to the node to be deleted. Before disposing of that node, the node before it must be linked to the node after it. There are two possible cases for the location of the node to be deleted: (a) it is at the head of the list or (b) it is at the middle or end of the list.

Let us consider an example of case (b). Suppose that the Foy node is to be deleted. Then, after a call to the SEARCH procedure, memory would contain

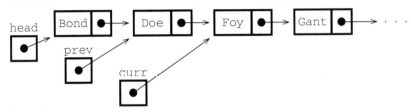

Question   Fill in the blanks in procedure DELETE.

```
procedure DELETE (var head: ListPtr;
                      KeyName: str20);

  var prev, curr: ListPtr;
      OnList: boolean;

  begin
    SEARCH(head, KeyName, prev, curr, OnList);
    if not Onlist then
      writeln (KeyName, ' is not on list')
    else
      begin
        if curr = head
          then _____
          else _____
        dispose (curr)
      end {main else}
  end; {DELETE}
```

Answer   then head := curr^.next
           else prev^.next := curr^.next;   • • •

26.7   LISTS WITH SEVERAL DATA FIELDS

The nodes in a linked list can contain more than one data field. For example, in the list displayed here, each node contains a name field, an IQ field, and a sex field, as well as a pointer field.

To declare the `ListPtr` type for the list, we will

1. First declare a record type for the data component of a node.

2. Then declare the `ListPtr` type and `NodeType`.

(Note the use of nested records.)

• • • • • • • • • •
Question Fill in the blanks. You will need to make up an additional identifier.

```
type
  InfoRec = record
    name: string[20];
    IQ: integer;
    sex: char
  end; {InfoRec}
  ListPtr = ^NodeType;
  NodeType = record
    _____ : _____ ;
    next: ListPtr
  end; {NodeType}
```

Answer You will need to make up a record identifier (such as `info`) for the data record field of the node.

```
        info: InfoRec;
```
                                                              • • •

Ordering of Lists In creating an ordered linked list, you may base the ordering on whichever field you choose. For example, the linked list at the beginning of this section could be ordered in terms of IQ, with the highest IQ given first.

Accessing the Data

• • • • • • • • • •
Question Suppose `ptr` points to the node depicted here.

(a) Give a `writeln` statement to output the name `Foy` stored in this node.

(b) Use a `with` statement to output `Foy 138 m`.

Answer **(a)** `writeln(ptr^.info.name)`

(b) `with ptr^.info do`
`writeln (name, ' ', IQ, ' ', sex);`   ● ● ●

26.8 **A MAJOR APPLICATION**

We are now in a position to write a fairly complex application program. It will maintain an existing sorted binary file of names and phone numbers for the John Doe Society. We assume that the binary file `member.dat` has been created by `program create` of Section 22.3, with the data entered in sorted order.

In `program maintenance`, the contents of this sorted file are read into an ordered linked list. The user chooses from a menu of options to maintain this file and may

- Insert a new member

- Delete a member

- Update a member's phone number

- Print the entire phone list

Finally, after exiting the menu, a test is made to determine if any calls to the menu options changed the list. (The boolean variable `ChangedList` is used for this purpose.) If `ChangedList` is `true`, then the data records of the new linked list are written back to the file.

Here is the program. In keeping with top-down programming, we give the program in skeleton form. Further discussion of the procedures will follow.

```
program maintenance;
{maintains an existing sorted binary files}
{using linked lists}
type
  str20= string[20];
  MembRec = record
    name: str20;
    phone: string[8]
  end; {MembRec}
```

```
   FileType = file of MembRec;
   MembPtr  = ^NodeType;
   NodeType = record
     info: MembRec;
     next: MembPtr
   end;   {NodeType}

var MembFile: FileType;
    head: MembPtr;
    ChangedList: boolean;
```

```
procedure READ_FILE_INTO_LIST goes here

procedure INPUT_ONE goes here

procedure SEARCH goes here

procedure INSERT_REC goes here

procedure DELETE goes here

procedure UPDATE goes here

procedure PRINT_ALL goes here

procedure WRITE_TO_FILE goes here
```

```
procedure MENU (var head: MembPtr;
                var ChangedList: boolean);

  var choice: char;
      NewRec: MembRec;
      KeyName: str20;

  begin
    repeat
      writeln ( ' 1 : INSERT');
      writeln ( ' 2 : DELETE');
      writeln ( ' 3 : UPDATE');
      writeln ( ' 4 : PRINT LIST');
      writeln ( ' 5 : QUIT' );
      write ( 'Enter choice number ' );
      readln (choice);
      case choice of
```

```
              '1': begin
                      INPUT_ONE (NewRec);
                      INSERT_REC (NewRec, head, ChangedList)
                   end;
              '2': begin
                      write ('enter name to be deleted ');
                      readln (KeyName);
                      DELETE (KeyName, head, ChangedList)
                   end;
              '3': begin
                      write ('enter name for phone change ');
                      readln (KeyName);
                      UPDATE (KeyName, head, ChangedList)
                   end;
              '4': PRINT_ALL(head);
              '5':       { quit program }
              else  writeln ('Invalid choice ', chr(7))   {bell}
           end {case}
        until choice = '5'
     end; {MENU}

  begin
     ChangedList := false;
     READ_FILE_INTO_LIST (MembFile, head);
     MENU (head, ChangedList);
     if ChangedList
        then WRITE_TO_FILE (MembFile, head)
  end.
```

INSERT_REC Procedure   In procedure INSERT of Section 26.6, a node was composed of just one data field and a pointer. By contrast, in procedure INSERT_REC, the data component of a node is a record. Thus, one must specify the full path to any data item.

• • • • • • • • • •

Question   Fill in the blank line.

```
procedure INSERT_REC (NewRec: MembRec;
                          var head: MembPtr;
                          var ChangedList: boolean );
   var prev,curr,betw: MembPtr;
       OnList: boolean;
```

```
begin
  SEARCH (head, NewRec.Name, prev, curr, OnList);
  if OnList then
    writeln (NewRec.name, ' already on list')
  else
    begin
      ChangedList := true;
      new (betw);                        {create a new node}
      _____

      betw^.info.phone := NewRec.phone;
      if curr = head then              {insert at head of list}
        begin
          betw^.next := head;
          head := betw
        end
      else
        begin
          betw^.next := curr;
          prev^.next := betw
        end {else}
    end {main else}
end; {INSERT_REC}
```

Answer   betw^.info.name := NewRec.name   • • •

Procedure READ_FILE_INTO_LIST   This procedure is similar to program create2 of Section 26.5. The two differences are

1. File member.dat is a binary file rather than a text file.

2. The data component of each node is a record rather than a single field.

Procedure INPUT_ONE   This prompts the user to enter one member's name and phone number and stores them in a record variable.

Procedure SEARCH   This is called by procedures INSERT, DELETE, and UPDATE. It is similar to the procedure SEARCH of Section 26.6.

Procedure DELETE   This is similar to procedure DELETE of Section 26.6.

Procedure UPDATE This echoes the name just entered, prompts the user to enter the new phone number, and updates the appropriate node of the linked list.

Procedure WRITE_TO_FILE This writes the data from the linked list to the external file, member.dat. It copies just the info component of each node.

REMARK Writing the previous procedures is Exercise 11. • • •

EXERCISES

1. Suppose p1 and p2 are both pointers of type integer. What will be printed by the following fragment? What will memory look like after these statements have been executed?

```
new (p1);
new (p2);
p1^ := 57;
p2^ := 94;
p2 := p1;
writeln (p1^, ' ', p2^);
```

2. Suppose that p and q are both of type ^string. What will be output by

```
new (p);
new (q);
p^ := 'Able';
p := q;
q^ := 'Baker';
p^ := 'Chen';
writeln (p^, ' ', q^);
```

3. Suppose that a linked list consists of a sequence of last names. Write a procedure that will count how many of these last names have a vowel as their second letter.

Longer Assignments

4. Write a program that uses a `for` loop to create the following linked list:

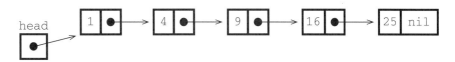

5. Write an interactive version of `program create2` of Section 26.5.

6. (a) Write a program that uses a procedure to create a linked list, ordered alphabetically by name, in which each record contains a student's name and IQ. The second part of the program should allow the user to specify an IQ range (upper and lower limit) and then should output the name and IQ of each student whose IQ is in that range.

   (b) Write a third part of the program to allow the user to update the linked list by inserting several more students.

* 7. Write a procedure to reverse the pointers in a linked list. For example, A → B → C → D would become A ← B ← C ← D. (*Hint:* You must change `head` and reverse each pointer.)

* 8. (a) Write a function to count the number of items in a linked list.

   * (b) Write a recursive function to count the number of items in a linked list.

* 9. Write a recursive subprogram to search a list for a given item.

* 10. Suppose that a list contains records with a person's name and age.

   (a) Write a procedure that will use two traversals of the list to delete the first person with the minimum age.

   (b) Write a procedure that will require only one traversal to delete the first person with the minimum age.

   (c) Write a procedure that will use two traversals of the list to delete all people with the minimum age.

   (d) Write a procedure that will require only one traversal to delete all people with the minimum age. (*Hint:* Keep a second linked list that contains pointers to the current set of cells with the minimum age. At the end, it is necessary to traverse this list and make the deletions from the original list.)

* 11. Complete `program maintenance` by writing the procedures `READ_FILE_INTO_LIST`, `INPUT_ONE`, `SEARCH`, `DELETE`, `UPDATE`, `PRINT_ALL`, and `WRITE_TO_FILE` (as described in Section 26.8).

Chapter

27

MORE ON SETS

• • • As you saw in Chapter 12, the use of *set* syntax makes it easier to write a test to determine whether a value is contained in a list of values. For example,

```
if (ch = 'a') or (ch = 'e') or (ch = 'i')
   or (ch = 'o') or (ch = 'u') then . . .
```

can be expressed more simply as

```
if ch in ['a', 'e', 'i', 'o', 'u'] then . . .
```

In this chapter, we discuss the syntax for set variables and operations on sets.

• • •

27.1 SET SYNTAX

Restrictions on Sets   In Pascal, a set is an unordered collection of values that are all the same ordinal type. Thus, a set cannot contain real or string values. The maximum number of values that a set may contain is 256. Moreover, sets of integer values may contain only values in the range 0 to 255.

Set Variable Declarations   Usually, a set variable is declared by first declaring a set TypeIdentifier using the syntax

```
type TypeIdentifier = set of base type;
```

and then declaring a set variable of that type.

For example, the set variables group1, group2, and vowels could be declared by

```
type
   IntegSetType = set of 0..255;
   CharSetType = set of char;
var
   group1, group2: IntegSetType;
   vowels: CharSetType;
```

The set variable CoinSet could be declared by

```
type
   coins = (penny, nickel, dime, quarter);
   CoinSetType = set of coins;
var
   CoinSet: CoinSetType;
```

REMARK   The set variables group1, group2, and vowels could also have been declared entirely in the var section by

```
var vowels: set of char;
    group1, group2: set of 0..255;
```
                                                                        • • •

Assignment Statements   A set variable holds *a set as its value.* You may assign a value to a set variable by listing all its elements within square *brackets* [   ], as in

```
CoinSet := [nickel, dime];
vowels := ['a', 'e', 'i', 'o', 'u'];
Caps := ['A'..'Z'];
```

Set Membership   The reserved word in is used to test whether a particular value is a member of a set. For example, the following kinds of tests are permissible:

```
if ch in vowels then . . . ;
if quarter in CoinSet then . . . ;
if 'g' in ['a', 'b', 'c', 'd'] then . . . ;
```

. . . .

Question   This program will count the number of vowels in a phrase input by the user. Fill in the blank.

```
program drill;
type characters = set of char;
var phrase: string[80];
    i, count: integer;
    vowels: characters;

begin
  count := 0;
  vowels := ['a','e','i','o','u','A','E','I','O','U'];
  write ('enter phrase ');
  readln (phrase);
  for i := 1 to length (phrase) do
  _____

  writeln ('phrase contains ', count, ' vowels')
end.
```

Answer   The completed `if-then` test should be

```
if phrase [i] in vowels then count := count + 1;
```    • • •

Set Operations   The *union* of the sets X and Y, denoted by $X + Y$, consists of all elements that are in at least one of the sets. Thus,

[1, 2, 5, 6] + [1, 2, 4, 7] equals [1, 2, 4, 5, 6, 7]

The *intersection* of the sets X and Y, denoted by $X * Y$, consists of all elements that are common to both sets. Thus,

[1, 2, 5, 6] * [1, 2, 4, 7] equals [1, 2]

The *difference* of the sets X and Y, denoted by $X - Y$, consists of all elements of X that are not in Y. Thus,

[1, 2, 5, 6] - [1, 2, 4, 7] equals [5, 6]

The Empty Set   The empty set, denoted by [ ], is a set with no elements. Note that

['a'..'z'] * ['A'..'Z'] equals []

We shall see two uses of the empty set. The first is to test whether two sets have any overlap, as in

```
if X * Y = [] then writeln ('No Overlap');
```

The second is to initialize a set variable before the start of a loop that will add elements to the set.

Comparison Operators   The four symbols =, <>, >=, and <= can be applied to sets.

X = Y is true when the sets are equal.

X <> Y is true when the sets are not equal.

X <= Y is true when x is a subset of Y—that is, when every element of X is also in Y

X >= Y is true when Y is a subset of X.

For example,

```
['a', 'e', 'i', 'o', 'u'] <= ['a'..'z'] is true.
['a', 'b'] < > ['b', 'c'] is true.
```

The set comparison operators can be used in Boolean expressions, such as

```
if x <= y then writeln ('Okay');
```

27.2 APPLICATIONS

• •

Outputting the Values of a Set   There is no simple command to output the values contained in a set. You should use a loop to output a set's values. For example, to output the values in the integer set group1, use

```
for i := 0 to 255 do
  if i in group1 then writeln (i);
```

Of course, for a set of enumerated type values, the loop to output its values would also need to translate the enumerated type values.

Building a Set One Value at a Time   A set may be built up by initializing its value to the null set and then repeatedly adding on values. In the next program, note the initialization

```
SkillSet := [ ];
```

• • • • • • • • • •

Example   An employer currently has one opening for someone who knows the computer languages BASIC, COBOL, and Pascal. The following interactive program will print on paper the names of all those applicants who meet this requirement.

Note that inside the body of procedure CREATE_SET, the applicant's

`SkillSet` is initialized to be the empty set. Suppose the current applicant knows BASIC, COBOL, and FORTRAN. During `CREATE_SET`, the user would enter `Y` for those three skills, and the screen display would be

```
Does applicant know Algol? (Y/N)   N
Does applicant know BASIC? (Y/N)   Y
Does applicant know COBOL? (Y/N)   Y
Does applicant know FORTRAN? (Y/N)   Y
Does applicant know Pascal? (Y/N)   N
```

Make sure you understand why `CREATE_SET` must call the function `TRANSLATE`.

```
program applicants;
uses printer;
{prints names of applicants with the needed skills}
type skills = (Algol, BASIC, COBOL, FORTRAN, Pascal);
     SkillSetType = set of skills;
     str7 = string[7];
var ApplicantSkills, NeededSkills: SkillSetType;
    name: string[20];

function TRANSLATE (skill: skills): str7;
  {translates enumerated type value into string value}
  begin
    case skill of
      Algol   : TRANSLATE := 'Algol';
      BASIC   : TRANSLATE := 'BASIC';
      COBOL   : TRANSLATE := 'COBOL';
      FORTRAN : TRANSLATE := 'FORTRAN';
      Pascal  : TRANSLATE := 'Pascal'
    end {case}
  end; {TRANSLATE}

procedure CREATE_SET (var SkillSet: SkillSetType);
  {interactively creates skill set of applicant}
  var skill: skills;
      ans: char;
  begin
    SkillSet := [];
    for skill := Algol to Pascal do
      begin
        write ('Does the applicant know ');
```

```
            writeln (TRANSLATE (skill), '?  (Y/N) ');
            readln (ans);
            if ans in ['y', 'Y'] then
               SkillSet := SkillSet + [skill]
         end {for}
   end; {CREATE_SET}

begin {main}
   NeededSkills := [Basic, COBOL, Pascal];
   write ('enter name of applicant or xyz to stop ');
   readln (name);
   while name <> 'xyz' do
      begin
         CREATE_SET (ApplicantSkills);
         if ApplicantSkills >= NeededSkills
            then writeln (1st, name);
         write ('Enter name of applicant or xyz to stop ');
         readln (name)
      end {while}
end.
```

REMARK   If the employer wanted to use this program to screen for a job opening that requires knowledge of the languages Algol, BASIC, and FORTRAN, the first statement in the main body would have to be changed to

```
NeededSkills := [Algol, BASIC, FORTRAN];
```

In Exercise 2, you are asked to make this program more flexible so that the skills needed by the employer can be entered interactively.   • • •

• • • • • • • • • • **EXERCISES**
• •

1. What will be output when the following program is run?

```
program SetOperations;
type
   IntegSet = set of 0..255;
var
   A, B: IntegSet;
   x: integer;
begin
   A := [3, 5, 6];
```

```
B := [3, 4, 6];
for x := 0 to 255 do
    if x in A * B then write (x, ' ');
writeln;
for x := 0 to 255 do
    if x in A + B then write (x, ' ');
writeln;
end.
```

Longer Assignments

2. Revise `program applicants` so that the employer can enter the skills needed interactively.

3. Write a program to make change using the fewest number of coins. Ask the user to enter the number of cents to be given in change. Within a `for` loop that runs from `quarters` to `pennies`, do the following for each coin:

> Call a function that determines how many of the particular coin should be given.

> Write the results using a TRANSLATE function.

4. Write a procedure that will randomly generate a set of six distinct positive integers from 1 to 54.

* 5. Write a program that will allow the user to play one game of Lotto. The program should first randomly generate a set of six distinct integers from 1 to 54 (see Exercise 4). Then it should allow the user to select a Lotto ticket consisting of six distinct integers from 1 to 54. If the user has selected all six of the random integers (in any order), he or she wins first prize. If the user has selected five of the six random integers, he or she wins second prize. The output should state how many of the random integers the user selected and which prize he or she won, if any.

Chapter

28

ADVANCED SORTING AND EFFICIENCY OF ALGORITHMS

• • • For a small array (say, 100 elements or less), it doesn't matter which sort you use since any sorting algorithm can perform the sort in a very short time. By contrast, for a very large unsorted array, one of the advanced sorts should be used since they are much quicker than any of the elementary sorts.

In this chapter, we begin by discussing a standard method of measuring the average efficiency of a sort—known as the order of magnitude of the sort. Then we calculate the order of magnitude of the Selection Sort and of the Bubble Sort. Finally, we present an advanced sort, known as the Quick Sort, and explain wherein its greater efficiency lies. In a rough sense, the Quick Sort resembles a binary search in that it repeatedly subdivides an array to be sorted into two smaller pieces. • • •

28.1 ORDER OF MAGNITUDE OF A SORTING ALGORITHM

Big-O

Big-O of an expression in n gives an order of magnitude measure of how quickly the expression grows large as n gets large; it does so by focusing on the expression's dominant term and ignoring constant factors.

Expression	*Its Order of Magnitude*
(a) $n^2 + 4n + 2$	$O(n) = n^2$
(b) $4n^2 + 3n$	$O(n) = n^2$
(c) $8n\log_2 n + 14n$	$O(n) = n\log_2 n$

Be aware that n^2 gets larger at a much faster rate than $n\log_2 n$ does. For example, when $n = 1{,}000$, $n^2 = 1{,}000{,}000$, whereas $n\log_2 n$ is approximately 10,000. Thus, when $n = 1{,}000$, both (a) and (b) are significantly larger than (c) even though (c) has the largest coefficients.

Efficiency of a Sort (Order of Magnitude)

Computer time during a sort is consumed by the large number of repetitions of certain basic operations, which are closely tied to the number of comparisons of array elements that the sort tends to make in performing the sort. Thus,

> The order of magnitude of a sort is equal to Big-O of the number of comparisons that the sort tends to make in sorting an average array of size n.

As you will see, each of the elementary sorts from Chapter 19 is of order n^2, whereas the Quick Sort, covered in this chapter, is of order $n\log_2 n$. Thus, to sort a very large array, there is no question that you should use an advanced sort such as the Quick Sort.

Selection Sort Is of Order n²

Let us calculate the number of comparisons performed in sorting an array of size n.

> During pass 1, it will make $n - 1$ comparisons.
>
> During pass 2, it will make $n - 2$ comparisons.
>
> And so on down to the last pass, when it makes 1 comparison.

Thus, the total number of comparisons is

$$n - 1 + n - 2 + \cdots + 3 + 2 + 1$$

The sum of these numbers is the number of terms $(n-1)$ times the average term $(1 + n-1)/2$. This product equals $(n-1)(n)/2$, which equals $\frac{n^2}{2} - \frac{n}{2}$. Thus, the selection sort is of order n^2.

Bubble Sort Is of Order n²

In version 1, the sort will make $n - 1$ passes. The total number of comparisons will be

$$n - 1 + n - 2 + \cdots + 2 + 1$$

which is equal to the same sum as in the selection sort and thus also of order n^2.

The question then is: Is the improved version of the bubble sort any better than order n^2. Note that, if an array has its smallest element in the last box of the array (worst case for number of passes), the improved version of the bubble sort will require $n-1$ passes before the array is sorted. (Do you see why?) Although for an average random array, the smallest element probably won't be in the last box, it is statistically quite likely that some of the smaller elements will be far enough to the right of the middle of the array so that the number of comparisons will be the same order of magnitude as in the worst case.

Thus, each version of the bubble sort is of order n^2.

28.2 THE QUICK SORT

The `QUICKSORT` sorting procedure presented here is a recursive procedure. Its body contains calls both to itself and to its subprocedure `SUBDIVIDE`. You should note that `SUBDIVIDE` does most of the work, and so not surprisingly the difficult coding is contained in `SUBDIVIDE`. (Also be aware that `SUBDIVIDE` is not recursive.)

In this section, we describe briefly what a call to `SUBDIVIDE` accomplishes, give the body of `QUICKSORT`, and then, present all the details of `SUBDIVIDE`. We conclude our discussion of `QUICKSORT` by explaining why it is of order $n\log_2 n$.

What the Subprocedure SUBDIVIDE Accomplishes

When `SUBDIVIDE` is applied to an array, it rearranges the array by focusing on the array's first element, which we shall call the *focus value*. For example, for the array

42	20	55	59	70	81	32	62	28

the focus value is 42.

A call to `SUBDIVIDE` accomplishes the following:

1. It ultimately puts the focus value in its correct position.

2. It moves the elements in the array so that by the end

    (a) all elements smaller than the focus value are to the left of the focus value, and

    (b) all elements larger than the focus value are to the right of the focus value.

After a call to SUBDIVIDE, the preceding array will look as follows, with the focus value in the fourth cell of the array:

Array After Call to SUBDIVIDE

32	20	28	42	70	81	59	62	55

• • • • • • • • • •

Question Suppose SUBDIVIDE is applied to the array

58	73	65	24	32	90	86	17	20	88	30

(a) In which cell will 58 end up?

(b) Will 65 end up to the left or right of 58?

(c) In exactly which cell will 65 end up?

Answer (a) 58 will end up in its correct cell—the sixth box.

(b) 65 will end up somewhere to the right of 58.

(c) You cannot answer this question until you have more details on how SUBDIVIDE works.   • • •

The SUBDIVIDE Header SUBDIVIDE will have four parameters—the name of the array to be sorted, the array's first and last indexes, and the index for the box in which the focus value will end up. Two of these parameters will be variable—the array name itself (since SUBDIVIDE will do some rearranging) and FocusIndex (the index for the box in which the focus value will end up). Here is the header for SUBDIVIDE.

```
procedure SUBDIVIDE (var list: listtype;
                     first, last: integer;
                     var FocusIndex: integer);
```

The QUICKSORT Procedure

After SUBDIVIDE has been applied a first time to the original array, the focus value will be in its correct place.

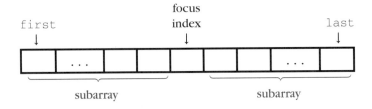

Thus, SUBDIVIDE reduces the original problem to that of sorting two shorter subarrays. This sorting can be done through two separate recursive calls to QUICKSORT.

. . . .

Question

Fill in the blank in the body of QUICKSORT. Note that QUICKSORT has three parameters—the name of the array to be sorted and its first and last indexes.

```
procedure QUICKSORT (var list: listtype;
                         first, last: integer);
  {sorts an array recursively}
  var FocusIndex: integer;

    ┌─────────────────────────────────────────┐
    │                                           │
    │  procedure SUBDIVIDE goes here.           │
    │                                           │
    └─────────────────────────────────────────┘

  begin {QUICKSORT}
    if first < last then
      begin
        SUBDIVIDE (list, first, last, FocusIndex);
        QUICKSORT (list, first, FocusIndex - 1);
        QUICKSORT ( _____ )
      end
  end; {QUICKSORT}
```

Answer

The second call to QUICKSORT sorts the subarray to the right of the focus value. The first index for this subarray is FocusIndex + 1; the last index remains unchanged. Thus, the missing line should read

```
QUICKSORT (list, FocusIndex + 1, last)
```
• • •

Details of SUBDIVIDE

You might imagine that SUBDIVIDE would first determine the correct position for the focus value and then do all its switching, but it works the other way around. By the time the correct position for the focus value is determined, most of the switching has already been done.

Recall that values larger than the focus value must end up to its right, and values smaller than the focus value must end up to its left. In SUBDIVIDE, each value from the left side of the array that is larger than the focus value is switched with a value from the right side that is smaller than the focus value.

The SUBDIVIDE Algorithm   SUBDIVIDE uses a left marker and a right marker. At the start, the left marker is at the left end, and the right marker is

at the right end. (The array shown here is the same one that was used in the discussion of SUBDIVIDE.)

At the Start

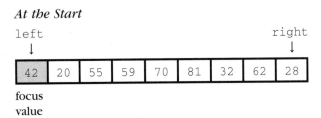

focus
value

Move the left marker to the *right* until you find the first element that is larger than the focus value.

Move the right marker to the *left* until you find the first element that is less than or equal to the focus value.

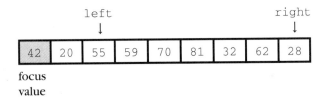

focus
value

Then switch these two values (in this case, 55 and 28).

After the First Switch

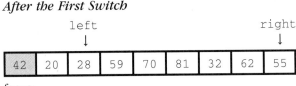

focus
value

Next, move the left marker farther to the right until you find the next element that is larger than the focus value. Move the right marker farther to the left until you find the next element that is less than or equal to the focus value. Then switch these two values (in this case, 59 and 32).

After the Second Switch

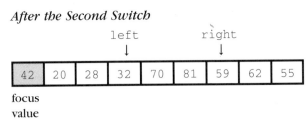

focus
value

Next, move the left marker to the right until you find the next element that is greater than the focus value. Move the right marker to the left until you find the next element that is less than or equal to the focus value. You do *not* switch these values, however, because the `right` marker has crossed over the `left` marker.

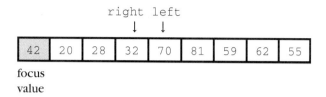

The final step is to switch the focus value with the value in the cell marked by the `right` marker.

At the Conclusion of SUBDIVIDE

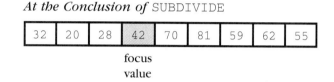

The SUBDIVIDE Procedure   We will use a `repeat-until` loop to keep switching larger values from the left side with smaller values from the right side. The `until` condition will determine whether the markers have met or crossed over.

```
until left >= right;
```

Note that the final switch will be done after the `repeat-until` loop. After the final switch, `FocusIndex` will be assigned the subscript for the correct position of `focus`. Thus, `FocusIndex` will be a variable parameter of the procedure so that this subscript value will be communicated back to QUICKSORT.

```
procedure SUBDIVIDE (var list: listtype;
                     first, last: integer;
                     var FocusIndex: integer);
{puts focus value in its correct position;}
{elements smaller than focus value will be to its left;}
{those larger to its right}
var focus: integer; {or whatever type of elements in array}
    left, right: integer;

procedure SWITCH (var x, y: integer);
  {switches the values of x and y}
```

```
    var temp: integer;
    begin
      temp := x;
      x := y;
      y := temp
    end; {SWITCH}

begin {SUBDIVIDE}
  focus := list[first];
  left := first;
  right := last;
  repeat
    {mark next value on left larger than focus}
    while (list[left] <= focus) and (left < last) do
      left := left + 1;
    {mark next value on right less than or equal to focus}
    while list[right] > focus do
      right := right - 1;
    if left < right then
      SWITCH (list[left], list[right])
  until left >= right;
  {put focus in its correct position}
  SWITCH (list[first], list[right]);
  FocusIndex := right
end; {SUBDIVIDE}
```

Why QUICKSORT Is of Order $n\log_2 n$

It is useful to analyze `QUICKSORT` in terms of levels in the following way:

Level 1: The first call to `SUBDIVIDE` on the full array. There will be essentially n comparisons of array elements since each of the other array elements will be involved in a comparison to the focus element. (See the `while` condition.)

Level 2: The two calls to `SUBDIVIDE`—one for each of the subarrays created by level 1. Since again every element of the original array of size n (except the focus elements of each of the subarrays) will be involved in *one* comparison with a focus element, there will be essentially n comparisons at this level.

Level 3: The four calls to `SUBDIVIDE`—one for each of the four subarrays created by the end of level 2. Again, there will be essentially n comparisons.

And so on for each of the levels.

The total number of comparisons for the full sort will be essentially the product of the number of comparisons at each level times the number of levels. Statistically for a random array of size n, most of the time the splitting into two pieces by SUBDIVIDE will be "roughly" in half. Therefore, the total number of levels will be of order $\log_2 n$, similar to the binary search.

Thus, the total number of comparisons will be of order

n times $\log_2 n$

Worst Case for the QUICKSORT

Ironically, the QUICKSORT does the worst in sorting an array that is already sorted. This is because the splitting at each call of SUBDIVIDE is not into two roughly equal subarrays. For example, the first call of SUBDIVIDE splits the original array into a subarray of 1 and another of size $n - 1$. This same kind of thing happens for each call. Thus, the number of levels will be n with n comparisons in each level, giving a total of n^2 comparisons for the full sort.

• • • • • • • • • EXERCISES
• •

1. How would SUBDIVIDE leave the following array?

55	40	58	32	20	12	29	80	70

2. Trace the effect of QUICKSORT on
    (a) the array

42	20	55	59	70	81	32	62	28

    (b) the array

1	2	3	4	5	6	7	8	9

    (c) the array

5	6	4	7	3	1	9	2	8

3. Write a program to
    (a) read 25 words into an array. (You may read them from a file that you have created.)
    (b) print the array.
    (c) sort the array using QUICKSORT.

(d) print the array in alphabetical order.

4. Write a procedure that uses a quick sort to alphabetize by name an array of records. Each record contains a name and a telephone number.

* 5. Write a program that

(a) stores in an array 200 randomly generated integers between 1 and 1,000. (See Chapter 14 for information on randomizing.)

(b) calls procedure BUBBLESORT.

(c) calls QUICKSORT.

(d) prints the number of comparisons and the number of swaps performed by each sort. (You must modify the sorts to keep track of these values.)

Make sure you send both sorts the same array.

6. Rerun your program from Exercise 5, using the integers 1 to 200 in order. Note how inefficient QUICKSORT is in this case.

Chapter 29

GRAPHICS

• • • Turbo Pascal provides graphics capability that is highly portable. In this chapter we present the following output commands:

`line`, `rectangle`, `circle`, `bar`, `OutTextXY`, and `PutPixel`

We also present the color setting commands

`SetColor`, `SetFillStyle`, and `SetBkColor`

Applications include a bar graph program, simple animation, and an exercise program to draw an American flag. • • •

29.1 GETTING INTO GRAPHICS

To compile Turbo Pascal graphics programs, you need the `graph.tpu` and `turbo.tpl` files. To actually run graphics programs, you also need a standard graphics adapter (such as VGA, EGA, CGA, or Hercules) and the `bgi` (Borland Graph Interface) driver file.

All graphics programs must declare the `graph` unit in the `uses` section.

Program to Draw a Slanted Line The following program assumes that the `graph.tpu` file and the `bgi` file are in the same directory as the Turbo compiler:

```
program TestingAdapter;
uses graph;
var grDriver, grMode: integer;
begin
  grDriver := detect;
  InitGraph (grDriver, grMode, '');
  line (0,100,200,200);
  writeln ('largest x coord ', GetMaxX);
  writeln ('largest y coord ', GetMaxY);
  readln;
  closegraph
end.
```

The first two statements in the body of the program initialize the graphics mode. Then after the next three statements are executed, the screen should display a slanted line with endpoints at (0,100) and (200,200) and messages telling you the largest possible x and y screen graphics coordinates for the particular graphics adapter you are using. For example, if you are using a VGA graphics adapter, the screen display will be

```
largest x coord 639
largest y coord 479
```
(not drawn to scale)

The `line` command and the built-in functions `GetMaxX` and `GetMaxY` are covered in Section 29.2.

InitGraph   The procedure `InitGraph` is a procedure from the graph unit, and `detect` is a constant from the `graph` unit. The following two statements are generally used at the start of a graphics program:

```
grDriver := detect;
InitGraph (grDriver, grMode, '');
```

They automatically initialize Turbo into the graphics mode of the *highest resolution* for the type of adapter that you have. (Note that in the call of `InitGraph`, `grDriver` had the value `detect` and `grMode` was uninitialized.)

CAUTION   The third argument of `InitGraph` specifies the path to the driver `bgi` file. The null string may be used when the `bgi` file is in the default directory. Depending on how Turbo was installed, it may be necessary to replace the third argument of InitGraph with something like `'c:\bp\BGI'` in Turbo 7.0 or `'c:\tp\BGI'` in Turbo 6.0. If the previous program did not run, it might be either because you don't have a suitable graphics adapter or because the computer was not able to find the `bgi` file.

The basic Turbo 6.0 package does not provide a simple method for generating hard copy of graphics output. Additional software for this purpose is available from Borland on request.   • • •

REMARK   The last two statements of a graphics program usually are

```
readln;
closegraph;
```

The empty `readln` keeps the graphics display on the screen until the user presses the ENTER key, and `closegraph` returns the computer to the text mode.   • • •

29.2   SOME BASIC COMMANDS

• •

A *pixel,* the smallest picture element that can be lit up on the display screen, is a tiny rectangle. The number of pixels on the display screen depends on the graphics adapter and the resolution mode used. Pixels are specified by giving their x and y screen coordinates. For example, for VGA graphics high-resolution mode

x coordinates range from 0 to 639

y coordinates range from 0 to 479

Thus, in VGA graphics, the screen is subdivided into a rectangular grid of 640 pixels by 480 pixels. The program of Section 29.1 can be used to determine the grid used for your adapter.

• • • • • • • • • •

Question   In the figure, the coordinates of several pixels are indicated. Give the coordinates of the pixels labeled A, B, and C. (The pixels have not been drawn to scale but have been enlarged so that they can be seen better.)

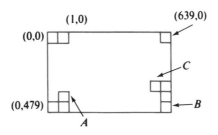

Answer   A = (1,478)   B = (639,479)   C = (638,477)   • • •

The line Procedure   The procedure call

```
line (X1, Y1, X2, Y2);
```

draws a line connecting the pixels (*X1, Y1*) and (*X2, Y2*). Thus,

```
line (10, 20, 50, 75);
```

will draw a slanted line connecting pixels (10,20) and (50,75).

GetMaxX and GetMaxY   After `InitGraph` has been called

`GetMaxX` gives the largest *x* coordinate
    (639 for both VGA and EGA)

`GetMaxY` gives the largest *y* coordinate
    (479 for VGA and 349 for EGA)

Since they are built-in functions (parameterless) of the `graph` unit, they do not need to be declared.

• • • • • • • • • •
Question   Draw a rough sketch for the screen display produced by

```
program lines;
uses graph;
var xCenter, grDriver, grMode: integer;
begin
  grDriver := detect;
  InitGraph (grDriver, grMode, '');
  line (0, 0, GetMaxX, GetMaxY);
  xCenter := GetMaxX div 2;
  line (xCenter, 0, xCenter, GetMaxY);
  readln;
  closegraph
end.
```

Answer   The first line will go from the upper left corner of the screen to the bottom right corner. The second line will be a vertical line cutting the screen in half.

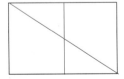

GetMaxX and GetMaxY help make programs independent of the particular adapter and resolution.

• • •

rectangle Procedure   The procedure call

```
rectangle (x1, y1, x2, y2)
```

draws an unfilled rectangle with upper left corner at (*x*1, *y*1) and lower right corner at (*x*2, *y*2).

circle Procedure   The procedure call

```
circle (a, b, r)
```

draws an unfilled circle with center at (*a, b*) and radius *r* pixels.

bar Procedure   The procedure call

```
bar (x1, y1, x2, y2);
```

is similar to the rectangle call except that the resulting rectangle will be filled in.

• • • • • • • • • •

Question   Fill in the blanks in the following program to produce the following screen display (assuming a VGA adapter). (The circle has radius 30 and its center in the center of the screen. Both the filled and unfilled rectangles are squares with side = 60.)

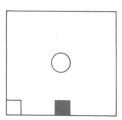

```
program figures;
uses graph;
var xCent, yCent, grDriver, grMode: integer;
begin
  grDriver := detect;
  InitGraph (grDriver, grMode, '');
  xCent := GetMaxX div 2;
  yCent := GetMaxY div 2;
  circle (xCent, yCent, 30);
  rectangle (0, GetMaxY - 60, _____, _____);
```

```
   bar (xCent - 30, _____ , _____ , _____ );
   readln;
   closegraph
end.
```

Answer   The pair of blanks in the `rectangle` call should give the lower right coordinates of the unfilled rectangle. Thus,

```
   60 , GetMaxY
```

The blanks in the `bar` call should be

```
   GetMaxY - 60 , xCent + 30 , GetMaxY                    • • •
```

OutTextXY Procedure   The procedure call

```
   OutTextXY (x, y, str1);
```

will display the string `str1`, starting at pixel (x,y). Thus,

```
   OutTextXY (0, GetMaxY div 2, 'HELLO');
```

would display

```
┌─────────────────────┐
│                     │      (not drawn to scale)
│  HELLO              │
│                     │
│                     │
└─────────────────────┘
```

After initialization by `InitGraph`, `OutTextXY` statements will be in

default font style, the horizontal direction, with font size = 1

The procedure call

```
   SetTextStyle (font, direction, size)
```

can be used to change one or more of these display specifications, where

font	range 0 to 4 (0 is default font, 4 is gothic)
direction	range 0 or 1 (0 is horizontal, 1 is vertical)
size	range 1 to 10 (1 is default size, 2 is twice as large, 3 is three times as large, and so on)

The statement

```
   SetTextStyle (0,0,2);
```

sets the font size to twice as large as was used to display HELLO before.

CAUTION   Using the same size parameter with different fonts does not produce characters of the same size.   • • •

PutPixel Procedure   The procedure call

```
PutPixel (x, y, PixColor);
```

lights up the single pixel (x,y) in `PixColor`. In VGA graphics, `PixColor` is in the range 0 to 15. Equivalently, the color constants (`black`, `blue`, `green`, `cyan`, `red`, `magenta`, `brown`, `LightGray`, `DarkGray`, `LightBlue`, `LightGreen`, `LightCyan`, `LightRed`, `LightMagenta`, `yellow`, and `white`) can be used instead of their numeral equivalents ($0-15$).

If nothing has been done to change the background color after initialization, an argument of 0 for `PixColor` will be the same color as the background color. (In VGA graphics, `PixColor = 1` gives the color blue.) Thus, in VGA graphics:

```
PutPixel (25, 25, 1);
delay (2000);
PutPixel (25, 25, 0);
```

will light up the pixel (25,25) in blue and then after a delay of approximately two seconds will erase that pixel (by restoring it to background color).

REMARK   Any program that uses the `delay` procedure must declare the `crt` unit.   • • •

• • • • • • • • • •

Example   (Animation)   The following program will first draw a vertical line using the `line` procedure and a small triangle by lighting up 49 pixels. Then the small triangle will move horizontally to pixel (170,80), moving one pixel to the right in each step.

```
program anim;
uses crt, graph;
var grdriver, grmode, i, x, y: integer;

procedure DRAW_TRIANGLE (x, y, onoff: integer);
  {Lights up a 49 pixel triangle with upper vertex (x,y)}
  var m, n: integer;
  begin
    for m := 0 to 6 do
      for n := 0 to m do
      begin
        PutPixel (x+n, y+m, onoff);
```

```
            PutPixel (x-n, y+m, onoff)
       end
  end; {DRAW_TRIANGLE}

begin
  grdriver := detect;
  Initgraph (grdriver, grmode, '');
  line (125, 0 ,125, 200);
  x:= 80;
  y:= 80;
  DRAW_TRIANGLE (x, y, 1);
  for i := 0 to 90 do
    begin
      delay (30);
      DRAW_TRIANGLE (x+i, y, 0);      {erases triangle}
      DRAW_TRIANGLE (x+i+1, y, 1)     {displays it 1 pixel}
                                      {to right}

    end;
  readln;
  closegraph
end.
```

REMARK   Note that the triangle erased the portion of the vertical line that it passed over. (See Exercise 10.)   • • •

29.3 **MORE ON COLOR**

A call to `InitGraph` initializes to white the color to be used by graphics commands without a color parameter. `SetColor` and `SetFillStyle` can be used to change the color setting for such graphics commands.

Color Constants   The following color constants can be used to specify the desired color: black, blue, green, cyan, red, magenta, brown, LightGray, DarkGray, LightBlue, LightGreen, LightCyan, LightRed, LightMagenta, yellow, and white. These colors can also be specified by the values 0 through 15, respectively.

SetColor Procedure   The procedure `SetColor` sets the color that will be used in executing

```
line, rectangle, circle, and OutTextXY
```

commands. It will not affect the color used in executing bar commands. Thus, if the following statements are executed immediately after InitGraph:

```
SetColor (red);
rectangle (0, 0, 50, 50);
bar (100, 100, 150, 150);
```

they will produce a red rectangle and solid white bar.

SetFillStyle Procedure The procedure SetFillStyle sets the color used in executing the bar command. The general form is

```
SetFillStyle (pattern, color);
```

where both arguments are of type word. Although normally we will use SetFillStyle with pattern = 1 (which produces bars that are filled in solid), pattern can be any integer from 0 to 11. (See Exercise 3.)

* * * * * * * * * *
Question What color output will the following produce:

```
SetFillStyle (1, yellow);
SetColor (blue);
circle (50,50,10);
bar (100, 100, 150, 150);
OutTextXY (200, 50, 'HELLO');
```

Answer The circle and HELLO will be blue, and the bar will be solid yellow. ● ● ●

SetBkColor Procedure InitGraph initializes the background color to black. A call of the form

```
SetBkColor (color);
```

will *immediately* change the background color to color.

29.4 BAR GRAPHS

We want to write a program to read data from the text file sales.dat and produce the bar graph shown.

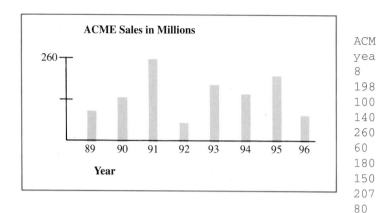

```
sales.dat
ACME sales in Millions
year
8
1989
100
140
260
60
180
150
207
80
```

Notice that the axes for the bar graph do not extend the full height and width of the "usable" screen. Instead, text is printed in the top and bottom margins as well as the left margin.

. . . .

Question Suppose the shaded area represents the region within which the bars (as opposed to the text) will lie. Suppose also that pixel A has coordinates (`Xleft`, `Yceiling`) and pixel D has coordinates (`Xright`, `Yfloor`). What will be the coordinates of pixels B and C?

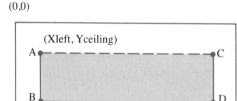

Answer   B = (`Xleft`, `Yfloor`) and C = (`Xright`, `Yceiling`)   • • •

. . . .

Question To reserve a left margin of 10 percent of the screen width for possible text, let

```
Xleft := round(0.1 * GetMaxX);
```

How would you reserve 10 percent of the screen height for top and bottom margins and 3 percent for a right margin?

Answer
```
Yceiling := round (0.1 * GetMaxY);
Yfloor := round (0.9 * GetMaxY);
Xright := round (0.97 * GetMaxX);
```
• • •

REMARK These values for Yceiling, Yfloor, Xleft and Xright cannot be declared in a const section because they depend on the values of GetMaxX and GetMaxY. In program BarGraph, we will treat them as "mock constants." We will assign values to these four global variables in procedure FOUR_FIXED. *For convenience, we will not bother to declare them as value parameters for subsequent procedures that use them.* • • •

Question The variable MaxSales will have as its value the maximum sales for the years in the file (for the data in our file, it was 260). Suppose that for the current i, sales[i] contains the sales for the *i*th year. There are two complications in determining the y coordinate for the top of the bar for that year.

(a) The *larger* sales[i] is, the *smaller* will be the y coordinate for the top of its bar.

(b) Suppose sales[i] equals 150. Then the number of vertical pixels for the height is not 150 pixels but must be scaled in terms of (Yfloor − Yceiling) and the fraction of MaxSales that 150 represents. The formula to use is

$$\text{NumVertPixels} = \frac{\text{sales[i]}}{\text{MaxSales}} \times (\text{Yfloor} - \text{Yceiling})$$

What will be the value of NumVertPixels when sales[i] = MaxSales?

Answer Plugging in MaxSales for sales[i], we get

```
Yfloor - Yceiling
```
• • •

REMARK When program BarGraph is run, it will produce the bar graph at the beginning of this section with the year labels 89, 90, 91, 92, 93, 94, 95, and 96 missing. In Exercise 4, you are asked to modify program BarGraph so that it also displays the year labels. (You should add code either to DRAW_BARS or WRITE_LABELS.) • • •

```
program BarGraph;
{Draws the bargraph of Section 29.4}
{This version will not print the year labels (89-96)}
uses graph;
type salestype = array[1..10] of integer;
var Yfloor, Yceiling, Xleft, Xright: integer;
    GrDriver, GrMode: integer;
    sales: salestype;
    width, NumOfYrs, FirstYr, MaxSales: integer;
```

```pascal
     title, XaxisTitle: string;

procedure FOUR_FIXED (var Yfloor,Yceiling,Xleft,Xright: integer);
  {sets borders for graph region}
  begin
    Yfloor := round (0.85 * GetMaxY);
    Yceiling := round (0.1 * GetMaxY);
    Xleft := round(0.1 * GetMaxX);
    Xright :=  GetMaxX
  end; {FOUR_FIXED}

procedure GETDATA (filename: string;
                   var sales:salestype;
                   var NumOfYrs, FirstYr, MaxSales:integer;
                   var title, xAxisTitle: string);
  var i: integer;
      SalesFile: text;
  begin
    assign (SalesFile, filename);
    reset (SalesFile);
    Maxsales := -1;
    readln (SalesFile, title);
    readln (SalesFile, XaxisTitle);
    readln (SalesFile, NumOfYrs);
    readln (SalesFile, FirstYr);
    for i := 1 to NumOfYrs do
      begin
        readln (SalesFile, sales[i]);
        if sales[i] > MaxSales then Maxsales := sales[i];
      end
  end; {GETDATA}

procedure DRAW_AXES;
  {Draws x and y axes and 2 hash marks on y-axis}
  var str1: string;
      Yhalf: integer;
  begin
    line(Xleft, Yfloor, Xright, Yfloor);             {x-axis}
    line(Xleft, Yfloor, Xleft, Yceiling);            {y-axis}

    line (Xleft- 10,Yceiling, Xleft + 10, Yceiling); {hash}
    yhalf := Yceiling + (Yfloor - Yceiling)div 2;    {marks}
    line (Xleft - 10, Yhalf, Xleft + 10, Yhalf)
  end;   {DRAW_AXES}
```

```
procedure DRAW_BARS (sales: salestype;
                     NumOfYrs, MaxSales, width: integer);
  {For each year calculates opposite vertexes for that year's bar}
  {and then draws the bar.}
  var i, X1,X2,NumVertPixels, Ytop:integer;
  begin
    for i := 1 to NumOfYrs do
      begin
        X1 := Xleft + (2 * i - 1) * width;
        X2 := X1 + width;
        NumVertPixels := Round((Yfloor-Yceiling)/MaxSales*sales[i]);
        Ytop := Yfloor - NumVertPixels;
        bar (X1, YTop, X2, Yfloor)
      end {for}
  end; {DRAW_BARS}

procedure WRITE_LABELS (title, xAxisTitle: string;
                        MaxSales: integer);
  {Prints titles and labels top hash mark with MaxSales value.}
  var y: integer;
      str1: string;
  begin
    str (MaxSales:3,str1);
    outTextXY (Xleft - 50, Yceiling, str1);
    y := round( 0.01 * GetMaxY);
    SetTextStyle (0,0,2);
    OutTextXY (Xleft + 40, y, title);
    OutTextXY (Xleft + 60, round (0.95 * GetMaxY), xAxisTitle)
  end; {WRITE_LABELS}

begin {main}
  GrDriver := Detect;
  Initgraph (GrDriver, GrMode,'');
  FOUR_FIXED (Yfloor, Yceiling, Xleft, Xright);
  GETDATA ('sales.dat',sales,NumOfYrs,FirstYr,MaxSales,
                                  title,xAxisTitle);
  width := round ((Xright - Xleft)/(NumOfYrs * 2));
  DRAW_AXES;
  DRAW_BARS (sales, NumOfYrs, MaxSales, width);
  WRITE_LABELS (title, xAxisTitle, MaxSales);
  readln;
  closegraph
end.
```

EXERCISES

1. Write a program to produce the following figure in the center of the screen. Let the circle have a radius equal to approximately $\frac{1}{6}$ of the screen height.

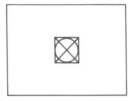

2. Write a program using a loop to display HELLO first written in each of the five font styles with normal font size and then with double font size.

3. Write a program that simultaneously displays on the screen 12 *filled* rectangles, showing the effect of each of the pattern constants from 0 to 11 in the bar command.

4. Modify BarGraph so that it also displays the year labels (89, 90, 91, 92, 93, 94, 95, and 96).

5. Modify BarGraph so that it produces four hash marks along the *y* axis and labels each of them.

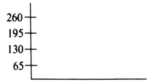

6. Write a program to produce the following line graph for sales.dat. Do it without using any commands not covered in this chapter (like moveto).

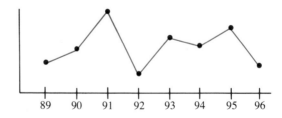

7. Modify BarGraph so that the title will be centered (no matter what its length is) in range 0 to 25 and where number of years is between 5 and 10.

8. Modify `BarGraph` so that the gap between bars will be half the width of each bar.

9. In `procedure DRAW_BARS`, replace the statement for `NumVertPixels` with

```
NumVertPixels := round (sales[i] * (Yfloor - Yceiling) / MaxSales)
```

Run the program, and explain what went wrong.

10. Revise the animation program of Section 29.2 so that the triangle does not erase the portion of the line it passes over.

* **11.** Write a program to display an American flag. The 13 stripes alternate between red and white (7 are red and 6 are white). Use white asterisks for the stars. The stars are in a box that has a blue background.

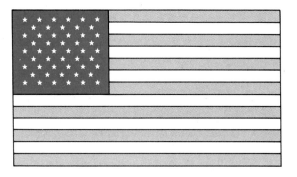

Chapter

30

OBJECT-ORIENTED
PROGRAMMING (5.5–7.0)

• • •   *Traditional structured programming* strives for programs that consist largely of self-contained modules that are easy to read, debug, and *revise.* Although structured programming was a great advance over unstructured programming, it has not been totally successful in its quest—most notably in the area of revising complex programs. There are still too many dependencies among the modules so that revision or improvement of some of the modules often necessitates adjustments in many other parts of the program.

    Object-oriented programming (OOP), which is best suited for large complex projects, represents a major advance toward further modularization. OOP keeps the interfaces between modules more free of details.

    OOP uses recordlike structures known as objects that bind together data fields and *methods* (procedures and functions) for manipulating those data fields. This binding together is known as *encapsulation.* Encapsulation greatly reduces the use of parameters because an object's data field values do not need to be passed to any of the object's methods (since they are already bound together).

    This chapter also discusses data hiding and inheritance. Polymorphism is mentioned briefly. These techniques can be used to facilitate revision and customization of software.   • • •

30.1   OBJECTS INTRODUCED

Declaring an Object Type   The syntax for declaring an object type is similar to that for a record type. In addition to data fields, however, there are also methods (functions and procedures) to manipulate the data. You first give the data fields and the headers for the methods. This is followed by the full declaration for each of the methods using dot notation to identify the object type to which the method belongs. This binding together of data fields and methods is known as encapsulation.

• • • • • • • • •
Example The following program contains two object variables, stud1 and stud2. The declaration of the object variables can be positioned after both the object type has been declared and the object methods defined. Alternatively, the object variables can be positioned immediately after the object type declaration *but before* the object methods have been defined.

Note that in the main body call to the initialization procedure

```
stud1.Init ('Smith', 80, 70);
```

The data fields for stud1 can be visualized as follows:

stud1

name	score1	score2
'Smith'	80	70

Similarly, after the call

```
stud2.Init ('Chang', 90, 93);
```

stud2 can be visualized as

stud2

name	score1	score2
'Chang'	90	93

```
program QuizScores;
type
  StudObj = Object
    name: string;
    score1: integer;
    score2: integer;
    procedure Init (nm: string; s1, s2: integer);
    function FindQuizAvg: real;
    procedure Report;
  end;
```

object
type
declared

```
procedure StudObj.Init (nm: string; s1, s2: integer);
  begin
    name := nm;
    score1 := s1;
    score2 := s2
  end;

function StudObj.FindQuizAvg: real;
  begin
    FindQuizAvg := (score1 + score2)/2
  end;

procedure StudObj.Report;
  begin
    writeln (name, ' had quiz average ', FindQuizAvg:5:1)
  end;

var stud1, stud2: StudObj;

begin {main}
  stud1.Init ('Smith', 80, 70);
  stud1.Report;
  stud2.Init ('Chang', 90, 93);
  stud2.Report
end.
```

object
methods
defined

object variables
declared

main body

The output will be

```
Smith had quiz average 75.0
Chang had quiz average 91.5
```

REMARK

1. In calling statements from the main body, the prefix (before the dot) is the object variable's name. In the header for a method definition, the object type must be given as the prefix. In the body of a method, a call to another of the object's methods has no prefix.

2. Note the reduced need for parameters. For example, the procedure call from the main body

```
stud1.Report
```

does not use any parameters since the only data values it needs are from the stud1 itself. ● ● ●

CAUTION Although it is legal for a main body statement to directly access the data fields of an object variable, this is considered extremely poor style. Thus, avoid a main body statement like

```
writeln (stud1.name)    {poor style}
```

Instead, data field values should be accessed (or changed) by the object's methods.   ● ● ●

The with Statement The syntax of dot notation and the `with` statement for objects are similar to those for records. Thus, the main body of `program QuizScores` could also have been written as

```
with stud1 do
   begin
     Init ('Smith', 80, 70);
     Report
   end; {with stud1}
with stud2 do
   begin
     Init ('Chang', 90, 93);
     Report
   end; {with stud2}
```

Terminology: Instance and Message A variable of an object type is known as an *instance.* `Program QuizScores` declares the object instances `stud1` and `stud2`. In OOP, the need for global variables that are not instances is greatly reduced. In this program, the only global variables were instances.

The procedure call

```
stud1.Report
```

is better thought of as `stud1` passing a *message* to itself.

● ● ● ● ● ● ● ● ●
Example   `Program MovingObjects` moves a smiley face and a heart across the screen. First the face and the heart are displayed at screen positions (2, 8) and (2, 15), respectively. (See part (a).) Then you see each shape moving horizontally. Part (b) shows a snapshot just after execution of `face.move (10);`.

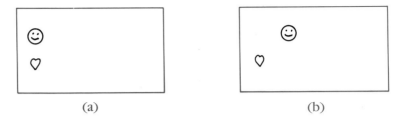

(a)   (b)

In traditional programming, if you wanted the main body to issue procedure calls to move a smiley face and a heart, you would need four global variables to keep track of the current screen positions of the face and the heart. You might use as global variables

```
FaceX, FaceY, HeartX, HeartY
```

Note that there is no need for such global variables in the following program because the screen coordinates of each figure are contained in the data fields of that figure's instance (object variable).

```
program MovingObjects;
uses crt;
type
  MovingObj = Object
     x: integer;
     y: integer;
     shape: char;
     procedure Init (xx, yy: integer; shp: char);
     procedure MoveHoriz (dist: integer);
  end;

procedure MovingObj.Init (xx, yy: integer; shp: char);
  begin
     x := xx;
     y := yy;
     shape := shp;
     gotoxy (x, y);
     write (shape)
  end;

procedure MovingObj.MoveHoriz (dist: integer);
  var i, increm: integer;
  begin
     if dist > 0
        then increm := 1
        else increm := -1;
```

```
      for i := 1 to abs (dist) do
        begin
          gotoXY (x, y);
          write (' ');
          x := x + increm;
          gotoXY (x, y);
          write (shape);
          delay (200)
        end
  end;

var face, heart: MovingObj;
begin
  clrscr;
  face.Init (2, 8, chr(2));
  heart.Init (2, 15, chr(3));
  face.MoveHoriz (10);
  heart.MoveHoriz (20);
  face.MoveHoriz (-8);
  readln
end.
```

• • •

REMARK

1. In traditional programming, the `MoveHoriz` procedure would need *four* parameters, not just one. In traditional programming, the shape of the figure and the distance would be value parameters, whereas the x and y screen coordinates of that figure would be variable parameters.

2. Note the use of value parameters instead of variable parameters in the initialization procedure `MovingObj.Init` and in the initialization procedure from the first program. This is in line with the desire to keep as much of the data as possible bound to objects. If variable parameters had been used, it would have required declaring extra (unbound) global variables. • • •

Data Hiding   Since the actual data is contained within an object and does not need to be passed to its methods, the data structures are to a large extent hidden from the main body. This is known as ***data hiding*** and is a result of encapsulation. Farming out such details is a further step in the direction of modularization.

For example,

```
face.MoveHoriz (10)
```

specified only the distance to be moved and not the current position or shape.

The advantage of data hiding goes beyond reducing the number of parameters. By localizing the data implementation to the object itself, OOP reduces the number of places where changes must be made when complex software is modified. Quite often the main body can remain intact.

Software Development and Data Hiding   An important issue in connection with most recent or "improved" versions of software library routines is whether old application programs that you wrote for an earlier version of the software will still work for the improved version. Software library routines that are written as object(s) contained within a unit can minimize or even eliminate the need for revising application programs.

Example   Suppose that you have software named `sort.pas` that can be used to read in club members' names and phone numbers from a text file that is *not* sorted alphabetically and then print them in alphabetical order. Note that `sort.pas` is a unit containing an object type named `ClubObj`.

Here is `sort.pas`.

```
unit sort;

interface
  uses crt;
  const maxsize = 50;
  type
    ClubObj = Object
      filename: string;
      size: integer;
      names: array[1..maxsize] of string[20];
      phones: array[1..maxsize] of string[12];
      procedure Init (fname: string);
      procedure Sort;
      procedure Print;
    end;

implementation

  procedure ClubObj.Init (fname: string);
  var
    MembFile: text;
  begin
    filename := fname;
    assign (MembFile, filename);
    reset (MembFile);
    size := 0;
    while not seekeof (MembFile) do
      begin
        size := size + 1;
```

```
      readln (MembFile, names[size]);
      readln (MembFile, phones[size])
   end;
  close (MembFile)
 end;
```

```
procedure ClubObj.Sort and procedure ClubObj.Print
implementations are left as an exercise for the reader
```

```
end.
```

Suppose that you wrote the following application program to make use of sort.pas:

```
program ClubSort;
{application of sort.pas}
uses sort;
var club: ClubObj;

begin {main}
  club.init('GleeClub.dat');
  club.sort;
  club.print
end.
```

• • • • • • • • •
Question Suppose that the software company has just sent you their most recent, improved version of sort.pas. In this improved version, the names and phone numbers are read into an array of records, whereas in the old version, they were read into parallel arrays. Will your application program have to be modified to be run with the improved software? If so, in what way?

Answer The old application program will run as is with the improved software. This is a direct benefit of data hiding.   • • •

Traditional Programming Version of sort.pas Consider, by contrast, if sort.pas had been written as a unit in traditional structured programming (that is, without objects). If the improved version of sort.pas changed the data structure from parallel arrays to an array of records, then *every* statement in the main body of the application program would have to be changed.

Old Traditional Main

```
begin
  INIT('GleeClub.dat', names, phones, size);
  SORT(names, phones, size);
  PRINT(names, phones, size)
end.
```

Revised Traditional Main

```
begin
  INIT('GleeClub.dat', members, size);
  SORT(members, size);
  PRINT(members, size)
end.
```

30.2 INHERITANCE

A new object type can inherit characteristics (data fields and methods) from a previously defined object type. This is known as ***inheritance.*** The new object type can extend the previous type by adding new data fields or methods. The new object type is called the descendant object, and the previously defined object type is called its ancestor.

To define a new object type that inherits from an ancestor, begin the type declaration with

descendant type identifier = Object (*ancestor type identifier*)

and then declare any *new* data fields and any totally *new* methods or any ancestor methods that will be *redefined*.

Example In program QuizScores, an object stud1 had three data fields (for the name and two quiz scores). There was not a data field for a final exam score. Suppose that a student's final course average is calculated by (final exam + term avg)/2. We want to create a descendant object type FullObj that has an additional data field for the final exam score. We will also need to redefine the procedures Init and Report for FullObj.

FullObj.Init will assign values to four (not three) data fields.

FullObj.Report will calculate and print the final course average.

Here is the type declaration associated with FullObj.

```
program drill;
type
   StudObj = Object
     Name: string;
     score1, score2: integer;
     procedure Init (nm: string; s1, s2: integer);
     function FindQuizAvg: real;
     procedure Report;
   end;

   FullObj = Object (StudObj)
     FinalExam: integer;
     procedure Init (nm: string; s1, s2, fe: integer);
     procedure Report;
   end;
```

• • • • • • • • •

Question   Here is a full program. Note that after the type declaration, all the implementations must be given.

(a)   What will the output be?

(b)   Why isn't the function `FindQuizAvg` redeclared by `FullObj`?

```
program FullScores;
type
   StudObj = Object
     Name: string;
     score1, score2: integer;
     procedure Init (nm: string; s1, s2: integer);
     function FindQuizAvg: real;
     procedure Report;
   end;
   FullObj = Object (StudObj)
     FinalExam: integer;
     procedure Init (nm: string; s1, s2, fe: integer);
     procedure Report;
   end;

procedure StudObj.Init (nm: string; s1, s2: integer);
   begin
     name := nm;
     score1 := s1;
     score2 := s2
   end;
```

```
function StudObj.FindQuizAvg: real;
  begin
    FindQuizAvg := (score1 + score2)/2
  end;

procedure StudObj.Report;
  begin
    writeln (name, ' just term average ', FindQuizAvg:4:1)
  end;

procedure FullObj.Init (nm: string; s1, s2, fe: integer);
  begin
    FinalExam := fe;
    StudObj.Init (nm, s1, s2)
  end;

procedure FullObj.Report;
  var FinalAvg: real;
  begin
    FinalAvg := (FinalExam + FindQuizAvg)/2;
    writeln (name, ' full course avg ', FinalAvg:4:1)
  end;

var StudTerm: StudObj;
    StudFull: FullObj;

begin {main}
  StudTerm.Init ('Henson', 90, 95);
  StudTerm.Report;
  StudFull.Init ('Jones', 70, 80, 95);
  StudFull.Report
end.
```

Answer

(a)

```
Henson just term avg 92.5
Jones full course avg 85.0
```

(b)   `FullObj` did not need to modify `FindQuizAvg`. By contrast, `FullObj` did need to modify the `Init` and `Report` procedures.   • • •

textcolor   `textcolor` is contained in the `crt` unit. `textcolor` takes an argument of type `byte` from a list of colors such as {green, blue, red, brown}. `textcolor` sets the current color to be used for current printing to the screen. Note that it does not change the color of previous screen printing.
    Thus, after

```
      textcolor (red);
      write ('A');
      textcolor (green);
      write ('B');
```

the screen will display a red A and a green B.

Example In the next application of inheritance, the moving objects will be given a color field for the objects' characteristic color. Then the main body statements

```
      ColFace.Init (2, 8, chr(2), red);
      ColHeart.Init (2, 15, chr(3), green);
```

will create a red face and a green heart.

```
      ColFace.MoveHoriz (10);
```

will move the red face.

• • • • • • • • • •

Question Fill in the blanks in the procedure ColObj.MoveHoriz.

```
program MovingObjects2;
uses crt;
type
  MovingObj = Object
    x: integer;
    y: integer;
    shape: char;
    procedure Init (xx, yy: integer; shp: char);
    procedure MoveHoriz (dist: integer);
  end;

  ColObj = object (MovingObj)
    color: byte;
    procedure Init (xx, yy: integer; shp: char; col: byte);
    procedure MoveHoriz (dist: integer);
  end;
```

```
procedure MovingObj.Init (xx, yy: integer; shp: char);
  Exactly as in program MovingObjects.  To save space we
  will not give it.
```

```
procedure MovingObj.MoveHoriz (dist: integer);
  Exactly as in program MovingObjects.
```

```
procedure ColObj.Init (xx, yy: integer; shp: char; col: byte);
  begin
    color := col;
    textcolor (color);
    MovingObj.Init (xx, yy, shp)
  end;

procedure ColObj.MoveHoriz (dist: integer);
  begin

    _____
    _____

  end;

var ColFace, ColHeart: ColObj;
begin
  clrscr;
  ColFace.Init (2, 8, chr(2), red);
  ColHeart.Init (2, 15, chr(3), green);
  ColFace.MoveHoriz (10);
  ColHeart.MoveHoriz (20);
  ColFace.MoveHoriz (-8);
  readln
end.
```

Answer
```
textcolor (color);
MovingObj.MoveHoriz (dist)
```
• • •

Software Implications   If you had software for the object `MovingObj`, notice how easily you could customize it to move *colored* objects. Note how little you would need to deal with the details of implementing `MoveHoriz`. Inheritance encourages the reuse of code. It lets you use and extend code you didn't write.

Polymorphism and Virtual Methods   A powerful advanced feature of objects is *polymorphism.* Polymorphism syntax allows an object instance to take on the ancestor's form or the form of any of its descendants. Polymorphism occurs when a single name is shared by a number of different methods, and yet a call to that name does not directly specify which method to use. How then does the compiler know which to use? Polymorphism uses *virtual methods* that permit *late-binding* (run-time resolution of which method to use). See an advanced textbook on OOP for the details of polymorphism syntax—look for the keywords `virtual` and `constructor`.

RESERVED WORDS AND PREDECLARED IDENTIFIERS

• • •   Recall that keywords are words that have built-in meanings in Turbo Pascal. There are two types of keywords: reserved words and predeclared identifiers.   • • •

RESERVED WORDS

Reserved words have a permanent meaning. Under no circumstances may you declare an identifier to have the same name as a reserved word. Here is a list of the reserved words in Turbo 7.0.

absolute	div	function	label
and	do	goto	library
array	downto	if	mod
asm	else	implementation	nil
begin	end	in	not
case	external	inherited	object
const	file	inline	of
constructor	for	interface	on
destructor	forward	interrupt	packed

```
private*      set         to          var
procedure     shl         type        virtual
program       shr         unit        while
public*       string      until       with
record        then        uses        xor
repeat
```

PREDECLARED IDENTIFIERS

A predeclared identifier is a word that has a built-in meaning in Turbo Pascal but whose meaning can be redefined by the programmer. Be aware that when a predeclared identifier is redefined, its original meaning will not be available.

The following list gives some of the most commonly used predeclared identifiers. Note that this list includes constants (c), functions (f), procedures (p), data types (t), and units (u).

(f) abs	(c) false	(p) read
(f) arctan	(f) filesize	(p) readln
(p) assign	(u) graph	(p) reset
(t) boolean	(p) insert	(p) rewrite
(t) byte	(f) int	(f) round
(t) char	(t) integer	(p) seek
(f) chr	(f) length	(p) seekeof
(p) close	(f) ln	(f) sin
(f) concat	(t) longint	(f) sqr
(f) copy	(c) maxint	(f) sqrt
(f) cos	(c) maxlongint	(p) str
(u) crt	(p) new	(f) succ
(p) delete	(f) ord	(u) system
(p) dispose	(f) pi	(c) true
(u) dos	(f) pos	(f) trunc
(f) eof	(p) pred	(f) upcase
(p) erase	(u) printer	(p) val
(f) exp	(f) random	(p) write
(t) extended	(p) randomize	(p) writeln

---

* Reserved words only within objects.

Appendix

B

ASCII TABLE

• • • The following table gives the ASCII numbers (codes) for the first 128 characters in Turbo Pascal.

For any given character ch,

```
ord (ch)
```

gives the ASCII number of that character. Inversely, for any given ASCII number n,

```
chr (n)
```

gives the character associated with that ASCII number.

The characters with ASCII codes 0-31 are control codes for various devices. Some of them are nondisplayable, whereas others appear as graphics characters. See Chapter 5 for a discussion of the chr and ord functions. The characters with ASCII codes 32-125 are displayable on all computers. The characters with ASCII codes 128-255 (not listed in the table) contain the IBM extended ASCII character set.   • • •

Some Uses of *chr*

Form Feed   If you include the form feed statement

```
writeln (1st, chr(12));
```

in your program, printed output that follows will be started on a new page.

The Bell statement

```
writeln (chr(7));
```

would produce a single beep.

Code	Char	Code	Char	Code	Char	Code	Char
0	Null	32		64	@	96	'
1	☺	33	!	65	A	97	a
2	☻	34	"	66	B	98	b
3	♥	35	#	67	C	99	c
4	♦	36	$	68	D	100	d
5	♣	37	%	69	E	101	e
6	♠	38	&	70	F	102	f
7	Bell	39	'	71	G	103	g
8	Backspace	40	(	72	H	104	h
9	Tab	41	)	73	I	105	i
10	LineFeed	42	*	74	J	106	j
11	Home	43	+	75	K	107	k
12	FormFeed	44	'	76	L	108	l
13	CarriageRet	45	–	77	M	109	m
14	♪	46	.	78	N	110	n
15	☼	47	/	79	O	111	o
16	►	48	0	80	P	112	p
17	◄	49	1	81	Q	113	q
18	↕	50	2	82	R	114	r
19	‼	51	3	83	S	115	s
20	¶	52	4	84	T	116	t
21	§	53	5	85	U	117	u
22	▬	54	6	86	V	118	v
23	↕	55	7	87	W	119	w
24	↑	56	8	88	X	120	x
25	↓	57	9	89	Y	121	y
26	Eof	58	:	90	Z	122	z
27	Esc	59	;	91	[	123	{
28	L	60	<	92	\	124	|
29	↔	61	=	93	]	125	}
30	▲	62	>	94	^	126	~
31	▼	63	?	95	_	127	DEL

Appendix

C

DOS AND
SUBDIRECTORIES

• • • DOS and Turbo are two different environments. Immediately after booting up, you are in DOS. After you load Turbo, you are in the Turbo Pascal environment. Almost all that you need to do to type and run Turbo programs can be done in Turbo Pascal. However, a basic understanding of how DOS handles files and of some DOS commands will prove invaluable. • • •

Default Drive   The default drive is the drive on which DOS file operations will take place by default. You can tell which is the default drive by looking at the DOS prompt. Suppose that the DOS prompt is A> or A:\>. In that case, the default drive is drive A. If you do not indicate a drive when specifying a file in a file command, the computer will assume that the intended drive is the default drive.

Files   Information can be stored together in a unit known as a file. A file name consists of a first part beginning with a letter and containing up to eight characters that are letters or digits, and an optional second part (extension) consisting of a period followed by up to three characters.

SUBDIRECTORIES

• •

Imagine that you have cut out and saved 100 newspaper articles on various subjects, such as Sports, Movies, Politics, and Science. One possible way to store these articles is simply to put them loose in one big folder. A better way to store them is to use additional folders so that all the Sports articles will be in a folder labeled Sports, all the Movie articles will be in a folder labeled Movies, and so on, and then put all these labeled folders in a big folder.

When DOS formats a diskette, it creates a main directory known as the root directory. (The root directory corresponds to the big folder.) The root directory may contain individual files. To make your filing system better organized, you may also create additional directories off the root directory, called subdirectories. (Subdirectories correspond to the labeled folders.) These subdirectories may contain individual files or further subdirectories of their own. (A subdirectory having its own subdirectories is like putting a Baseball folder within the Sports folder.) Even further nesting is possible. This gives rise to a tree-structured filing system.

PATHNAME—SPECIFYING A PARTICULAR FILE

The pathname tells DOS not only the name of the file but also where the file is located in the directory system. A pathname consists of a sequence of subdirectory names followed by a file name. Each subdirectory name is separated from the previous one by a backslash (\\).

```
C:
├─ LAB
│      PROG1.PAS
│      PROG2.PAS
├─ LECTURE
       NOTES.TXT
```

For example, suppose drive C: had the directory structure as shown in the diagram. The full pathname for prog1.pas would be c:\lab\prog1.pas, and the full pathname for notes.txt would be c:\lecture\notes.txt.

Using Wildcard Characters   The two wildcard characters * and ? enable a single command to refer to a whole collection of files. The asterisk (*) used in a file name or file name extension indicates that any character can occupy that position or any of the remaining positions in the file name or extension. The question mark (?) in a file name or file name extension indicates that any single character can occupy that position.

DIRECTORY COMMANDS

Command	Function
CD	**C**hange **D**irectory
MD	**M**ake **D**irectory
RD	**R**emove **D**irectory
DIR	**DIR**ectory listing

• • • • • • • • •
Examples **cd c:\dos**
Changes the current directory to c:\dos.

dir c:\dos
Lists all the files in the dos subdirectory.

md a:\examples
Creates a new subdirectory on drive a: called examples.

rd a:\junk
Removes the directory called junk from drive a: (provided junk has no files in it). • • •

COPYING FILES—COPY AND XCOPY

• •

Files can be copied in DOS by using the DOS copy or xcopy command. xcopy provides additional copy options like copying subdirectories also.

The syntax for the copy commands are

Copy *sourcefile targetfile*

• • • • • • • • •
Examples **copy a:\lab\prog1.pas b:**
Copies the file prog1.pas to the b: drive.

copy a:\prog1.pas b:\prog2.pas
Copies the file prog1.pas to the b: drive with the new name of prog2.pas.

copy a:*.* b:
Copies all the files from the root directory of drive a: to the root directory of drive b:.

xcopy a:*.* b:\ /s
Copies all the files from drive a: to drive b:, including subdirectories and all the files within them. • • •

Erasing Files—Erase and DEL   To erase a file, we can use the erase or del command. Erase and del are functionally equivalent.

• • • • • • • • •
Example **erase a:\lab\prog1.pas**
Erases the file prog1.pas from the subdirectory lab that exists on drive a:.

• • •

Appendix

D

FURTHER EDITOR FEATURES

• • • Some Turbo editor commands were discussed in Chapter 2. This appendix presents some additional commands. • • •

SEARCH AND REPLACE OPERATIONS

The search and replace feature allows you to replace some or all occurrences of a particular string with a specified substitute string. Suppose, for example, that in a program you wish to change all occurrences of the variable named balance to the new name, amount.

To search and replace in Turbo 6.0–7.0

- Press **CTRL-q-a.** (This is the hot key combination for the Replace choice from the Search submenu.)

- Type balance in the Text to find box, and press **TAB.**

- Type amount in the New text box, and again press **TAB.**

(*Caution:* Do not press ENTER at all during the entire process.)

- The cursor is now in the Options box. Since you want the replacement to be done for all occurrences without prompting, you must erase the [X] by Prompt on replace.

To do so, position the cursor at the X, and hit the spacebar. (The spacebar toggles between a blank and an X.)

- Press **a** for change all.

REMARK   In the Options box you can mark with an X as many options as you wish. By contrast, the Direction, Scope, and Origin boxes require that exactly one of two alternatives be marked with a dot. (The arrow key acts as a toggle.)   ● ● ●

BLOCK OPERATIONS

You can mark a portion of text as a block. This block can then be moved, copied, or deleted.

To mark the beginning of the block

- Position the cursor at its beginning, and press **CTRL-k-b.**

To mark the end of a block

- Position the cursor beyond the block, and press **CTRL-k-k.**

All the text in the block will be highlighted. Only one block may be highlighted at a time. Any time that you wish to unmark a block that has been marked, move the cursor to any position above the marked block and press **CTRL-k-k.**

While a block is marked, you can perform various operations on it.

Block Operations within a Single File

CTRL-k-v   Moves the block to wherever the cursor is currently located.
CTRL-k-c   Makes a duplicate copy of the block at the current cursor position.
CTRL-k-y   Deletes the block.

Copying a Marked Block from One File to a Second File   This can be done most easily using the clipboard. See Appendix E.

Appendix

E

WINDOWS IN 7.0

• • • Windows (available in Turbo Pascal starting with 6.0 and not to be confused with Microsoft Windows) makes it easier to manipulate files by allowing the user to keep multiple files open at one time. This is very useful when doing more complex programming and makes it easy to copy or move text between files. • • •

ACTIVE FILE VERSUS OPEN FILE

Each time you open another file, the Edit Window becomes smaller, and the names of all the open files remain on the screen. Of these open files, only one is directly available for editing—it is known as the active file and is marked with a double-line border. When you open a file (by pressing F3 and specifying the file name), that file becomes the active file. You can change which of the open files is the active file either by pressing the F6 key to activate the next open file or by using a mouse. You can close a file by first making it active and then selecting the Close command from the File submenu or by using the hot key ALT-F3. If you wish to see text from all the open files simultaneously, you can use the Tile command from the Windows submenu.

Common Functions When Working with Windows

ALT-F3	Closes the active window
F6	Activates next window
SHIFT-F6	Activates previous window
Zoom (F5)	Enlarges active window to full screen

| ALT-w-t | Arranges the open windows in a tile layout |
| ALT-w-a | Arranges the open windows in a cascade layout |

USING CLIPBOARD TO INSERT A BLOCK FROM ONE FILE TO ANOTHER

• •

The clipboard is a holding area that can be used to store block(s) of text. To insert a copy of a block from fileA to a position in fileB

- Open both of these files, and then keep pressing **F6** until fileA is the active file.

- Mark the block of text from fileA that you wish to insert in fileB by typing **CTRL-k-b** to mark the beginning and **CTRL-k-k** to mark the end or by using a mouse.

- Press **CTRL-INS** to move a copy of the block to the clipboard. (Note that CTRL-INS is the hot key combination for the Copy choice from the Edit submenu.)

- Press **F6** until fileB is the active file. Position the cursor to where you want to insert the block, and press **SHIFT-INS.** (Hot keys for the Paste choice from the Edit submenu.)

Viewing the Clipboard   Select the Show clipboard from the Edit Submenu to view the current contents of the clipboard.

You should verify the following features of the clipboard:

1. After copying a block to the clipboard, only the just-copied block will be highlighted in the clipboard.

2. The Paste choice copies the clipboard block that is highlighted to another file.

3. The clipboard can be Edited.

4. Pressing F6 activates the next window (leaving the clipboard open) whereas ALT-F3 closes the clipboard window.

Appendix

TURBO BUILT-IN DEBUGGER

• • • Turbo's built-in debugger makes it easy to trace the flow of execution of a program and watch the values of variables as they change. • • •

BASIC TRACE

If you wish to step through a program line by line to observe the flow of execution, you can do so by repeatedly pressing the F7 hot key (for run/trace).

The following program will be used to illustrate such a trace:

```
program drill;
var x, y: integer;
begin
  writeln ('Hello');
  x := 5;
  writeln ('Type An Integer and Press Enter ');
  readln (y);
  if x > y
    then x := x + 1
    else y := y + 1;
  writeln (x, ' ', y)
end.
```

Type in the program, and then initiate the debugging trace by pressing F7. The program will remain on the screen, and the word `begin` from the main body will be highlighted. Each time you press F7, the line that is currently highlighted will be executed, and the next line to be executed becomes highlighted. In an `if-then-else` test, the highlighting will indicate whether the flow of execution is to the `then` or the `else` branch.

Exiting the Debugger Mode   Upon execution of the last line of a program, Turbo Pascal automatically takes you out of the Debugger. Note, however, that in the case of an infinite loop, you will need to press **CTRL-F2** to exit from the Debugger.

CAUTION   If the built-in debugger does not seem to respond as described, the default compiler settings may have been modified. If this occurs, try adding the compiler directives `{$D+ , $L+ }` to the top of the program. (For a more permanent solution, see Appendix G on how to check or reset compiler directive defaults.)   • • •

TRACING USING WATCH VALUES
• •

The built-in debugger allows you to set up a watch window to watch the values of certain variables change as you execute a program one line at a time.

Adding Variables to the Watch Window

Method 1: For each variable that you would like to watch, press CTRL-F7, type the variable's name in the dialog box (overwriting anything already in the box), and press ENTER. The variable will be added to the watch window at the bottom of the screen. At this stage, each such variable will be an unknown identifier.

Method 2: If the Edit Screen is active, you can add a variable without having to type the variable name. Simply move the cursor to any character of a variable that you wish to add. Then press CTRL-F7 and the ENTER key.

F6 and SHIFT-F6 as a Toggle   Pressing F6 moves you to the watch window while SHIFT-F6 moves you back to edit mode.

Tracing the Program   Now you are ready to run the program one line at a time. Each time that you press F7, the currently highlighted program line will be executed, and the current values of all "watch" variables will be displayed in the watch window. If the watch window does not appear at the bottom of the screen, press SHIFT-F6 to display it. (Be aware that any watch variables that your program has not yet assigned a value will have a garbage value.)

Deleting a Watch Variable   While in the watch window mode, use the ↑ or ↓ arrow to move the highlight to a variable that you wish to delete, and then press the DEL key. *Watch variables can be added or deleted at any time during a trace.*

Restarting a Trace   To restart a trace, press **CTRL-F2.**

Data Structures as Watch Variables   A watch variable can be any type of variable; the display of the variable will vary according to the variable's data structure.

> **Arrays**   When an array is used as a watch variable, the current contents of the array are displayed within parentheses, as in

```
(15,22,18,19)
```

If the array is two dimensional, it is displayed as a nested list. For example, a 3×2 array of integers would be displayed as

```
((8,12), (9,25), (8,7))
```

> **Records**   When a record is used as a watch variable, the current contents of the record are displayed within parentheses. The fields are separated by commas, as in

```
('Smith',45,6.50)
```

TRACING A PROGRAM WITH PROCEDURES
• •

When a procedure call is highlighted, you may either continue the line-by-line execution or have the whole procedure executed at once. To step through the procedure body one line at a time, just keep pressing **F7.** To execute the entire procedure call with a single keystroke, press **F8** (instead of **F7**).

Tracing Values of Variables with the Same Name   If the same name is used for a global variable and a value parameter or a local variable, the current watch value will depend on whether the line being executed is in the procedure body or the main body.

• • • • • • • • •
Example   To see how the values change, trace the following program. Set watch variables of w, x, and y and use F7 to execute the procedure body line by line.

```
{$D+,L+}
program drill;
{tracing a program with a procedure}
var x, y: integer;

procedure JUNK (x: integer;
                    var y: integer);
  var w: integer;
  begin
    w := 5;
    x := x + 40;
    y := y + 40
  end; {JUNK}
begin {main}
  x := 2;
  y := 2;
  JUNK (x, y);
  writeln (x, ' ', y)
end.
```

REMARK

1. Notice that the current watch value of x depends on whether the line being executed is in the procedure body or the main body.

2. Notice what happens to w in the watch window when the line being executed is in the main body. • • •

BREAKPOINTS

• •

Instead of tracing a program line by line, you can skip over groups of lines by using breakpoints—*breakpoints* are points in the program where Turbo temporarily suspends execution. When you run a program that includes breakpoints, Turbo will execute the program until it comes to a breakpoint. At the breakpoint, Turbo will temporarily halt execution and return control to you, giving you the opportunity to carry out other operations. You might inspect watch variables, start single-step tracing, or resume execution. By using breakpoints, you can eliminate line-by-line tracing of code in which you are not interested, such as long loops or sections of code that have already been debugged.

Setting Breakpoints   Breakpoints are set in the Edit Window by moving the cursor to the line at which you want to set a breakpoint and then pressing

CTRL-F8. Repeat these steps for each breakpoint you want to create. Each line with a breakpoint will be highlighted.

To initiate a run of the program, press **CTRL-F9.** Execution will proceed until a line with a breakpoint is reached. Before that line is executed, Turbo will suspend execution and place you back in the Edit Window. To resume execution until the next breakpoint, press **CTRL-F9** again. To start single-step tracing instead, press **F7.**

REMARK

1. Breakpoints should be set only on lines with executable statements.

2. A maximum of 21 breakpoints is allowed.　　　　　　● ● ●

Clearing a Breakpoint　To remove a breakpoint, position the cursor on the breakpoint line and press **CTRL-F8.**

Clearing All Breakpoints　To clear all breakpoints, type **ALT-d** to bring up the Debug submenu, press **b, c,** and answer yes if you are prompted for confirmation, and then press **ESC** to return to the Edit Screen.

"Go to cursor"　Another form of the breakpoint is the "Go to cursor" feature. The Go to cursor function is invoked by pressing the F4 key. Turbo then executes the program until it finds either a line previously defined as a breakpoint or the line where the cursor is currently located, whichever comes first. If you press F4 again or **CTRL-F9,** Turbo will resume execution, going to either the cursor or the next breakpoint. Or you can press F7 to resume single-step tracing. For example, you could use F4 to get you to the beginning of a procedure and then use F7 to trace through it.

CTRL-BREAK　You can also halt program execution by pressing CTRL-BREAK. This command causes Turbo to break at whatever line it was executing and return you to the Edit Window, with the highlighted line to be executed next. This method of generating an immediate breakpoint generally is used to regain control so that another operation can be performed.

Appendix

G

COMPILER DIRECTIVES

• • • Compiler directives can affect the way Turbo Pascal processes a program. They can either be placed in the program itself or selected from the Options submenu. Here is a list of some commonly used "switch" compiler directives, where + means the directive is activated, and − means it is disabled.

• • •

BOOLEAN EVALUATION

The default mode {$B-} is short circuit boolean evaluation. That is, evaluation of a boolean expression halts as soon as its value is determined. For example, suppose count = 0 when the following expression is evaluated using boolean evaluation:

```
if (count > 0) and ((sum / count) > 75) then
```

This will not produce a 0 divide run-time error since evaluation of the compound condition halts when the first condition is found to be false. By contrast, under {$B+} this test would produce a run-time error of division by 0 since *complete evaluation* would be used (all the expressions would be evaluated).

RANGE CHECKING

For the default mode {$R-} there will be no detection of run-time out-of-range errors. For {$R+} range checking will be performed on array and string subscripts as well as assignments to subrange and ordinal variables. Refer to Chapter 16 for more details.

DEBUGGER

To ensure that the built-in debugger is activated, a program that is run using the debugger should contain the directive {$D+,L+}.

EXTENDED NUMERIC PROCESSOR

The directive {$E+,N+} should be included when extended real data types (single, double, extended) are used and your program does a lot of mathematical calculations of real variables. Single real requires 4 bytes of storage and allows either 7 or 8 significant digits. Double real takes up 8 bytes and allows 15 or 16 digits. Extended real uses 10 bytes and provides 19 or 20 digits.

SETTING DEFAULTS IN
THE OPTIONS SUBMENU

The Compiler choice within the Options submenu allows you to set compiler directives that you want to be set by default. This is instead of having to include them at the top of each program like {$R+}.

To set defaults, press **ALT-o** then **c**, which brings up the Compiler Options window. Use the TAB key to move from one group to the next and then the arrow keys to highlight the option you wish to change. Then use the spacebar to toggle the setting—X means activate it, and blank deactivates it. Press ENTER when done.

TUTORIALS AND USING THE TEXTBOOK DISKETTE

● ● ●   The diskette that accompanies the book contains the following:

(a) Sample programs contained in the book

(b) End-of-Chapter Lab Exercises

(c) Lab Activities and Tutorials

Descriptions and instructions for these items follow.   ● ● ●

Sample Programs Contained in the Book   The textbook programs on the textbook diskette are named by page number with each chapter having its own subdirectory off the root directory. For example, the program on page 116 in Chapter 7 has the full file name A:\CH7\P116.PAS. Note that most, but not all, of the programs from the book are on the textbook diskette.

We assume that you have the textbook diskette in the A drive and that you are already in Turbo Pascal. To load the program from page 116 of Chapter 7:

- Press **Alt-f** then **c** to bring up the change directory submenu.
- Type **A:\CH7** in the Directory Name box and press **ENTER**.
- Press **F3**.
- Press **TAB**, highlight **P116.PAS**, and then press **ENTER**.

End-of-Chapter Lab Exercises   At the end of most chapters you will find a section called Lab Exercises, which contains a list of canned programs (their file names and what they are about) to debug. Their files are on the textbook diskette in the directory for that chapter. For example, the file lab3-1.pas listed in the Lab Exercise section for Chapter 3 is in the ch3 subdirectory on the textbook diskette with the filename lab3-1.pas. To load a debugging exercise use the same procedure that was given for loading a sample program.

Lab Activities and Tutorials   Step-by-step Lab Activities, grouped into the following three topics, are given in this Appendix:

> *I.* Basics of DOS

> *II.* Elements of Editing

> *III.* More Advanced Editing

Each Lab Activity can be used in a stand-alone mode by simply following that Lab Activity's printed instructions; or if you wish you can also use an accompanying tutorial file while working on the Lab Activity.

Using a Tutorial File

For Lab Topic I

1. Get into Pascal and put the book diskette in drive a:.

2. Press **F3** and type **a:\lab\basicdos.pas**.

3. Read the material on the screen. When you are ready to do a lab activity, shell out to DOS by pressing **Alt-f** and then **d**. At the DOS prompt follow the steps outlined in the specified lab activity. To return to the Turbo screen containing the expository text, type **exit** and press **ENTER**.

For Lab Topics II and III

1. Get into Pascal and put the book diskette in drive a:.

2. Press **F3** and type the appropriate expository text filename:
   - For topic II type **a:\lab\elemedit.pas**.
   - For topic III type **a:\lab\moreedit.pas**.

3. Read the material on the screen. When directed to do the lab activities press **Alt-F3** to close the expository text file and then continue with steps outlined in the specified lab activity. If you wish to continue to review the expository text, simply repeat steps 2 and 3.

LAB TOPIC I—BASICS OF DOS

Activity A—Disk Drives and DOS Version

We assume that you are in DOS now. You should see the DOS prompt ending with >.

To find out which is drive A   Suppose that the computer has two diskette drives and you would like to be certain of which is drive A.

- Place a formatted diskette in the drive that you think is drive A. (You could use the textbook diskette for this activity.)
- Type **a:** and as you press **ENTER** look at the disk drives to see which drive's light momentarily turns on—that is drive A. (If nothing happens when you do this try typing **dir** and press **ENTER**, and check which light comes on.)

CAUTION   If you encounter the following error message

Not ready reading drive a:
Abort, Retry, Fail?

it means that the computer expects there to be a formatted diskette in drive A, but there isn't one. To get rid of this error message, you should put a formatted diskette in the indicated drive and type **r** for Retry.   • • •

To produce the above error message and then get rid of it
- Remove the diskette from drive A and type **a:** and press **ENTER**.
- Try getting rid of the error message by pressing **ENTER** or **ESC**.
- Now try putting a diskette in drive A, and press **r** for Retry.

To find out the version of DOS being used by the computer
- At the DOS prompt, type **ver** and press **ENTER**.

Activity B—Copying a Diskette

We assume that you are in DOS now. You should see the DOS prompt ending with >. Read the following two methods of making a backup copy of the textbook diskette.

NOTE   For this activity we assume that drive A is a 3.5″ drive. The textbook diskette is a 3.5″ low density diskette. If your blank diskette is also 3.5″ low-density, then you can use either method. Otherwise, you will need to use the second method which uses the xcopy command.   ● ● ●

Using the DISKCOPY Command

- Put the textbook diskette in drive A.
- At the DOS system prompt, type **diskcopy a: a:** and press **ENTER**.
- Follow the instructions displayed on the screen.
- After the copying process is completed, press **n** to exit the DISKCOPY program.

Using the XCOPY Command

- Put the textbook diskette in drive A.
- At the DOS system prompt, type **xcopy a: b:/s** and press **ENTER**.

  If you have only one diskette drive, that drive will act as both the A and B drives. When the system is ready to write to drive B, you will be directed to insert the diskette for drive B, which refers to the target (blank) diskette.

Activity C—dir and tree Commands

The following diagram is the directory and file structure of the LAB directory, which is on the textbook diskette.

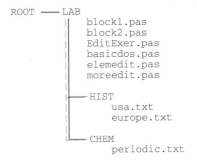

```
ROOT ── LAB
         ‖    block1.pas
         ‖    block2.pas
         ‖    EditExer.pas
         ‖    basicdos.pas
         ‖    elemedit.pas
         ‖    moreedit.pas
         ‖
         ├── HIST
         ‖        usa.txt
         ‖        europe.txt
         ‖
         └── CHEM
                  periodic.txt
```

Put the textbook diskette in drive A and change the default drive to drive A. The DOS prompt should be A:>.

To see which files and subdirectories are in the LAB directory

- Type **cd \lab** and press **ENTER**.
- Type **dir** and press **ENTER**. (Note that LAB's two subdirectories, HIST and CHEM, are enclosed in < >, whereas its files are not.)

To see which files are in the HIST subdirectory

Method 1—completing path in dir command

- Type **dir hist** and press **ENTER**. (Note that HIST contains the two files shown in the diagram.)

Method 2—changing the current directory to HIST

- Type **cd hist** and press **ENTER**.
- Type **dir** and press **ENTER**. (Note it is the same two files.)

To see which files are in the CHEM subdirectory

- First back up to the parent of the current directory by typing **cd . . .**
- Then type **dir chem**.

To see the tree structure of LAB (including not just its subdirectories but also the files within its subdirectories)

- Type **cd \lab** and press **ENTER**. (The prompt should be A:\LAB>.)
- Type **tree** and press **ENTER**. (This lists subdirectories only.)
- Type **tree /f** and press **ENTER**. (This includes files.)

To create another subdirectory (BIOL) in LAB and then remove it

- Type **md biol** and press **ENTER**.
- To see that this created BIOL, type **tree /f** and press **ENTER**.
- Type **rd biol** and press **ENTER**.
- Type **tree /f** and press **ENTER**. (Note that directory BIOL has been removed.)

Activity D—Copying and Erasing Files

Put the textbook diskette in drive A and change the default drive to drive A. The DOS prompt should be A:>.

Other forms of the dir command

- Compare the effects of the following three commands: **dir**, **dir /w** and **dir /p**.

To make another copy of a file with a different name but in the same subdirectory

- Type **cd \lab** and press **ENTER** to move to the LAB subdirectory.
- Type **dir** and press **ENTER**.
- Type **copy block1.pas examp5.pas** and press **ENTER**.
- Type **dir** and press **ENTER** or type **tree /f** and press **ENTER**.

Note that the new file examp5.pas is in the directory.

To use the wildcard ∗ to copy all the files from one subdirectory to another
- Type **md sociol** and press **ENTER** to create a new subdirectory.
- Type **copy hist\∗.∗ sociol** and press **ENTER** to copy all the files in HIST to SOCIOL.
- Type **tree /f** and press **ENTER**.

    Note that the sociol subdirectory now contains all the files also contained in the hist subdirectory.

To erase the files created in this activity
- Type **erase examp5.pas** and press **ENTER**.
- Type **erase sociol\∗.∗** and press **ENTER**.
- Type **y** to confirm deletion of all files.
- Type **rd sociol** and press **ENTER**.
- Type **tree /f** and press **ENTER**.

The tree structure of LAB should be as it was originally in the diagram on page A-22.

LAB TOPIC II—ELEMENTS OF EDITING

Activity A—The Editor and Pulldown Menus   We assume that you have the textbook diskette in the A drive and that you are already in Pascal.

To change the default directory to drive A:\LAB
- Press **ALT-f c**.
- Type **a:\lab** in the Directory Name box, and press **ENTER**.

Typing, Compiling and Running a Simple Program
- Press **F3** to open a file.
- Type **people** in the dialog box, and press **ENTER**.
- Type in the following program.

```
program people;
begin
   writeln ('People Make Mistakes');
   writeln ('It Takes a Computer')
   writeln (' To Really Mess Things Up')
end.
```
- Press **F2**. This saves the above program in the LAB subdirectory with the filename people.pas.
- Press **CTRL-F9** to compile and run the program.
- Press **ALT-F5** to recall the output screen.
- Press **ESC** to get back to the Edit Screen.

To temporarily go to **DOS** to execute **DOS** commands
* Press **Alt-f d**.
* Type **dir a:** and press **ENTER**. (The file people.pas should be in the listing.)
* Type **exit** and press **ENTER**.

When you are ready to exit completely from Turbo Pascal, press **Alt-f x**.

Activity B—Retrieving Files

The programs in the textbook diskette are named by page number with each chapter having its own subdirectory off the root directory. For example, the program on page 57 in Chapter 4 has the file name A:\CH4\P57.PAS.

CAUTION Most but not all of the programs from the book are on the textbook diskette. $\qquad$ • • •

We assume that you have the textbook diskette in the A drive and that you are already in Turbo Pascal.

To load the program from page 57 of Chapter 4
* Press **Alt-f c** to bring up the change directory submenu.
* Type **A:\CH4** in the Directory Name box and press **ENTER**.
* Press **F3**.
* Press **Tab**, use the arrow key(s) to highlight **P57.PAS**, and press **ENTER**.

To load the program from page 60 of Chapter 4, it is not necessary to change the directory since the default directory is already A:\CH4.
* Press **F3**.
* Press **Tab**, highlight **P60.PAS**, and press **ENTER**.

To load the program from page 87 of Chapter 6
* Change the directory to A:\CH6 using the edit method.
* Press the left arrow key until the cursor is under the 4, and then press the **Del** key, type 6, and press **ENTER**.
* Press **F3**.
* Press **Tab**, highlight **P87.PAS**, and press **ENTER**.

Activity C—Creating Files Under Subdirectories from within Pascal

We assume that you have the textbook diskette in the A drive and that you are already in Turbo Pascal.

Create and save the file A:\LAB\CHEM\EX1.PAS.

- Press **Alt-f c**.
- Type **a:\lab\chem** in the Directory name box, and press **ENTER**.
- Press **F3**.
- Type **ex1.pas** in the File name box and press **ENTER**.
- Type in the following line for the actual file:

```
This is EX1.PAS within the CHEM subdirectory
```

- Press **F2** to save that one-line file.

Create and save the file A:\LAB\HIST\EX2.PAS.

- Press **F3**.
- Type the file name **a:\lab\hist\ex2.pas** and press **ENTER**.
- Type the following line for the actual file:

```
This is EX2.PAS within the HIST subdirectory
```

- Press **F2** to save it.

Note that in this step we created the file by specifying the full pathname as opposed to changing the current directory to a:\lab\hist and then creating the file.

Activity D—Using Turbo Windows

We assume that you have the textbook diskette in the A drive and that you are already in Turbo Pascal.

To open multiple windows

- Press **F3** to open a file.
- Type **proj1** in the Open File box and press **ENTER**.
- Type **This Is Window One**.
- Press **F3** to open another file.
- Type **proj2** in the Open File box and press **ENTER**.
- Type **This Is Window Two**.

To toggle between windows and save the active window

- Press **F6** to activate the first window.
- Press **F2** to save.
- Press **F6** to activate the second window.
- Press **F2** to save.

To work with three windows and tile them for a better view

- Press **F3** to open a file.
- Type **proj3.pas** in the Open File box and press **ENTER**.
- Press **Alt-w t** to tile the open windows.
- Press **F6** to activate next window.

- Press **Shift-F6** to activate previous window.
- Press **Alt-F3** to close the active window.
- Press **Alt-w t** to re-tile the remaining open windows.
- Press **Alt-w a** for a cascade view of the open windows.

LAB TOPIC III—MORE ADVANCED EDITING

Activity A—Cursor Movement and Deleting

Get into Turbo Pascal, place the textbook diskette in drive a: and then load the text file **a:\lab\editexer.pas**.

Experiment with advanced Cursor Control keys

- Press the **down arrow** key (↓) until you come to the line which reads "The following program etc.".
- Press **Ctrl-→** four times and note the effect.
- Press **Ctrl-←** two times and note the effect.
- Press the **End** key and note where the cursor is now located.
- Press the **Home** key and note where the cursor is now located.
- Compare the effect of **Ctrl-Home** versus **Ctrl-End**.

Compare the Effects of DEL key versus the Backspace key

- Move the cursor to the middle of a line with at least seven words in it.
- Locate the Backspace key (←). It is not the (←) key grouped with the other cursor arrow keys.
- Press the **Del** key 3 times.
- Press the **Backspace** key 3 times.

Compare the effect of Ctrl-q y versus **Ctrl-y**

- Move the cursor to the middle of a line and press **Ctrl-q y**.
- Move the cursor to the middle of a line and press **Ctrl-y**.

Restore the line that was just erased

- Press **Alt-e r**.

Activity B—The Search and Replace Commands

Get into Turbo Pascal, place the textbook diskette in drive a: and then load the text file **a:\lab\editexer.pas**.

Change all occurrences of the variable sum to SqSum throughout the program without prompting.

- Press **Alt-s r**.
- Type **sum** in the Text to find box.
- Press the **Tab** key.
- Type **SqSum** in the New Text box and press **Tab** again.

CAUTION   Do not press **ENTER** during the entire process.   • • •

The cursor is now in the Options box.

- Position the cursor at the X next to Prompt on replace and then press the **space bar**.
- Press **a** for Change all.

Change some but not all occurrences of Writeln   Add to the program the following lines before the end statement:

```
writeln ('So long');
writeln ('Good bye');
writeln ('Adios');
```

Use the Prompt on replace option to replace two of the writeln statements (you decide which ones) to writeln(lst, . . .)

- Press **Alt-s r**.
- Type **writeln (** in the Text to find box.
- Press the **Tab** key.
- Type **writeln (lst,** in the New text box.
- Press the **Tab** key.
- Make sure there is an [X] next to Prompt on replace.
- Press **a** for Change all. You should be prompted by:

      Replace this occurrence? Yes   No   Cancel

  for each occurrence of writeln (

- Press **y** for those you wish to replace with writeln (lst,

Activity C—Moving Blocks Within a File

1. Get into Turbo Pascal and place the textbook diskette in drive a:.

2. Load the file **block1.pas** containing the following text:

```
1) This is line one
2) This is line two
3) This is line three
```

3. Mark the block consisting of line 3 and insert a copy of it between lines 1 and 2. Thus, the text should become:

```
1) This is line one
3) This is line three
2) This is line two
3) This is line three
```

- Move the cursor to the **3** of line 3 and press **Ctrl-k b**.
- Move the cursor to the end of line 3 and press **Ctrl-k k**.
- Move the cursor to the end of line 1 and press **ENTER**. This creates a blank line between lines 1 and 2.
- Press **Ctrl-k c**.

4. Move line 1 to the end so that the lines are now 3), 2), 3), and 1).

- Move the cursor to the **1** of line 1 and press **Ctrl-k b**. (Do not be alarmed that some text is already highlighted—Turbo remembers the location of the end marker, which you still need to change.)
- Move the cursor to the end of line 1 and press **Ctrl-k k**.
- Move the cursor to a blank line at the end of the file and press **Ctrl-k v**.

5. Move the block consisting of lines 2 and 3 to the end of the file by the method used in Step 3. The lines should now be 3), 1), 2), and 3).

6. Delete line 3 from the top by first marking it and then pressing **Ctrl-k y**. The file should be back to the way it was when it was first in step 2.

Activity D—Copying Blocks to Another File

1. Get into Turbo Pascal, place the textbook diskette in drive a:.
- Load the file **block1.pas**.
- Also load the file **block2.pas**.

2. Make block1.pas active and mark the block consisting of lines 2 and 3.
- Press **F6** as necessary to make block1.pas active.
- Move the cursor to the **2** of line 2 and press **Ctrl-k b**.
- Move the cursor to the end of line 3 and press **Ctrl-k k**.

3. Copy that marked block so that it is inserted between the next to last line and the end line of the program in file block2.pas.
- Press **Alt-e c** to copy that marked block to the clipboard.
- Make block2.pas the active file by pressing **F6**.
- Move the cursor to a new line before the end line of block2.pas.
- Press **Alt-e p** to paste the marked block from the clipboard.

4. Display the current contents of the clipboard.
- Press **Alt-e s**.
- Press **F6** a few times to make block1.pas active again.

5. Copy the block consisting of line 1 from block1.pas to block2.pas so that it is inserted before lines 2 and 3.
   - Press **F6** as necessary to make block1.pas active.
   - Move the cursor to the 1 of line 1 and press **Ctrl-k b**.
   - Move the cursor to the end of line 1 and press **Ctrl-k k**.
   - Press **Alt-e c** to copy that marked block to the clipboard.
   - Make block2.pas the active file by pressing **F6**.
   - Move the cursor to a new line before line 2 in block2.pas.
   - Press **Alt-e p** to paste the marked block from the clipboard.

6. - Press **Alt-e s** to display the clipboard. (Note that only the most recent block sent to the clipboard is marked there.)

SOLUTIONS APPENDIX

Chapter 1

1. The identifiers in (b), (e), and (f) are illegal: (b) because no spaces are allowed in identifiers, (e) because an identifier must begin with a letter, and (f) because identifiers may contain only letters, digits, and the underbar.

2.
```
program prog8;
var feet, inches: integer;
begin
   feet : = 5;
   inches := feet * 12;
   writeln (inches)   {the semicolon can be omitted before an end}
end.
```

3.
```
x equals 5
58
5equals x
```

4. **(a)** `10510`   **(b)** `10 5`   **(c)** `x = 5`

                              `10`   `y = 10`

5.
```
TotCents := 10 * dimes + pennies;
writeln (dimes, ' dimes and ', pennies, ' pennies');
writeln ('equals ', TotCents, ' cents.');
```

Chapter 2

2. The program output appears on the User Screen. Press Alt-F5 to go from the Edit Screen to the User Screen and press any key to move from the User Screen to the Edit Screen.

4. No, it will not save your program but will simply return you to the Edit Screen.

5. Alt-x causes a permanent exit from Turbo Pascal whereas the DOS shell choice temporarily transfers you to DOS and allows you to return to where you left off in Turbo Pascal by typing exit.

6. You can see a list of *all* the files in the current directory of your disk by pressing F3 and then typing a:*.* in the name box.

7. After making sure that you are in the insert mode move the cursor to the end of the line after which you want to type in a new line and then press enter.

Chapter 3

1. **(a)** `1,437`   **(b)** `.5462`

2.
```
824.2
824.18
 8.2417600000E+02
```

3. The zero is missing before the decimal in the number .25.

4. **(a)** `64`   **(c)** `4`

5. **(a)** y^2 **(b)** `4`   **(c)** `1`

6. (a) 13   **(c)** 32   **(d)** 1

7. (a) `(x + y)/(2 * w)`   **(b)** `(5 * x - 3 * y) / 2`

8. Syntax errors are caught when the program is compiled. Execution errors are caught when it is run. Logical errors are ideally caught by hand checking.

9. (a) You will get a syntax error when the program tries to compile `y := x/2; x/2` will give you a real answer and `y` is an integer variable.

(b) `avg := total/n;` will given you a divide by zero error at run time.

10. This fragment will set `salary` to -31536 because of the integer declaration which allows only whole number values between -32768 and 32767.

11. The misspelled `skore2` will be reported as an unknown identifier error, because the variable declared was `score2`. The variable `total` will be reported as an unknown identifier because the variable declared was `sum`.

12. `hundreds := num div 100;`

Chapter 4

1. `age < 21`

3. There should not be a semicolon seperating the `then` and `else` branches.

4. false

5. (a) maybe   **(b)** yes

7. (a)
```
if (ht < 72) and (wt > 200) then ...
                              else ...
```

(b)
```
if (ht >= 72) or (wt <= 200)
   then writeln ('maybe OK')
   else writeln ('overweight');
```

Chapter 5

1. (a)
```
ABCDEFG
      431
       57
   431
   431
```

2.
```
ABCDEFGH
 675  42
  18   5
```

3. (a) 32 33   **(b)** 4 2.0

4. (a) 5   **(c)** 2   **(e)** R   **(f)** D

6.
```
program older;
var name: string;
    age: integer;
begin
  write ('What is your name? ');
  readln (name);
  write ('How old are you ', name, '? ');
  readln (age);
  writeln ('You look much older ', name, '.');
  writeln ('I thought you were at least ', age + 5, '.')
end.
```

Chapter 6

1. **(a)** ```
hello
hello
hello
good day
so long
```
**(b)** 30    **(c)** 4    **(d)** 5.00

2. **(a)** `Joe` will be printed 11 times.

   **(b)** `Joe` will be printed once.

3. Sometimes.

4. It is not necessary to initialize the variable `wage`, because the previous value of `wage` is not used in computing the current value.

5. **(b)** The memory cell for `sum` might have garbage as its starting value. If you do not initialize `sum`, then your answer will be off by the starting value of `sum`.

6. ```
6 7
11 12
16 17
16 29
```

7. **(a)** ```
x = 28OK
x = 26
x = 24OK
x = 22
x = 20OK
```

**Chapter 7**

1. **(a)** ```
6
11
```

   (b) The computer will keep outputting 1 in an infinite loop, since the loop body is the single statement `writeln (n)`.

   (c) 1

2. **(a)** ```
5 9
7 10
9 11
11 12
13 13
15 14
```

3. False

4. **(a)** ```
50
5
32
8
18
3
```

5. **(a)** ```
8
9
7 9
x = 7y = 9
```

**Chapter 8**

1. **(a)** ```
1 4
3 10
5 22
7 23
```

2. **(a)** 1 5 1 6 1 7 2 5 2 6 2 7 3 5 3 6 3 7   **(b)** 1 5 1 6 1 7
                                                           2 5 2 6 2 7
                                                           3 5 3 6 3 7

Chapter 9

1. **(a)** The associated file variable   **(b)** The associated file variable

   (c) An `assign` statement

2. **(a)** The `reset` statement prepares the file for reading by the program. The file must already exist. A rewrite statement prepares the file for writing by the program. If the file already exists, the contents are lost. If the file does not exist, it is created.

   (b) Whatever the original file contains is lost.

3. ```
   assign (file1, 'prog1.inp');
   reset (file1);

   close (file1);
   assign (file2, 'prog1.out');
   rewrite (file2);
   ```

4. If you are entering the external file name interactively you don't need quote marks. If the actual file name is written in the assign statement then quote marks will be necessary.

5. ```
   StudFile: text;
   reset (StudFile);
   while not seekeof (StudFile) do
   readln (StudFile, name);
   readln (StudFile, score);
   close (StudFile)
   ```

Chapter 10

1. ```
   Smith 85.0
   Jones 71.5
   ```

2. `yrs` is undeclared in the main body of the program.

4. ```
   program height;
   var feet, inches: integer;

   procedure HEIGHT_IN_INCHES (feet, inches: integer);
     var InchTotal: integer;
     begin
        InchTotal := feet * 12 + inches;
        writeln ('your height is ', InchTotal, ' inches')
     end; {HEIGHT_IN_INCHES}

   begin
     write ('enter height in feet and inches ');
     readln (feet,inches);
     HEIGHT_IN_INCHES (feet, inches)
   end.
   ```

7. **(a)** 1   **(b)** 1
          0   0

8. **(a)** Since each new call to the procedure initializes the value parameter, `total`, to 0, the statement

   ```
   total := total + pay
   ```

   assigns to `total` the current employee's pay.

• • • • • • • • •
Chapter 11

1. **(a)** 2

2. **(a)** A variable parameter does not receive its own memory cell. It uses the memory cell of the corresponding variable in the calling statement—a constant or expression would not have a memory cell.

4. **(a)** 13 14
13 6
25 26
25 6

5. 6 30 15 6
5 30 15 5
6 55 25 6
5 55 25 5

6. **(a)** 7 2 4 7
8 2 6 8
7 8 2

8. 25 5
5 25

• • • • • • • • •
Chapter 12

1. **(a)** Hi   **(b)** Ho

2. a A
b b
c C
d d
else
e d
else
f d

3.
```
procedure HONORS (gpa: real);
   var hon: string [9];
   begin
     if gpa >= 3.75 then
       hon := 'Summa'
     else if gpa >= 3.50 then
       hon := 'Magna'
     else if gpa >= 3.25 then
       hon := 'Cum'
     else
       hon := 'No honors';
     writeln ('Graduate with ', hon)
   end; {HONORS}
```

4. String and real data types cannot be used as selectors in case statements. The selector must be of an ordinal type.

5. There should be no begin after case selector of. A colon should not be used after the keyword else in a case statement.

• • • • • • • • •
Chapter 13

1. A function call cannot stand by itself. It must be used in place of an expression in a statement.

2. (a) This type of use is reserved for a recursive function and should not be done otherwise.

   (b) Although it is legal to include a writeln or readln statement in the body of a function, it is bad style to do so.

3. (a)
```
i equals 1
one
three
i equals 2
two
three
i equals 3
two
three
four
```
(b)
```
3  4 81
3 64 81
27 64 81
```

4.
```
function POWER (x: real; n: integer): real;
  {finds x to the n for n a positive, negative or zero}
  var i: integer;
      prod: real;
  begin
    prod := 1;
    for i := 1 to abs(n) do
      prod := prod * x;
    if n < 0 then prod := 1/prod;
    POWER := prod
  end;
```

6. (b)
```
writeln (FIND_SUM (101, 500):0:4);
```

• • • • • • • • •
Chapter 14
• • • • • • • • •

1. Approximately 20 times, because it has a 1-in-5 chance of being printed for each i.

Chapter 15

1. If the variable x were a local variable of a procedure that called a second procedure, x would be nonlocal to the second procedure.

2. Yes, the declaration of procedure B would have to appear before the declaration of procedure A.

4. There is an unknown identifier error because y is neither declared in WORK nor is it declared in any of the other containing blocks.

5.
```
4 4
2 4
y in WORK = 100
0
```

6. The procedures will be called in the order B, C, D, B, and C.

• • • • • • • • •
Chapter 16
• • • • • • • • •

1. Since each data type name within a procedure header must be a legal identifier we can define a global type identifier in a type declaration and then use it in the procedure header.

2.
```
ord_diff := abs (ord(day1) - ord (day2));
if (ord_diff = 1) or (ord_diff = 6)
  then writeln ('The two days are adjacent')
  else writeln ('The two days are not adjacent');
```

•••••••••
Chapter 17

1. 10 0 0 9 0 19

2. {$R+}

3. (a) With {$R+} there will be a range check error when you try to run the program because you are trying to access an array subscript beyond its bounds.

5. (a) 36 30 24 24 30 36

6. 44 15 44 44 44 44

7. (b) 1 1 2 6 24 120

8. 0
   1
   1
   2
   0
   0

10. (b) Here are two possible solutions:

Solution 1

```
procedure INTERTWINE (arr1, arr2: fivearray; var result: tenarray);
  var i: integer;
  begin
    for i := 1 to 5 do
      begin
        result[2 * i -1] := arr1[i];
        result[2 * i] := arr2[i];
      end;
  end; {INTERTWINE}
```

Solution 2

```
{procedure INTERTWINE (arr1, arr2: fivearray; var result: tenarray);
  var i, ct1, ct2: integer;
  begin
    ct1 := 1;
    ct2 := 1;
    while ct1 < 10 do
      begin
        result [ct1] := arr1[ct2];
        result [ct1+1] := arr2[ct2];
        ct1 := ct1 + 2;
        ct2 := ct2 + 1
      end
end;}
```

•••••••••
Chapter 18

1.

11	22	33
4	22	33
4	4	33
4	4	4

3. (a) *first*   *second*

15	25	35
20	30	40
25	35	45

15	16	17
20	21	22
25	26	27

4. (a)
```
for i := 1 to n do
    sum := sum + a[i, i];
```

(b)
```
for i := 1 to n do
    sum := sum + a[i, n + 1 - i];
```

6. (a)
```
for i := 1 to 5 do
    write (mat[i, 3], ' ');
```

• • • • • • • • •
Chapter 19

1. (a) 14 26 25 40 32 12 18 49 6

2. (a) 2 4 9 45 23 16 44 11 33 29

(b) 4 2 11 16 9 23 29 33 44 45

4. (a) 3 executions, `first = 1`, `last = 3`

• • • • • • • • •
Chapter 20

1.
```
ST A STITCH
TC  IN T STIME
```

2. (a)
```
cuter
commuter
str = commuter part = mcommuterut
```

3. (b)
```
E AN **
THMF**
THE MAN FROM TENNESSEE
```

4.
```
procedure PRINT_NAME (name: str20);
{prints first name followed by last name}
  const comma = ',';
  var first, last: str20;
      CommaPos: integer;
  begin
    CommaPos := pos (comma, name);
    last := copy (name, 1, CommaPos - 1);
    first := copy (name, CommaPos + 2,
                   length (name) - (CommaPos + 1));
    writeln (first, ' ', last)
  end; {PRINT_NAME}
```

• • • • • • • • •
Chapter 21

1.
```
type
   companyrec = record
     name: string[24];
     sex: char;
     pay: real
   end; {companyrec}
   companytype = array[1..30] of companyrec;
var company: companytype;
```

2. (a) `writeln (employees[4].name, ' ', employees[4].age);`

(b)
```
for i := 1 to 30 do
   with employees [i] do
      if salary > 25000
         then writeln (name);
```

• • • • • • • • •
Chapter 22

1.
```
type
   memberrec = record
     name: string[24];
     sex: char;
     age: integer;
     occupation: string[20]
   end; {memberrec}
   memberfile = file of memberrec;
var fileA: memberfile;
```

• • • • • • • • •
Chapter 24

1. Positions 7, 5, and 3

2. (a) The human could leave more matches than were there when the turn began. The human could take more than two matches or take none. The human could leave −1 match.

• • • • • • • • •
Chapter 25

1.
```
function FACT (n: integer): longint;
   {recursive function that computes n!}
   begin
     if (n = 0) or (n = 1)
       then FACT := 1
       else FACT := n * FACT (n-1)
   end; {FACT}
```

2.
```
function POWER (x:real; n: integer): real;
   begin
     if n = 0
       then POWER := 1
       else POWER := POWER (x, n - 1) * x
   end; {POWER}
```

3.
```
function SUM (a: arraytype; n: integer): integer;
   begin
     if n = 1
       then SUM := a[1]
       else SUM := SUM (a, n - 1) + a[n]
   end; {SUM}
```

• • • • • • • • •
Chapter 26

1. 57 57

2. Chen Chen

3.
```
procedure COUNT_SEC (head: ListPtr);
   {counts how many names have a vowel as the second letter}
   var ptr: ListPtr;
   begin
     ptr := head;
     while ptr <> nil do
       begin
```

```
          if copy (ptr^.name,2,1) in ['a', 'e', 'i', 'o', 'u']
             then count := count + 1;
          ptr := ptr^.next
       end {while}
    end; {COUNT_SEC}
```

Chapter 27

1. 3 6
3 4 5 6

Chapter 28

1.

12	40	29	32	20	55	58	80	70

FocusIndex will have the value 6.

2. (a) First QUICKSORT will be called with first = 1 and last = 9. Using 42 as the focus value, SUBDIVIDE will rearrange the array to be

32	20	28	42	70	81	59	62	55

and will give FocusIndex the value 4. Then the left subarray will be sorted. QUICKSORT will be called with first = 1 and last = 3. SUBDIVIDE will rearrange the first three elements of the array to be

[1]	[2]	[3]
28	20	32

and will give FocusIndex the value 3. Then QUICKSORT will be called with first = 1 and last = 2. SUBDIVIDE will put the first two elements in order and give FocusIndex the value 2. The calls QUICKSORT (list, 1, 1) and QUICKSORT (list, 3, 3) will do nothing, because first will not be less than last.

Next, the right subarray will be sorted. QUICKSORT will be called with first = 5 and last = 9. Using 70 as the focus element, SUBDIVIDE will rearrange the subarray to be

[5]	[6]	[7]	[8]	[9]
62	55	59	70	81

and will give FocusIndex the value 8. Then QUICKSORT will be called with first = 5 and last = 7. SUBDIVIDE will rearrange the elements in boxes 5 to 7 to be

[5]	[6]	[7]
59	55	62

and will give FocusIndex the value 7. Then the call QUICKSORT (list, 5, 6) will rearrange the elements in boxes 5 and 6.

The call QUICKSORT (list, 5, 5) will do no rearranging.

Finally, the calls stemming from QUICKSORT (list, 8, 9) will do no rearranging.

INDEX